Eye on the Struggle

Eye on the Struggle

ETHEL PAYNE,
THE FIRST LADY OF THE BLACK PRESS

James McGrath Morris

Amistad

An Imprint of HarperCollins*Publishers*

HarperCollins books may be purchased for educational, business, or sales promotional use. For information, please e-mail the Special Markets Department at SPsales@harpercollins.com.

All images courtesy of the Library of Congress unless otherwise noted.

FIRST EDITION

Designed by Suet Yee Chong

Library of Congress Cataloging-in-Publication Data has been applied for.

ISBN: 978-0-06-219885-3

15 16 17 18 19   OV/RRD   10 9 8 7 6 5 4 3 2 1

In memory of
Gertrude Keaton
1909–2004

CONTENTS

PART THREE

We are soul folks and
I am writing for soul brothers' consumption.

—ETHEL PAYNE, 1967

A PRESIDENTIAL PEN

S THE SEVEN O'CLOCK HOUR NEARED ON THE EVENING of July 2, 1964, President Lyndon Baines Johnson took a seat before a table at one end of the East Room in the White House. Nine months earlier the ornate room had been a somber place when President John F. Kennedy's body lay in repose on the catafalque that had been made for President Abraham Lincoln's casket in 1865. In contrast, the mood on this night was exuberant.

Resting on the table, to the left of a green blotter, was the final draft of the Civil Rights Act that had been approved less than five hours earlier by overwhelming numbers in the House of Representatives. The venerable *New York Times* hailed the new law as "the most sweeping civil rights legislation ever enacted in this country" and reported that civil rights leaders regarded it "as a Magna Carta in the struggle to secure equal treatment and opportunity for the Negro."

All that remained now was for the president to add his signature to the bill. For that, Johnson needed an audience. Arrayed before him in rows of gold-colored chairs on the Fontainebleau oak parquetry and awash in klieg light sat two hundred and fifty of the nation's most powerful and recognizable politicians, officials, and activists whose work, in one way or another, had led to this moment. The remainder of America watched on living room televisions.

When the president looked up through his wire-rimmed glasses he saw a vista of familiar white faces punctuated only occasionally by a dark countenance and almost entirely devoid of women. But sitting six rows back was a figure both female and black. In assembling a guest list suitable to the magnitude of this event, the White House had not failed to include Ethel Lois Payne.

WHILE UNRECOGNIZED BY MANY of the whites in the East Room, fifty-two-year-old Payne was an iconic figure to readers of the nation's black press. The granddaughter of slaves and the daughter of a Pullman porter, the South Side Chicago native at midlife had inspiringly traded in a monotonous career as a library clerk for one as a journalist at the *Chicago Defender*, the country's premier black newspaper. In a matter of a few years she had risen to become the nation's preeminent black female reporter of the civil rights era, and during the movement's seminal events in the 1950s it had been her words that had fed a national black readership hungry for stories that could not be found in the white media.

Her unflinching yet personable reporting had enlightened and activated black readers across the country and made her a trusted ally of civil rights leaders. Among those in the White House audience that night, labor leader A. Philip Randolph remembered her as far back as 1941 when she worked with him on his March on Washington Movement. For Clarence Mitchell Jr., the potent lobbyist for the NAACP, she had been a dependable confederate in the White House press corps during the Eisenhower administration. And Martin Luther King Jr. had first been the subject of her perceptive reporting during the initial days of the Montgomery, Alabama, bus boycott when Payne crafted the earliest account of the black clergy's ascension to the leadership of the civil rights movement.

On this night Payne was in temporary exile from her craft, serving as a Democratic Party functionary. But when she had sat in the ranks of the press, crowded together on the other side of the East

Room, she had given black America a voice and presence at the highest reaches of power that could not be ignored. From challenging the white occupants of the White House and courthouses to reporting firsthand on events from Alabama to Africa and Asia, Payne had traveled the length of the civil rights movement that led to the legislative victory celebrated this evening. In doing so, she had served as both an emissary from and a representative for a large group of Americans long neglected by the mainstream media. She was, as she would later be called, "the First Lady of the Black Press."

DESPITE A STORIED HISTORY dating back to 1827, the black press that employed Payne had unremittingly chronicled racism, eloquently protested injustices, impassionedly educated its people, and remained—like most African American institutions—completely out of sight of white America. "To most white Americans the black press was a voice unheard, its existence unknown or ignored," said Enoch P. Waters, an editor at the *Chicago Defender.* "It was possible for a white person, even one who believed himself well informed, to live out his three score years and ten without seeing a black newspaper or being aware that more than 150 to 250 were being published throughout the nation."

Until the civil rights movement made its mark, African Americans were absent from the pages of the nation's white newspapers unless they were accused of a crime. When Payne was growing up, her hometown *Chicago Tribune* chose words like *negress* or *southern darky* when it mentioned the city's black residents. The important events of their lives such as graduations, marriages, and deaths were not commemorated in the white press. The useful news African Americans wanted about church, schools, entertainment, sports, not to mention politics, was nowhere to be found. It was in this capacity that Payne's employer the *Chicago Defender* and other members of the black press had found their initial role.

But the *Chicago Defender,* the *Baltimore Afro-American,* the *New York Amsterdam News,* the *Pittsburgh Courier,* and other black newspapers grew to have circulations beyond their cities and an influence greater than their press runs would lead one to believe. "The most predominant media influence on black people was the black newspaper," recalled veteran reporter Vernon Jarrett, whose *Negro Newsfront* was the first daily radio news broadcast in the United States created by an African American. "They were—our internet. They were our cement that helped keep us together."

DRESSED IN A DARK SUIT, President Johnson faced a bank of four large cameras arrayed in front of the table. Between them stood a blue and black metal box that held within it a glass screen on which the text of his speech was projected. He was the first president to make use of this new technology being called a TelePrompTer.

In a thick voice laced with a Central Texas drawl, the president began by invoking the gathering that 188 years ago had produced the Declaration of Independence, which embodied the American ideals of equality and inalienable rights. But, he said, these rights and these blessings of liberty had been denied to Americans "not because of their own failures, but because of the color of their skins."

Such unequal treatment was impermissible under the Constitution, he said, "and the law I will sign tonight forbids it." It will provide no special treatment for any group. Rather, Johnson continued, "it does say that those who are equal before God shall now be equal in the polling booths, in the classrooms, in the factories, and in hotels, restaurants, movie theaters, and other places that provide services to the public."

His speech concluded, Johnson drew the first nib pen from a supply sticking up from a rack like porcupine quills. He dipped it into an ink bottle and began to write. Using each of the pens before him, and more brought by an aide, he inscribed "Lyndon B. Johnson, approved

July 2, 1964, Washington, D.C." at the bottom of the engrossed legislation before him, adding dashes and dots, and putting periods in *D.C.*
so as to extend his use of pens to more than seventy-five, creating with
each one he touched a much-sought-after political trophy.

The crowd surged forward and encircled the desk. Johnson gave
the first pen to Senators Everett Dirksen and Hubert Humphrey
as a reward for their work in breaking the fifty-seven-day filibuster
mounted by Southern senators and ending the longest debate in that
chamber's history. House members Republican William McCulloch
and Democrat Emanuel Celler were given pens for their work as the
bill's managers in their chamber. Attorney General Robert F. Kennedy was handed six pens to distribute to Justice Department aides.
Then reaching over his left shoulder, grasping Martin Luther King's
hand, and pausing for the cameras, the president bestowed a pen on
the civil rights leader.

Ethel Payne too rose from her seat and slowly made her way to the
front. Standing five feet three inches tall, she wore a striped skirt and
jacket. A small soft white beret, angled to her right side, completed
the outfit. As the crowd thinned around the president, Payne moved
closer to the desk until she stood at its front edge.

Johnson looked up. Payne smiled, and her face, with its skin a
warm shade of nut brown, took on a disarming countenance. In
many a time and place, it had been a mollifying power. The president
reached his arm across the table and placed a pen in Payne's hand.
The journalist, whose reporting had both chronicled and inspired the
movement, clutched the writing instrument and said, "Thank you,
Mr. President."

PART ONE

CHAPTER 1

THROOP STREET

I N 1901, TWENTY-ONE-YEAR-OLD WILLIAM A. PAYNE MADE his way across the marble floor of the cavernous Illinois Central Station in downtown Chicago. The son of black Tennessee farmers, he had just debarked from the storied Illinois Central Line that ran up from New Orleans. He had made the journey north in search of a better life. He was not alone. Black men and women throughout the South were beginning to drop their tools in the cotton and tobacco fields, abandon their shanties, and join a silent exodus from the feudal life to which they had been confined since emancipation from slavery. One yoke had been traded for another.

A train ticket north held the promise of freedom. But with his one-way ticket clutched in his hand, Payne was among the trailblazers. When he reached Chicago, African Americans made up less than 2 percent of the city's population. Within a decade the vanguard, of which Payne was a member, would grow into a torrent of six million migrants entirely reshaping the social, cultural, and political landscape of Northern cities.

Well used to hard labor, Payne found work as a cooper assembling barrels in the vast stockyards that stretched over hundreds of blocks in South Side and whose stench spread for miles. The hours were long and Sunday was the only day of rest. Within a year he met and fell in love with Bessie Austin, a Hoosier who had moved to Chicago to join a brother who held a coveted job in the post office. In January 1903, the two newcomers were married.

The newlyweds faced a daunting task in finding a place in Chicago to start their new life together. Landlords and real estate agents conspired to confine African Americans to a few South Side neighborhoods. But the Paynes were blessed with good luck. Nine miles southwest of central Chicago, they came upon a set of tidy freestanding wooden houses open to them, one of the very few enclaves outside what was known as the "Black Belt" that permitted African Americans. Remarkably the four-by-six-block neighborhood, known as West Englewood, was not solidly black. White European immigrant families lived in several of the houses on each block.

At first the Paynes rented a series of places, a block apart, to accommodate their growing family. By the end of 1910, seven years into their marriage, the Paynes had three girls and one boy and Bessie was pregnant with another child. For the only time in their marriage, they left West Englewood and rented a house three miles to the east in West Woodlawn. There, on August 14, 1911, Bessie gave birth to their fifth child, whom they named Ethel Lois Payne, the name suggested by her aunt Clara Austin Williams. Her parents considered their newest progeny so winsome as to enter her into a baby contest at the local church. Ethel came in sixth out of eight contestants and brought home a one-pound box of chocolates.

IT WAS NOT LONG before the Paynes and their new baby were back in West Englewood, renting yet another in a succession of houses, this time on Loomis Boulevard and Throop Street. But their fortunes were improving.

William had left the stockyards and gone to work as a porter on the famed Pullman sleeping cars that each night carried as many as 100,000 pajama-clad travelers along the nation's rails. Next to working in the post office, it was one of the most sought-after jobs among

African Americans. Pullman porters wore suits to work, traveled the length of the land, and became leaders in their churches. The job put one atop the Negro social world in Chicago. The work, however, was hard. Porters seldom got more than a few hours of uninterrupted sleep, were gone from home for long stretches of time, and had their patience tested by wealthy white patrons who alternately called them "Uncle," "Joe," "Sam," or "George" (Pullman's first name) when not using "Boy" or even "Nigger."

Earning a Pullman salary and tips, William was able to accomplish a rare thing among African Americans in Chicago at the time. He purchased a home. In late 1917 the Paynes moved into a twenty-five-year-old two-story white clapboard house with a basement at 6210 South Throop Street. "It was one of the very few houses that had electricity when we moved in," remembered Thelma, the second-eldest child. "One of its wonders was that the upstairs and downstairs front hall light switches worked so that you could turn both lights on or off from either end, and our friends used to come over and play with this marvel."

ALTHOUGH STRICT WITH their children, Bessie and William fashioned a home full of joy and affection. When he was home between train runs, William loved to take the children to ride ponies at carnivals or to see a parade, and occasionally to Gary, Indiana, where much of Bessie's family still lived. "He was a big man, both physically and in personality possessing both temper and kindness," said Ethel. "His temper could be as hot as the desert sands at noon one day; yet he was gentle, with a great sense of the responsibility of the strong to help the weak."

The family's love of a carnival enticed three-year-old Ethel to wander away from the new house. A mischievous child, she may have been providing a hint of her life to come. But in the meantime she gave her parents a scare. The family frantically launched a search, enlisting neighbors, firemen, and policemen. At last she was located at a street fair four blocks away. Bessie wanted to administer corporal punishment, according to Ethel. "But Grandpa admonished her saying, 'Ain't no use in fanning her. Won't do no good. That child was just born with itching feet.'"

Bessie kept the home on a firm schedule: washday on Mondays, ironing on Tuesdays, baking on Wednesdays, and mending on Thursdays. Saturday mornings began with the children downing a dose of castor oil, followed by a couple of gingersnaps before setting off to do their assigned chores. Sundays were reserved for church.

Bessie's family had been members of the African Methodist Episcopal Church for generations. As it happened, the Greater St. John AME Church, the oldest Negro church in Englewood, moved from its storefront home a block away and built a proper brick church directly across the street from the Paynes' Throop Street house. In no time St. John's became a focal point of the family. "Church, church, church," recalled Ethel, "she was very strong on church." Once her mother caught Ethel playing hooky from St. John's with a boyfriend. "When Bessie Payne caught me, I was marched back to the sinner's bench, chastised, and prayed over mightily," Ethel said.

Bessie's parents, who came to stay for long periods of time, often accompanied the family to services. "When Grandpa would 'get happy' in church," Ethel said, "he would take out his handkerchief and wave it vigorously." One Sunday, however, the handkerchief he pulled from his pocket was not a go-to-church linen one kept in the dresser drawer but rather one that his wife had made from old sacks with the word *sugar* clearly stenciled on it. "Mama, who shared his devotion to church," Ethel said, "was mortified to see the sugar sack floating in the air."

ETHEL, HER OLDER SISTERS Alice Wilma, Thelma Elizabeth, Alma Josephine, her older brother, Lemuel Austin, and her younger sister, Avis Ruth, were never without something to do. Outside, they played hide-and-seek or raced up and down the block with other neighborhood kids. Inside the house, Bessie maintained a serene atmosphere interrupted only by music emanating either from the Victrola or from the violin that Lemuel, the only boy in the family, reluctantly practiced. There was no shortage of games and amusement. Once, for instance, the children and young adults staged a "Billion-Dollar Wedding" at Hope Presbyterian Church, a block away. They impersonated members of the Astor, Morgan, Gould, Armour, and other millionaire families. Six-year-old Ethel served as the ring bearer.

Books and stories were a favorite source of entertainment for Ethel and her sisters. Each Saturday the family walked into the surrounding white neighborhood to a city library in Ogden Park, one of several open spaces the city created as a safety valve for the burgeoning tenement districts. Access to the well-stocked library intended for white citizens was one of several advantages the Paynes enjoyed over African Americans cooped up in the Black Belt to the east. Most black citizens were kept at bay from good schools, well-stocked libraries, and green parks by the city's segregated housing. Rather than using laws, as in the South, housing confined blacks together and preserved the whiteness of public amenities. But in West Englewood, courageous black families such as the Paynes walked to better schools, libraries, and parks that were beyond reach for others of their race elsewhere in the city.

Ethel's sister Alma came home with the full limit of books each week. "She would read half the night if Mama didn't see the light was still on," said Thelma. Leisure time was devoted to reading the scads of books borrowed from the library or procured at rummage sales. "As I look back now," Ethel said many years later, "I see this as perhaps the greatest influence on the direction of my life."

In particular, Ethel was drawn to Paul Laurence Dunbar, an African American poet who had become famous before his early death at age thirty-three in 1906. While his work was written mostly in conventional English, it was his poems in Negro dialect that gained him fame, much to his dismay and annoyance. His poem "Sympathy" with the line "I know why the caged bird sings" resonated with black audiences. Ethel and her siblings put on plays, acting out Dunbar's poems, especially those about life on the plantation. They even formed a little theater company that included other children from the neighborhood.

Ethel and her siblings delighted in hearing family stories. On innumerable nights, Bessie recounted how her mother, Josephine Taylor Austin, and her family escaped from slavery in Kentucky, fleeing before daybreak at the end of a weekend. Drinking water from rain puddles, they found shelter with a courageous family of freed slaves, crossed the Ohio River on a skiff piloted by a white agent for the Underground Railroad, hid in a river cave with old cooking implements left by previous escapees, and finally boarded a boat that took them upriver to freedom.

Bessie's father, George Washington Austin, a short, bald man with a twinkling eye, was a master storyteller. On sizzling hot Chicago summer evenings the children were sent out to lie on straw mattresses arrayed under the porch. As the youngsters drifted off to sleep, their grandfather told his tales. Unlike his wife's family, he and his parents had not been freed from slavery in Tennessee until the end of the Civil War. He recalled vividly how, at age seven, his family was placed on the auction block on a snowy New Year's Day. After being examined by prospective buyers for the soundness of their limbs and teeth, the family members were sold to separate plantations.

But tall tales were George Austin's specialty. On those summer nights on the porch he would trade story after story with a neighbor. One time Ethel's grandfather and a neighbor named Spencer tried to outdo each other with their storytelling. "Finally at midnight," said

Ethel, "Mr. Spencer rose, shook hands with Grandpa, and said, 'You win, Brother Austin.'"

As with the Ogden Park Library, the family's good fortune of living in West Englewood gave Ethel and her siblings access to schools better than those that served virtually all African Americans in Chicago. Schools here were not legally segregated. With 90 percent of the city's African American population confined to the Black Belt, there was no need. The races remained almost entirely separate, confined to their neighborhood schools. But as a result some white schools counted African Americans among their ranks—in small numbers, to be sure.

Ethel began her school at Copernicus Elementary School, where a dozen or so black students were also allowed to enter the handsome four-story building three blocks north of the house. Although he had not gotten far in school, her father, William, shared Bessie's dedication to obtaining a good education for their children. Once Thelma asked her father for permission to join her friends working summer jobs at an apron factory. "No," he said, "the money will seem so good to you that you won't want to go back to school." It fell to Bessie, who had been trained as a Latin teacher, to keep the children on track when it came to school. "She knew the importance of regular attendance at school and did not cheat any of us by keeping us at home for her convenience," Thelma said. "Since our father had to be away on his job so much, she ruled the roost, served as business manager, disciplinarian, cook, seamstress, teacher, and manager."

Accompanying Ethel to Copernicus each day was her brother, Lemuel. A skinny and frail boy, he was close in age to Ethel, especially in comparison to her sisters. "I was down the ladder quite a bit, so I really didn't have that close rapport with my older sisters,"

Ethel said. "They were almost like one generation, and I constituted another one."

Each day's walk to Copernicus brought Ethel and Lemuel to a setting with advantages unattainable in the overcrowded, understaffed, underfunded schools that served the Black Belt. For most black children, school took place in aging buildings, many of which didn't even have bathrooms. On the other hand, no Chicago white school could be regarded as hospitable to black students. School officials had no reservations about publicly expressing their fear about the mixing of races. "When it comes to morality, I say colored children are unmoral," explained an assistant principal of a high school with a few black students. "The colored and white children here don't get mixed up in immorality; they are too well segregated. Not that we segregate them: the white keeps away from the colored."

At school and at home, Ethel came to be regarded as somewhat of a tomboy. "I didn't bother too much with dolls," she admitted. Lemuel, on the other hand, was a frail, skinny boy who got picked on and sometimes beat up by other boys his age. "Oh, I just hated it," Ethel said. Coming out of Copernicus one afternoon, she heard that her brother was in a fight. "I waded into this batch of boys," she said, "and I was just throwing them right and left." When she reached Lemuel, he looked up at her and said, "Go on home. Girls aren't supposed to fight. Go on home!"

CHAPTER 2

RED SUMMER

O N SUNDAY, AUGUST 27, 1919, EIGHT-YEAR-OLD ETHEL Payne chased bugs and grasshoppers and put them into mason jars and tin cans with punched-in paper tops that she kept under the porch. It was a blistering hot summer day. Not far from where she played, five young black teenagers sought relief from the stifling heat by jumping a ride on the back of a produce truck heading toward the cooling waters of Lake Michigan. Chicagoans loved their beaches, especially the thousands of working-class families for whom the lake provided inexpensive Sunday recreation. But they didn't leave their racial attitudes behind. Just like the city, the beaches were segregated.

In South Side, some eleven miles of beaches reaching all the way to Indiana were reserved for whites, leaving only a small stretch of waterfront to its north to serve as the "colored beach." But the boys went instead to an inlet and boarded a small raft they had made on a previous visit. Paying no attention to the southerly direction in which the draft drifted, they entered troubled waters. Unbeknownst to them, the sanctity of the white enclave had already been challenged earlier in the day by the entry of several black bathers. Mobs had gathered, both black and white, until the whites outnumbered the blacks and the invaders were chased off.

As the raft passed an outcropping that demarcated the segregated beaches, a man by the water's edge began throwing rocks at the boys. The boys dove into the water to seek protection, but a rock struck fourteen-year-old Eugene Williams on his forehead and he disappeared under the surface. The other teenagers reached shore, ran to the black beach, and returned with the lifeguard, who dove into the water looking for Williams. It was too late.

Using a grappling hook, the police retrieved his body and brought it to the white beach. The surviving boys singled out a white man in the crowd as the rock thrower. But the white police made no effort to arrest the man and thwarted a black officer's attempts to do so. Word spread quickly across the city. Soon as many as a thousand angry black Chicagoans gathered at the entrance of the white beach, demanding the police turn over the rock thrower and the white officers. A black man discharged his gun and was immediately killed by a jittery policeman.

By nightfall a race war had begun. Armed whites, members of so-called athletic clubs with such names as Ragen's Colts, Hamburgs, Dirty Dozen, and Our Flag, combed the streets attacking blacks. They took to automobiles and sped through black neighborhoods in the dark, unloading their guns at men, women, and children on the street. Unrestrained by the police, the gangs believed they had license to kill. Unprotected by the police, blacks took their own measures to resist. They stationed themselves behind windows or in the cover of darkened porches and fired back.

The South Side became a battle zone. Confined economically in poor neighborhoods, families were now also trapped by violence. At day, the white gangs expanded their attack to go after blacks returning from work in the stockyards. Black men were dragged from streetcars and assaulted. Few dared to venture out from their homes. At night, entire blocks were enshrouded in darkness as rioters shot out the streetlights and in a silence broken only by the sound of pistol and rifle shots.

The Payne family huddled in their Englewood house. The police designated their neighborhood a "danger zone" when rioting broke out at four different spots within blocks of the family's house and a police platoon was dispatched to quell the outbreaks. Making matters more terrifying, their father was not home.

All but a few of the Chicago Pullman car porters, cooks, and railroad employees had reported for work when the riot first began. They found themselves imprisoned on their trains, unable to get home. The railroads stopped black workers from debarking in Chicago. "We drew up new running schedules," said one railroad official, "making the porters and other employees double back out of town instead of resting here."

Finally, on the third night of violence, Payne got off a New York train. Hiding from marauding mobs, probably using his knowledge of the maze of railroad yards that honeycombed the city, he reached his house just before midnight. Awakened by the sound of his return, Ethel went into the front bedroom, where she found her father loading a rifle. In her innocence, she clasped her hands in excitement. "Shut up," yelled her father, "get down on the floor." The street below was enshrouded in darkness broken only by the light of an occasional flashlight or gasoline lamp. Bessie began to sob and pray. "My mother was praying," said Ethel, "and he was cursing!"

"Hello, Bill," came a voice from below. "Can you come down?" It was a white police officer and, more important, one of the few trusted white neighbors. Payne consented to come out of the house but he brought his rifle. The policeman promised that more officers were on their way to protect the neighborhood. But just then a small white mob appeared out of the darkness. Telling Payne to put down his rifle, the policeman drew his revolver. "I got some pretty good target practice at Belleau Wood," he told the mob, referring to an epic World War I battle. A clap of thunder and a sudden downpour of rain rendered his threat unnecessary, and the men dispersed. Under the drenching rain, Payne gripped the police officer by both shoulders and thanked him.

Several days later the police gained the upper hand and the violence abated. Chicago had not been alone in experiencing racial violence in the summer of 1919. The season was soon nicknamed "Red Summer" after rioting broke out in more than three dozen cities, mostly whites attacking blacks.

WHEN CALM DID COME, life did not go back to what it had been. The Paynes' few white neighbors decamped. Before the riots, a white couple from Eastern Europe lived next door, as did another white couple, with French and German ancestry, down the block. By 1930, the block was entirely black except for one lone white couple who had recently arrived from the Netherlands. The same was true throughout Chicago. Whites moved away and landlords further tightened the real estate cordon around blacks, leaving them no choice but to remain in the overcrowded neighborhoods of South Side. The wall of segregation became firmer than ever. As Payne entered her teenage years, her neighborhood was solidly black. "It was sort of an island in the midst of a white sea," she said.

Excluded from Chicago, African Americans began building their own city within a city. Turning, as one observer put it, "segregation into congregation," they set about strengthening their own institutions. Several miles to the northeast of the Paynes' home, Grand Boulevard became the hub of all things black. Here African Americans could purchase anything they needed. One could cash a check at the Binga State Bank, Chicago's first black-owned bank; pick up a new supply of High-Brown Face Powder from the Overton-Hygienic Company; make a payment on a life insurance policy at Supreme Life; pay respects to a deceased relative at the Jackson Funeral System; consider a new house at the Julian A. Black real estate office; take in a show at the Regal Theater; or hail a cab from the Supreme Taxicab Company. "Because cabs wouldn't come in," said one longtime South Side resident, "we created our own."

An African American newspaper, the *Chicago Bee*, christened the emerging community Bronzeville. And, as it did with all its other needs, the city within a city created its own vibrant Fleet Street. Two blocks from the *Bee*, which occupied a magnificent Art Deco building on State Street, the *Chicago Defender* moved into an equally imposing edifice. Although it was the *Bee* that gave Bronzeville its name, the older *Defender* was its newspaper. "The *Chicago Defender* was the paper," said Payne. "You couldn't grow up in Chicago and be black if you didn't know the *Chicago Defender*."

The *Defender* was the brainchild of Robert Sengstacke Abbott. Born in Georgia in 1868 to former slaves, Abbott had lost his father while still an infant. John H. H. Sengstacke, a German immigrant who had been raised in Georgia, became Robert's stepfather, and the child was raised in small towns in Georgia. Abbott briefly attended two colleges before pursuing training as a printer at Hampton Normal and Agricultural Institute in Hampton, Virginia, which counted Booker T. Washington among its alumni. After graduating in 1896, Abbott came to Chicago, Illinois, where he earned a law degree from Kent College of Law.

Finding the practice of law in Chicago mostly closed to African Americans, Abbott hit upon the idea of creating a newspaper for black readers. He already had printing skills and experience as a reporter with the *Savannah Tribune*; his stepfather had once established a newspaper. Converting his landlady's apartment kitchen into an editorial office, Abbott ordered up a 300-copy press run of the *Chicago Defender* on May 5, 1905. The four-page, six-column broadsheet weekly was a hit.

TAKING A PAGE FROM Joseph Pulitzer and William Randolph Hearst, Abbott gave his copy a sensational sheen and packed his headlines with a melodramatic vocabulary. Living up to its name, the *Defender* chronicled every racist injustice, from atrocities such as lynchings in the South to discrimination in the North, under its thunderous motto "American Race Prejudice Must Be Destroyed."

Within a decade of its founding, the weekly's circulation exceeded 50,000. But the actual number of readers was far greater. "Copies," said one reader, "were passed around until worn out." African Americans in the South dared not receive the *Defender* through the U.S. mail. To do so would tip off watchful whites that they were reading the incendiary sheet, banned by law in some communities. Instead, the paper devised another system to get its issues into the hands of its Southern subscribers. It formed an alliance with Pullman porters, rewarding them financially with payments and editorially with coverage. Each week the men would get bundles of the *Defender*, store them in their personal lockers on the trains, and drop them off at barbershops and churches along their Southern routes. By 1920, two-thirds of the newspaper's 130,000 circulation was outside of Chicago. The *Defender's* national readership was considered so threatening to racial order that the U.S. government military intelligence created a 64-page report on its circulation growth, complete with maps, as if charting the progress of an invading force.

The *Defender* was no more solely a Chicago newspaper than the *New York Times* was merely a New York newspaper. It was America's black newspaper. Southern readers were fed an endless diet of stories about the prosperous life that awaited blacks in Chicago, accompanied by graphic reminders of the horrors at home. It sparked a migration fever. In turn, the *Defender* fueled it by providing hard-to-find transportation and resettlement information and each week covered the migrants' arrivals in Chicago. "I bought a *Chicago Defender*, and after reading it and seeing the golden opportunity, I have decided to leave this place at once," wrote a Tennessee man. As a poem the *Defender* made popular exclaimed:

I'll bid the South good-bye
No longer shall they treat me so,

And knock me in the eye.
The Northern States is where I'm bound.

In short, Chicago became the Promised Land.

As ETHEL PAYNE NEARED the completion of her years at Copernicus Elementary School, the city completed the construction of Lindblom Technical High School. Towering over the squatting wooden
bungalows of West Englewood and consuming an entire block, the
massive stone edifice was fronted by stout Ionic limestone columns
and ornamented in Beaux-Arts style. It was an emblem of civic pride.
"The finest high school in the country," proclaimed the *Chicago
Tribune*.

Just as its design was inspired by Chicago's new passion for Classi-
cal Revival–style architecture, triggered by the 1893 World's Colum-
bian Exposition, its education philosophy reflected the fashionable
progressive notions of Chicagoans like John Dewey. It offered the
usual array of vocational classes in pharmacy, automobile repair, and
printing, as demanded by the business community, but the centerpiece of its curriculum was a four-year college prep program.

Lindblom's facilities and top-notch faculty were intended for
white students. But because Payne's house fell two blocks inside
its enrollment district, this educational paradise was open to her.
Reaching the school, on the other hand, was not easy. Payne's parsi-
monious parents were unwilling to pay the daily fare for the streetcar
that rattled down nearby Sixty-Third Street. So instead Payne had to
walk the mile to the school and cross Loomis Boulevard, a frontier
line past which blacks were not welcomed. "And when you crossed it,
boy, you were in all-white territory," Payne said. She endured taunts,
epithets, and the occasional rock thrown at her. "Sometimes I stood
my ground, sometimes I got a bloody nose from fighting," she said.
"But that was the way it was."

It was not much easier for Payne inside the building. She was only one in a handful of black teenagers among the 2,500 students roaming the cavernous, high-ceilinged halls. And there was little sentiment that they were welcomed in their ranks. Only the year before, rough play in a basketball game against a Negro school emptied the stands and sparked a brawl involving more than 200 students. Razors and revolvers were flashed in the melee before police reached the gymnasium. The blame for any violence of this sort was always put on the black students. "White parents are cautious about stirring up trouble," said one principal, "for they know the emotional tendency of the colored to knife and kill."

ETHEL PAYNE FOLLOWED LINDBLOM'S college prep curriculum, taking history, English, algebra, geometry, botany, French, and four years of Latin, a requirement her mother, the former Latin instructor, placed on each of her children. But she struggled academically. "I think it was because I was under stress and trauma all the time," Payne said. She was also, by her own admission, "a daydreamer." However, to Bessie's delight, history and English appealed to her, especially English. "My mother, early on, discovered that I had a flair for words and writing, and she encouraged that," Payne said.

Miss Dixon's English class provided a second endorsement. A compact woman with black hair parted and drawn back and somewhat masculine features, Margaret Dixon had come to Lindblom from Oak Park, where she had been a favorite teacher of the teen-aged Ernest Hemingway, whose novels *The Sun Also Rises* and *A Farewell to Arms* had just turned him into a household name. The veteran teacher had left her mark on students. "I don't believe I ever had any professors at Dartmouth or Illinois who were better instructors, and I majored in English," recalled one of her Oak Park students. Filled with a kind of nervous energy, she talked rapidly and loudly, pushed students to make creative use of their imaginations, and left little doubt about her opinion of a student's work. "She was," said another student, "salty in her criticism, proud and full of praise for our efforts, and quite ready to rip at what was not good."

Payne fell under Dixon's spell. "She encouraged me to write, and she asked me to do little short stories." Seeking a subject for a composition, Payne wandered out of her neighborhood and headed northeast to Maxwell Street, well-known for its open-air pushcart market manned by Eastern European Jews. Although the neighborhood was now inhabited mostly by African Americans, Jews continued to remain an important presence on the street. There she found a quiet spot to sit, notebook in hand, taking it all in. "I thought the people on the row were like characters out of a book," Payne said. She was happy simply recording what she saw. "You could smell the fish frying, you could smell meats cooking and hear the banter that would go on from upstairs and downstairs, as the women sat in the yard and did the quilting."

At home she read aloud from her efforts to describe what she found on Maxwell Street to anyone in the family willing to listen. Her mother, who was a good writer herself, was a patient listener and would occasionally offer a criticism. "It usually was on grammatical construction more than content," said Payne. "I don't think she ever criticized what I was trying to say, so much as she wanted me to have it correct in punctuation and grammatical patterns."

Payne's story about Maxwell Street was published in the school newspaper. But despite her journalistic contribution to the paper, joining its staff was not an option for Payne. "It just wasn't the code at the time," she said. "It just wasn't. So the fact that I have even had this accepted was really something."

One day as English class began, Dixon handed Payne back some of her work. Dixon had scribbled illegibly in the margins. Payne approached her desk. "Miss Dixon, what did you write?" she asked. Smiling, Dixon replied, "Your handwriting reminds me of another pupil I used to have when I taught in Oak Park, Illinois," referring to her now-famous student.

It was, for Payne, a treasured affirmation.

ONE MONTH AFTER PAYNE started her new life at Lindblom, her father came home from work complaining of a headache. Forty-six years old, strong, and physically fit, William was rarely ill. But this time was different. He soon developed a fever and a rash that turned patches of skin a brownish gray. The pastor's son, who had just graduated from medical school, was called to the house. He concluded that William had contracted a bacterial infection known as erysipelas, or more commonly called Saint Anthony's fire, perhaps from the soiled linens on his train runs. In addition, his kidneys were failing. There was little that could be done in the preantibiotic days of the 1920s.

Thelma, the second-oldest child, who was now twenty years old and nicknamed the Boss by her father, mounted the stairs to peek in the room where their father lay. None of the other children were permitted to see him because the doctors feared his condition was contagious. He asked Thelma if she had taken care of the bills that he wanted paid. "I said yes, and he seemed satisfied," she recalled. "To the last, he was a responsible person looking after the needs of his family."

On the evening of February 2, 1926, at a few minutes before ten, William Payne died. Ethel couldn't cope. "It was my first real encounter with death, because people didn't die that fast in Englewood," she said. "I was so hysterical about it that a neighbor took me in and kept me." She even avoided the funeral three days later at St. John's. "I just couldn't deal with the idea of death. It was just too alien to me."

The following month was the snowiest on record in Chicago. Bessie faced a future with six children and no husband to provide for them. William had left a small life insurance policy, and thankfully, the house was paid for. But the loss of his wages was devastating. Bessie's only remaining income came from her job teaching Sunday school at St. John's and from her hobby of painting china. Alice, the oldest child, was working at a dressmaking shop, and Thelma, the second eldest, was employed as a public school teacher. Lemuel left school and took a job as a runner with an insurance company but continued taking classes at night. Ethel remained at Lindblom.

In the fall of 1929, Ethel posed for her yearbook photo with a large corsage of small white flowers, her hair tightly combed back, exposing her earrings, and a long strand of pearls falling across her open-necked dress. On January 31, 1930, she received her diploma in a midyear commencement held to accommodate students who entered the school in the winter rather than in the fall. But no inspiring oration or uplifting recessional music could lift the pall cast by the descending economic storm.

CHAPTER 3

DRIFTWOOD

THE 1930S DID NOT GREET ETHEL PAYNE'S GRADUATING class with open arms. The fury of the Great Depression lashed Chicago's South Side with devastating force. Merchants on State Street and Grand Avenue, at the center of Bronzeville, shuttered their storefronts, and the Binga Bank closed its doors. At the Royal Gardens Cabaret, where a jazz orchestra once wailed into the night, eight hundred men slept in long rows of army cots.

Like canaries in a coal mine, black workers were the first to feel the effects of the Great Depression. "It is well known that when an unemployment wave strikes the country," warned the *Chicago Defender* in the early months of 1930, "race workers are the first and hardest affected, as many jobs which they hold ordinarily are taken from them and given to white workers."

The Payne family was more fortunate than most. Ethel joined her brother doing clerical chores for an insurance company while her older sisters clung to their jobs in the schools and the youngest one toiled in a dress shop. Among African Americans in Chicago, nearly 60 percent of the men and almost 45 percent of the women were without work. But even holding jobs, the Payne family was destitute. By April 1931, the Chicago school system ran out of funds to pay its teachers. For the next two years, the two oldest Payne sisters received real paychecks only four months out of the year. The remainder of the time they were given scrip that they could redeem for eighty to ninety cents on the dollar, at least until the banks and stores lost faith in the IOUs and ceased accepting them.

But no matter how dire their circumstances, Bessie refused charity and remained determined to keep her family together and get her last child through school. She took on domestic work and turned their residence into a boardinghouse by stuffing the six children into two or three bedrooms. At every turn, she devised a way forward. Meeting as a council, the family decided to pool its resources so that the youngest child, Avis, could go to college. "So we would all save up," Ethel said. "I would work or go work in people's houses, clean, and I'd put aside a little money, maybe a dollar." The funds, combined with a scholarship, sent Avis to West Virginia State University.

Bessie's indomitable spirit remained an anchor for the children throughout the turmoil of the Great Depression. Even when bone-tired she never let up in providing structure and stability for her family. At night, when the children were at the dining room table finishing their homework, an exhausted Bessie would manage to call down instructions from upstairs.

"Bed the fire."

"Yes, ma'am."

"Don't forget to wind the clock"

"Yes, ma'am."

"Don't forget to empty the icebox pan."

"Yes, ma'am."

As for herself, Bessie's strong faith and her job as a Sunday-school teacher gave her strength to carry on. "My mother," said Ethel, "was the most devout, religious person you'd ever want to meet. She just prayed, prayed, and prayed all the time." The children found respite in the family's abiding habit of reading. "This was our entertainment, as well as a broadening of education and culture," said Thelma. "So if we were poor in purse, we had a wealth in books and an appreciation of the classics to an uncommonly high degree."

At night the family took turns reading aloud from the Bible and treasures such as Charles Dickens's *Great Expectations* and Louisa May Alcott's *Little Women*. Alcott's enduringly popular novel about four daughters growing up with a mother and a much-absent father mirrored Ethel's own life. In the Payne family, Ethel was Jo March, a tomboy frustrated by social limitations, infatuated with reading, and driven ceaselessly to write. Marmee March, Jo's mother, could well have been Ethel's own mother, holding the family together through difficult times, providing unconditional love to her children, and dispensing sage counsel. Until the end of her life, Ethel said she could recite *Little Women* by heart, just as she never forgot her mother's advice. "You may not have what you want or what you even need," Payne said her mother used to tell her, "but always remember that using what you have to improve your mind is more important than material things."

IN THE MIDST of the hard times, Ethel Payne pressed on with her education. She hoped to become a lawyer. "Just as I was fierce about protecting my brother, I had a strong, strong, deeply embedded hatred of bullies," she said. "I just felt that if you're strong, you had no right to pick on weak people."

The odds, however, were stacked against her. Less than 3,500 of the nation's lawyers were female. Few professional schools were open to African Americans. And she certainly did not have the kinds of grades a law school required. Undeterred, she entered Crane Junior College, which was near West Englewood. Open to African Americans, who made up 15 percent of its student body, Crane was a haven for low-income students who hoped to eventually enter the University of Chicago or Northwestern University. But Payne was soon bored. "I was just majoring in English and history, the routine things that most people did," Payne said. "But I was always thinking of doing something else more creative." That thing was writing.

When she began at Crane, Payne learned of a national essay contest for high school and junior college students sponsored by the American Interracial Peace Committee, a group of African Americans allied with the American Friends Service Committee and under the direction of Alice Dunbar Nelson, who had once been married to Payne's favorite poet Paul Laurence Dunbar. The essays, one to two thousand words in length, were to address subjects ranging from general ones such as "Youth Looks at World Peace" to rather specific topics like "Russia and China in Manchuria."

Payne decided to enter the competition and submitted an essay about "Interracial Relationships as a Basis for International Peace." It made the then rarely heard link between domestic racial justice and decolonization. The peace committee winnowed down the entries to nine finalists and sent them off to a group of judges that included, among others, W. E. B. Du Bois, the most famous African American intellectual and civil rights leader of the time, and Carter G. Woodson, the founder of the Association for the Study of Negro Life and History, who had recently established Negro History Week, the forerunner of Black History Month. When the winners were announced in July, Payne was on the list. First place went to a Harvard University student. Payne tied for fourth and earned a $10 prize.

Despite this success, Payne's writing ambition was neither in essay writing nor in nonfiction. She wanted to be a writer of stories and novels like Jo March in *Little Women*. And like March's mother, Bessie Payne encouraged her daughter. "I happen to be one of the great mass of aspiring writers," Ethel confessed in a letter at the time, "who hope to some day pen the 'Great American Novel' and earn a place in the sun."

THE GREAT DEPRESSION HAD NOT put an end to cultural life in South Side. Rather, in some ways the hard times reinvigorated musical and literary enterprises, which were well used to surviving on the economic margins.

In the fall of 1930, newsstands in South Side and other centers of African American populations carried a new magazine. Publisher Robert S. Abbott, working off his phenomenal success with the *Chicago Defender*, had launched a new general-interest magazine bearing his name. "*Abbott's Monthly* has just made its bow," reported the *New York Amsterdam News*, "and its contents warrant the expectation that it will be the magazine the people have been waiting for." Monthlies catering to black readers then were primarily the NAACP's *Crisis* and the National Urban League's *Opportunity*. Unlike the two civil rights–oriented publications, however, Abbott's new entry was more akin to the *New Yorker*, which had been launched five years earlier. Magazines that served white readers were flourishing, and Abbott's faith in his publication seemed to be confirmed by its initial reception. "There have been many literary ventures of this sort, and magazine upon magazine, but not of the caliber of *Abbott's Monthly*," reported the *Detroit Independent*. "It has outstripped the imagination of all and upon perusal proves to surpass any other endeavor."

Abbott's Monthly put out a call for work from writers and artists in Chicago, an acknowledgment that by 1930 the center of African American cultural life had shifted away from the East and Harlem. Payne immediately sent off a short story. To her delight, it was accepted for publication.

Well-crafted and clever, Payne's tale was heavy in autobiographical overtones but with dark notes her mother could not have applauded. In the story, entitled "Driftwood," eighteen-year-old Madge Barton, whose father died when she was twelve years old, moves to a great Midwestern city in hopes of becoming a novelist. "Eighteen had seen the dawning of her conviction," Payne wrote. "She would forge ahead and strike out for herself." In contrast to her roommate Vivian Lasham, "the embodiment of all the spirit of wild, revolting youth," who haunts stage doors in hopes of becoming an actress, Madge devotes her time to writing.

Vivian's failure to obtain work drives her into the arms of a sleazy white-suited gambler with black patent leather shoes brilliantly shined and a black-banded tan derby worn angularly and whose plump fingers at the end of oily hands sported ruby and gold rings, "Hello there, baby. C'mon. Come sit with papa," he says upon spying Madge.

Her roommate's descent into the gambler's world solidifies Madge's literary plans. "The idea had been playing in Madge's mind for weeks that she would write a novel dealing with the sordidness of the dens of vice and evil and the evils of the city," wrote Payne. "Why! She would make this her masterpiece; she would point out all the evils so as to bring about great reform."

She works day and night, alone in her apartment now that Vivian has deserted her. But publishers promptly reject the first draft of her novel. A successful novelist consoles her. "Madge," he says, "you haven't had enough experience with hardships. You think your trouble is hard, but you must learn to face defeat bravely. Victory comes in getting up after you are down, and trying again."

With renewed energy, Madge trims the sentimentality and weak portions of her manuscript. Convinced it is now bound for success, she goes out to consign it to the mail. On her way to the post office, she encounters a broken-down and haggard Vivian, abandoned by her gambler. Madge helps her into a nearby drugstore and over hot chocolate invites Vivian to live with her again. "Kid," Vivian replies, "I know you mean it, but it's too late to start again. I'm just driftwood, floating along, getting nowhere."

Several days later Madge returns to her room. She is months in arrears on the rent. There she finds her manuscript at her door, once again rejected. She sinks into despair and rushes out into the night. From the shadows emerges a slender sinister-looking man ogling her.

"Hello, baby, going my way?" he asks.

Madge prepares, as she had before, to give him a stare intended on sending him away. But instead she throws her head back, issuing "a laugh of despair and abandonment that lingered on the night air in haunting echoes." Taken aback, the man stares at Madge. "Sure," she says, "anywhere you say, daddy."

"They melted into the night and the great grimy shadows of the city swallowed them up."

CHAPTER 4

AN ABUNDANCE OF NERVE

I N NOVEMBER 1931, TWENTY-YEAR-OLD ETHEL PAYNE SAT before her typewriter in the house on Throop Street, placed a piece of paper in the roller of her machine, and put her fingers to the keys. "My dear Dr. DuBois," she began. "Fate and circumstances have a curious way of coinciding to achieve a common purpose. So it is with a good deal of presumption that I take it upon myself to write to you at this time."

Presumption was the right word because her letter was directed to W. E. B. Du Bois. Sociologist, activist, and cofounder of the National Association for the Advancement of Colored People (NAACP), he was the most nationally prominent African American of the day. Payne was proposing to write his biography. "Of course, I realize that this is a tremendous undertaking that requires wide experience and a broad range of material to draw from, as well as nerve," she wrote. "At the present time the only one of these three that I have in stock is nerve, and that is in abundance." If Du Bois replied, the letter was lost to history.

Despite her determination and early good fortune with her fiction, Payne was learning—as Madge had—that a black woman had little hope of making a living by writing in the 1930s. A more practical career plan was in order.

Payne left Crane College, which was struggling to remain open, and entered the Chicago Training School for City, Home, and Foreign Missions run by the Methodist Episcopal Church. The tuition-free college had a Bible-centered curriculum that offered basic medical and social work training likely to make one employable. Payne found its religiosity a bit overwhelming but she stuck it out, majoring in social services with minors in fine arts and religious education. She earned her highest grade, an A–, in a storytelling class. But overall her work, or lack of it, resulted in yet another lackluster academic performance.

In her spare time, she continued to write her stories for *Abbott's Monthly*. Her choice of subjects and her style was like those of Émile Zola, the French writer known for his natural style in writing about violence, alcohol, and prostitution. One of her tales featured a minister who had an affair with a parishioner, and another described a black prostitute's day in court. The magazine was evidently happy with her contributions and promoted her work in display advertisements in the *Defender*. "You remember the story 'Retribution' in the March issue by Ethel L. Payne, whose fiction and facts are so closely interwoven that one marvels at the unfolding of her story," said the advertisement. "This month Miss Payne has written 'Cabaret.' In it the glamour of the night life is brought into the open day."

Payne's success with *Abbott's Monthly* was no small achievement. Since its start, the magazine had grown in circulation to more than 100,000 and attracted some of the nation's best black writers, such as Chester Himes, who would later write *If He Hollers Let Him Go*, and Richard Wright, who was struggling to launch himself as a writer, tearing into pieces most of what he wrote. But he was sufficiently pleased with one story called "Superstition" that he submitted it to *Abbott's Monthly*. It became his first published work.

IN THE SPRING OF 1934, Payne neared the completion of her studies in social service at the Chicago Training School. In the *Torch*, the student annual publication to which she was a contributing editor,

Payne published a lengthy semifictional account of washday in an alley behind her house. "'The row' is like an alien intruder or an ill-favored child," wrote Payne in introducing the place. "Complacently it squats in its ugly, squalid surroundings while the rest of Englewood haughtily lifts its skirt and passes around it."

On the evening of June 15, 1934, Payne graduated from the Chicago Training School. She was still not a scholar and finished eleventh out of her class of thirteen. For her yearbook, Payne selected words from Henry Wadsworth Longfellow, "All things come round to him who will but wait." She still retained hope of a law career and asked the school to send her transcript to the University of Chicago. While the university had accepted black students as early as 1870 and by the 1920s had more than sixty African Americans in its student body, it would be another decade before a black woman would graduate from its law school. With her grades, Payne was not a feasible candidate.

Instead Payne used her newly minted degree to land a job at the State Training School for Girls in Geneva, Illinois, about forty miles west. The reformatory housed about 400 to 500 girls sent to it by juvenile courts from around the state, mostly on charges of immorality and incorrigibility. "Those girls," Payne said, "some of them 15, 16, 17 years old, and they'd had experiences of people 40 years old or more—street hustling, prostitution, into drugs and things."

When Payne arrived she found a campus-like setting situated on the sloping banks of the Fox River. The inmates were housed in about a dozen two-story-tall brick cottages, each with a dayroom, kitchen, dining room, and matrons' quarters on the first floor and bedrooms with barred windows on the second. The day was given over to classes, vocational training, and religious services. In their free time, the juveniles engaged in sports such as croquet, basketball, and even roller-skating on the half mile of paved sidewalk.

Payne was hired as a matron. Each cottage housed about thirty-five girls with two women who were on duty all the time except when the relief matron took a turn for a day each week. Payne had to wake the girls and get them off to classes or to their jobs within the reformatory such as working in the laundry. "I was like a jail warden," Payne said.

Payne's wards were all black girls. About one hundred girls, or a quarter of the population, were African American, the high number a reflection of the eagerness of Cook County courts to lock up black youths compounded by the refusal of other state reform institutions to house black inmates. The black cottages, with such names as "Faith" and "Lincoln," were overcrowded, and the residents received less-than-adequate treatment. In fact, the professional staff neglected them except when white girls were discovered having sex with the black inmates. The racial indiscretions horrified the staff more than the sexual transgressions.

The job was exhausting and the girls were a challenge. "They put me to a test, and they would do all kinds of things to see how strong I was," Payne said. "They had lived hard lives crowded into their very young years." After a while she reached an accommodation with many of the girls, and some, Payne felt, came to respect her. "I don't know how many lives I actually affected, because it was too much of an experience for a young person who had been sort of sheltered."

But after a year and a half, her mother finally told her, "Stop it. Stop it and come home." Payne returned to Throop Street. The best job she could find was as a nursery school teacher in settlement houses and public schools at $80 a month. She kept the job for three years, earning enough to get by comfortably. But she was now in her late twenties, more educated than most in her neighborhood, and yet Chicago remained shuttered to her. It was as Chicagoan Bigger Thomas said in Richard Wright's *Native Son*, "Half the time, I feel like I'm on the outside of the world peeping in through a knothole in the fence."

IN JUNE 1939, Payne instructed the Chicago Training School to send her transcript to the Chicago Public Library Training School.

Admitted and trained, she swapped tending children for working with books and became a junior library assistant, with a 40 percent hike in salary.

The aspiration to be a writer, however, remained alive in her. She signed up for a two-credit evening course in short story writing at Northwestern University's Medill School of Journalism; the class was taught by John T. Frederick. Lanky, thin, with wire-rimmed glasses resting on a Roman nose, he looked every part the professor. However, the farm-raised Frederick, who rode a pony to school, was actually an accomplished author, editor, and host of a CBS radio show about books. During the Great Depression, as regional director of the WPA Writers' Project, he had worked with such Chicago writers as Richard Wright and Nelson Algren, who would become one of the best-known American writers in the 1940s and 1950s.

Payne stayed with the class and signed up for Frederick's advanced short story writing class in the second semester. She wrote weekly class assignments of all sorts ranging from recollections to short stories, from plays to dialogues. Her papers came back carefully marked up with encouraging remarks such as those Miss Dixon used to write at Lindblom Technical High School.

"You have a good feeling for words," Frederick told Payne. "More than that, you have a rich and significant experience to share."

CHAPTER 5

MUSKETEER

MONOTONOUSLY STAMPING LENDING SLIPS OR SORT-ing books at the Chicago Lawn Branch Library was hardly the life Ethel Payne had imagined for herself. "Work at the library was boring for me," she said, "and I'm almost sure I was a bore to it." But Chicago remained intransigently inhospitable for an ambitious young black woman. Seven out of ten employed black women worked as domestic servants. Other than that, the few jobs that could be had were in eating and drinking establishments, clothing stores, and, with the right credentials, black schools. A professional black woman was as rare in the Windy City as a warm day in winter.

Preparations for war in 1940 reinforced the resolute racism. The conflagration in Europe fueled a government armament-spending spree that fired up the economy and wiped out the last vestiges of the Great Depression. But the economic growth left most African Americans behind, a bitter reminder of the racial divide. Nearly one in two blacks in Illinois remained without work. Picking up a copy of the *Chicago Defender* was discouraging. The paper's Los Angeles correspondent reported finding only one Negro among the thousands employed in the city's booming aircraft industry. A plant manager in New York told the *Defender* there was no company policy against hiring Negroes. "He said that objections to working with Negroes undoubtedly would come from the men already in the plant and that the company did not wish to experiment at this present time because of the possibility of labor difficulties or the impairment of the morale of its workers."

Following the disheartening racism of the 1920s and 1930s, the stoicism of urban African Americans reached its limit. In the fall of 1940 three black leaders met with President Franklin D. Roosevelt to seek an end to segregation in the military and defense industries. Roosevelt listened sympathetically, but the White House soon made it clear that it would not alter the policy prohibiting the intermingling of colored and white soldiers.

The White House tried to mollify the black leaders. But A. Philip Randolph, the founding president of the Brotherhood of Sleeping Car Porters, was not to be placated. As he rode the train into the South, he brooded over the impasse. By the time he reached Savannah, Georgia, Randolph had a plan. Proposing his idea first to small gatherings and then finally to the nation in January 1941, Randolph called on African Americans to march on Washington as had Coxey's Army of unemployed workers in 1894 and the Bonus Army of unpaid war veterans in 1932.

Over six feet tall, elegant in gestures, and possessing a baritone voice once described as being as musical as an organ, Randolph rallied his people with an eloquence in speech and writing that belied his limited education. "The virtue and rightness of a cause," he said, "are not alone the condition and cause of its progress and acceptance. Power and pressure are at the foundation of the march of social justice and reform."

The planned protest struck terror in the administration. Roosevelt turned for help to his wife, who enjoyed considerable respect among African Americans. With the date of the march drawing near, an anxious Eleanor Roosevelt pleaded with Randolph to call it off. If the arrival of thousands of blacks in the nation's capital, still a deeply segregated city whose hotels and restaurants barred Negroes, triggered an incident of any sort, it would set the cause back, she wrote. "You know that I am deeply concerned about the rights of Negro people, but I think one must face situations as they are and not as one wishes them to be."

To the president, his wife, and such allies of theirs as New York City mayor Fiorello La Guardia, such a protest march was unfathomable, especially in wartime. This fear was Randolph's trump card. The march, he promised, "would wake up and shock official Washington as it has never before been shocked" because "Negroes are supposed not have sufficient iron in their blood for this type of struggle. In common parlance, they are supposed to be just scared and unorganizable."

He invited African American laborers and lawyers, doctors and nurses, mechanics and teachers, men and women, young and old, to join in. The black press, with the exception of the *Pittsburgh Courier*, supported the plan. "To get 10,000 Negroes assembled in one spot, under one banner with justice, democracy and work as their slogan would be the miracle of the century," proclaimed an editorial in the *Defender*. "However, miracles do happen."

TWENTY-NINE-YEAR-OLD PAYNE was among the believers. Randolph had long been a respected figure in her house for having organized the Pullman porter union. But professional frustrations and her reporter-like observations of life in South Side also fueled Payne's discontent. "Already," she said, "I was beginning to have the seeds of rebellion churning up in me."

She was an active member of the Chicago branch of the NAACP, honored for recruiting more than twenty new members. The chapter was fighting the housing covenants that blocked blacks from living in 80 percent of the city and was campaigning to get blacks employed in defense factories. Payne had also organized a community improvement program in her neighborhood through the Modern Women Social and Charity Club that she helped establish at St. John AME Church. The program included a story hour for children at the YMCA, a community council aimed at reducing juvenile delinquency, and a college scholarship fund. Payne, with three volunteers, raised the scholarship money by going door-to-door and soliciting funds from merchants and organizations. Within a few years it provided $500 annually to a college-bound Englewood student.

Nor was she sheepish about speaking her mind. When President Roosevelt sought to weaken the Supreme Court in 1937 by expanding its membership, Payne denounced the plan in a letter published not in the *Defender* but in the *Chicago Tribune* calling the court the "final, greatest hope for political, moral, and economic justice" for American Negroes.

Throughout the spring and into the summer of 1941, no one in South Side could escape the buildup to the march. Each week the *Defender* reported on the growing plans as well as administration efforts at preventing its occurrence. Finally, with only a few days remaining before the march, the president capitulated. On June 25, 1941, Roosevelt signed Executive Order 8802 creating the Fair Employment Practices Committee (FEPC) and requiring that companies with government contracts not discriminate on the basis of race or religion. Randolph called off the march. In its place, he redirected the planned protest into the March on Washington Movement aimed at solidifying the gains and making sure the new employment committee lived up to its promise.

Hammering away at the military's discriminatory policies, the lack of jobs in taxpayer-supported defense industries, and the Red Cross's refusal to use Negro blood, Randolph announced a series of mass meetings in major cities. In mid-February he brought his campaign to St. John AME Church across the street from Payne's house. Payne enlisted and was given the post of chairman of the planning committee for the mass meeting in the city's Coliseum.

It fell to Payne to turn out a crowd for the rally planned for the Coliseum on June 26, 1942, one of three events the movement planned over the course of the year in large cities with black populations. By April the group opened an office in the center of Bronzeville and installed a telephone and typewriter. But trouble brewed behind the flurry of activities and the veneer of unity.

The prickly personalities of the various male Chicago leaders stirred up friction, made worse by their mulish resistance to put any of the women volunteers in leadership posts. "I had hoped that we might proceed in the greatest harmony possible," Payne reported to Randolph, "but it seems as if there are some squalls which come up and must be weathered." Payne chafed at the slow pace of the organizing work, caused by what she saw as a needless redrafting of letters and flyers by Charles Wesley Burton, a member of Randolph's executive committee. She felt blocked at every turn by him. "I am to work in close cooperation with the chairman of the city wide committee, but if I go ahead and take action, I am constantly reminded that I am usurping authority," Payne complained. She warned, "I cannot sit by and wait for orders to proceed."

IN THE END THE WORK moved sufficiently forward. WAKE UP, NEGRO AMERICA! blazed the headline on the Chicago group's flyer. "Do we want to work? Do we want our full rights? Do we want justice?" it asked, inviting black Chicagoans to send in a dime for membership dues, attend Friday-night meetings at the YMCA, or volunteer to work on the Coliseum rally.

Armed with the flyer, Payne and two volunteers canvassed neighborhoods on foot until a supporter offered the use of an automobile. "So you can imagine our raves," reported one of the tired women, "when he stands in our planning committee meeting and quite nonchalantly offers the use of his car without any strings attached, except that most of the time we shall have to furnish our own driver."

As the day of the rally neared, Payne drew up instructions for Bronzeville businesses to close their doors and extinguish their lights, inside and out-, on the night of the event. The gesture, borrowed from wartime blackouts in London, was intended to symbolize the manner in which African Americans were "blacked out" of American democracy. Payne dispatched dozens of volunteers sporting armbands to visit merchants and small-businessmen. The request to join the protest was hardly an invitation. "Stores that refuse to cooperate," Payne wrote in her instructions, "should be blacklisted, boycotted and picketed as enemies to the fight for Negro rights."

The work paid off. From her perch on the stage of the Chicago Coliseum, Payne watched as thousands streamed in. Walter White, the executive secretary of the NAACP, warmed up the crowd before Randolph's appearance. At length he explained that the federal government's racist policies stemmed from the inordinate influence of Southerners, who controlled 50 percent of the congressional committee chairmanships.

"In the light of the control of our government by these men who spit upon democracy whenever the Negro is involved, is there any wonder that meetings like this are tragically necessary at a time like this?" White asked. "Or that, irony of ironies, we Negroes must fight for the right to fight when the world is threatened with destruction?"

Then, after a theatrical play whose humor brought the house down, and several more speakers, Randolph finally took to the stage at 11:00 PM. He recounted how at American train depots, USO canteen workers rushed out to greet white soldiers with cigarettes, candy, and drinks but refused to provide such service when the trains pulled in with Negro soldiers.

After detailing a litany of military discrimination and war industry prejudices, Randolph told the thousands that it was their responsibility to wage the struggle. "History shows that Jews must depend upon Jews to fight the battles of the Jews; Catholics must depend upon Catholics to fight the battles of Catholics; women must depend upon women to fight the battles of women; Negroes must depend upon Negroes to fight the battles of Negroes."

Surely, he said, Negroes can't be expected to fight for democracy in Burma when they don't have it in Birmingham.

THE NEWS COVERAGE of the event was gratifying. On the *Defender's* front page, headlined with 12,000 IN CHICAGO VOICE DEMANDS FOR DEMOCRACY, was a photograph of Payne wearing one of her many hats, a fashion accessory for which she would retain a preference until the end of her life. Other black papers increased the crowd estimates and carried long excerpts from the speeches. Even the white press felt it necessary to say something. The *Chicago Tribune* included a short report buried on page 20 that 10,000 Negroes had gathered to protest what it called "alleged discrimination" in the armed forces and war industry.

The rally took in $1,449.71, Payne excitedly reported to Randolph. "The main questions now being asked by the man on the street are what's next and how are you going to keep interest alive?" Exercising his tendency to aggrandizement, Randolph told Payne that her work contributed to "making the great Coliseum Meeting the biggest demonstration of Negro power ever witnessed in the history of the world." With the success of the rally Payne became, in Randolph's words, one of the movement's Three Musketeers.

The rally over, the planning committee disbanded. But Payne didn't let up in her efforts. When the *Pittsburgh Courier* accused the movement of intensifying racial antagonism and weakening support for the war among African Americans, Payne rushed to its defense. Taking a cue from Randolph's hyperbolic style, she wrote to the editors that the executive order opening factory gates to blacks was the most important victory since the Emancipation Proclamation. For too long the Negro has "depended upon the interest and sympathies of his white friends to intercede for him." Instead, the movement is based on a principle "that the salvation of the Negro people comes from within."

She took the lesson to heart. While holding down a full-time job in the library, she maintained the movement's office after hours and worked on a mammoth tea party intended to sustain interest among Chicago women. For two weeks straight, she did not get to bed before one in the morning. In mid-December, Payne awoke complaining of a persistent headache and went to see her doctor. He told her that if she did not curtail her many activities she would have something far worse than a bothersome headache, namely a complete breakdown.

At home that night, Payne wrote to Randolph. "I am feeling at my lowest physical ebb so much so that I can scarcely hold the pen." While she reported that the outlook for the organization was better than at any time since the Coliseum rally, there remained much to be done. New members needed to be managed, a constitution or bylaws had to be written, and planning had to get under way for the proposed May conference. "Now as egotistical as it may sound," Payne wrote, "the strain of trying to balance these pressures is really telling on me. I think that if some of that burden were lifted I would not be so worried and nervous."

With rest, Payne recovered her strength by summer's end and was able to be among the sixty delegates who assembled in Detroit in September to design a permanent structure for the movement. The group voted to hold a national convention in Chicago the following year. Randolph thanked Payne for her participation but again voiced some trepidation about her Chicago colleagues. "I hope," he wrote to Payne, "they will drop all bickering and grievances and concentrate on the conference."

IN 1943, WITH THE UNITED STATES in its second year of the war, the movement redoubled its efforts. As the summer approached,

Payne took a short leave of absence from her job at the library to work full-time on preparations for what was now being called the "We Are Americans, Too" convention set for the end of June. For her efforts she was paid $500, a considerable sum for the cash-strapped organization. Knowing that Randolph was the movement's biggest draw, to publicize the convention she booked him for four community meetings in churches serving the city's burgeoning black population.

Once again rebellion surfaced among Chicago members. This time the insurrectionist was Payne. Free labor from women, particularly admiring ones, had made it possible for Randolph to run his movement on a shoestring budget. But he regularly disregarded their advice and never considered them equal to men. During the previous year's campaign, Payne had gotten a taste of this when Randolph had done nothing to help when male Chicago organizers undercut her. Many of Randolph's numerous female supporters tolerated his paternalistic treatment of women, but not Payne.

She picked up the telephone and called Randolph. She told him that she wanted her duties and powers clearly spelled out. The call was insufficient. She took pen to paper. "I simply refuse to be treated like a worrisome child and patted on the head and told to run along," she told him. "This is your brainchild and I simply want to help it grow, but if you're going to be indifferent I don't see why in hell I should get my blood pressure up for nothing. I refuse to be taken for granted and I hope I made myself clear."

Payne had reasons to worry. The men in the movement remained uncomfortable with women in positions of authority. "Too many bossy dames around here," complained one male organizer. When she was done itemizing her complaints in the letter, she closed with a promise. "I know," she wrote, "you are relieved that this is all I am going to say, but if you don't straighten up and fly right there's more yet to come."

Randolph got the message and Payne resumed her organizing work. The convention's agenda was announced. The focus would be on ending "Jim Crow in uniform" and the conference would include strategy sessions on eliminating military segregation and creating a program to do the same with American civilian life. Patience among Negroes was at an end, Randolph warned. "The pulse beat of the nation is being quickened by this restless volcano that disturbs men's souls."

RANDOLPH WAS PRESCIENT in a way that he did not anticipate. Roosevelt's executive order, although weakly enforced, had given blacks access to the lowest-paid jobs in the defense industries. Their presence, however, created animosity among white workers in Northern cities who feared that their jobs would be threatened.

On a warm Saturday June evening, a week before March on Washington delegates reached Chicago for their meeting, a fight broke out between black and white youths at Detroit's Belle Isle Park. Fueled by rumors, the clash escalated and spread into the Motor City, creating the worst urban riot in more than twenty years. It took three days for authorities to restore order. Thirty-four people died, twenty-five of whom were black, and 760 were injured.

The riots in Detroit, as well as ones at the Beaumont, Texas, shipyards, created a sense of urgency when the conference opened in late June. Randolph laid the blame for the outbreak of violence on the doorstep of the White House. "Riots are the result of the government policy of segregation of and discrimination against Negroes," he said. Once again the specter of a march on the nation's capital appeared as the gathering approved a resolution giving the executive committee the power to set a time and date for one.

Payne had all the details well planned out for the gathering. For five days, 109 delegates from fourteen states, meeting inside the South Side's Metropolitan Apostolic Community Church, debated and voted on resolutions ranging from supporting the war and opposing the Communist Party to demanding a revision of the Atlantic Charter to include the darker races and require the Allied nations to give up their colonies.

During the meeting Payne intermingled with emerging civil rights leaders such as Edgar D. Nixon, who a decade later would organize the Montgomery, Alabama, bus boycott, and Bayard Rustin. Only thirty years old and working as Randolph's youth coordinator, Rustin had caught the attention of many activists for his principled devotion to nonviolent direct action inspired by Mahatma Gandhi's struggles against colonial British rule in India. The year before, Rustin had refused to give up his seat in the front of a bus while traveling in the South and had not fought back when police officers beat him. He now faced prison for draft resistance. His presentation on this new strategy moved the delegates to act audaciously. Under the watchful eyes of FBI informants, Payne and other delegates formally pledged to adopt nonviolent direct-action tactics. At the time, a fourteen-year-old Martin Luther King Jr. was preparing to enter his final year at Atlanta's Booker T. Washington High School.

The 1943 Detroit riots not only agitated the conference delegates but also panicked politicians throughout the United States. In Illinois, Republican governor Dwight Green looked anxiously at his 1944 reelection bid. He won the office in 1940 when support for the New Deal was waning. Voters were now preparing to reward him for three years of dependable service free from the chicanery of the Chicago Democratic political machinery. A riot could upset his reelection plans.

The concern was real. "It CAN happen here, because at the present time, living conditions here are worse than any city I've been in," wrote a Pullman porter to the *Defender*. "Someone should wake up and look around Chicago if they want to avoid trouble here, because it is more serious than you realize." The NAACP called on its interracial committees in nineteen potential trouble spots to persuade newspapers to suppress unsubstantiated rumors that could incite violence. Even CBS Radio joined in by airing an anti-riot program featuring thirty famous actors and writers.

Governor Green was not taking any chances. "We have been alarmed," he said, "by recent outbreaks of interracial strife in other states and we are determined to prevent any such tragedies in Illinois." To that end he selected seven white and seven black citizens from around Illinois to serve on an interracial commission aimed at easing racial friction. For its black members, Green selected two prominent pastors, a funeral director, a vice-president of the Brotherhood of Sleeping Car Porters, a physician and former track star, a housing bureau official, and one other.

"I hereby appoint you to be a member of the Interracial Commission for Illinois," Green wrote to Payne in late July, "for the purpose of investigating means, not only of preventing racial strife, but of effecting permanent improvement of racial relations in the State." Her appointment stood out. Payne was one of only two women on the fourteen-member panel; the white side had a female elected politician. More striking, Payne was the only one without a post of some stature.

The March on Washington Movement had made Payne into a prominent Chicago activist with a reputation that reached the corridors of the state capitol.

CHAPTER 6

TIME TO LEAVE

IN SEPTEMBER 1943, ETHEL PAYNE RODE UP TO THE CHI-
cago Loop and walked into the twenty-two-story La Salle Hotel,
one of the city's toniest hotels, a world away from South Side.
There she joined the Interracial Commission for its inaugural meeting. The governor, underscoring his support for the group's work,
attended the session. "I'm looking to this commission for advice and
counsel on a program that will lead us nearer to the American ideal
of equal opportunity for all our citizens," Green told the panel's members, hoping his words would win him support among African American voters.

Getting down to business, though its members remained in the
dark as to exactly what work they were empowered to do, the commission urged that similar organizations be established in Illinois communities that had substantial black populations. Payne brought her
industriousness, her activism, and her impatience to the work. From
the start, commission members turned to her for help in preparing
reports and drafting resolutions.

In one of its earliest meetings, the commission identified housing
as central to improving relations between the races. It charged Payne
and two other commission members, a white judge and a black physician, to draft a resolution that could be quickly adopted. But compromise would have to be the order of the day to obtain an agreement

from the biracial group. In its final version, a watered-down resolution urged that laws be enacted to tear down unsuitable housing, prohibit overcrowding, prevent overcharging rent, and secure cooperation from landowners to provide new housing. In only one instance in the seven-point resolution was discrimination even mentioned, and only in reference to public housing. The commission was hardly going to promote the change Payne believed was necessary.

Payne's impatience for the weak declarations of the commission soon surfaced. She had met the night before with fellow commission member Catholic bishop Bernard J. Sheil, who was known for his outspokenness. He shared Payne's more ambitious hopes for the commission. "Justice for minority groups is the ultimate test of our domestic processes," Sheil told the press, "and this commission must proceed fearlessly to lead in this grave problem for Illinois and America."

Payne described to her fellow members the plans she and Bishop Sheil had devised. "We both arrived at the conclusion that we feel it would be well to recommend to this commission that we hold a series of regional meetings, because we cannot adequately cover the problem unless we are on home ground," she said. The meetings should particularly be held in areas of tension such as East St. Louis. The commission agreed to the idea but limited the hearings to a single day. When Payne complained, the chair told her the discussion was over.

When members turned to talk about instructions they believed should be provided to law enforcement in case of riots, Payne interrupted. "May I inject this thought," she asked. "I have noticed that this commission was created out of an emergency because we thought there was enough racial tension throughout the state to warrant the establishment of this commission." Now she wondered if the commission believed the tension had eased to the extent that there was not much to worry about. The chair replied, "The most dangerous situation in America regarding race relations is the tendency to feel we have gotten over the hump." Then he quickly moved to the next item of business, closing off further discussion of Payne's concerns.

Frustrated, Payne nonetheless remained on board. In contrast to her dull work at the library, the commission gave her status and a sense that she had a platform. But she was keenly aware that the commission, like most such political contrivances, lacked teeth. It was a point a *Defender* editor drove home when he appeared before the panel. He urged them to seek policing powers such as those granted to the Federal Fair Employment Practices Committee. "You would be wasting your time and energy," he told them, "to sit here philosophying on social conditions and racial tensions, housing, etc., if you do not have the power to act upon those things."

PAYNE'S WORK WITH THE March on Washington Movement was so rewarding that in the fall of 1943 she applied for a job as a fieldworker at the NAACP. Randolph promised to talk to Roy Wilkins, then the editor of *Crisis* magazine, on her behalf. In the meantime, she received a surprising letter from the U.S. Department of Justice. Two years earlier, she had taken a civil service test and had earned a sufficient rating to be a government librarian. The letter asked if she would be interested in a library post. "Unquestionably," Payne replied.

In Washington on a lobbying trip for Randolph a few months later, Payne stopped in at the Department of Justice to seek out Matthew McKavitt, the librarian whose signature had been on the letter. Directed to the fifth floor of the department's new building, which was decorated with WPA art, Payne found McKavitt. Although he greeted her warmly, McKavitt told her that her name had been struck from the list of candidates. "From some of the statements on my application," said Payne, "it was ascertained that I was colored and so the conversation revolved around the difficulties which would arise upon having a Negro on the staff."

There were, indeed, Negro women running the elevator, McKavitt said, and five Negro men working as messengers and clerks. No thought, however, had been given to having a Negro in a professional position. In fact, after learning of Payne's destination, the receptionist who had greeted her downstairs had already called McKavitt to warn him not to hire her. All the while praising her qualifications, McKavitt apologetically said his superior from Georgia would oppose giving her the job. The next morning Payne sought out the Civil Service Commission. The best the staff there could do was to offer her a junior clerk's position if she was willing to take yet another exam.

Payne retreated to Chicago by overnight train. When Randolph heard of Payne's Washington ordeal, he immediately wrote to Attorney General Francis Biddle, saying that he was sure Biddle would not tolerate this kind of discrimination if brought to his attention. Press savvy as he was, Randolph also gave a copy of his letter to newspapers.

Hardly anyone paid attention. Segregation, while frowned on by some in the North, was widely accepted as a matter of fact, and jobs in Washington's federal bureaucracy continued to be off-limits to African Americans unless they wanted to operate elevators, run messages, serve food, or clean bathrooms.

THE FAILURE TO GET the job in Washington or one with the NAACP intensified Ethel Payne's despondency at being stuck at her Chicago library job. Her life was dull, punctuated only by volunteer work at a community house and the occasional Interracial Commission meeting. "I was definitely ready for a change, something more challenging," she said. Even Chicago, her birth city, discouraged her by its lack of progress. "When I ride down South Parkway now or State Street or similar streets, I get a bitter nausea at the grimy squalor of Chicago's South Side. It makes me ashamed, disgusted and fighting mad that a city of this size should allow such."

The massive immigration of African Americans to Chicago

worried her. Like many of the established black settlers, Payne was not immune to developing an antipathy toward the newcomers and what she saw as their general rowdiness and bad conduct as well as the crime and disease that accompanied them. "They even trespass the quiet somber decency of my own street and I resent it. They're like barbarians overrunning the civilization that I've known," she said. "I know they are my own people and somehow they must be taught the better way of life."

The March on Washington Movement occasionally showed signs of life, but Payne recognized that its time had passed. "It was good to see you again and to hear you speak in this old familiar way," Payne wrote Randolph after hearing him talk in September 1945. "It brought back memories of old times." She retained some optimism that the end of the war might reinvigorate the movement. "I am hopeful," Payne told Randolph, "that the Negro who has been deaf to all warnings of coming cutbacks and indifferent to problems of his own welfare will now have time to and cause to think and act. Soon the field should be ripe for reorganizing. Something has to be done."

The war's end was bringing a more tangible and personal change for Payne. Her brother, Lemuel, had enlisted in the Army and joined the approximately 125,000 African Americans who went overseas. Now he would soon be home and the family would once again be together. "Although he is anxious to return home," Payne wrote to Randolph, "he dreads the thought of returning to the old American discrimination after he has had a chance to see some of the liberalism of such places as Paris, Belgium, and even some parts of Germany where the German people despite the *verboten* of fraternization have heartily welcomed Negro troops."

As desired as it was, the international peace renewed economic challenges for African Americans. Returning white veterans displaced the black workers who had taken their places. (The same held true for those women who had worked during the war.) "The collapse of Japan this week," the *Defender* told its readers, "boo-meranged on Negro workers here with the devastating effect of an atomic bomb, blasting thousands from their well-paying wartime jobs." Even those African Americans who served the country were behind the eight ball. Holding the lowest ranks in the military, they were often discharged later than white soldiers, and by the time they got home, most jobs were already filled. The peace, it seemed, would be no easier than the war. African American living standards rapidly deteriorated. By 1947, the unemployment rate for blacks was twice that of whites.

ON A HOT AUGUST DAY in 1947, Payne and her sister Avis came home from a picnic. When they got off the bus at the corner of Six-tieth and Racine in Englewood, they spotted police officers arresting a group of black men in front of a tavern and loading them into a paddy wagon.

"What's going on?" Payne said.

The question prompted two plainclothes police officers to cross the street, cursing at the two women as they approached. "Get the hell out of here!" they yelled.

"This is not Mississippi or Alabama," a furious Payne replied.

One of the officers struck her and dragged her to the paddy wagon across the street while Avis screamed and ran home. Their mother was on the front porch when she arrived. "Somebody get the bail money together," she ordered, adding to send for her son-in-law the attorney.

The wagon delivered the two dozen or so arrested men, along with Payne, to the police station about five or six blocks away. An aging Irish captain asked, "Now what's the trouble?" Payne lit into him. "This is an abuse of citizens' rights," Payne exclaimed, citing her membership on the Interracial Commission.

Her brother-in-law arrived and listened to the captain's explanation. "Well," he said in an apologetic manner, "the boys got a wee rough. They just went a wee bit far, but you didn't do anything really wrong."

"You book me," Payne insisted, "because I want to go to trial. This is police brutality. You book me."

"Let's just settle this. Let's go and have a peaceful weekend."

"No, you book me. I want to be booked."

So in due course the police officers fingerprinted her, booked her, and asked what else they could do.

"You let those people out of their cells downstairs, that's what you can do. You let those people out."

The officer, probably glad to be rid of Payne, relented. The others were released, and a month later a judge threw the case out. The incident became a favorite in Payne family lore.

IN 1948, NOTICES BEGAN APPEARING in newspapers that the U.S. Army wanted to hire at least 250 single women between the ages of twenty-five and forty for staff service club posts overseas. The chief Army hostess for the Far East command told the press there was a "desperate need" among enlisted men for organized recreation. The ideal hostess, she said, "must be of a high type, capable and energetic, and must bring a wholesome feminine touch to the service club."

During World War II, when the Red Cross previously operated these social clubs, Payne had considered trying to obtain work in one. "I'm glad that I didn't now," she wrote Randolph when the war was over, "because the stories of discrimination and restrictions on staff workers are too convincing. I might have been frustrated and anything could have happened." Instead, Payne did get a job for nine months as a hostess at Camp Robert Smalls, part of the Great Lakes Naval Training Station in North Chicago, where the Navy was training African American enlistees, including a group who became the service's first black commissioned and warrant officers.

In March Payne submitted an application for the position of assistant service club director. She had the prerequisite two years of college and, more important, the Camp Smalls experience. Within a few weeks Payne got word that she had the job. She was given the choice of being assigned to Korea or Japan. She chose the latter. The Army remained segregated, "so I knew in advance I would be going into an all-Negro unit," Payne said.

At the Throop Street house, she called her brother, sisters, and mother together for one of their family councils. She told them the news. Her sister Wilma objected. "Why can't you settle down and be satisfied?" she asked. "You've got a good job with the Chicago Public Library. Why can't you be satisfied with that?"

Bessie sat quietly listening to her children take different sides. "Well," she said, joining in at last, "she's been raised to know the difference between right and wrong, and she's been raised in a religious atmosphere. At this point in time, I think it's up to her to decide what she wants to do with her life. So if she wants to go, she has my blessing."

CHAPTER 7

JAPAN

ER MOTHER'S CONSENT SECURED, ETHEL PAYNE PRE-
pared for her departure. She had several bad teeth pulled,
fearing that dental care might be hard to procure in Japan,
and even gave her insides a flushing by dosing herself with magne-
sium citrate. For the sea voyage, she laid in a stock of seasickness pills,
dry crackers, and lemons. Japan was an uncommon destination for a
South Sider. For a thirty-six-year-old single black woman in 1948, this
was a journey of courage.

Japan put a pause on her romantic life. Since her teenaged years
when she had her first love, a boy a year younger than she from a
Mississippi family that had moved into the neighborhood, Payne
had dated frequently. But by this point in her life, only one man,
whom we know only as Paul, had asked her to marry him. A postal
employee, Paul was "not particularly, you know, dashing or anything like that," said Payne. "It would have been a marriage, maybe
a good marriage, but it wouldn't have been exciting and full of
adventure." As the date of her departure neared, Paul asked Ethel
when she would return. "I'll come back in a year," she promised.
"So," Payne laughingly told an interviewer four decades later, "I left
him at the dock."

Setting off by train in early June, at the same time that President
Harry Truman passed through Chicago on a train similarly bound

for the West, Payne spent several days as a tourist in San Francisco, riding the cable cars and eating at Fisherman's Wharf. The final leg of her overland trip brought her to Seattle, where an Army transport ship bound for Japan awaited. After checking in with the military authorities in charge of her ship's voyage, Payne went off to explore downtown Seattle. She ditched her uniform, feeling conspicuous in it. "Evidently," she said, "there aren't many colored girls going through here in uniform."

Her sightseeing agenda, however, was altered as she found herself in a sea of 100,000 people flooding the streets for a peek at President Truman. In the late afternoon sun, hundreds of flags along the parade route snapped in the breeze and buckets of confetti poured down from office building windows when Truman appeared in an open automobile. "I says to myself," Payne wrote that night, "'Look here, Harry, who's chasing who? Darn if we ain't bumped into each other all the way from Chicago to Seattle.'"

ON JUNE 15, Payne boarded her ship. Unlike during the war, when ships sailed under the cover of darkness, the ship steamed into Puget Sound at lunchtime and out to sea before sunset. During the passage across the Pacific, Payne spent time with the other women who had been selected as club directors and hostesses. They came from all parts of the United States, and while the military remained segregated, the white and black women traveled as a group, although they did sleep apart. At times it got to be a bit much for Payne. In particular, one white woman from Michigan was genial to a fault. "What she doesn't know," said Payne, "is that you can't run this brotherly love down everybody's throat and besides she don't understand I can take only so much of white folk trying to be nice."

After nearly two weeks, on the morning of June 28, the ship docked at Yokohama, just south of Tokyo, and awaiting buses ferried the new recruits to their quarters. As she got off her bus, still without her land legs, Payne felt the ground moving under her feet. It was an earthquake, centered in Fukui, less than three hundred miles to the west. While it devastated that city, the damage was minimal around Tokyo. "It was over in a few minutes," according to Payne, "but I said, 'Oh, what a welcome. What a welcome.'"

Payne was assigned to a small house just off the main part of the Tokyo Quartermaster Depot in Shinagawa, right on Tokyo Bay. A flimsy and drafty cottage with no cooking facilities and a Japanese-style shower, it had lodged a group of Red Cross hostesses getting ready to head home. Payne and another woman were to take their place as the Army took over running the social clubs.

The Seaview Club, where Payne was to work, was the only facility with a black staff in the Tokyo-Yokohama area. It was housed on the grounds of the massive depot, the largest of its kind in the world, charged with supplying all the U.S. forces in the Far East. Housing and life on the depot was not all that different than Chicago. Four months after President Truman had issued his executive order directing the desegregation of the military, the depot remained segregated, with white and black soldiers housed at either end of the facility. Payne's club was solely for the black soldiers.

"There were rules and the 'unwritten rules' for blacks," recalled Vivian Lee, an African American woman who was a child growing up on the depot at the time. "Black soldiers in my stepfather's company had to be immaculately dressed and groomed before my stepfather, Sgt. Frank Little, would issue them a pass because the white Military Police would deliberately target them."

Being kept apart from whites, however, did not mean that African Americans in the occupying forces were denied other benefits of life in the military. The Army provided dependable salaries and benefits, generous in comparison to civilian life back home, decent housing, abundant food, and affordable clothing. Moreover, what couldn't be gotten from the military could be easily bought from Japanese destitute from the destruction of their country in the war. For example,

African Americans, including Payne, were in the unusual situation of hiring servants of a different race. "Their dish washing, suds busting, and scrubbing days are over for a while," declared a *Chicago Defender* who was a frequent critic of the military. He was so astounded by what he found that he called his piece WELL SHUT MY MOUTH.

Black soldiers, who were not in combat units, were given the military's most menial positions. At the depot they were used primarily to unload, store, and transport equipment and supplies. The work was hard and long. On the other hand, by the nature of their assignments, African Americans came into greater contact with the Japanese than whites did. On the docks, for instance, Japanese stevedores were hired in large numbers and were often under the supervision of black noncommissioned officers. In turn, as base life mirrored segregated life in the United States, African Americans had a greater incentive to find recreation outside the confines of the facility. But they had to exercise caution because white soldiers, bringing their American racial customs with them, frequently succeeded in occupying and marking certain entertainment districts as exclusively white zones.

Even so, life in Japan could offer a new racial experience for young African Americans. For instance, a twenty-one-year-old black New Yorker heading home said Japan had been, for him, a place where "colored and white soldiers are working, eating, sleeping, drinking and 'balling' together, and it works out just fine."

AT THE SEAVIEW CLUB, Payne enthusiastically took to her job of creating entertainment for the black servicemen and their families. "I lead the life of a squirrel on a treadmill always racing around in circles," Payne told her family. Picnics by the bay were organized. Soldiers were recruited for musical shows that grew sufficiently popular to be performed for civilians off the base. "These boys are just like little children," Payne reported, "you have to bear down on them to make them stay in line." Payne even recruited the wives of enlisted men to put on fashion shows. The first of these featured clothing from China, India, the Philippines, Japan, and Korea. A later edition of the show was elevated to a United Nations Fashion Revue and included the participation of representatives from various embassies. The soldiers, in turn, took an immense liking to Payne and trusted her. "The soldiers kind of flocked around her," recalled one observer.

On a Saturday, only two months into her stay, a new friend, Marguerite Davis, asked Payne to accompany her to Yokohama. A Louisville, Kentucky, native of mixed-race parents (her father was African American; her mother, German), Davis was Payne's age and they shared a background of civil rights activism in their native cities. Of the two, however, Davis was the seasoned Asia hand, having worked for three and a half years with the Red Cross in New Guinea and the Philippines and most recently as club director for the all-black 24th Infantry Regiment in Okinawa.

Davis wanted to expose Payne to a heartrending problem stemming from the behavior of the men whom their clubs served and for whom the female club directors often acted like den mothers. Since the arrival of the occupation troops, a growing number of Japanese women had become pregnant by U.S. soldiers. To military officials the infants, known as "occupation babies," were none of their concern. It was forbidden to collect data on the extent of the problem and the subject was not to be publicly discussed. Only the month before, a reporter for the *Saturday Evening Post* had been expelled from the country for writing about occupation babies. Simply put, the subject was taboo. If blame was to be assigned, the military said it lay with licentious Japanese women who "made good clean American boys go morally wrong."

Being of mixed race, the babies were so unwanted by the Japanese, who abhorred what they viewed as the tainting of their blood, that they were frequently abandoned upon birth. In one case, a train passenger unwrapped a cloth bundle she spotted on the luggage rack to discover the corpse of a black Japanese baby.

Military law freed U.S. soldiers "of all but moral responsibility" unless they formally admitted paternity. But if the authorities were to push soldiers, specifically African American ones, to claim paternity or to marry a Japanese woman, it would challenge American opposition to mixed-race relationships and, more to the point, contradict existing prevailing state anti-miscegenation laws. As a result, the children of these relationships were regarded as pariahs by both societies, even more so in the case of those with black fathers.

To cope with the growing problem, the nuns of the Franciscan Missionaries of Mary opened an orphanage inside the Yokohama general hospital. As Davis and Payne approached the place, Payne already knew something of the issue. "We have a case in our club now of one of our Japanese girls who is pregnant by a master sergeant," she had told her family. "We talked and talked to him to try to get him to help in some way, but he will do nothing. There is no law requiring him to do so."

But Payne was unprepared for what she would see. As she and Davis made their way down the hall of the hospital they found the infants in a segregated corner of the facility. "Here were 160 foundlings of all mixtures, about 50 of them 'Spookinese,' Negro and Japanese," said Payne. "Some beds had three babies they are so crowded."

The nuns were doing the best they could with the large population of abandoned infants thrust into their care, but their resources were severely limited. "They need canned milk and Karo syrup for formulas, mosquito nets, all the children's clothes they can get, powder, baby oil, diapers, money," Payne wrote home. "Yes, I'm afraid you are all in for another project. If you could see these helpless babies, your heart would really go out for them."

Before leaving to return to the base, Payne talked with the mother superior about the pregnant Japanese employee at the club. She agreed to take in the woman and care for the baby when it was born, but Payne remained skeptical that the offer would be of use. "The girl would rather have an abortion."

As her first Christmas in Japan neared, Payne tried to raise money and find needed items for the orphans, including those at Our Lady of Lourdes, "where," Payne added, "the brown babies are." The club brought in a group of orphans for a holiday show with a trick bicycle act and a visit from Santa Claus.

Christmas in Tokyo was Payne's first away from South Side Chicago. For her and other Christian foreigners, the festive preparations for the Japanese celebration of the New Year substituted as an "Occupation Christmas." During the day, women in kimonos, their hair piled high, dashed about getting foods for the holiday, and in the evenings the trains and streets were full of, in Payne's words, "sake-happy" commuters. A few stores had bunting and some even displayed Christmas signs in a tribute to the occupiers, but it was, said Payne, a "far cry from Marshall Field's."

On New Year's Day, Payne sampled the style of celebration at the house of a Japanese artist who worked for the club. The family served her sake, several kinds of raw and dried fish, bean and rice cakes, preserved persimmons, fresh oranges, pickled spinach, sweet potatoes, and green tea. "After two hours I could take no more of the bitter cold nor the strange dishes so I bowed myself out laden with gifts," she said. Back in the cottage she downed a double dose of Ex-Lax, hot lemonade, aspirin, and soda.

As her second year in Japan got under way, the separation from home became harder. In the spring, her mother shared an anxiety about municipal plans that might alter the neighborhood. Ever the activist, Payne fretted. "I have not slept well since I got the letter," Payne wrote. "Being 8,000 miles away and not being able to jump in and fight has me just about frantic." Her alien surroundings and the distance from home grew increasingly taxing, as the letters from

Paul ceased to come. He had even forgotten her birthday. Although she worked in a sea of men, her other options were limited. "Hundreds of soldiers pass through my hands," Payne said, "but the romantic possibilities for me are very few." The men were either so young they could conceivably be her children or else they were what Payne called career military "hoboes" not interested in marriage. Nonetheless, there was no absence of suitors. "An American Negro woman is a rare object to an extent over here, and even if you look like 'Lena the Hyena'" somebody will make passes at you."*

IN JAPAN, PAYNE LIVED TWO LIVES. Inside the depot she was an exemplary and industrious worker bee, earning letters of commendation and eventually a promotion to club director. Outside the base, Payne was a consummate explorer. Free time meant one thing to Payne: a chance to see Japan and meet its people.

At Nara Park, south of Tokyo, she fed the deer, considered by the Shinto religion to be messengers from god. At Nikko, to the north, she climbed the many steps to the shrine and spent time talking to "the withered old lady who had the tea shop at the head of the stairs who spoke English with a New York accent and who remembered vividly lunching with Eleanor Roosevelt on a visit by her to Mount Holyoke College." At Kamakura, she stood before the Great Buddha. In Tokyo, she attended a performance of the all-male Kabuki theater, where she witnessed its renowned dance piece the *Heron Maiden* (*Sagi Musume*), which includes four onstage rapid costume changes. "The make up and costuming alone is something to behold," Payne wrote home, "but the acting! is a revelation."

But Payne's interest in Japan was far deeper than that of an ordinary

---

* Lena the Hyena, regarded as the ugliest woman in the world, was the 1946 creation of cartoonist Al Capp for his *Li'l Abner* strip; she was a resident of Lower Slobbovia.

tourist. Rather, her writerly instincts were energized, and her diary, which she had kept since boarding the ship to Japan, became her book. At last, she believed, she had the material with which to break into writing.

She attended the war tribunals, which were nearing their end, and she sought out audiences with everyone. "I had a very, very great curiosity," Payne said. "I just tried to mingle as much as I could with the population." She chivied the Japanese who worked at the club for invitations to their homes and gained entrée to well-known members of the deposed government. She was especially curious to learn what prompted the war and how the Japanese were dealing with defeat. Her self-initiated home visits included ones with Mamoru Shigemitsu, the foreign minister who had signed the surrender on board the USS *Missouri,* and Toshikazu Kase, a high-ranking member of the ministry recently released from prison. She found the two officials to be welcoming and unsurprised to be plied by questions from an American Negro female. "I thought I had information that very few people had, the fact that I had been there and had been on the scene and could talk to these people and get their feelings," Payne said.

AT THE END OF A YEAR and a half in Japan, Payne earned home leave. On December 8, 1949, she boarded the USNS *General Edwin D. Patrick* in Yokohama, bound for San Francisco. She spent Christmas with her family and was feted by her friends. More than two hundred South Siders turned out to hear her give a talk at the Parkway Community House, an important social and cultural center of Bronzeville. Payne delivered a colorful account of her life in Japan matched by the bright red heavily brocaded Chinese mandarin gown she wore for the occasion. The *Defender*'s account called Payne "Englewood's 'Favorite Daughter.'"

Soon, however, the holiday ended, and Payne was back on a ship. In Japan, Payne resumed her private after-work investigations. They were all done, Payne noted, "sans press card and only nerve." Her hope was to write a magazine article upon her return to the United States.

Payne even found time to work with the Great Books program that was founded three years earlier in Chicago, offering to select books from Asia that could be included on an expanded list.

Payne's superiors remained pleased with her performance at the Seaview Club, giving her an A+ for personality and emotional stability in her employment file. In early June she requested a yearlong extension to her contract as a GS-6 earning $3,450 a year. But within two weeks, life for Americans in Japan suddenly changed.

At dawn on Sunday morning, June 25, 1950, North Korean troops poured across the 38th parallel, a temporary division line drawn at the end of World War II, and swept down into the south. Convinced that no small nation would be safe if the communist regime in North Korea were permitted to force its way into the south, President Truman promised aid and military troops to back up the United Nations' condemnation of the invasion.

The occupation forces in Japan, only 700 hundred miles to the east, were called into action. Overnight, the Tokyo Quartermaster Depot took on the primary duty of providing the logistical support for the troops being sent into combat on the peninsula. "I don't know when I have ever worked as hard or been as tired," an exhausted Ethel wrote to Thelma two months into the war. "Hospitals are No. 1 on our schedule now. A lot of volunteers are doing all they can, but still there are some neglected soldiers."

The men whom Payne entertained at the Seaview Club suddenly found themselves in a shooting war. By September, two of them were among the casualties, shot by snipers as they moved supplies. Conditions were harsh. One soldier wrote Payne that he had his first bath in weeks when he found an abandoned oil drum. Correspondence acquired a new urgency. Tired as she was, Payne took up her pen daily to reply to the many men who wrote her from Korea. "If you don't write, they send such pathetic notes that you feel so debased and cruel that you just drop everything else to grind away."

The burdens of war fell heavily on African Americans. At the time there were almost 100,000 blacks on active duty. A dismal lack of opportunities in the United States for African Americans continued to make the military an attractive option. "Negro lads," reported the *Pittsburgh Courier* in late July, "were swarming into recruiting offices." But because of General Douglas MacArthur's intransigency when it came to Truman's edict to integrate the Army, they went into combat in segregated units.

The war also brought a new scrutiny to Ethel Payne.

CHAPTER 8

CHOCOLATE JOE

O NE OF ETHEL PAYNE'S FAVORITE DESTINATIONS IN Tokyo was the Foreign Correspondents' Club, which was housed in a five-story redbrick building tucked into an alley a few minutes' walk from MacArthur's headquarters. Run-down and somewhat on the seedy side, the place was nonetheless the center of social life for many, white and black, in the Western community. It was a popular spot to get a drink or a meal, read hard-to-find newspapers, and even play the slots. One correspondent described the place as combining "some of the features of a make-shift bordello, inefficient gaming-house and black market center."

Over drinks at the bar in the fall of 1950, Payne met reporters L. Alex Wilson of the *Chicago Defender* and James L. Hicks of the *Baltimore Afro-American*. Both World War II veterans, the two reporters had been assigned to cover the role of black soldiers in the Korean War. Everything that went to the Korean peninsula, including report-ers, came through Tokyo. Over drinks, Payne told the two about her life in Japan and what she had observed about black troops. Spending time with two men who earned their living as writers, one of whom came from her hometown newspaper, was exhilarating.

Hicks was impressed with Payne. He came out to Seaview to see her at work. "This reporter," he wrote after touring her workplace, "has seen and visited many such Special Service Clubs but never yet seen one which received the all-out support and program participation which both colored and white members on the base give the Seaview." While the place remained a black club, there were no rules prohibiting whites from entering, and quite a few white soldiers had taken to doing so. Once, when an integrated unit took up quarters near the club and white soldiers began patronizing it, a detachment's sergeant ordered his white men to stay away from the club. The white soldiers complained. The depot's commander, Hicks said, "promptly issued orders that the club was 'on limits' to all personnel on the depot."

But what really caught the attention of Hicks and Wilson was what Payne told them about black soldiers and Japanese women. Describing the harsh economic realities of postwar Japan, Payne described how many Japanese women had been drawn to soldiers with their ready cash and easy access to the post exchanges that bulged with Western goods. Unlike in the United States, the fair-skinned Japanese women were not put off by the men's dark skin. In fact, many found that black soldiers were kinder and more generous than the white ones.

"By tradition," Payne told the reporters, "the Japanese woman is submissive." If a soldier wins the affection of one, he will be showered with affection and servitude. "Then there is the color factor," she continued. "The hue of the girls ranges from very fair to nut brown. Hence it can be easily understood why our boys fall for them."

"A stock comparison with American women would be: Too independent. Won't take anything off a man or wait on a man," Payne explained. GIs called their docile Japanese companions "mooses," picking up on *musume*, the Japanese word for girl. "The *musume* fetches the GI's shoes, washes, cooks, and irons. Keeps quiet, when asked. Never talks back. Laughs easily. All of which is very soothing to the male ego.

"*Musume* has played it cool," she continued. "Her very helpless-ness has been a powerful weapon and an asset to her and she is using it fully."

BY THE STANDARDS OF RACE journalism in 1950, this was one hell of a story about violating the taboo of sex across race lines. Hicks rushed an account to his paper. "This is a story that I hate to write," explained Hicks to his readers. "Colored women on civilian duty in occupied Japan are being ignored by colored soldiers stationed here to the point that many of the women swear once they get 'stateside' again, they will never so much as speak to a colored soldier who has been stationed in Japan." Hicks's article, however, made no mention of Payne, and he deliberately left out all names. Wilson, on the other hand, had different reporting plans.

Like Payne, Wilson had also taken an interest in writing when he was a child, but with greater success. As a male armed with a college degree and time spent studying journalism at Lincoln University in Jefferson City, Missouri, he had risen up in the ranks of black journal-ists. The six-foot-three-inch lanky reporter, who favored a black suit and a white fedora, was a prodigious workhorse. With his clipped and sonorous voice and formal demeanor, he projected the air of one who planned to single-handedly cover all aspects of African American involvement in the war.

Payne and Wilson hit it off. They conferred regularly at the press club, and one night Payne even organized a dinner in his honor with several other Chicagoans. For Payne, time with Wilson gave her a rare opportunity to share her passion for writing with a professional. For Wilson, Payne was a valuable source. After all, for three years Payne had been spending her spare time acting like a reporter and dutifully keeping notes on her encounters and observations.

Wilson filed a report with the *Defender*. Headlined WHY TAN YANKS GO FOR JAPANESE GIRLS, the lengthy article quoted Payne,

unlike Hicks's earlier piece for the *Afro-American*. But Wilson was
not done yet. He had his eye on Payne's diary filled with stories and
observations that she had brought to their meetings. "You know," Wilson said to Payne, "the folks back home don't know what's going on,
particularly about the GIs and Japanese women. Why don't you just
let me share this with them?"

Payne agreed. Although later she would feign innocence, claiming that she had actually forgotten about giving Wilson the diary, she
certainly knew what she was doing. After years of failed attempts to
launch some kind of writing career, providing her articles and notes
to Wilson was hardly an act devoid of motivation in the world of
journalism. She knew the editors at the vaunted *Defender* would read
her work. Letting Wilson take it back to Chicago was like earning a
literary lottery ticket.

When Wilson was back in the office, he handed editor Louis Martin the diary. "I read the manuscript and I could hardly believe it,"
Martin said. Wilson confirmed its contents but warned that Payne
could be fired if they published it. "The day the U.S. fired her, she
could have a job with the *Chicago Defender*," said Martin.

About a month later, one of Payne's sisters called from Chicago.
Ethel was in the paper again, but this time on the front page with
a bylined article. SAYS JAPANESE GIRLS PLAYING GIS FOR SUCKERS,
"CHOCOLATE JOE" USED, AMUSED, CONFUSED, read the headline.
The editors had taken Payne's diary and cobbled the entries into two
articles. "They rewrote it," said Payne, "and they put it into the prose
that was adapted to the paper."

THE ARTICLE, PATCHED TOGETHER as it was from the diary, lacked
the cohesion of a unified piece of writing. It opened with a rambling
discourse about changes in Japan under the occupation, touching on
a wide range of topics from fashions and the Japanese fascination with
the Sears, Roebuck catalog to a noticeable growth in height among

children because of changes in diet. Halfway through, however, it came to its incendiary point.

"To get back to 'Chocolate Joe,'" Payne wrote, "for him it was the opening of an entire new life. Surrounded by tons of army regulations, nevertheless, life in Japan became an escape from the irking confinement of the social caste system and segregation which he had left behind in the States." With even the pay of the lowliest private, Payne reported that a black soldier could live like a king and retain the pleasures of a *musume*. Some of what she said had already appeared verbatim in Wilson's article, but in this instance, here was an employee of the military detailing in a public forum how soldiers paid the rent for their girlfriends, ordered goods for them through the Sears, Roebuck catalog, obtained ration cards at the PX for them, and converted military script to yen on the black market.

The paper told its readers that the following week it would run a second article by Payne in which, "from her feminine point of view, she gives further evidence of her charge that the Nipponese girls are playing GIs for suckers."

The identical headline above the second installment promised more on how Japanese women were taking advantage of black soldiers. But though it was again a disjointed work, the article provided a more nuanced account of the lives of the soldiers. It was indeed true, Payne wrote, that the men had a wide range of choice among "almond-eyed femmes." But the real issue related to race and the startling experience of the black soldier in Japan. "It all added up to one thing," Payne said. "Despite the encumbrances of Army policies on racial quotas, restrictions, limitations, etc. he was less of a Negro here than he had been at any time in his life. In his heart, he was an expatriate."

Racial attitudes in Japan were hard to fathom because it was, after all, a conquered nation whose citizens were obliged to give respect and obedience to the occupying forces, wrote Payne. But she accused MacArthur of trying to foster an acceptance of segregation among the Japanese, well used to a rigid class system.

Defender editors ended her article on a far more sympathetic note than the first installment, which had painted the women as self-serving Oriental temptresses. The women and the "crop of sloe-eyed curly topped brown babies" were the first victims of the Korean War, Payne said. The future for the women and their children was dim, left on their own as their men were sent off to battle, probably never to return to Japan. "This means then with the passing of years without a steady income, the mother, unless she has unusually strong love for the child, may not be able to resist the hardships of social ostracism and inevitable abandonment may be the fate of the child."

"If there was a storm in Chicago" after the publication of the articles, Payne said, "there was a tornado in Japan and Korea." It was not long before her white superiors heard about the article as well. The War Department published a weekly "Report of Trends in the Colored Press" that was circulated among the higher ranks of the military. Payne received the dreaded summons to Allied headquarters. Only bad news came with such an invitation.

MacArthur's aides gave her a dressing-down. They accused her of disrupting the morale of the troops. From her years on the Tokyo bases, Payne knew that there was no appeal from their judgment. She was removed from her post and shunted away to be a secretary at command headquarters. She hired an American attorney in Tokyo and awaited her punishment.

ETHEL PAYNE'S RESCUE came by way of one of the century's greatest lawyers.

In the early months of the war, both the black troops, who were undertrained and ill equipped, and the white troops were unable to hold back the invaders. But unlike the white regiments, who could draw on vast reserves, the all-black regiments could be reinforced only with black soldiers. "It is a fact that enormous casualties suffered by the 24th Infantry Regiment and the 159th Field Artillery Battalion, both all Negro outfits, might have been lighter had there been replacements for them," Payne wrote. "The wanton die-hard attitude of segregation has been a costly and needless waste of life."

Concerned with survival in the face of overwhelming odds and lacking faith in their white officers, black soldiers deserted. Military police stationed on the roads leading away from the battlefields arrested them. Sixty black soldiers were charged with cowardice before the enemy, and about half of them were convicted in trials that often lasted less than an hour and were given sentences ranging from the death penalty to a term of imprisonment. Only eight white soldiers were similarly charged during the period, and only four of them were convicted.

When word of the drumhead trials reached the NAACP, it instructed its chief counsel Thurgood Marshall to investigate. At first MacArthur balked at the notion of having a lawyer snooping around his command, but under pressure, he relented. In early 1951, Marshall arrived in Tokyo to begin his work. He soon discovered the Foreign Correspondents' Club and obtained a guest membership. There he found that over whiskey he could pump members of the press for information. He also found a diversion. "The slot machines at the press club are real one-arm *Bandits*," he wrote in his diary.

At the club, Marshall met Payne and a group of her supporters. She detailed what had happened to her since the articles appeared in the *Defender* and the threat of further punishment. Marshall used his meetings with MacArthur and his staff to bring up Payne's case. The command conceded that they would drop the matter and let Payne return to the United States two months before the end of her contract.

Meanwhile, hearing about Payne's rough treatment at the hands of the military and that she would be returning home, the *Defender's* Louis Martin remained true to his word and called Payne. "Come on home," he told Payne. "We have a job for you." The call was well timed. "I was going through a very psychological repression," Payne said. "I'd been humiliated and chastised and all that, and then I was put in isolation, so to speak. So it was a relief to me. I had been there three years, so I welcomed the opportunity."

In early March 1951 Payne asked for a seat on a homebound plane.

GETTING HOME WAS NO EASY TASK. The eighth day of waiting rolled around and the Military Air Transport Service (MATS) still had no seat for Payne on an outbound plane. With several hours to kill between the check-in times at the MATS office, Payne went out among the downtown crowds. It was a brilliant springtime Sunday full of promise. The day, said Payne, was "so brilliant with sunshine and so intoxicating with the champagne of spring that in a moment of sheer abandon you could forget there was a war and rumors of more war." The *sakura zensen*, the name given to the latitudinal line marking the flowering of cherry blossoms, was moving north. The buds on the trees in Tokyo were only days short of bursting open. French sailors with berets, Australian soldiers with slouched hats, and American GIs with garrison caps intermingled with the crowds of Japanese strolling in front of the Imperial Palace, all grateful the warm breezes from the south had come to free the island of its winter cold.

The MATS office was just down the street from the Dai-ichi, where MacArthur made his headquarters, so Payne decided to take in, perhaps for the last time, what was called the "daily review." For more than five years MacArthur's daily comings and goings from the building had grown into a well-attended ceremony of sorts. By the time Payne reached the Dai-ichi, there was already a densely packed crowd of spectators of old hunched-over women and young mothers with their babies, workmen with sweatbands around their heads and students in black suits and peaked caps. "Blue uniformed

Japanese policemen importantly waved back the forgetful ones who stepped across the yellow lines back into place."

At the front door of the building, a chauffeured 1950 Chrysler Crown Imperial, the largest car made by the manufacturer, stood by, idling. Suddenly a Japanese policeman dashed to the corner and rang a bell, and his uniformed colleagues brought the traffic at the busy intersection to a standstill. The chauffeur opened the Chrysler's door and two American guards took their positions on the pavement. "The people craned," Payne said, "and Douglas MacArthur flanked by his aides strode majestically out, erect, proud, disdainful of the admiring glances of his subjects yet fully aware of his role as Destiny's chosen to rule some 80,000,000 people."

When Payne checked next with the MATS office, they reported she had a seat on a flight to San Francisco. Just after midnight on March 19, 1951, Payne's DC-4 taxied out to a runway at Haneda Army Air Base at the edge of Tokyo Bay and waited for clearance. As the propellers on the plane's four Pratt & Whitney engines noisily sliced into the night air and the craft ascended into the sky, Payne looked out her window at the twinkling lights and the glimmer of the moon on the bay.

THOUSANDS OF MILES from the DC-4 making its way across the Pacific that March night, Barbara Rose Johns was also making a change in her life. The sixteen-year-old Johns attended the all-black Robert Russa Moton High School in Prince Edward County, deep in Southside Virginia, home of the state's most isolated and conservative communities. Under any circumstances her school would have been regarded as an inadequate facility for children. But in comparison to the new white high school, it was a galling injustice.

In enormous disrepair, Moton's classrooms lacked suitable desks, were dotted with strategically placed pails to catch leaks on rainy days, and were so cold that in the winter the students rarely shed their coats. To cope with overcrowding, the school board had recently consented to erect some tar-paper shacks, hardly sturdier than chicken coops, heated with woodstoves. Anything the board provided its black students was shoddy and deficient. The students were even forced to ride each day in buses discarded by the white school.

The month before, the board had faced down an angry crowd of black parents at one of its meetings. The board members promised they would buy land for a new colored school but would make their decision known in due time and on their own schedule. In the meantime, they told the black families to stay away from board meetings.

Johns decided one day to talk to her approachable music teacher about the school's deplorable conditions. "Why don't you do something about it?" asked the teacher. The question might have discouraged a less imaginative teenager. Instead, it stirred Johns. Although she was quiet and introspective, Johns was also worldlier than many of her classmates. She knew about what other African Americans in the South were doing to fight Jim Crow laws from her uncle Reverend Vernon Johns, who was an outspoken civil rights advocate in Montgomery, Alabama. "Soon," she said, "the little wheels began turning in my mind."

She secretly enlisted the help of some other students. Meeting on the bleachers at the edge of the athletic field, whose grass was overgrown and unattended, the teenagers plotted. On the appointed day, one of them called the principal's office and said that students were spotted at the Greyhound station and were in trouble with the police. With the principal out of the building, a forged note went to all the classrooms telling the teachers to bring their students to an assembly.

When the curtain in the auditorium drew open, rather than the principal, there stood Johns and a group of students. She asked the students to join her in going out on strike. The protest, she said, would aim not merely to win a new facility but to gain the right to attend school with whites. Banging her shoe on the podium, Johns urged everyone to join her. "Don't be afraid," she said, "just follow us." And as a group, the 450 students rose, left the school, and marched to the courthouse, carrying protest signs they had made earlier and stored in the carpentry classroom.

Johns and another student then sent a letter to NAACP lawyers Spottswood Robinson III and Oliver Hill in Richmond. Coincidentally, the two attorneys had recently met with Thurgood Marshall, from the NAACP's national office. He had urged them to find a Virginia school to use in a lawsuit against segregation itself, abandoning the years-old strategy of winning improvements in black schools by filing cases based on the separate but equal doctrine of the half-century-old *Plessy v. Ferguson.*

Robinson and Hill drove down to meet with Johns and the protesting students. Deeply impressed by the courage of the young strikers and the support they had from their families, the lawyers agreed to go to court on their behalf. The case would eventually reach the Supreme Court, but not under its name. Instead, the justices consolidated four similar cases under the name of *Brown v. Board of Education.*

Johns's actions that spring were only the start. All across the nation, a fuse of impatience was igniting a new form of activism among African Americans. Nine decades after emancipation, the yoke of Jim Crow was being directly challenged.

THOUSANDS OF FEET ABOVE the Pacific, Ethel Payne's plane sped out of the night and toward the rising sun. In a few months she would turn forty. After two decades of waiting, she knew that a writing job was finally hers as a reporter on the nation's premier black newspaper. What she didn't know was that the biggest story in the history of the black press since the Civil War was breaking. The DC-4 was bringing Payne closer not just to home but to a journey through the civil rights revolution.

PART TWO

CHAPTER 9

CUB REPORTER

I N EARLY APRIL 1951, ETHEL PAYNE STOOD ON THE SIDE-walk before the three-story headquarters of the *Chicago Defender*. Situated on Indiana Avenue in the heart of Bronzeville, the paper's three-story headquarters was fronted by a brick-and-cement facade that attempted to mask its former life as a synagogue. The halls where worshipers once reverently gathered now echoed with the sound of thunderous printing presses. The rooms reserved for contemplation and study were full of reporters on telephones, editors in conference, composers setting type, and sales-men extolling the virtue of advertising in America's leading Negro newspaper. If the African American press was black America's secu-lar church, then the *Defender* was one of its best-known and -loved incarnations. "Everyone read the *Defender*," said the South Side activist and historian Timuel Black. "Every copy was read four or five times. People who didn't get it would ask others to let them see it."

In stark contrast to the *Chicago Tribune*, the *Defender* carried information that mattered to African Americans. In a typical issue that April, news of brutal police tactics in Jackson, Mississippi, the election of Arizona's first Negro state legislators, and the publication of an article in a UNESCO bulletin by the director of the School of Library Science at the historically black Atlanta University all merited space. The flagship of black journalism, the paper was a chronicler of racial injustice and a consummate publisher of ascension stories that provided hope. "Oh, the *Defender* was Mr. Big," said a black radio broadcaster.

Although it covered national news and had readers all across the country, the paper remained loyal to South Side. If you were a black Chicagoan, you could count on the *Defender* to carry news of your graduation, wedding, job promotion, retirement, and death. It celebrated its city as if it were the capital of all things African American. In particular the *Defender* supported, and in some instances set up, civic and social Bronzeville organizations, as its readers were excluded from most of the city's established institutions. "The things the *Defender* created and sustained were vital to the health of the community," said Black. "It gave folks something to look forward to. It gave some belief that there was a land beyond this one, and hope beyond this life."

As she faced the *Defender*'s building that day in April, Payne had little idea what the editors had in mind for their new hire. Louis Martin, the editor in chief who had offered Payne the job, had been vague about her potential role. Payne had no training or experience in reporting or news writing, aside from a smattering of writing courses she took at the Chicago Training School and the Medill School of Journalism. This was an almost entirely male trade and certainly the province of the young. But as she had told W. E. B. Du Bois two decades earlier, she had nerve, plenty of it. She opened the building's glass door, walked in, and made her way to the second-story newsroom and Martin's office.

IN THE *DEFENDER*'S FIRST FOUR DECADES, Louis Martin was among the most successful men to have had the editorial helm of the paper aside from the founder, Robert Sengstacke Abbott. Unlike other African Americans from the South, the thirty-eight-year-old editor had a fortunate upbringing: he was educated in Catholic schools, attended a high school operated by Fisk University, and obtained a college education at the University of Michigan. In 1936, two years after getting his degree, Martin came to work as a reporter for the *Defender*. John H. Sengstacke, who was being groomed by his uncle Robert to take over the paper, was impressed by the young reporter and enlisted him to launch the *Michigan Chronicle*, rewarding him with a share of the ownership. In 1947, Martin returned to the *Defender* to become its editor in chief. By 1951, he was not only a part owner of the growing Sengstacke publishing company but also an important political figure whose advice was solicited by emerging black politicians as well as white politicians looking to gain support from the black community.

A natty dresser who favored a straw skimmer, Martin had a flair for the unusual and a keen eye for talent. He had seen Payne's Japanese diary entries and knew she could write well. As he had learned the trade of journalism on the job, there was no reason to think that she couldn't as well. He and city editor Enoch P. Waters decided to start Payne out writing features and soft news stories, the bread and butter of the inside pages of the paper and an ideal training spot for her. "All they did," Payne said, "was to tell me to go ahead and to use my good judgment and to make it factual. That was the main thing that they asked. They didn't want any big errors or misstatements that they would have to apologize for or even be subject to libel."

Pen and pad in hand, Payne set out to rediscover Chicago.

PAYNE SAW HER NATIVE CITY with the eyes of both an insider and an outsider. Having lived in a different culture, Payne had ceased to take her own world for granted. For despite the continued segregation in the Army under MacArthur and the resolute xenophobia of the Japanese, Payne's time as an expatriate had been a singularly liberating experience for her. Just as it had been for the soldier she had poignantly described in the *Defender*, Payne had been less a Negro in Japan than at any point in her life.

But in Chicago everything conspired to remind one of one's race. As had been true for decades, the only housing open to African Americans remained in the Black Belt running south from Twenty-Third Street. Despite the continuation of the Great Migration, the city had made no accommodation for the hundreds of thousands of new arrivals. In one apartment house, for instance, a thousand people were crammed into its seven stories, many of the rooms so overcrowded that the tenants had to sleep in shifts.

An elaborate system of restrictive housing covenants, collusive real estate operators, and compliant politicians continued to keep black families bottled up. The housing apartheid was so absolute that when black families challenged the system they faced a legal struggle stacked against them and sometimes violence. Carl A. Hansberry faced this when he tried to move his family into a white area. Carl's daughter Lorraine Hansberry imortalized their ordeal in the play *A Raisin in the Sun*. "You mean you ain't read 'bout them colored people that was bombed out their place out there?" asks Mrs. Johnson, a character in the play. "Ain't it something how bad these here white folks is getting here in Chicago! Lord, getting so you think you right down in Mississippi."

Health care, even emergency care, was restricted. Only a few of the city's seventy-seven hospitals would accept black patients, and did so on a limited basis, leaving only the massive, overcrowded, and understaffed Cook County Hospital and the African American–operated Provident Hospital to provide the bulk of medical care. When Richard Wright took a menial job in a Chicago hospital, the racial division of the city was brought home his first morning when he saw two long lines of women coming toward him. "A line of white girls marched past, clad in starched uniforms that gleamed white; their faces were alert, their steps quick, their bodies lean and shapely, their shoulders erect, their faces lit with the light of purpose," Wright wrote. "And after them came a line of black girls, old, fat, dressed in ragged gingham, walking loosely, carrying tin cans of soap powder, rags, mops, brooms. . . . I wondered what law of the universe kept them from not being mixed?"

In the spring of 1951 Payne moved back into her mother's home on Throop Street. Despite some economic improvements brought about by wartime employment, life in South Side was much as it had been in Chicago before she left. All that had changed was Payne herself.

FOR ETHEL PAYNE, journalism was love at first sight, and the *Chicago Defender* reciprocated. Her personality traits, her ambition, and her skills were a recipe for success. A beguiling gregariousness gained her entry, and her obvious earnestness won over the trust of sources. Her ambition, stoked by years of closed doors, gave her the energy to match younger reporters. And in the end she delivered dependable copy, the kind editors craved to fill a newspaper's seemingly insatiable appetite for words.

In no time, her stories were taking up full pages of each week's edition of the *Defender*. One week she was reporting on a trade unionist's four-month-long trip to Africa and his observation that Africans harbor suspicion about the United States because of its treatment of Negroes. Another week she was off writing about a mason trained at the Tuskegee Institute who was donating his labor to build a house for an Italian American veteran who lost his legs in the war.

As she became more skilled in the conventions of journalism— writing a lede, crafting a nut paragraph, and using quotations—the editors gave her increasingly free rein. Soon Payne picked up the responsibility for an ongoing series about employment in Chicago called "Industry USA." The subject was of immense interest to readers. Before World War II, only 9 percent of the city's African Americans held jobs in manufacturing. Now 30 percent did.

The articles were classic *Defender* fare that combined journalism with advocacy. They reported on progress in interracial hiring, rewarding forward-thinking employers with good publicity; exposed the lack of progress, putting recalcitrant employers in a bad light; and offered readers a guide to employment in the city. When Payne visited Inland Steel, she reported that not only were a majority of employees African Americans but the union leadership was also black. "I saw Negroes working side by side with whites on welding machines, planking presses, cutting machines, lithographing presses, and other equipment," she wrote. "Full integration in industry like full democracy has a long way to go, but along the forward march we can say, 'Good work: keep going.'"

On the other hand, Payne was quick to point out where progress was absent, as at the South Side packinghouses, where 50,000 Chicagoans were employed slaughtering and processing 15,000 to 20,000 cows, 11,000 to 15,000 hogs, and thousands of calves and sheep a day. None of the big three—Swift, Wilson, and Armour—employed any blacks in clerical, managerial, or executive positions.

Her output was prodigious. In the July 14 issue alone, Payne had three lengthy articles, including the first of a two-part series on sumo wrestling in Japan culled from her stockpile of diary material. Although the *Defender* obligingly published a number of her articles about her experiences in Japan, Payne's hope to use her research to break into a national magazine were dashed. She submitted her work to *McCall's* and *Ladies' Home Journal* with no luck. It was as Payne's fictional Madge experienced. "On the whole, there are few black women who can really get into publication in the major publishing houses," she said. "That's just the way it is."

By the end of her first six months, Payne had churned out more than two dozen features. One could not pick up a copy of the *Defender* when it hit the streets on Saturdays without coming across an article with the byline "Ethel Payne."

ON A SUNNY NOVEMBER MORNING, in her first autumn with the paper, Payne sat in a South Side apartment watching a familiar ritual. Just as her dad used to do, Golden William Smith was finishing off his packing by placing two iconic items into his suitcase: a small whisk broom—the kind used to brush off a suit—and the blue uniform of a Pullman porter. Notebook in hand, Payne had come to Smith's apartment to gather material for a three-part series on the life of a Pullman porter. She selected Smith to be the center of the series because he was a veteran whose service dated back to the years when her father, William Payne, worked as a porter. Getting ready for his 615th run on the *City of Los Angeles*, his forty-second year as a porter, and the beginning of his seven millionth mile on the rails, Smith was, for Payne, "the symbol of an occupation familiar to millions."

Twenty-six years after the death of her father, Payne composed a loving and public tribute to her dad. To do so, she followed Smith from his modest apartment to the rail yard where he boarded Car 1032, named Los Feliz. There she watched as he adjusted the heating controls, made the beds according to strict Pullman standards, and checked his supplies. Until the train rolled into the nearby Northwestern Station and he drew back the door and stepped onto the platform to welcome his passengers, Smith fussed anxiously. Slapping the porter on the back, a buffet car worker interjected, "You've been married to trains so long that you see them in your sleep. And, why the night before you go out, you're worse than an old hunting dog, fidgeting for the bugle to blow."

As the train headed out into the night and began its forty-hour run to Los Angeles, Payne shadowed Smith fluffing pillows, taking drink orders, helping his passengers settle in for the night, and standing discreetly back as a newlywed couple got off the train for a brief nighttime view of the husband's hometown when the train paused in Council Bluffs. In between, Smith told Payne tales from his four decades on the rails that she recorded for use in her articles.

When they reached Los Angeles, Payne was not yet done. She accompanied Smith to the house he had purchased two years before, where his wife awaited him, and remained there overnight as their guest. He planned to work for three more years before retiring. "In the meantime," Payne wrote, "Golden William Smith, symbol of the 10,320 porters serving thousands of customers, would continue to uphold an old tradition of fine service."

In the early months of 1952 the *Defender* published her reports in a three-part series entitled "Knight of the Road" and included a photograph of Payne debarking from the train in Los Angeles. "Radiant from a luxury trip aboard the City of Los Angeles, reporter Ethel L. Payne gets an assist from the train by Porter Smith after journey to Los Angeles to get inside story on a Pullman porter." In the pages of the *Defender*, Payne was becoming as well-known as the subjects of her articles.

In fact, the Newspaper Guild selected Payne's earlier series on African American employment for honorable mention in the 1951 Heywood Broun competition, named after an intrepid New York reporter. The judges said they were particularly impressed by various series they had read "written by Negroes concerning the place of the Negro in American life."

CHAPTER 10

MORE UNWANTED BABIES

WITHIN A FEW MONTHS OF RETURNING TO CHICAGO, Ethel Payne embarked on a mission of sorrow. With a *Defender* photographer to chronicle the moment, Payne traveled to Buffalo, New York, bringing with her an urn containing the ashes of a two-month-old child of a Japanese woman and her husband, a black soldier who had gone missing in action in Korea. She delivered the remains to the soldier's mother, who was campaigning to win a visa for her daughter-in-law and a surviving granddaughter.

Payne had not shaken off her experience with the Japanese orphans. Looking around Chicago, Payne discovered that black orphans in Chicago faced a dismal fate similar to that of the tan orphans of Japan. They weren't wanted. The nation treated all of its citizens unequally, including babies. The offspring of unmarried white women received care and found a path to adoption from a bevy of foster homes and adoption agencies. But such agencies in Chicago might as well have posted a "whites only" sign on their front doors. Black mothers were told they could be charged with child abandonment if they tried to put their child up for adoption.

As a result, few institutions accepted black babies, and those that did struggled to find them a home. Adoption by families other than black ones was completely out of the question. In fact, white parents were permitted by the courts to return a child whose pedigree later revealed black ancestors.

In the spring of 1952, Payne began visiting the city's adoption agencies. In one orphanage, she met seventeen-month-old Davey, who had been abandoned by a mother too young to care for him. "Davey has a pair of the biggest, most beautiful sad eyes in the world," wrote Payne. "There is a haunting depth to them which makes one remember him long after the first sight."

"The instinct to be loved makes Davey reach out his arms to be cuddled every time one of the nurses comes near him," said Payne. "But the busy nurses, who have 200 other children to look after, have only the time to give him an occasional pat on the head as they hurry about their duties."

Payne made Davey the center of the first installment of a series of articles, which appeared in mid-April. But after introducing the cute toddler to her readers, Payne explained that Davey was one of thousands of children looking for a home. "What makes his problem a little different than many of the other children in the institution is that Davey is a Negro child and there are not enough qualified applicants for the adoption of Negro children."

Consequently, most black children would remain in orphanages or foster homes, Payne said. "Or worse still, remain with their mothers and grow up under the blighting stigma of illegitimacy." Sixty percent of the children put up for adoption were born out of wedlock. But at the time thirty states still prohibited or restricted the advertisement or sale of contraceptives. So Payne crafted her next comment carefully so as not to mention sex, offend readers, or transgress the line of what could permissibly be said about the issue. There is, she wrote, "a basic need for educating people on what are the causes of the problem and how a more intelligent approach to it can be taken."

For four weeks the *Defender* splashed Payne's series on the front page and included, on the inside pages, a guide on how to adopt, a report on cases of successful adoptions, and a heartrending account of children in foster care. Seventy-three of every hundred children under the care of Chicago's Children Division were black because there weren't enough foster homes for them. At the end of the series, Payne pleaded with her readers to help. "It's a grand feeling," she wrote, "to know that you have not only saved a child, but you have done your share toward making better citizens for tomorrow."

The series was a smash hit. Within weeks the city's welfare offices reported an uptick in adoption applications from African Americans and an increase in the number of families volunteering to provide foster care. Her profiles, her feature articles, the series on employment, and her investigation into the plight of orphans taught Payne a valuable lesson about reporting. "Early on," she said, "I decided that my best bet in newspapering was to build up a bank of contacts, and it proved very worthwhile, because people began to, well, admire me for my aggressiveness in going after something. So they cooperated by giving me information."

THE EDITORS ASSIGNED PAYNE to do a follow-up series of stories on the mothers of the orphaned babies. To illustrate their plight, Payne settled on using the experiences of Amy Lester to tell the story of the others. "She was pert, pretty, young and sick with fright and worry," wrote Payne in her front-page story. "Clutching a brown suitcase as she shuffled through the crowds coming down the ramp in the railroad station, she was unaware that she was one of a hundred thousand women in the same embarrassing condition." Some 25,000 white and black pregnant unmarried women leave the small towns they grew up in and seek the anonymity of life in a large city, where, according to Payne, "they wait out their time to deliver the results of an illicit love affair away from the prying eyes and the wagging tongues of neighbors and friends."

Payne followed Lester as she registered under the name Mrs. Carl Brewster in a dingy hotel and watched as the desk clerk took her cash payment for a week's stay. After Lester settled into the room, Payne said the clerk called an abortionist to alert him of a new prospect. "All that is left now for the abortionist to do is to make contact with Amy and find out how much money she has or can get without arousing suspicion," explained Payne. Unless she could get care from a licensed welfare agency, Lester, like others in her condition, had only two options: "Either seek relief from the ever-present abortionist or very often abandon the child shortly after birth."

In subsequent installments, Payne reported on the opinions of social workers and highlighted the stigma borne by these women, not unlike like that of Hester Prynne's scarlet letter. "Today, a century later, it is still the woman who pays and pays for the crime of bastardy; because the cruel and inequitable fallacy still exists that it is the woman's fault in all cases," Payne wrote. "On the other hand," she continued, "the father of the illegitimate child is looked upon as merely a youth having its fling and to some extent, indulgence of this laxity goes to the point where it becomes a huge joke as to how many 'outside children' 'so and so' is the father of."

Lester did not succumb to the abortionist's offers, Payne informed her readers at the conclusion of her series. Instead, she was taken in by a maternity home. There she awaited the birth of her child with twenty other young women. After consultation with a minister, a psychiatrist, and a psychologist, Lester decided to give up her child for adoption and try to continue her college education in Chicago.

There was little doubt where Payne stood. In a world in which unwed mothers were pariahs, Payne was not going to join the condemnation. "There need not be illegitimate children or illegitimate parents," Payne wrote. "It is an illegitimate society which fails to give each one of its members a chance to make good."

The series resonated with other journalists. The Illinois Press Association selected it for first prize among feature stories appearing that year in communities with populations greater than 10,000. In writing this series, more so than her previous two on employment and adoption, Payne had found her journalistic voice.

CHAPTER 11

A TASTE OF NATIONAL POLITICS

I N THE SUMMER OF 1952, DEMOCRATS GATHERING IN CHI-
cago for their presidential convention gave Payne an opportunity
to try her hand at some political reporting. Until now, with the
exception of a couple of press conferences, her reporting had been
solely devoted to features and profiles. But a gathering of national
political leaders a couple of miles west from the office sent Payne into
her first political arena as a reporter.

For the *Defender*, the big story of the convention was civil rights,
which threatened party harmony as it had in 1948, when a group of
Southern Democrats bolted and nominated Governor Strom Thurmond of South Carolina to run as the States' Rights Party's nominee.
Four years later, Southern Democrats had returned to the fold. But
it was not long before they and Northerners began arguing over the
party's civil rights plank.

Payne, who was paired by her editors with another *Defender*
reporter, headed over to Chicago's International Amphitheatre and
the Conrad Hilton hotel to see the fireworks. The two arrived in time
to see New York senator Herbert Lehman, a member of the platform
drafting committee, squash any talk of compromise. He was demanding a civil rights plank that called for new Senate rules to break fili-
busters.

This was a direct attack on Southern senators who had success-

fully used the tactic in the Senate to forestall federal civil rights legislation. Lehman's speech deepened the chasm between the Southern
and Northern delegates and increased the likelihood of a floor fight.
"I should regret a floor flight," Senator Lehman said, "but I will press
for a strong civil rights plank even if it makes such a battle inevitable."

Lehman wasn't the only national figure that Payne witnessed
campaigning for civil rights. "Fighting also for the respect of individual dignity and first class citizenship for Negro Americans was
Minnesota's fiery senator, Hubert Humphrey," Payne noted. It was,
indeed, an unusual spectacle for Payne. With the exception of Chicago African American congressman William Dawson, who was on
the platform committee, here were white politicians publicly fighting to advance the cause of civil rights. They were motivated by the
changing color of voters, Payne concluded. Keenly aware that the
Negro vote had delivered Ohio and Illinois in the 1948 election, they
wanted to capture a larger share of the vote. The fight, Payne concluded, "demonstrated the vast importance of the Negro vote."

Instead of seeking time with the Democratic leaders who supported her cause and rewarding them with flattering pieces, Payne
took an entirely different tack. She decided to enter the enemy's lair.
She sought an audience with the die-hard segregationist senator
Richard Russell Jr., one of the four leading candidates for the presidential nomination. His membership in the Democratic Party, like
that of other segregationists, raised the hackles of the NAACP. "If
the Democrats win," asked its magazine *Crisis*, "won't the Dixiecrat-
GOP coalition kill civil rights?"

Slender in build, with a Roman nose and large ears made more
pronounced by his close-cropped hair, Russell graciously received
Payne in his ninth-floor room of the Conrad Hilton. He represented
the bulwark of resistance to federal civil rights laws and was the wili-
est of opponents. When he first reached the Senate in 1933, Russell
had taken it upon himself to become the chamber's most astute par-
liamentarian. He skillfully opposed every effort that he deemed a

threat to the Southern way of life. He fought against anti-lynching bills, removal of poll taxes, and equal employment opportunity measures and linked such plans to communism.

Sitting before Payne with a coterie of staff members hovering behind him, Russell affably told her that Georgians were unalterably opposed to integration of any sort. If integration were to come to schools, for example, he promised the state would shut down its public schools and replace them with private ones.

"Will you support whatever civil rights plank the Democratic Party platform will contain?" Payne asked.

"I believe I can support the kind of civil rights plank which the party will produce. I am absolutely opposed to a compulsory jailhouse FEPC,* which will throw a man in jail for not hiring somebody. I believe the Constitution guarantees civil rights to all persons. We must use the education approach to the problem, not the compulsory one. The method of approach should be left to the states."

At this point Russell broke off from his well-honed speech about states' rights to launch into a complaint about extremists. His sycophantic staff members nodded approvingly.

"What do you mean by 'extremists'?" she asked.

"The senator," said one of the staffers, taking up the question, "means the radicals on both sides; the ones who want to push integration by force and the few who don't want to see Negroes have anything. Now believe me, the senator is just as fair as he can be about trying to see that the Negroes get just as much as anybody else; and believe me, he's a lot more honest than this crowd that runs around making a lot of promises they don't mean."

The interview at an end, Russell rose, shook Payne's hand, and

* The Federal Fair Employment Practices Committee, which was created by President Roosevelt's executive order. Truman had sought to make it a permanent commission, but Southern senators had prevented the passage of the legislation.

apologized for not having more time for her. But Senator J. Lister Hill of Alabama caught up with Payne in the hallway as she was leaving to lecture her further on the segregationist cause. Back at the *Defender* she tried to make sense of the experience. What Russell said did not upset her, she told her readers. She had anticipated his answers. Nor did Senator Hill's impassioned hallway speech get under her skin. It wasn't even the denunciation by Russell's staff of radicals that troubled her.

"What really upset me," Payne wrote, "I guess is what poet Robert Burns describes as the 'Unco good' or the 'rigidly righteous' who so firmly believe they are right. It's the same kinds of fanatic religious who freely quote the scriptures to [support the] righteousness of Prime Minister Daniel Malan of South Africa to back up his claims for white supremacy." Payne was confounded to find that not only did Russell earnestly believe he was right but also he had the temerity to tell her he was the best friend the Negro has ever had in public office. "Negroes," he had told Payne, "have absolutely nothing to fear from me."

The convention provided Payne with her first exposure to the federal legislative battleground for civil rights. This was an Alice in Wonderland world where Northerners were attacked as hypocrites and Southerners resolutely proclaimed that Negroes back home lived in harmony with whites, accepting their respective social roles. If they complained, it was only because they had been instigated to do so by Northern meddling.

Her time with Senators Russell and Hill made it clear to her the immense and entrenched national power held by opponents of desegregation. "I came away from the interview," said Payne, "feeling depressed and sick."

THE ELECTION DID NOT GO as the Democrats had hoped. Instead, the nation's voters selected war hero Dwight D. Eisenhower, sending the first Republican to the White House in twenty years. Thirty-three percent of African Americans, almost all in the North, voted in the election. They supported Adlai Stevenson, the Democratic candidate, by a margin of three to one. Yet Eisenhower did not engender the enmity of their community. In a sense, no verdict had yet been rendered on the civil rights record of the general who like Cincinnatus had assumed power.

Having recently lost its Washington correspondent, the *Defender* dispatched Payne for the inauguration. The choice made sense. She was now among the paper's most visible reporters, with a story on the front page once every four or five issues in 1952. Her coverage of the Democratic convention had demonstrated her skills as a political journalist.

Reaching Washington on the eve of the swearing in, Payne found the city jammed with visitors. Republicans euphorically converged in record numbers. Pullman cars parked in the rail yard were being used as temporary hotels, and apartments in a not-yet-occupied building had been filled with cots. At noon on January 20, 1953, Payne watched as Eisenhower took the oath of office and Pennsylvania Avenue was overtaken by a massive inaugural parade made up of 22,000 military and 5,000 civilian participants, 350 horses, 3 elephants (and even an Alaskan dog team), 65 bands, and floats from all states.

That evening, in the company of her sister Thelma Gray, Payne made the rounds of the social events. They first attended a gathering of Howard University faculty wives and then made their way to the east side of Washington to the National Armory, where one of the two inaugural balls was under way; there they listened to Lionel Hampton leading his band and blues artist W. C. Handy.

Payne was enchanted by the gala's glitter and glamour. Dozens of the most prominent black judges, lawyers, professors, doctors, publicists, and politicians dressed in tuxedoes and glistening evening gowns mingled freely among Washington's power elite. *Defender* columnist Marion B. Campbell ceded her Mostly About Women space entirely over to Payne for a who's who of the festivities. Gushing about the "breathlessly radiant" women with "sparkling warm personalities," Payne filled an entire page of the paper, dotting her account with well-known names, all set in caps and surrounded by photographs.

A more demure version of Payne's reporting was reserved for the front page. There she updated readers on the black cabinet, the nickname given to the Federal Council of Negro Affairs that had been created in the Roosevelt years as an informal advisory group of African Americans. Composed of blacks who had been appointed as special assistants to cabinet secretaries, the group advised the administration, acted as liaisons with the African American community, and represented the administration in the Negro press. It had included Walter White, Robert C. Weaver, and Mary McLeod Bethune, among others.

"As the last strains of the last band in the inaugural procession died away," Payne reported, "jockeying for position in the 'new black cabinet' grow more intense and capital corridors hummed with predictions." At some length, Payne ran through all the rumored judicial, administrative, and diplomatic appointments that might include an African American.

The celebrations at an end, Washington settled in under its new administration and Payne headed back to Chicago.

AFTER THE GLAMOUR and excitement of Washington, Chicago took on a dull sheen. Instead of national politics and high society, Payne found herself covering meetings of the American Library Association, press conferences, and endless church leadership meetings. Not that the church was not important. To the contrary, *Defender* readers were very religious, and the church was one of very few institutions over which blacks exert unfettered control.

But her stories slipped to the inside pages of the paper. In the following eight months, her reporting made it to the front page only six times, one of which was a story on the awarding of an honorary degree to her publisher. Such stories as "Prayer Guides Lives of St. Jude Nuns" or "3,000 Attend Christian Congress" weren't exactly page one material. But even the two substantive series she wrote that year, one of which was about the integration of the State Street shopping district, didn't merit front-page treatment. "I really didn't have an inclination or a desire to do straight, mundane, local reporting," Payne said. "I just didn't have a feel for it."

On the other hand, the work did put Payne on the road. She covered AME church leadership meetings in New Orleans, Philadelphia, Nashville, Atlanta, and Houston. She loved the travel and the perks, such as a steak dinner at the Top Hat Lounge in Nashville, tea at the Ministers Wives and Daughters Alliance of New Orleans, and a performance of the play *Portrait in Black* at Ohio's Wilberforce University, the nation's oldest private, historically black university.

Quite to her surprise, the Southern cities won Payne over. "I've fallen in love with the South—some parts of it. So far I'm torn between Atlanta and Nashville," she wrote during one of her trips. "There are slums here just as in every other city: but compared to the litter of Chicago's sore spots, the streets were far cleaner." Later she added Houston to her list of favorite cities. There she found a black family residing in a residential community with large homes and front lawns, quite unlike anything available to blacks back in Chicago. "Yes, this is the South!"

While in Tulsa, Oklahoma, in mid-August to cover a church conference, Payne met with Edward L. Goodwin Sr., who owned the *Oklahoma Eagle*, the city's black newspaper. A successful businessman, Goodwin had entered law school and was looking for someone to run his paper. "You know," he told Payne, "I think you're just the person I need." He offered her the post of managing editor with complete control over the paper, a salary of $300 a month, which was a little less than she earned at the *Defender*, and an option to buy up to 49 percent of the paper's stock. Payne told Goodwin she would consider it and he had his lawyer draw up a contract stipulating that she would report to work in early October.

An *Eagle* staff member drove Payne out to the Tulsa airport to catch a flight back to Chicago. It was unusual for African Americans to take to the skies. Those who traveled at the time did so mostly by car, bus, or train. The bible for black travelers was the *Green Book*, published by Victor H. Green, a Harlem postal worker. Frequently updated, *The Negro Motorist Green Book*, sometimes called *The Negro Traveler's Green Book*, listed those businesses that blacks could safely use to get their cars repaired, find a meal, get their hair done, or spend the night. A traveling African American blindly entering a business establishment, particularly in the Jim Crow South, risked danger or even death.

Seating in airplanes was not segregated, but airports in the American South certainly were to different degrees. When Payne flew into Atlanta, she found the lounges to be integrated but colored and white signs above the bathroom doors. National Airport, a federal facility that served the nation's capital, had only recently opened its restaurants to blacks and only after President Truman interceded.

After securing her seat on a Chicago flight at the Tulsa airport, Payne and her companion from the paper decided to get some coffee. At the restaurant the waitress told them they could not be served. When Payne complained, the assistant manager said that she was only following state Jim Crow laws. The establishment was operated by the Sky Chef chain, whose executives had instructed its staff that it would be to their peril to overlook local customs. With no other option, Payne waited for her flight without coffee.

WHEN SHE RETURNED TO WORK at the paper, she wrote up a page one item about her treatment at the Tulsa airport and vowed that she and the *Eagle* staffer would sue both the airport and the restaurant chain. She let the threat die because she had another, more pressing item on her agenda.

She drafted a request for a leave of absence and left it on Louis Martin's desk. "You would have thought I had released an atomic bomb," Payne said. "The place went up in smoke." Martin said it was out of the question.

"See," Payne said, brandishing her offer from the Oklahoma paper in front of Martin, "if you don't appreciate me, then here's somebody who does." Martin took the papers and looked them over. "He acted like a Philadelphia lawyer before the Supreme Court," said Payne.

If she took the proffered job, he said, she would make less money, work harder, and lose the prestige and advantage of working for the *Defender*. More important, she would give up the national reporting opportunities for which the paper was grooming her.

It all gave her a splitting headache. "The only reason why I listen to Mr. Martin at all is because he is respected as one of the smartest men in the newspaper game, white or colored," she wrote to a friend. "The biggest thing which is swaying me at the moment and something which he knew would hit home with me was my fear of taking a long-shot gamble and losing."

Holding Payne's documents in his hands, Martin snorted.

"Forty-nine percent? Forget it!" he said. "If you don't have fifty-one percent, you ain't got nothing.

"You know," he continued, "if you're so restless, I'll tell you what. Why don't you go down to Washington?"

CHAPTER 12

WASHINGTON

O
N THE MORNING OF FEBRUARY 10, 1954, ETHEL PAYNE made her way across Washington to the Executive Office Building, a massive gray stone structure adjacent to the White House that had once housed the entire Departments of State, War, and the Navy. Under a cloudy sky, the temperature would hardly reach the forties that day, but Payne was seething.

Five days earlier the choir from Howard University, the capital's historically black college, had been asked to perform, along with singers from Duke and Emory Universities, at the annual Lincoln Day Dinner held by Washington Republicans. Happy at long last to have one of their own in the White House, about 8,000 Republicans crowded into the Uline Arena, a cavernous vaulted hall named for an ice mogul. When the two Southern white choirs reached the entrance, they traversed the security cordon without any delay. But when the bus carrying the Howard choir arrived, the police refused to let it pass.

The officers insisted that the bus had to come in through a different entrance, so the driver obediently pulled around to the other side of the building. Once again it was blocked from entering. The dean of the university's school of music, who had accompanied the students, agreed to wait while a police officer went to talk with an event organizer. But during the first officer's absence, another policeman

ordered the bus to move immediately because the president's lim-
ousine was expected at any minute. The dean's patience ran out. He
instructed the driver to take the choir back to the university.

The exclusion of the black singers, unreported in the press, wasn't
the only aspect of the celebration that had gotten under Payne's skin
over the weekend. In putting together a program to honor the great
emancipator, the Republicans had included Jack Powell, an aging
white vaudeville actor with a minstrel routine. Powell came onstage
dressed in a cook's outfit, in blackface and wearing a wig of kinky hair.
According to the announcer, the actor was included in the program
by special request of Sherman Adams, Eisenhower's chief of staff.
The morning after the event, Payne fired off a telegram to Adams.
"Surely," she wired, "there could have been some representation of
the Negro people on such an occasion more dignified and in keeping
with the progress of the race."

Now, heading to the Executive Office Building, Payne planned
to take up the matter with Adams's boss. At 10:30 AM, Eisenhower was
set to hold his twenty-seventh press conference of his administration.
Since her arrival in Washington three months earlier, Payne had yet
to ask a question at a presidential press conference. Today she was
going to make sure she did.

A FEW MONTHS EARLIER, when editor Louis Martin asked Payne
if she wanted to go to Washington, he had been motivated by more
than a desire to retain a star reporter who was feeling unappreciated.
The skinflint newspaper had lost its Washington correspondent to
a better-paying job and Payne's unhappiness was an opportunity
for the *Defender*. "Go on down to Washington and try your hand,"
Martin told Payne. "If you don't like it, come on home after six
months." He was hedging his bet. By giving Payne the option of
coming home, he preserved for himself the excuse to bring her back
if her work did not measure up.

Since the end of World War II, the *Defender* had continuously maintained at least a part-time correspondent in the capital. Some had been government employees, like Al Smith, who wrote a column under the pen name Charlie Cherokee. In recent years, Venice Tipton Spraggs, a tall, striking woman with prodigious work habits, had ably served the paper. But she had taken a job with the Democratic National Committee, leaving the *Defender* bereft of representation in Washington, DC.

With the fanfare of a front-page story, the paper announced, "Miss Ethel Payne, one of the *Chicago Defender*'s crack news and feature writers, has been assigned to Washington." Publisher John Sengstacke sung her praise. "We purposely waited to fill the Washington assignment in our organization until we were satisfied that we had a person capable of doing the same superb job of giving our readers the most accurate coverage possible of the Washington scene in the same excellent manner as Mrs. Spraggs and Al Smith who preceded her," he said, giving the appointment the sheen of forethought.

If the segregation still prevalent in Chicago had been a jarring readjustment for Payne upon her return from Japan, Washington had worse in store for her. By constitutional designation, the city was the nation's capital. In all other respects, from the Southern congressmen who ruled over the powerless federal enclave down to school officials and city administrators, it was a Southern town through and through, with an approach to racial matters not unlike that prevalent in Atlanta, Georgia, or Richmond, Virginia.

E. Frederic Morrow, a black Republican who had worked for both the NAACP and CBS, was also moving to Washington at the time. He had served as the liaison between the black community and the Eisenhower campaign in 1952 and had been promised a White House job. He found white cabbies would not pick him up, restaurants would not serve him, and hotels had no rooms. A dark-skinned visitor's best chance at obtaining lodging in a hotel was to wrap his head in a turban and register using a foreign name, according to a report on segregation in Washington. "This maneuver was success-fully employed not long ago at one of the capital's most fashionable hotels by an enterprising American Negro who wanted to test the advantages of being a foreigner."

In late November, after unpacking her belongings in a flat on Vernon Street in a black neighborhood in northwest Washington, Payne went to call on Spraggs. "I felt like a child trying to step into grownup's shoes," said Payne. The seasoned correspondent received her warmly and, over home-cooked meals, provided her with an introductory course in the ways of Washington. Unlike many other correspondents sent to Washington, Payne did not feel it was beneath her to take lessons. Her insecurity about reporting on national affairs after only a couple of years of local reporting left her open to sage advice. It also permitted her to consider Washington events with a fresh perspective. From Chicago, city editor Enoch Waters praised her early work in Washington and spurred her onward. "Of course it did not measure up to the standard of which you are capable," he wrote. "Keep up the good work old girl and remember everybody here is pulling for you."

A FEW WEEKS AFTER Payne settled in, Sherman Briscoe, an alum-nus of the *Defender* who now worked in the Department of Agricul-ture, came calling. He made it a habit to help members of the black press and had come to escort Payne to a meeting of the Capital Press Club.

That night Maxwell M. Rabb was the guest speaker. A Boston lawyer who had helped organize the movement to draft Eisenhower, Rabb now worked in the White House. "For those of us in the black press," Louis Martin said, "Max Rabb, short, plump, and person-able, was the principal figure in the White House to whom we addressed racial problems." Accepting an invitation to speak at the Capital Press Club certainly fit his job description. The club had been established in 1944 because membership in the National Press Club was closed to African Americans.

Rabb and other political operatives in the Eisenhower administration were convinced that Negro voters might be drawn away from the Democratic Party. After all, it had been only two decades since they abandoned the Republican Party. "Negroes as a whole admire the President, and with proper public relations this can be turned into votes," wrote Val J. Washington, who as an assistant to the Republican national chair was the highest-ranking African American in the GOP.

In his talk, Rabb played the Washington game of journalistic flattery. He was a master at the art and could "really butter people up," according to Morrow, who a year into the administration was still waiting for his promised White House post. Before his largely black audience, Rabb praised the *Defender*, holding aloft a copy of that week's issue with Payne's front-page story on Attorney General Herbert Brownell Jr., who had written a brief urging that the Supreme Court overturn school segregation in the *Brown v. Board of Education* case currently before it. With no previous exposure to the duplicitous flirtations of Washington movers and shakers, Payne accepted the flattery as a compliment. "He was referring to the headline and the story on the Brownell brief," Payne wrote to Waters at the paper. "Gee, I was glad for us."

In the corridor following his talk, Rabb told Payne he would assist her in obtaining White House press credentials and invited her to come by his office. Press credentials were not routinely granted to a black reporter. In fact, until the 1940s the credentialed Washington press corps had been exclusively white. "Letting a colored reporter have equal news gathering status with white and foreign correspondents in Washington was unheard of," said an NAACP lobbyist. In fact, according to Payne's boss, "a black reporter had as little a chance of interviewing a cabinet officer as of getting an interview with God."

By the time Payne came to Washington, the press committees of journalists that governed access to Capitol Hill and the White House had provided credentials to only two black reporters. The senior of the two was Louis Lautier, a Louisiana native, who worked for the National Negro Publishers Association. White reporters valued the presence of the prim and dapper Lautier. Because of his lengthy service as a legal stenographer for the Justice Department, Lautier was in demand at the end of press conferences by reporters wanting to check the accuracy of the quotes in their notes. The other accredited black reporter was Alice Dunnigan.

DUNNIGAN, A REPORTER for the Associated Negro Press (ANP), was the first African American female journalist accredited by Congress and the White House. The daughter of a Kentucky sharecropper, at thirteen Dunnigan had set her sights on being a reporter and never let any obstacles get in her way.

In 1948, for instance, when Truman took off on a fifteen-day, 9,000-mile train trip that would presage his famous fall campaign whistle-stop tour, Dunnigan paid her own way by taking out a loan after her boss at the ANP, Claude Barnett, refused to approve the $1,000 travel costs. Her boss's stinginess was a result of sexism rather than parsimony. "I did not think a woman could do the best job on a jaunt of that kind," he said.

Female reporters had first been seen at presidential press conferences during the Franklin D. Roosevelt administration, when two women joined the all-male White House press corps. But their entry didn't signal an acceptance of women on the hard news side of the media. In fact, two years earlier Barnett had only hired Dunnigan to work for the ANP because all the men he approached turned down the pitiful salary he offered. She took the job in return for the title of Washington bureau chief and a low piece rate that was eventually converted to a salary of $25 a week.

To make it work, she moved into a basement apartment of a white family's house, tending the furnace and hauling the ashes to reduce her rent, eating Sunday meals of pig ears and turnip greens, and pawning her jewelry when her paycheck was late.

When she boarded Truman's train in June 1948, Dunnigan was the first black newspaperwoman to travel on a presidential trip. She was such a rarity that when the train stopped in Cheyenne, Wyoming, a white military policeman thought she didn't belong in the phalanx of reporters walking down the street behind the car ferrying the president to the capitol building. "Get back there behind this line where you belong," the police officer called out. When Dunnigan continued to walk, he grabbed her and tried to forcibly direct her toward the sidewalk.

But before he could, a young correspondent for the *Nashville Tennessean* stepped in. "I want you to know," he told the MP, "you are messing with the party of the president of the United States. You know this woman is with us. She has her badge and she has it on." The MP backed off.

A couple of days later, Dunnigan sat in her train compartment, her shoes off, her bare feet on the seat, and her typewriter on her lap, when there was a knock on her door. In walked Truman. "I didn't know what to do," she said. "I tugged at my skirt. I couldn't find my shoes. I knew I should be standing up, but I couldn't move."

"I heard you had a little trouble," Truman said in a quiet voice. "Well, if anything else happens, please let me know."

AT FIRST, NEITHER OF THE TWO black White House correspondents welcomed Payne's arrival. Lautier was a lifelong Republican. "For twenty years of the New Deal," a reporter noted, "he was the most outspoken defender of the Republican Party in the Negro press." Now, with Eisenhower in office, he was deferential at press conferences. Payne considered him "a water boy for the administration."

Lautier also held women reporters in low regard and had worked against Dunnigan's entry into the press corps. For Dunnigan, Payne's arrival was financially costly. The *Defender* canceled the unsigned column she wrote for the paper and the subsequent loss of $75 a month represented the reduction by a quarter of her already paltry income.

Payne decided to work on gaining her White House press pass first and then concentrate on obtaining the necessary credentials to cover Congress. The rules governing the accreditation of newspaper reporters, both at the White House and on Capitol Hill, required that the applicant work for a daily publication. The clients of the news services that employed Lautier and Dunnigan included at least one daily newspaper. But Payne's *Defender* was still a weekly. However, with Rabb eager to curry favor with African American voters and the changing political sensitivities of those who enforced the rules, White House press secretary James Hagerty assured Sengstacke that Payne would be cleared. By the beginning of 1954, Payne possessed her White House press credentials.

AS SHE ENTERED the Executive Office Building that February day, Payne's displeasure over the Howard choir incident fueled her every step as she made her way down the black-and-white tiled corridors, She found a seat among the 204 reporters who had gathered in the ornate Treaty Room, in which the president held his meetings with the press.

Despite her fury, Payne was terrified at the prospect of asking Eisenhower a question. "It was just unheard of for blacks to be standing up and asking presidents impertinent questions and particularly a black woman," Payne recalled. But at a previous press conference, she had learned, "the chances of getting the coveted nod depended upon your dexterity in leaping to your feet and crying 'Mr. President!'"

"Mr. President!" Payne shouted, her voice quavering. "Mr. President!"

Eisenhower looked over, smiled, and gave her the nod.

"Mr. President," she began, reading the question she had carefully written out, "last Friday evening at the Lincoln Day box supper at the arena, the Howard University choir, which was scheduled to sing, was barred from the hall by District police."

"Who?" asked the president.

"The Howard University choir," Payne answered, "even though they had their instructions, and had followed out those instructions. Consequently, they were forced to return to the campus without appearing on the program; but in the meantime, two other singing groups, the Duke and Emory University glee clubs, were admitted without incident. I wonder if you had been informed of that, and if you had looked into it."

Eisenhower turned to his press secretary. Briefly the two conferred. "I not only had not been informed of it," said the president, turning back to the reporters, "I am just told, for the first time that I have heard about this, I am told by Mr. Hagerty that the bus driver was instructed to go around to the door by which I entered, and he refused to go around to that place.

"I hope there is no connection between those two facts," said Eisenhower, to the laughter of the reporters. "But anyway, that is just what I have been informed." Turning serious, Eisenhower added, "I would say this: if that choir was barred by the reason that you seem to fear, of anything about race or of color or anything of that kind, I will be the first to apologize to them. I just don't believe that could have happened."

When the press conference concluded, white reporters swarmed around Payne, wanting to know the details of the incident. One reporter offered some advice. "I know how nervous you were, but keep at it," he said. "It was a good question, but take a tip, on your next one, don't read it. They'll be sure to think it's planted and then Jim

Hagerty will want to have you investigated as a suspected lobbyist."

Payne's question to the president about a topic that in the scheme of national and international politics was not a major event revealed her potential power as a member of the White House press corps. By asking the president about the incident, she single-handedly caused the white press to pay attention and publicize the injustice done to the Howard choir. The next day the *New York Herald Tribune* reported EISENHOWER MAY APOLOGIZE IN MIX-UP ON NEGRO CHOIR and the *Los Angeles Times* ran an article entitled RACIAL INCIDENT CRITICIZED BY EISENHOWER. Even the *Washington Post,* which had ignored what was after all a local story, felt compelled to publish an account under the headline OFFERS APOLOGY: IKE BLAMES MIXUP FOR CHOIR "BAN."

Payne was no longer in the comparatively uncompetitive world of black journalism of her native Chicago. After three months in Washington, Payne was coming to terms with being part of a larger and more combative press corps. "If I was going to succeed at all, I would have to learn to be aggressive and tough as the rest of the persons in the pack," she said. At first the handicaps of being a woman, being black, and working for a weekly minority newspaper that was not in the same league as the major papers pushed her to the periphery of the press corps. But her success at the February presidential press conference empowered her.

"From then on," said Payne, "I decided I was going to have the same privileges as anybody else."

TWO DAYS AFTER THE PRESS CONFERENCE, Rabb welcomed Payne and her boss, Louis Martin, to his office. On their way to Rabb's second-floor office, Martin, a Democrat, noticed things to like about the Eisenhower administration. He spotted several African Americans, including the first one to ever work as a secretary in the White House, a "pretty lass," in his eyes. "I also counted three brothers with important looking papers in their hands walking through the corridor on the first floor, and the receptionist is a handsome brother who is as smooth and suave a greeter as Grover Whalen," said Martin, referring to the prominent New York City politician and public relations figure.

Dressed in a charcoal-gray flannel suit, Rabb conducted himself like a gregarious salesman eager to convince Martin that his initial impressions in the hall were correct. It was his second time making such a pitch to the *Defender*. Two weeks earlier he had held a private off-the-record meeting with Payne in which the two went over a wide variety of topics from the absence of African Americans in the Department of Agriculture to pending legislation. "Smooth-talking Max has found his lap the repository of some real hot potatoes," noted Payne.

In both meetings Rabb succeeded in making his case that the President was on their side. "The President is personally determined to clean out racism in the Federal area," Martin wrote in the *Defender* when he returned to Chicago. "He is going to put his own house in order and proceed from that point forward." But Martin, more experienced than his Washington correspondent, added a caveat at this end of his complimentary description of progress under this administration. "Here I suppose I ought to confess that I also believe in miracles."

Rabb was not the only Washington fixture that caused Payne to lower her journalist guard in the early months of her life as a Washington correspondent. She was transformed into a gossip queen when she attended a reception given by the National Council of Negro Women to honor Pat Nixon, the wife of the vice-president. It was, she told her readers, "the top drawer event of the social season since the beginning of the Republican administration for my money."

"The sparkle of names and personalities mingling in the Crystal Room of the Willard Hotel," she wrote, "matched the brilliance of the smart gowns and accessories worn by the throng who turned out to do homage to a very charming woman." Wandering about, Payne gaped at the cadre of Washington's notable women who had come for the event, including the "fabulous and almost legendary" Alice Roosevelt Longworth.

A doyen of the group took Payne in tow and introduced her to the wives of cabinet secretaries, White House functionaries, and ambassadors. Payne filled her notebook with details of each woman's looks, choice of dress, and jewelry. Later, at her desk in her small cramped apartment, Payne gushed about those she had met. The Pakistani ambassador's wife was "one of the most beautiful women I have ever seen," the Korean ambassador's wife sported a dress "with huge butterfly sleeves," and the wife of the Ethiopian ambassador had "eyes as limpid and deep as clear pools." The domestic representatives at the event were feted as well. When introduced to Ruth Rabb, wife of Maxwell, Payne saw "a stunning blond woman with classic features and a flowered cloche atop her waves."

It was a world far removed from South Side Chicago.

CHAPTER 13

FEARED NEGRO

E THEL PAYNE WAS PLEASED WHEN SHE WAS TOLD THAT her question about the Howard choir at the February press conference had made her the "most feared" Negro journalist in Washington. At the same time, however, she rushed back to Rabb's office in case her new reputation damaged her access. "I have tried to emphasize that I intend to be as factual as possible without slanting the news," she reported to *Defender* publisher Sengstacke following the meeting.

She was concerned that any rumor that she was to be feared might endanger her request to interview Vice-President Richard Nixon. After a 68-day, 38,000-mile trip around the world, Nixon had returned to the United States publicly convinced that legalized racism at home was hurting the nation's standing overseas and providing a wedge for communism. "The elimination of racial discrimination in the United States is one of the most important things we all have to do," Nixon told business and industrial leaders in late December.

Payne submitted twelve questions focused mainly on how the "color problem" was seen from outside the United States and if Nixon was willing to join efforts to desegregate interstate travel and reduce discrimination in employment. To bolster her chances at gaining the interview, Payne emphasized that in addition to the *Chicago Defender* she now also represented the *New York Age Defender*, the *Michigan Chronicle*, the *Tri-State Defender*, and the *Louisville Defender*, all owned by Sengstacke. Inside the vice-president's office the names of these black publications carried little weight. "Dotty, do you know anything about these papers?" wrote a staff member on whose desk the interview request had landed.

In the end, Nixon's office told her it was unlikely an interview would be granted because, as an aide explained, "the V.P. could not give out interviews for fear that what he said would be interpreted as speaking for the administration." In addition, Payne learned that the White House didn't very much appreciate what Nixon had been saying. "The V.P. is being gagged because he has latterly been making some forthright statements on the color question," she shared privately with her boss. "The gagger is Sherman Adams."

But as much as Payne presented herself to Rabb and others in the administration as an objective reporter with a nonpartisan agenda, behind the scenes it was a different story. In February a source provided her with confidential information concerning the Republicans' plans for the fall elections. Fearful that any action taken by the administration sympathetic to Negro causes could increase voter registration and benefit Democrats, the Republicans were planning to hold off taking favorable civil rights positions until after the deadline for voting registration had passed. "The information is of tremendous value to the Democratic Party, and at the urgent request of the source, I have turned over the materials to Congressman Dawson," she told Sengstacke.

To some, Payne's actions violated the accepted journalistic codes of conduct that dictate reporters not take sides on an issue or engage in partisan work. But for Payne, what she did was not comparable to the actions of a reporter who favored a candidate or a political cause. At stake here were fundamental constitutional rights denied to African Americans. Supporting the Democratic Party, in a moment like this one, was the only viable means to advance civil rights. "The only people who can afford to be neutral in a situation are those who are untouched by what's going on," Payne said years later. "And any time there's a racial injustice, it involves me, just as much as the person who's directly involved."

IN THE SPRING OF 1954, while African Americans anxiously anticipated the Supreme Court's decision in *Brown v. Board*, Payne was drawn to another long-running Washington story. Senator Joseph McCarthy's four-year-old crusade to ferret out Communists in the government consumed vast amounts of ink and airtime. This was, however, not true with regard to the black press.

Communists had never been regarded as much of a threat to the black community. In Chicago during the Depression, recalled Payne, "when people were evicted, communists would come and move the furniture and everything else back into these houses, and they would bring baskets of food." And for a group lacking civil rights, the fact that McCarthy tramped all over civil liberties hardly mattered. The Wisconsin Republican senator had so far merited only an occasional mention in the pages of the *Defender*. But in the spring of 1954 Payne changed that.

She believed McCarthy and his Senate Permanent Subcommittee on Investigations of the Committee on Government Operations were dangerous, damaging, and destructive. "To me he was savage in the way he operated. I thought that McCarthy was a modern-day Savonarola," Payne said, referring to the fifteenth-century Florentine Dominican friar who ruthlessly tried to create a puritanical republic. "He was just really savaging people, destroying people in the process." Whenever she could find the time she would attend the hearings, sometimes dropping in between chasing down other stories.

In early March, Payne found the means to make McCarthyism a story for her readers. The committee had summoned Annie Lee Moss, a forty-nine-year-old African American widowed mother who worked in the Pentagon. Washington had treated the South Carolina native well up to this point. She had started off life working in cotton fields at age five, followed by years of domestic service, laundry work, and factory labor. With the outbreak of World War II, she and her husband came to Washington, where the demands of war opened federal employment to black women. By 1954, although now widowed, she was making good wages as a clerk in the Pentagon.

Preparing to launch a set of hearings on Communist infiltration of the Army, McCarthy focused on Moss when an FBI informant claimed she was on a list of dues-paying Communist Party members. A Communist working as an Army Signal Corps communications clerk, Moss seemed to the senator to be the perfect target. "Who in the military," asked McCarthy, "knowing that this lady was a Communist, promoted her from a waitress to a code clerk?"

Payne made sure to be on hand when Moss answered the committee's summons, accompanied by her attorney, whom McCarthy immediately labeled as a Communist. The planned showdown with Moss, however, failed to get under way. She was sick with bronchitis and looked exhausted. "If she says on the stand that she is not a communist," intoned McCarthy, "she will be committing perjury, and I do not want to send a sick woman to jail." Although there was nothing more than an unsubstantiated charge against Moss and she had not had her day before the committee, the Army skittishly suspended Moss from her job.

On March 11, a healthier Moss returned to Capitol Hill, with her attorney, to face the committee. Payne took her seat just to the side of the witness table in the classically designed grand Senate Caucus Room, with a floor of Italianate black-veined marble and a ceiling of gilded flowers, leaves, and a ribbon of Greek key pattern. Unlike her white colleagues at the table, to whom Moss was only one more in an interminable line of witnesses, Payne had made an effort to learn about the woman. She had interviewed her pastor, who said that Moss was a good Christian who had belonged to the Friendship Baptist Church for a decade, along with her twenty-three-year-old son.

To Payne, the gray-haired, widowed mother was a pawn in McCarthy's battle against the secretary of the Army, who refused to permit his officers to testify before the committee. "She was a woman of limited education, she was a very humble person," Payne said. "The three things in her life were her son, her grandson, and her church, besides her job. And other than that, she knew very little about the world outside."

WITH THE TELEVISION CAMERAS rolling, McCarthy swore in Moss and began with his questioning. First he sought to learn about any coded messages she might have handled as a clerk in the Pentagon. Moss said she had never been in the code room and was charged only with filing and passing on messages of unknown classification. Then the senator signaled Roy Cohn, the committee's chief counsel, to launch his often-repeated line of questioning.

The committee, said Cohn, had information that Moss had been a member of the Communist Party.

"Not at any time have I been a member of a Communist Party, and I have never seen a Communist card," Moss said.

"You have never seen a Communist card?"

"That's right."

McCarthy resumed the questioning, repeating essentially the same questions that Cohn had tried. The back-and-forth continued, with no admissions made by Moss. Then McCarthy drew what he thought was the ace up his sleeve. He asked about Robert Hall, a white man who used to deliver the *Daily Worker* to her house years before when her husband was still alive. In a quiet voice, Moss replied that he might have been at the house once, years ago, to see her late husband, but she was absent at the time. The diminutive bespectacled Moss, clad in a black coat with a small white hat, quietly and respectfully held her ground, thwarting McCarthy at each point.

"She answered the questions with disarming candor and won the sympathy of many of the spectators and newsmen crowded into the room," said Payne.

A discouraged McCarthy suddenly excused himself from the hearing room, and Senator Stuart Symington Jr., who as a newly elected Democrat from Missouri was already earning the enmity of McCarthy, resumed the questioning of Moss. He asked her to tell the committee more about Hall, the alleged white Communist leader in Washington who had supposedly brought the *Daily Worker* into her house.

"Is the Robert Hall that you know a colored man?"

"Yes, sir."

"You sure about that?"

"Yes, I am pretty sure that he is colored."

"Does he look like a colored man, or does he look more like a white man?"

"The man that I—I—have in mind as Robert Hall was a man about my complexion."

In turn, further friendly questions revealed that Moss wasn't even sure about the meaning of the word *espionage* and that there were as many as three other women in the city with a name similar to hers. The hearing went from bad to worse for the absent McCarthy.

"Did you—did you ever—to the best of your knowledge, have you ever talked to a Communist in your life?" asked Symington.

"No, sir—not to my knowledge."

"Did you ever hear of Karl Marx?"

"Who's that?"

The hearing room burst into laughter. Cohn took to the microphone and made one last attempt to regain the upper hand by restating that the committee was in possession of information that Moss was a party member. But emboldened senators halted him.

"Mr. Chairman," interrupted Senator John McClellan, a Democrat from Arkansas. The witness has already been cross-examined, he said. "To make these statements that we have got corroborating evidence that she is a communist, under these circumstances I think she is entitled to have it produced here in her presence and let the public know about it—and let her know about it." The audience applauded. "I don't like to try people by hearsay evidence," he added, triggering yet more applause.

Outside the caucus room, a jubilant Moss recognized Payne among the throngs of journalists and rushed over to thank her for her reporting. Embracing her, Moss exclaimed, "Honey, I want you to tell the world that if you just trust in God, everything will come out all right!"

Payne went back to her apartment. At her typewriter, she wrote, "With dramatic intensity, the case of Mrs. Annie Lee Moss, Pentagon clerk accused of being a former card-carrying communist, blew up last Wednesday in the face of Sen. Joseph McCarthy." Quoting what Payne called "corridor opinion," she concluded her report by saying that "the senator from Wisconsin took a real beating."

The following week Edward R. Murrow devoted an episode of *See It Now* on CBS to Moss's appearance before the committee, a week after his landmark attack on McCarthy. It was becoming clear that the senator's days were numbered.

By APRIL 1954, when Washington's famed cherry blossoms opened, Payne had settled comfortably into her new role as a national correspondent. While she still had a great deal to learn, particularly about the pitfalls of national politics, there was no talk of bringing her back to Chicago. In fact, it was quite the opposite in the offices on Indiana Avenue. The paper even ran circulation advertisements listing its famous writers and citing Payne's reporting as a reason to subscribe to the paper. "From such brilliant minds as Walter White, Mary McLeod Bethune, Langston Hughes, and Ethel Payne (D.C. Correspondent), you begin to know what's what and why."

Payne's growing confidence permitted her to remodel the job of Washington correspondent for the *Defender*. While she dutifully continued to send home reams of copy on standard government stories, she also began to assume a far broader beat, that of civil rights. Typical of her efforts in this new direction were two lengthy articles appearing in the April 3, 1954, issue of the *Defender*. Easily two to three times the length of her usual pieces, the two works dominated the pages of the paper.

The first was a detailed analysis of pending civil rights legislation in Congress that included a survey she had administered to at least forty members of Congress. At question was the future of efforts to ban segregation on interstate travel, anti-bias amendments to existing labor laws, and the admittance of Hawaii and Alaska, which proponents of civil rights believed would strengthen their hand in the Senate because of the states' multiracial populations. Her report revealed a gloomy prognosis. "Progressive legislation either directly or indirectly pertaining to civil rights is really getting the run around in Congress these days," Payne told her readers. "Unless some drastic action is taken to goad the lawmakers into action, they are slated for the graveyard."

Payne's second, even longer article was a review of President Eisenhower's record on civil rights in his first fifteen months in office. She was immensely proud of the piece and pushed editor Waters to display it prominently. "I'd like to get full dress treatment as I think it will mean a lot to us," she told him. "I want a whole lot of care because on the outcome a lot of things are hinged, a good job as I know we can do, and more inside tracks for me to get the real dope on things."

Waters followed Payne's request and the piece was laid out on a full page with fourteen photos. The text was a panegyric to the president. "For months after the inauguration the administration dragged its feet in giving Negroes a place in the sun in running the government," wrote Payne. "And then suddenly, the executive

machinery began moving in high gear, and to the delighted aston-
ishment of all but the reactionaries, color bars began tumbling in
rapid succession."

Eisenhower moved to desegregate restaurants in the nation's
capital, filed a brief in support of desegregating schools nationally,
and gave visible posts to blacks. "Appointments of Negroes in choice
positions began to fall like ripe plums from a tree," wrote Payne. But
E. Frederic Morrow, who had worked on the campaign, was still
biding his time as an assistant to the secretary of commerce. "Rumor
persists that he will move up to a berth on the presidential staff,"
Payne said. "At any rate Morrow is highly respected by the President
for his capabilities."

Payne's flattering assessment of Eisenhower gained national
attention. Mainstream newspapers from the *New York Herald
Tribune* to the *Washington Post* reported that the *Defender,* a
pro-Stevenson publication, was praising Eisenhower. Even *Life*
magazine took note.

At the White House, Max Rabb, who had been given an advance
peek at the article, told Payne how pleased he was with the work,
especially "the very friendly approach you took in reference to this
problem." He promised to bring the article to the president's attention. Morrow sent his congratulations to Payne, praising what in
his eyes was her fairness. "The other remarkable feature about the
article," he said, "is the fact that the *Defender,* true to the newsman's code, prints the news as it is, despite the fact that the paper
was not necessarily a supporter of the President during his campaign." The Republican National Committee staff was ecstatic.
The committee issued a two-page press release quoting extensively
from the article.

Two weeks later, a happy Rabb lent Payne a hand in putting on a
version of the *What's My Line?* television game show at the Capital
Press Club, the black alternative to the segregationist National Press
Club. He served as the mystery guest and panelists had to guess his

occupation. The love between the administration and the African American press was such that Sengstacke and other black newspaper publishers, accompanied by Payne, presented to the president the National Negro Publishers Association John B. Russwurm Award, in memory of the publisher of the first black newspaper.

For now, Ethel Payne was the White House's favorite Negro reporter.

CHAPTER 14

TURNING LIKE A SPINNING TOP

A S SHE HAD EACH MONDAY FOR SEVERAL MONTHS, ON May 17, 1954, Ethel Payne joined a group of lawyers and reporters at the neoclassical-styled Supreme Court building on Capitol Hill in hopes of being present when the court handed down its long-awaited decision in the *Brown v. Board* case. Payne had covered the final oral arguments five months earlier. Then the chambers had been packed and the press section was overflowing with reporters, including many foreign correspondents. When NAACP attorney Thurgood Marshall, along with his mother and wife, passed by the press box he paused to tell reporters, "If any of you are in touch with the man upstairs, you can put in a good word for us on this case please."

Presenting the opening arguments was Spottswood Robinson III. He had represented the children from the Robert R. Moton High School in Virginia, where student Barbara Johns had led the student body out on strike. Representing the other side were such Southern stalwarts as Virginia's assistant attorney general, who, Payne noticed, peppered his speech with the word *nigra*, and John Davis, who invoked an Aesop's fable as a warning that integration might cause Negroes to lose the gains they had already made. "By the time Thurgood Marshall took to the floor for the rebuttal,"

wrote Payne, "he was in his best fighting form as he coolly repudiated all the arguments of the opposition."

For three days the lawyers waged verbal battle over racial segregation while the justices listened and questioned. Presiding for the first
time was their new chief justice, Earl Warren, whom Eisenhower
had appointed. Schoolchildren were at the heart of the case, but the
principle at stake was greater. Ever since 1896, the South had built
a legal rampart around its segregationist culture on the principle
enunciated in *Plessy v. Ferguson* that separate but equal treatment
of blacks was permissible under the Constitution. Should the court
now overturn this principle when it came to schoolchildren, other
forms of segregation would certainly be doomed. A decision was
expected before June on a Monday, the day the court handed down
its decision.

The Mondays of winter and spring had come and gone, and June
was now only two weeks away. But when Payne and her colleagues
reached the pressroom on the ground floor of the Supreme Court
building that morning, they were told that it looked like a quiet day.
At noon the justices took their seats, entering the chamber through
an opening in the red velvet curtain. In the audience were fewer
than a dozen African Americans, but among their ranks were Thurgood Marshall and two other NAACP attorneys. The day before,
Marshall had received a phone call in Mobile, Alabama, suggesting
he might want to be at the court the next day. Reporters made little
note of the presence of the NAACP attorneys or the fact that all nine
justices were in attendance, including one who had been recently
hospitalized for a heart attack. The consensus that this was not the
day for the ruling seemed to be confirmed when the justices began
disposing of some routine business and announced a decision in a
dairy monopoly case.

But as the time on the wall clock neared 12:45 PM, a pneumatic
message descended to the pressroom. After reading it, the court's
press officer stood up, put on his jacket, and told the reporters as he

left the room that the "reading of the segregation decision is about to begin in the courtroom." Payne and her colleagues raced up the marble steps and took their seats in the press box.

AT 12:52 PM, Chief Justice Warren picked up a document before him. Normally printed copies of a court's decision were distributed to the press at this moment. Not this time. "I have for announcement," Warren said, "the judgment and opinion of the Court in No. 1—*Oliver Brown et al. v. Board of Education of Topeka.*" The Associated Press alerted its newspaper and broadcast clients. Bells on wire machines in newsrooms around the country began to ring. In Chicago, the *Defender* halted its presses 8,000 copies into the run of its national edition.

Slowly and deliberately Justice Warren read from the opinion, reviewing the history of segregation, the arguments in the current case, and alternative solutions. Fifteen minutes into Warren's reading, Payne, the reporters, the lawyers, and the lucky members of the public who were in the audience could not yet tell which way the court was ruling. The first clue came when Warren asked, "Does segregation of children in public schools solely on the basis of race, even though the physical facilities and other 'tangible' factors may be equal, deprive the children of the minority group of equal educational opportunities?

"We believe that it does," he said. The Associated Press rushed out another bulletin and Warren read on. He reviewed more case law and took the unusual action of referring to the opinions of social scientists, most notably those of Kenneth and Mamie Clark. Their experiments with black and white dolls had revealed a preference for white dolls among all children, thereby buttressing arguments that segregation internalized racism among black children.

At last Warren came to the point. "We conclude," he began. Then, deviating from the text before him, he inserted the word "unanimously" and continued reading, "that in the field of public education the doctrine of 'separate but equal' has no place." At that moment it was clear to all what had transpired. Even from his bench above, Warren felt the audience's reaction. "When the word 'unanimously' was spoken," he recalled years later, "a wave of emotion swept the room, no words or intentional movement, yet a distinct emotional manifestation that defies description."

For Payne it was beyond belief. "There I was—right in the middle of it and almost out of my mind!" she wrote, trying to explain the moment to her readers. "I'm so excited, like I'm drunk. I'm turning around like those spinning tops." The Associated Press was finally able to report to its clients the entirety of the court's decision. In thirty-four languages the Voice of America flashed the news around the world on its network of shortwave stations. Within a few hours, listeners from tiny Albania to the vast reaches of Communist China heard the news in their own languages along with explanations that the issue was settled by law rather than mob rule or dictatorial fiat. In Farmville, Virginia, sixteen-year-old Barbara Trent, a Moton High School student, burst into tears when her history teacher announced the decision. "We went on studying history, but things weren't the same, and will never be the same again."

When the decision was broadcast on the radio in Washington, the mostly black cabbies celebrated their jubilance with a cacophony of blaring horns. Now rolling quietly, a taxi picked up Payne on the steps of the courthouse. She gave the driver an address on Park Place, where Sarah Bolling, a widow, and her two young sons lived. One of her sons had been refused admission to Sousa Junior High School four years earlier. His legal case, *Spottswood Thomas Bolling v. C. Melvin Sharpe*, was one of the five school desegregation cases that comprised the court's decision.

A gangly but athletic boy, the sixteen-year-old Spottswood did not relish the publicity. When he came around the corner and spotted the photographers at his house, he started to back away. "Heck," he said, "I thought those guys would give up and go home." Payne won admission to the house and sat down to talk with Sarah Bolling, who had been let off early from her government bookbinding job when word of the ruling came down.

"At first," she told Payne, "I couldn't realize that it had really happened." She had been anxious during the ordeal. Some had tried to discourage her from using her son as a test case, and she didn't want to stir up antagonism among her neighbors. Happy the matter was at an end, she told Payne, "I wish that all the people could understand that we want for our children the same rights as any other human beings."

EVEN THOUGH ITS ATTORNEY GENERAL had filed a brief in support of the NAACP's case, the White House puzzled over how to react to the unanimous decision. The first indication of the president's public sentiments came at his weekly press conference two days after the ruling. He stayed clear of recognizing Payne, Dunnigan, or Lautier. The white reporters he selected launched into questions about the McCarthy hearing. At last a correspondent from South Carolina asked Eisenhower about the *Brown v. Board* ruling. "Mr. President," he said, "do you have any advice to give the South as to just how to react to this recent Supreme Court decision banning segregation, sir?"

"Not in the slightest," Eisenhower replied. "I thought that Governor Byrnes [of South Carolina] made a very fine statement when he said, 'Let's be calm and let's be reasonable and let's look this thing in the face.' The Supreme Court has spoken and I am sworn to uphold the constitutional processes in this country; and I will obey." Two more questions on the case followed. But again reporters asked only about the political implications of the ruling and how it might affect the administration's standing in the South, coming, as it did, under a Republican administration. The president curtly replied, "The Supreme Court, as I understand it, is not under any administration."

Given a chance to call on members of the press who represented readers most directly affected by the Supreme Court ruling, Eisenhower opted not to. Given the opportunity to use the presidential bully pulpit to urge citizens to follow the court's edict because it was morally right, Eisenhower demurred. He said only that he would obey the decision. In seconds, it was back to the McCarthy hearings. The chasm between the black reporters and the white ones was so deep that the person constitutionally obligated to enforce the court's edict—the most significant advancement of civil rights since the Emancipation Proclamation—could escape a press conference with only a few light questions on the most important court ruling for African Americans in sixty-one years.

CHAPTER 15

ASKING QUESTIONS
NO ONE ELSE WOULD

P RIOR TO MAY 19, 1954, THE PRESIDENT HAD BEEN TAK-
ing Ethel Payne's questions at press conferences. "Eisenhower was probably very democratic, probably the most
democratic, because he gave recognition to the smaller newspapers,"
Payne said. "He didn't just deal with the titans." In April she had
put an elaborately composed query to him. "Mr. President, in your
housing message to Congress on January 25th you said the administrative policies governing the operations of the several housing agencies must be, and will be, materially strengthened and augmented
in order to assure equal opportunity for all of our citizens to acquire,
within their means, good and well-located homes. Then there was a
further reference to the misuse of slum clearance laws to dislocate
persons. I would like to know what administrative regulations have
been issued by the housing agencies to implement this part of the
message?"

"You have asked a question," Eisenhower replied, "that I will have
to ask Mr. Hagerty [Eisenhower's press secretary] to look up for next
week. I know this: I know that every administrative part of government

knows my policy and is trying to do it. Now, they may be slow getting around to it, sometimes."

A few weeks later, a tenacious Payne followed up on her housing pursuit. "Mr. President, I would like to refer to the question asked you on April 7th, as to whether the several housing agencies had issued any regulations to implement the statement in your housing message to Congress, that everything should be done to assure good and well-located homes for all citizens. You said then that you would have an answer later for this. So far as we have been able to learn, no such specific regulations have been forthcoming. May I cite to you the situation at Levittown in Pennsylvania as an example where members of minority groups are being barred. I would like to know if you have any information at this point on this matter."

"Just a minute," said Eisenhower. He leaned over and conferred with Murray Snyder, a former New York City reporter who had come on board as an assistant in the press operation. "Mr. Snyder," Eisenhower resumed, "tells me that there have been some reports come to the White House, but they are of a general character; and the only hope of getting a detailed report, such as you describe, is to go to the FHA [Federal Housing Administration] people themselves, that department."

Payne's two attempts to pin the president down on a matter of federal housing policy, clearly an issue important to her readers, failed to elicit much of an answer. But she had no plans to cease trying. Just asking paid dividends. In the six months she had been in Washington, Payne had learned, no matter what assurances Rabb— Eisenhower's point man on race issues—gave privately, that matters of importance to black Americans remained absent from the public agenda in the capital. "The white press was so busy asking questions on other issues that the blacks and their problems were completely ignored," she said. Presidential press conferences offered a national forum at which these issues could be raised. "So therefore I would think carefully about what kinds of questions I would ask the president, and before I did, I would research it and I went to the one man who I considered an authority and that was Clarence Mitchell Jr., the director of the Washington Bureau of the NAACP."

PAYNE COULD NOT HAVE SELECTED a better ally. Mitchell was an old hand in Washington who was also press savvy, having once worked for the *Baltimore Afro-American*. He first came to Washington in 1941 to take a job in the Negro employment and training branch of the Office of Production Management. The work, he said, quickly gave him a taste of what he was up against. "After a long conference with the vice-president of Goodyear Rubber Company in Akron, Ohio, about the importance of using all the nation's manpower in defense plants without racial discrimination, he concluded the meeting by asking me, 'Do you know where I could find a good cook?' "

Following his stint with the government, Mitchell moved to the NAACP's Washington office, eventually rising to become, by the time Payne met him, the organization's chief lobbyist and director of the bureau. In the halls of Congress, the sight of dark-skinned, professionally dressed Mitchell—like the sight of Payne and her two black press colleagues—was rare. It had been only a few years, said Mitchell, since "on the floor of the U.S. Senate, the voice of Bilbo* could be heard yelling 'nigger' as often as the prayers of the Senate chaplain."

Payne made it a habit to frequent Mitchell's office in a small brick building on Massachusetts Avenue a few blocks from the Capitol. Wise now to political journalism, she rewarded Mitchell with a

---

* Mississippi senator Theodore Bilbo, an apostle of segregation, was famously the author of *Take Your Choice: Separation or Mongrelization*.

long and flattering profile in the *Defender*, a typical favor that journalists routinely do when forging a relationship with an important
source. Regardless of her intent, her description of Mitchell's skills
was spot-on. "Mitchell has developed an uncanny instinct for behind
the scenes maneuvering and he knows the habits and background of
most of the government officials that it is hardly necessary for him to
consult the unique and extensive card file in which he keeps voting
records and other pertinent facts relating to each."

"You know," she would say in her meetings with Mitchell, "I want
to raise a question next week at the press conference. What do you
think I should ask the president about?" Mitchell would then brief
Payne on the status of legislation important to African Americans,
and the two would craft a question that might draw out the president's
sentiments, reluctant as he was to show his hand in matters of civil
rights. Unknown to Payne, Mitchell was playing the same game with
Dunnigan, although she was far more timid than Payne in pursuing
her quarry.

Payne appreciated the help. Unlike her white colleagues in the
press corps who had offices with desks and support staff, she was a
one-person shoestring operation. "My office," she quipped, "was the
cluttered living room of my small apartment and the murky depths
of a battered bag." She slept little and kept a grueling schedule of
cranking out three, four, or even five stories at a time to make up for
the paper's lack of wire services. Sometimes she had to head out into
the night at two or three in the morning to get her stories into the
mail in time to reach Chicago before the weekly's deadline. "I got to
be known among the cabdrivers and they sort of formed a benevolent protective association," she said. "One of them, one of this crew,
would wait for me until I came out. 'Come on, it's time for you to go
home. You shouldn't be out by yourself.'"

But Mitchell was rendering more than just assistance. His coun-
seling and eventual partnership with Payne provided a sense of a mission larger than reporting alone did. "I really, actually, became the

conduit for getting questions directly to the president and then the information would come back," said Payne, "and I felt I was doing a real service that way."

LOUIS LAUTIER DIDN'T SHARE Payne's view of her work. In fact, he used his column in the *Afro-American* to sarcastically chastise her and Dunnigan for competing with each other as to who could ask the longest question. While he was right about the length of their questions, the pair weren't in a competition. Rather, they were working together. "Alice Dunnigan and I," Payne said, "put our heads together and decided to team up so that each week there would always be a question on some phase of civil rights."

Mitchell publicly rebutted Lautier's criticism. He published a letter in the *Afro-American* expressing the NAACP's delight with the pursuit of the president by Payne and Dunnigan. Specifically he explained that Payne's questions on housing were of vital importance because nothing had been done to act on the president's promise to reduce discrimination in the assisted housing program. "I am grateful that these questions have been asked," wrote Mitchell, "and I hope that they will continue because, after all, that is what a press conference is for."

The president resumed taking Payne's questions when *Brown v. Board* ceased to be as newsworthy. In mid-June, Eisenhower told Hagerty that he had deliberately called on Payne during the spring because he didn't want to give the impression he was ignoring the black press even though he considered many of her questions foolish. "You know, Jim," said Eisenhower, "I suppose nobody knows how they feel or how many pressures or insults they have to take. I guess the only way you can realize exactly how they feel is to have a black skin for several weeks. I'm going to continue to give them a break at press conferences despite the questions they ask."

Two days later he did just that. Getting the nod, Payne once again pursued her line of questioning about civil rights. On her mind was a recent incident on an interstate bus bound for Atlanta. Police officers had forcibly separated a white student from Italy from his seat next to his black friends in the Jim Crow section of the bus. After telling the president about the incident, Payne said there were several pending measures in the House to ban segregation in interstate travel. "I understand that the attorney general was asked to render an opinion on this. I would like to know if you plan to use any action to get these bills voted out of committee?"

"The attorney general hasn't given me any opinion on the bills; I haven't seen them; I know nothing about them," Eisenhower answered. "I think my general views on this whole subject are well known, and you also know that I believe in progress accomplished through the intelligence of people and through the cooperation of people more than law, if we can get it that way. Now, I will take a look. I don't know what my opinion is, really, at this minute on that particular law."

And so the president and Payne resumed their cat-and-mouse game.

CHAPTER 16

IRKS IKE

THE BROWN DECISION FIRED UP THE CIVIL RIGHTS COMmunity, who had grown increasingly impatient with the pace of change. The NAACP was the hero of the day, while the more accommodation-minded organizations came in for criticism. Inside the National Urban League, one of the organizations whose approach was now being questioned, a behind-the-scenes battle broke out for control. Unfortunately for Ethel Payne, she took an interest in the story.

For forty-four years, this civil rights organization had focused its energy on opening up employment opportunities for black Americans, a tactic that now seemed docile in light of the NAACP's legal victory. The Urban League's executive secretary, Lester Granger, came under attack from critics who believed he kowtowed to white business leaders, especially as so many members of the organization's board were white. His defenders argued that Granger was simply remaining true to the league's original mission. In fact, they said that Granger's close relationship with industrialists, and now with the Eisenhower administration, had opened thousands of new jobs for African Americans.

If for no other reason than it gave ink to Granger's opponents, any reporting Payne did on the dispute would strengthen their hand. But she went further. Payne published accusations about James E. Dowling, Granger's most important ally, without checking on their veracity. In an unsigned column, Payne referred to Dowling as "one of the nation's biggest real estate manipulators" who had financially supported the construction of a housing project that excluded blacks. She reported that he was closely connected to U.S. Steel, which was resisting efforts to increase its minority hiring, and threw in a charge, for good measure, that he got into *Who's Who* only by virtue of his connection to the league.

Shortly after the column appeared, *Defender* editors began extensively editing Payne's dispatches on the dispute, and full paragraphs disappeared in the published versions. In addition, Granger was given the opportunity to rebut Payne's charges on the front page of the paper. He claimed that it was Urban League policy not to reply to what he called "slanderous gossip," but because the "malicious stories" continued to be circulated, he agreed to answer selected questions that been put to him by "genuinely interested reporters." The questions, not surprisingly, were contrived opportunities for Granger to defend his record.

Payne complained to editor Louis Martin. "I have noticed recently," she wrote him, "a consistent pattern of censoring all material submitted by me relating to Mr. Lester Granger and the current unrest within the Urban League." She felt that the items she had filed were neither slanted nor opinionated but were news. "I am concerned because it seems to be a radical departure from the liberal atmosphere and policy of the *Defender* to print the news favorable and unfavorable. I certainly do not mind being criticized or checked up when I have been guilty of being biased, but it becomes a matter of personal freedom when the pattern is consistent," she wrote. "I would appreciate having your views on this matter so that I may know how to proceed in the future." She certainly got them.

Four days later, in Chicago, Martin took to his typewriter. "Dear Miss Payne," he frostily began his two-page, single-spaced response. "Until you exercise the elementary, basic and fundamental journalistic principle of presenting, or attempting to present, both sides of highly controversial issues in your copy, you leave us no choice but to rewrite it, complete it or throw it out." Martin, the most politically connected member of the *Defender* organization—in fact, he often worked for politicians on the side—was apoplectic.

From the start, Martin told her, she had skewed her coverage of the dispute in favor of the rebellion inside the Urban League. He further accused her of ignoring his suggestion that she check with those being attacked before running accusations. "This was not done because you deliberately did not wish to present but one side of the issue, the side that you are personally convinced is the right one."

Martin tore to shreds her unsigned article, listing the unsubstantiated charges and criticizing the nonsensical comment about Dowling's *Who's Who* entry. "Such silly, below the belt writing makes us look far more ridiculous in the eyes of intelligent people than it does Dowling." In short, because she was in a highly visible post and both whites and blacks were carefully reading her work, her shoddy journalism had diminished the paper.

Payne owed her career to Martin and he reminded her of the fact. "I also feel responsible to some extent for sending you there," he said. "I wish you well and, up until this incident, I thought you were on the ball." His fury continued unabated to the last line of his letter. "Let it not be true," he told Payne in closing, "that we with our pens in our hands are no more civilized than the monkey with the shotgun in his hands."

Granger and Dowling carried the day. A chastised Payne tried to shake off Martin's verbal beating and threw herself back into her work. But she soon experienced the wrath of another powerful person.

ON THE MORNING OF JULY 7, 1954, Eisenhower greeted the 165 reporters who came that day for his regular press conference in the Indian Treaty Room. After congratulating the press on the media's efforts to reduce casualties from fireworks during the recent Fourth of July celebrations, the president took questions.

A UPI reporter asked: Would Eisenhower support the admission of Red China to the United Nations? A *New York Times* correspondent wanted to know: Did the pending farm bill meet with the administration's approval? One reporter after another plied the president with the usual questions on politics, policy, and foreign affairs.

Seventeen minutes into the conference, Eisenhower looked over at Payne and gave her the nod. "Mr. President," she began, "we were very happy last week when the deputy attorney general sent a communication to the House Interstate and Foreign Commerce Committee saying that there was a legal basis for passing a law to ban segregation in interstate travel. Mr. Rogers also said that in view of the recent decision by the Supreme Court in the schools cases, that such legislation ought to be enacted by Congress at this time, and the Bureau of the Budget approved it. I would like to know if we could assume that we have administration support in getting action on this?"

The president drew himself up into his military posture. "I don't know what right you say that *you* have to have administration support," Eisenhower barked like a general affronted by the temerity of a grunt. "He became very angry," Payne said. "Oh, he was so angry."

"The administration is trying to do what it thinks and believes to be decent and just in this country, and is not in the effort to support any particular or special group of any kind. These opinions were sent down, these beliefs are held as part of the administration belief, because we think it is just and right, and that is the answer."

This brusqueness from the usually affable Eisenhower startled the room. Nor was it lost on the reporters that the president had just suggested that African Americans and their quest for equality were tantamount to a special interest group. The UPI reporter stood up and switched the subject to the potential for Hawaiian statehood. At the end of the press conference, as the reporters broke up, Edward

T. Folliard, a veteran reporter from the *Washington Post*, came up to Payne. "You asked the right question," he told her. "In fact, we should have asked those questions sooner."

Payne was gratified by Folliard's words. When she returned to her apartment, which still doubled as her office, the phone was ringing off the hook. From Chicago, her Republican mother intoned, "Now, sister, I don't think you ought to be down there making the president mad." Next it was Martin and Sengstacke calling from the paper to tease her about picking on presidents. The *Washington Star*, the city's afternoon paper, carried the page one headline: PRESIDENT ANNOYED BY QUERY ON TRAVEL RACE BAN SUPPORT. Under the headline EISENHOWER NO CHAMPION OF ANY SPECIAL GROUPS, the *New York Times* told its readers that the "President made the statement with considerable heat when a Negro reporter asked if 'we have Administration support' in seeking legislation to outlaw segregation in interstate travel." Payne's question even made news outside the United States. US NEGRO REPORTER DRAWS IKE'S WRATH, reported the *Panama Tribune*.

Payne's own paper led its front page with the headline DEFENDER QUERY ANGERS IKE. "The president's remarks made at his weekly press conference," read the unsigned article likely to have been written by Payne, "were interpreted as meaning that he regarded the passage of the bill as favoritism towards Negro citizens and his outburst of temper marked a new low in relations with the Negro Press."

DUNNIGAN RALLIED TO PAYNE'S DEFENSE. In a guest column, she told readers of the *Defender* that for months Eisenhower had repeatedly been vague in answering civil rights questions or had put off replying, claiming he needed more information. "The president's lack of knowledge on many racial issues, raised by reporters of Negro newspapers, seems to have become embarrassing after a while, and his impatience began to show," Dunnigan wrote.

While white journalists reported on the president's discourteous behavior, Lautier chose instead to attack the two black women pursuing this line of questioning, Dunnigan explained. "This unethical journalist action has resulted in a running word battle between the man reporter and those who would dare speak out in defense of the women." Lautier's behavior, she claimed, was spreading to other male columnists "who are joining the fray and vehemently tossing word stones of unpleasantness at those who would dare go to bat for issues affecting ten percent of America's population."

But Lautier didn't restrict himself to solely hurling brickbats. Rather, according to Dunnigan, he informed Hagerty that both women were earning incomes from groups other than their news organizations. By now Hagerty had grown weary of Payne and probably regretted having made it possible for her to be part of the White House press corps. Four months earlier she had applied for credentials to attend Mamie Eisenhower's meetings with reporters. On the application, Hagerty scrawled a note to the First Lady's secretary. "Stall on this one until you talk to me, will you? I would like to give you the fill-in on this orally and not in writing."

Hagerty summoned Payne to a meeting in his large office directly across from the Cabinet Room. Spartan in furnishings so that it could hold meetings of several dozen reporters, it was decorated primarily with political photographs. Hagerty had entered politics in 1943 when he left his job as a *New York Times* reporter in Albany, New York, to become Governor Thomas Dewey's press secretary in 1943. He subsequently handled press relations in the governor's two runs for president. Eisenhower, running in 1953, tapped Hagerty for the job on his campaign and after his victory appointed Hagerty press secretary.

When Payne entered Hagerty's office, she found that Murray Snyder, the assistant press secretary, was also present. "Looking like a pair of executioners, the charges were read to me." Hagerty made no mention of the press conference incident. Rather, he took another tack. In his hands was a report from the clerk of the House of Representatives that had been filed by the Congress of Industrial Organizations (CIO) political action committee reporting its contributions and disbursements in compliance with lobbying laws. "I see here," Hagerty said, "that you were paid by the CIO at the same time you were serving as an accredited news correspondent at the White House.

"We can't have that," he continued. "It's against regulations. The CIO-PAC is a political organization and I'll have to report this to the standing committee of correspondents." Payne admitted that she had indeed been paid for doing some editorial work for the labor group to supplement her meager salary from the *Defender*.

"Are you still on the CIO payroll?" Hagerty asked.

"Absolutely not," replied Payne. "It is correct that I received a payment from the CIO on September 10, but that was the last payment I received. Furthermore, I only edited campaign material. I had nothing to do with making policy." Hagerty brought an end to the meeting. He told Payne that if he found another instance of her doing work for an organization while serving as a White House correspondent, he would refer her case to the standing committee of the congressional press galleries.

The rules of the standing committee, which governed the congressional press galleries and influenced press credentialing throughout the capital, were vague. They did not prohibit freelance writing. Rather, the arcane rules prohibited admission to those who could not satisfactorily document that they were not engaged "in paid publicity or promotion work." Payne was certainly not alone in doing work for others. Many reporters wrote articles for publications other than their own and gave paid talks. "So what this was," said Payne, "was clearly a harassment tactic, and it was an effort to get rid of me, because I had become a nuisance." She stormed out of Hagerty's office.

"I was put into deep freeze and given the silent treatment by the White House," Payne said. The president had called on Payne seven times since she asked her first question five months prior. He would call on her only two more times during his remaining seventy-nine months in office.

CLARENCE MITCHELL WAS FURIOUS. He worked to make sure the incident with the president did not undermine Payne's standing at the *Defender* as the earlier Urban League fiasco had. "I hope that your readers and the public generally will understand that in Washington there will always be those who want reporters to refrain from asking any questions on racial matters," Mitchell told Enoch Waters, now the paper's executive editor. "No doubt Miss Payne could be the darling of these interests if she kept quiet at press conferences and was content to enjoy the prestige of being a White House correspondent."

Then one of the best-known civil rights leaders, Mitchell gave her work a ringing endorsement. Payne, he said, could curry favor in Washington circles by sticking to reporting minor squabbles and reporting on personalities. "Fortunately for your paper and the public generally," he wrote, "she is a reporter who seeks the news and does not attempt to color it."

The White House remained unhappy with Payne, but she was back in the paper's good stead. She resumed her duties, sending in a prodigious amount of copy. One moment she would be crafting a lengthy explanation of why after a dozen years Congress was no closer to creating a fair employment practices commission. She wrote in what was developing into a folksy style that directly connected her readers with seemingly obtuse governmental issues. "Politicians prattle about equal opportunity for all people and have overworked the phrase 'voluntary methods rather than compulsion' until the words have become nauseous gobble de gook, particularly with the people most affected—the worker barred from a job solely because of the color of his skin." The next moment Payne would be detailing the defeat of improvements in public housing by the Senate's acceptance of a compromise bill. The vote, she said, "took another yank at the hangman's knot around public housing, thus sending it on its way to sure death."

After clawing her way into the Washington press corps, enduring assaults from her colleagues for being black and female, surviving a fight with her editors, and standing up to the president, Payne was no longer the hesitant Chicago features reporter. Instead she had forged herself into a hybrid journalistic role as both an emissary from and a representative of African Americans in a media whose whiteness kept readers in the darkness about civil rights. "Like Folliard said, they hadn't paid much attention to it," Payne said. "They were talking about the Middle East or whatever, you know. Everything was more important than civil rights."

Her reporting grew aggressive and her writing took on an explanatory tone. The line between journalism and advocacy blurred. Looking back years later, Payne offered an explanation. "If you have lived through the black experience in this country, you feel that every day you're assaulted by the system itself," she said. "You are either acquiescent and you go along with the system, which I think is wrong, or else you just rebel, and you kick against it. That was just my feeling that somebody had to do the fighting, somebody had to speak up. So I saw myself as an advocate as much as being a newspaper person."

In the time Payne had been in Washington, she had come to love her new life. Money remained an issue. She rented an apartment that served as both her office and her living quarters, and this in combination with the expenses associated with being a correspondent strained her budget. Her annual salary of about $5,000 was the same she had earned for the last two years. This wasn't a bad salary, especially considering Payne was without a college degree.

It was roughly equal to what a professional woman could expect to earn working for the federal government. In April, when she had asked for a salary increase, Martin had made a verbal promise to hike her wage at some point that year. She sat down to remind Martin of his pledge, addressing Waters in the letter as well.

"I am fully aware of heavy financial obligations of the paper plus some anger which occurred when I broached the subject some time ago," she wrote. "I want by all means to avoid any unpleasantness because the discussion of money with me, believe it or not, can be very painful. I would much rather leave it to your discretion and the confidence which I have always had in you (despite some differences).

"Can I get biblical," she said in closing, "and ask 'Is the Servant worthy of his hire?'?" Her question, however, went unanswered.

But as with journalists everywhere, she thrived in being in a profession that every day brought a new challenge. At any moment she could be writing about important civil rights legislation, a court ruling, or the president's press conference. She never knew what the day might bring.

FOR A NEWSPAPER THAT RARELY RAN much in the way of international news, the front page of the *Defender* on January 7, 1955, was out of the ordinary. Under the large headline AFRICAN, ASIATIC LEADERS TO MEET, the paper reported that five Asian prime ministers were organizing a meeting of African and Asian leaders later that spring in Indonesia. At first glance, the reader might assume this would be yet another gathering of international leaders. However, a more careful examination of the announcement, like that employed by officials in Washington, revealed why the *Defender* thought it to be front-page material. The idea that as many as thirty nonwhite nations, representing a quarter of the landmass and more than half the world's population, would meet on their own without inviting, consulting, or notifying the Soviet Union or the United States sent shock waves through Moscow and Washington. One correspondent called the planned meeting "the biggest time-bomb set for 1955 which puts our State Department right on the hot seat."

Payne's phone rang. It was her publisher calling. "How would you like to go to Indonesia?" Sengstacke asked.

CHAPTER 17

BANDUNG

JOHN SENGSTACKE WAS SERIOUS. HE WANTED HIS NEWSPAper's star reporter Ethel Payne on the scene of the planned April gathering of African and Asian leaders in Bandung, Indonesia. It was growing daily into a big story not just for the African American community but internationally as well.

In Paris, writer Richard Wright was astonished to hear about the conference. "Only brown, black, and yellow men who had long been made agonizingly self-conscious, under the rigors of colonial rule, of their race and their religion could have felt the need for such a meeting," he said. He called his wife into the living room and handed her the newspaper.

"Why, that's half the human race!" she exclaimed when she finished reading the article.

"Exactly," said Wright. "And that is why I want to go."

On the floor of the U.S. House of Representatives, Congressman Adam Clayton Powell Jr., who represented Harlem, rose to urge that the government pay attention to the conference. Although the United States was not invited, Powell pleaded with the Eisenhower administration to send an integrated team of observers as a sign of support. "We need to let the two billion colored peoples on the earth, without whom we cannot continue much longer as a first-class power, know that America is a democracy of the people," Powell said.

It was the last thing Eisenhower's secretary of state wanted to hear. When the conference was first announced, John Foster Dulles saw it as a threat to U.S. interests, particularly since Zhou Enlai, the premier of the People's Republic of China, was expected to attend. Simply put, the conference was a rejection of the Cold War division of the world into two camps. Instead these nations wanted to fashion a third, nonaligned way.

The administration told Powell he should not go. Until that moment he had not yet decided if he would attend. Furious, he now told the White House he was going even if it meant paying his own way. "Immediately all hell broke loose," Powell said. The State Department tried to buy him off with a red-carpet trip to Asia and Africa if he would stay clear of Bandung. But nothing would dissuade him. "Bandung was a pilgrimage to a new Mecca," he said.

THE BLACK PRESS JOINED in Powell's enthusiasm. By the time Sengstacke called Payne, the National Negro Publishers Association had declared it was sending Louis Lautier to cover the conference. Marguerite Cartwright, a Hunter College professor and columnist for the *New York Amsterdam News*, also made known her plans to go.

The flurry of announcements of Bandung travel plans made by black reporters was no accident. Figuring it could not block Powell and others from attending, the White House had adopted the course of trying to make sure the "right" journalists got to Bandung. As one memorandum put it, "State is aware of the leanings of all who plan to attend. The plan seems to be to balance out representation rather than refuse permission."

On the suggestion of Marquis Childs, chief Washington correspondent for the *St. Louis Post-Dispatch*, the White House focused its attention on Lautier, the lone black reporter loyal to Republicans. An idea was submitted to Nelson A. Rockefeller, who served as special assistant to the president for foreign affairs charged with developing a regime of psychological warfare against the Soviets in the international arena. Why not pay for Lautier's trip and obtain the services of a friendly Negro reporter on the scene? "Lautier is aware that in order for him to make the trip, some financing will have to be arranged because the National Negro Press Association cannot afford to send him," said an aide. He suggested that Rockefeller's brother John pay or that money be taken from the American International Association for Economic and Social Development, a philanthropy run by Rockefeller. "If both of these previous suggestions cannot be worked out, it is not impossible for the CIA to finance it indirectly," added the aide.

Meanwhile, unaware that the administration was already at work on damage control, C. D. Jackson, a former member of the Office of Strategic Services (OSS) and now a Time-Life executive, wrote Rockefeller an anxious letter. The correspondence, labeled personal and confidential, was one that would catch Rockefeller's attention because Jackson, who had been his predecessor in the job, had not entirely left government service. He was part of Operation Mockingbird, a secret CIA project to support the anticommunist attitude of the American media.

"One of *Life*'s editors, an old friend of mine who also happens to be a Negro, called me over the weekend in a state of considerable agitation," Jackson told Rockefeller. According to his source, Jackson claimed that "three American Negroes"—Powell, Cartwright, and Lautier—with communist sympathies were heading to Bandung. "Maybe he had changed his beliefs," Jackson said of Powell, "but there was a time not so long ago when his Communist flirtations were pretty shocking." In Cartwright's case, her husband "is reported to be at best a Fellow Traveler, at worst a card holder." About Lautier, Jackson had little to say except to remind Rockefeller that he "was the one who recently got into the Press Club after considerable furor."

Rockefeller turned to his aide and asked him to look into the matter. The man reported that nothing could be done about Powell that the State Department had not already tried. And nothing should be done about Lautier because he was on their side. Nor, as it turned out, would he need financing. "He has been highly recommended to attend by other responsible newspapermen," the aide said, "and is endorsed by Lester Granger of the National Urban League, one of the most conservative Negro organizations, which is financing his trip."

IF NOT MONEY, political pressure was being brought to bear to make sure the "right" black reporters would make the trip to Indonesia. In the eyes of the government, Carl Rowan was the dependable anti-Communist they wanted. He was the *Minneapolis Tribune*'s star black reporter and had entered journalism about the same time as Payne had, beginning at Minnesota black newspapers before being hired, with considerable fanfare, by the *Tribune*. In 1951, when the Newspaper Guild cited Payne for her work, Rowan was the other Negro writer they honored.

He had just returned from a State Department–funded tour of South and Southeast Asia. Allen Dulles, head of the CIA and brother to the secretary of state, called Rowan's publisher John Cowles Sr. After hanging up with Dulles, Cowles got Rowan on the phone and asked if he knew about the Bandung conference.

Of course, replied Rowan.

"Dulles called me to say it would be a service to the nation if you were there," Cowles said. "Allen says you would have access to the key people who will be there well beyond the access available to anyone in the Foreign Service. Think about whether you want to go."

"Mr. Cowles, I don't have to think about it," Rowan replied. "I could never pass up a chance to cover a meeting as important as this one will be."

Even Richard Wright's trip from Paris to Bandung was being made courtesy of the U.S. government. Unable to obtain backing from an American foundation for his trip, Wright turned to the Congress for Cultural Freedom. Founded five years earlier by a group of internationally minded intellectuals, the congress had put on gatherings "in defense of culture" so pleasing to the CIA that it indirectly funded the congress to combat communist propaganda. The congress agreed to provide support for Wright's travel expenses, and in turn, the writer obtained a pledge from the organization that he would attend the meeting as an independent journalist and not be censored in any manner.

Cartwright, the Hunter College professor and columnist, got wind of the behind-the-scenes machinations. Writing about the journalists with plans to go to Bandung, she disclosed, "One rather dramatic elaboration on the story was the rumor that the trips of both Mr. Lautier and Miss Payne were being financed by Nelson Rockefeller, to make certain—the story goes—that an ideologically 'pure' report would be disseminated in the Negro press."

With all this government money flowing surreptitiously to reporters and writers, it was likely that the *Defender* was among the beneficiaries of the government munificence. A few months earlier Sengstacke had accepted a promise of a $2,000 payment from the Haitian embassy in Washington to support the paper's coverage of President Paul Magloire's visit to the United States. Payne knew about the Haitian payment and was aware that her colleagues were now using funds from various sources other than their newspapers to support their travel to Bandung. In fact, she reported to editor Louis Martin that Lautier and his wife's journey was not being paid for by the National Urban League, as Rockefeller's aide believed, but rather by the Crusade for Freedom, an organization that raised money for Radio Free Europe but also served as a conduit for CIA funds.

But if it was true that the government was helping to pay Payne's $1,428.15 airfare, and for hotels, food, and taxis, she remained blissfully unaware. Payne publicly assailed Cartwright for having published the rumor that her travel had been paid for by the government. "Bunk pure and simple," said Payne. And, in a private note to Martin, Payne wrote, "The remarkable thing is that the *Chicago Defender* is sending somebody on its own with no strings or under the table deals with somebody else."

ON APRIL 13, 1955, Payne found herself once again on a plane above the Pacific Ocean. But what a difference four years made. In 1951 she had ridden in a military transport; now she traveled in the Pan American Clipper *Polynesia*, an 86-passenger Douglas DC-4. Instead of being an obscure employee of the military, Payne was now a highly regarded journalist whose departure had been covered on the front page of the *Defender* and touted in display advertisements.

As the plane gained altitude, Payne felt she was on her way to a rendezvous of great personal and historical significance. "As a reporter, it was my assignment to relay the events of the Asian-African conference," she said. "More important, as a black American, it meant the emotional experience of interrelating my own ethnic background with those individuals of other 'colored' origins."

The conference also fed one of Payne's long-term passions. Ever since she wrote her award-winning essay at Crane College on "Interracial Relationships as a Basis for International Peace," Payne had maintained a steady interest in the world beyond America's borders. As a Washington correspondent, Payne had taken every opportunity she could find to write about issues that surfaced in the capital relating to Haiti, Liberia, and African colonies.

Attending the Bandung conference would put Payne in the midst of the world's majority, quite unlike being a black reporter in white Washington. "The impact of that realization profoundly affected me in ways that are hard to describe," she wrote later. "From henceforth, I would be in search of that newly found ego and the linkages between it and the ethos of the larger community of the darker races of the world."

Including a refueling stop in Hawaii, Payne's flight took almost twenty-two hours to reach Manila, where she was to spend the night and change planes. As soon as she debarked, the first thing she spotted was Adam Clayton Powell speaking with reporters. "He was talking about the conference and what a great thing this was," Payne said, "because this was going to be strictly all colored people, colored people of the earth, and no Western nations were included, and he thought this was a phenomenal thing, which it was."

In the short time in Manila, Payne found time to file a short dispatch highlighting the enthusiasm in the Philippines for the Bandung meeting. "Here in Manila," she wrote, "there are impromptu discussions in parks, street corners, clubhouses, and other gathering places. The consensus will be an opportunity for the Republic to assert itself strongly as a vital force in world affairs."

At the airport the next morning Payne ran into Carlos Peña Rómulo, a Philippine Pulitzer Prize–winning journalist who now served as his nation's ambassador to the United States. A dapper man, barely five feet four in shoes, Rómulo was leading the Philippine delegation. He invited Payne and Powell to fly the next leg of the journey to Jakarta in a plane provided by his government. Payne boarded the craft and found it already contained the prime ministers of Pakistan and Ceylon, among other dignitaries. In awe, Payne moved quickly past the group. "I kind of shrank up into a little ball in the back of the plane," she said.

Under an array of the twenty-nine flags of the participating nations, musical bands greeted the plane as it landed in Jakarta, the Indonesian capital city. Payne waited patiently for the prime ministers, their entourage, and the delegates to debark. Through the window she spotted what looked like students with pads and pencils waiting around. She presumed they were at the airport to take notes during the welcoming ceremonies. At last Payne came out of the plane, but before she reached the bottom of the stairs, the young crowd surrounded her. "We want your autograph," they yelled in English.

"Autograph?" replied Payne. "Well, I'm just a reporter. I'm not a VIP. There are all the VIPs over there."

"No, no, no! We came to see the American Negro," said one member of the group. "We heard you were coming, and we want to talk to you. We want to learn all about you, we want to learn about what's happening in your country, to Negroes in your country."

Reaching the tarmac, Payne obligingly answered their questions. Powell stood not far away. He was fuming that no American diplomat had met his flight. "Never to my knowledge has the United States government let down a member of the United States Congress more completely than it let me down," Powell said, "and in doing so, let down all the American people, on Friday afternoon, April 15, 1955, in Indonesia."

Nor were the students tending to Powell. "As light-skinned as he was," said Payne, "there was some skepticism on the part of the locals about his true identity." In fact, as Richard Wright observed, Powell was whiter in color than many whites. Here, far from America's racial divide, Wright said, "the congressman had to explain that he was 'colored,' that his grandfather had been branded a slave." After taking only so much of the group's adulation of Payne, Powell came over. He put his arm around Payne and, according to her, said, "Me colored, too!"

CHAPTER 18

THE *DEFENDER'S* NELLIE BLY

A S THE SMALL PLANE FERRIED ETHEL PAYNE ON THE last short leg to Bandung, a stunning scene unfolded before her. The mountains that rimmed the city were green—yellow green if in the sun, blue green if in shadow. "But sometimes," noted a reporter, "the blue green would darken to gray and be indistinguishable from the heavy, wet clouds that shrouded the peaks, producing a continuity of land, air, and moisture that seem peculiarly tropical."

The city of 165,000 had been working for months to prepare for the gathering. Many streets had been repaved and the houses along the main thoroughfares repainted. Those students who spoke passable English were enlisted to serve as guides. A white-helmeted militia carrying submachine guns made its presence known in the hopes of controlling the crowds, warding off the guerrillas said to be in the nearby hills, and comforting the arriving luminaries.

The city's fourteen hotels, all spruced up for the occasion, and thirty houses were commandeered for the 2,000 delegates, observers, and members of the press. Payne was given a room in a house about five blocks from the conference center. Three others shared the house with Payne. In the room next door was Valentina Scott, Moscow correspondent for the London *Daily Worker*, who was married to an African American and had lived in the Soviet Union since the Great Depression.

The purpose of the conference, as Payne explained to her readers, was to promote cooperation between Asia and Africa, to examine the problems nations on the two continents faced, and to look for cooperative ways to achieve world peace. The organizers were an independent-minded bunch. They recognized and invited China but excluded the South African government because of apartheid.

The work got under way in earnest on Monday morning when the delegates made their way to the Gedung Merdeka, an aging Dutch club that had been remodeled for the occasion. When the bulk of them had found their seats, the most prominent attendees paraded in: the Philippines' Rómulo, in a Barong Tagalog; Iraq's Muhammad Fadhil al-Jamali, in a morning coat; Egypt's Gamal Abdel Nasser ("the most handsome man I've ever seen in my life," gushed Payne), in a khaki uniform; and China's Zhou Enlai in a Sun Yat-sen tunic suit.

Without question the star attraction was Zhou, the drama of whose participation was heightened by the fact that assassins had blown up a chartered plane heading to the conference on which they mistakenly assumed he was a passenger. "Of all the great world figures who came to the conference," Payne said of Zhou, "his was the most towering personality." A *New Yorker* writer described the amount of attention lavished on the Chinese leader as "very reminiscent of the way they rushed Great Garbo any time this actress shows up on Fifth Avenue."

The excitement of the opening ceremonies seized Payne. "A freedom fever swept the 29-nation African-Asian conference on its opening day at this mountain resort," she wrote, beginning her first dispatch from Bandung. The fever took hold, Payne wrote, when the African National Congress and the South African Indian Congress, whose nation was not invited, delivered a thirty-two-page document asking that the conference provide aid against apartheid. The call for freedom continued as observers from Tunisia, Morocco, and Algeria, all parts of France's empire, presented a document demanding their independence.

Payne's enthusiasm turned her prose purple when Indonesian president Sukarno welcomed the assembled delegates. Delivering his speech in English, apparently only the second time he had ever done so, and with a sparing use of gestures, Sukarno captivated his audience for a full hour. "For sheer eloquence and artistry, he is a master," Payne told readers. "He plays with words like an organist coaxing crescendos and pianissimos and blending them together in a tremolo which sends the blood tingling through your veins."

She was charitable in her reporting, holding the authoritarian Sukarno to a standard that back home Eisenhower would have been grateful for. Deferential to a fault regarding the conference's leading figures, Payne was more on her game when writing about the issues before the gathering. The presence of the Chinese at a conference from which Western nations had been excluded led to the assumption that the Reds would gain the upper hand at Bandung. This notion became even more prevalent when the South African anti-apartheid activists announced they would accept communist aid. But Payne correctly perceived that the delegates were no more interested in being dominated by the Chinese than by the Americans.

For Payne, the drive for self-determination was most evident when on the first day Iraq's prime minister Muhammad Fadhil al-Jamali opened the conference by denouncing communism as "a new form of colonialism much deadlier than the old one." During al-Jamali's speech, Payne looked over at Zhou. He was listening but remained silent, betraying no annoyance. On the other hand, Jawaharlal Nehru of India stormed out. He complained to reporters that baiting Zhou could cause the conference to turn into a Red versus anti-Red battleground. His fears were unwarranted. The real challenge for the conference was finding common ground. After all, as Payne told her readers, "a colonial history is about the only thing the conference members have in common."

BANDUNG WAS THE MEETING PLACE of the world's underdogs, and it attracted its share of sympathizers. W. E. B. Du Bois and singer, actor, and activist Paul Robeson hoped to come but were denied passports by the State Department. Instead they sent greetings that were read aloud to the delegates. Among the many who were able to make the trip were authors James Michener, Vincent Sheean, Norman Cousins, and Homer A. Jack, a Unitarian minister and social activist who had worked with Payne on the Chicago Council Against Racial and Religious Discrimination.

Payne discovered that her race—along, perhaps, with a treasured talisman—worked magic. In addition to her credentials, she wore around her neck a ceramic locket made by her sister Thelma Gray. It was turquoise blue with decorative black squiggles that looked like Arabic. Every day when Payne approached the conference hall the soldiers would lift their bayonets and let her pass, including into sessions closed to reporters. Not one to question her access, she continued entering each day.

On the fourth day, Chet Huntley, an NBC radio reporter who a year later would become coanchor of television's *Huntley-Brinkley Report*, fell into step with Payne. When the pair reached the checkpoint, Payne strolled right in, but the guards would not let Huntley pass. Laughing, Payne said from the other side of the security cordon, "Now you know what it means to be a minority." An interpreter standing nearby looked at Payne and stared intently at her necklace. "Aren't you attached to the Saudi Arabian delegation?"

Payne spent most of her time with delegations and only rarely met with the various national figures leading them. She had brief encounters with Nehru and Zhou. Of the leaders whom she met, Payne was most struck by U Nu, the prime minister of Burma. A devout Buddhist, U Nu was also a spiritual leader in his nation, as well as an accomplished author, novelist, and playwright. Payne spent a long interlude with him, discussing philosophy and religion. "He was almost monastic, in that he was deeply religious," she said. From her perspective, Payne thought he "tried to mute the militant tones at the conference with his philosophy of peace and love."

After each long day of speeches, meetings, and sudden rainstorms, nightfall brought political receptions. Each nation sought to outdo the other. According to Payne, Saudi Arabia's Prince Faisal was the uncontested winner. He provided a buffet dinner, complete with roasted pheasant cooked in Paris, allegedly at Maxim's, and flown to Bandung at the cost of $36,000. Not to be outdone, Zhou held a reception, inviting both Rowan and Payne, at which the Chinese gave out beautiful reproductions of antique Chinese paintings. The artwork would decorate the office walls of both journalists for years to come. In Payne's case, her new friend Chet Huntley was worried about the gifts. "He said that it was a communist ploy, you know, and I, as a black woman, was particularly vulnerable," Payne said. "So he just hoped that I wouldn't fall victim to that.

"Years later," Payne continued, "I always giggled when I would watch Huntley and Brinkley on the evening news and say to myself, 'Chet, old boy, wouldn't you be surprised to know that those paintings are hanging on my apartment walls, and I'm waiting for the FBI and the CIA to charge me with Communist collaboration.'"

When all the participants found their way back to their lodgings for a night of sleep, it was then that Payne would pull out her small portable typewriter and begin banging out her stories, hunting and pecking for each letter with her index fingers. "It was an exhausting thing, but there was so much excitement about it," she recalled, "that I felt like I had taken on a major thing that was different from any other experience I'd ever had." When done, Payne had to locate the special courier employed by the conference who flew out to Jakarta each day and could put her articles on a flight to the United States.

FOR THE TRIP Payne had intended on packing four or five cans of Sterno, jellied alcohol that burns while still in its container. Payne needed a flame to warm a metal comb that she used to straighten her hair. "There was no such thing as going about with nappy hair," Payne said. "You straightened your hair." But when her sisters helped her pack during the few days she was in Chicago before leaving on the trip, one of them thought she was taking too much stuff. As it was, Payne would already have to pay overweight charges on her luggage. To cut down on what she was taking, her supply of Sterno was reduced to one can.

In the humidity of Bandung, Payne's Sterno ran out quickly. Wearing a scarf to cover her hair, she ran into Richard Wright. He was staying in the same compound of houses, and the two found they had much in common from their years in Chicago to their strong personal reasons for coming to Bandung. "He said he was trying to find a link for his own identity with what was happening at the conference," Payne said.

"Oh," she said upon seeing Wright, "I don't know what to do about my hair! My hair is just . . ."

"What's the matter?" Wright asked.

"The Sterno is gone. I didn't have but the one can of Sterno!"

"Well, don't worry. If there's any Sterno in Bandung, I'll find it for you."

Late that night Payne got back to her room after attending one of the endless series of social events. As her room had only a Dutch door, or half door, that could not be locked, she would often find gifts on the table from one of the delegations. Payne spotted a bottle wrapped in white paper. She presumed it was a present, and not being much of a drinker, she left it unopened and went to bed. At about three in morning she heard a voice from outside.

"Ethel! Ethel! Please answer me! Ethel! Are you all right?" It was Wright.

"What is it?" she asked him when she let him in.

"Did you open that bottle?"

"No, I was too tired."

"Well, thank God!"

"What's the matter?"

"I couldn't find any Sterno, so I got some pure alcohol."

"Well, what do you do with that?"

"You got any cotton?"

Payne did. They put the cotton in a saucer and Wright poured the alcohol over it and lit it. Then the pair took turns heating the comb and pulling it through Payne's hair.

"Together," said Payne, "we were frying my hair. It was the wildest thing you ever heard of!"

NOT A SINGLE ONE of the 600 delegates to the conference was a woman. And although the 387-member press contingent included women, they were very few in number. As a result, Payne attracted the attention of a group of reformist Muslim women. Interested in the American women's rights and civil rights movements, the women invited Payne to a tea. When she arrived, she discovered they were angry about the actions of two leading men at the conference. The Pakistani ambassador had divorced his wife for a woman of mixed English and Asian blood, and their own president, Sukarno, had taken a second wife. "And these women were—I guess they could be described as feminists, but they were very upset about this."

The Indonesian women asked Payne what she thought.

"You are predominantly a Moslem country, aren't you?" Payne asked.

"Yes," they replied.

"Well," Payne said, "I thought it was a custom to have plural wives."

The women claimed it was an ancient practice to ensure that war widows were cared for, but it was no longer needed. "And that," Payne realized, "was my first lesson in real feminism, you know, for equal rights and everything."

Following the discussion, the women wanted to demonstrate their knowledge of American culture. One of them read poetry by Walt Whitman and one sat down at the piano and played "Old Black Joe," a Stephen Foster tune. At its conclusion, Payne stood up.

"I thank you for your hospitality," she began. "You're so gracious. But let me tell you a little bit about the history of that particular piece of music. It represents a very sad, a very bleak picture in the history of our country. It goes back to slavery days when my people were in slavery, and 'Old Black Joe' represents the kind of denigration that we had. So we don't accept that anymore. We think it's a pattern back to a day that we would like to put behind us."

When she finished speaking, there was silence in the room. One of the women said the sheet music had been brought over by other Americans as an example of music favored in the United States, but they hadn't known it was offensive. Then another woman stood and went to the piano, grabbed the music, and tore it in half. "We will never again sing that song."

"It was," Payne said, "a high moment, a very high moment."

DESPITE THE POTENTIAL PITFALLS, such as the opening-day attacks on communism as the new imperialism, the Bandung conference was free of conflict. At its end, the delegates agreed on a ten-point declaration that mirrored many of the principles in the United Nations Charter and called on Third World countries to further exchange technical assistance to lessen their dependence on industrial nations.

The conference achieved nothing concrete beyond its declaration, yet it was clear to all who had been there that it had been a historic moment. "Bandung was more important as ceremony than as conference," wrote Norman Cousins upon his return home. "The ceremony, of course, was the graduation exercises of two continents into equality in the family of free nations."

Delegates and others packed up to return home with a sense of optimism about what had occurred. As one writer put it, the gathering was "the voice of the voiceless." Adam Clayton Powell found himself changed by Bandung. "It made me over into an entirely new man," he said. He shed his nationalist beliefs to embrace an internationalist sense. "Whereas previously I had thought of civil rights in terms of rights for Negroes only, I now thought of civil rights as the sole method by which we could save the entire United States of America."

Likewise, Payne was exuberant. "I felt that I was witnessing something that had never happened before in the history of the world and probably would not happen again," she said. But unlike the other American attendees heading east to the United States, she boarded a flight going west. The *Defender* was milking the trip all it could. There was more reporting to be done.

AT A TRAVELING SPEED that would have impressed Nellie Bly, who famously emulated Jules Verne's *Around the World in Eighty Days* for the *New York World* in 1889, Payne flew west, setting down briefly in Ceylon, India, Pakistan, Italy, Switzerland, Germany, and France. From each stop she sent the paper an impressionistic piece filled with local color and anecdotes about her sightseeing. They were like postcards home.

"This is the hottest spot I've hit yet," said Payne of Ceylon. "The winds blowing in from the Arabian Sea sear you like tongues of flame and everything is parched brown." In Karachi, Pakistan, "graceful young girls in baggy trousers balance jars of water on their head and move along with [the] rhythm of ballet dancers." At Alfredo's restaurant in Rome "six handsome waiters descended on me, smiling and talking away with their shoulders and eyes and hands—the Italian way."

Only in Germany did she put back on her reporter's cap, and for good reason. About 12 percent of the more than 150,000 servicemen stationed in Germany were African American. Payne traveled about to several cities with large bases to get a sense of their lives. Her three years of service on a base in Japan made her feel at ease among troops. In the interviews she conducted, she learned that in the prior two years there had been a marked decline in racial friction and brawls. At the headquarters of the 37th Engineer Group (Combat), an eight-year veteran of European service told her that the primary reason for the improvement in race relations was the Army's efforts to weed out those resisting integration.

In fact, Payne found that the U.S. military in Germany had opened up college courses, such as those run by the University of Maryland, to black soldiers and had worked to end the racial restrictions she had known in Japan. "On duty, at chow time, in their sleeping quarters, at post recreation facilities, mixing is the normal procedure of routine," she said. However, the improvements ended at the base's gates. "When it comes to fraternizing over a beer or visiting a dance hall or nightclub," Payne said, "separation becomes an automatic thing, self imposed by the troops and not by military authorities."

According to Payne, if black soldiers frequented a beer cellar, then the "fräuleins," as Payne referred to the barmaids, fraternized with the soldiers while the proprietors informed the white soldiers that the bar is for the use of the black troops. "Conversely, it's the same with the white soldiers," Payne said. "Wherever they take over, it's understood it is their domain and the fräuleins will have nothing to do with the colored GIs."

If a soldier crossed this informal color line, he would be thrown out of the establishment. For that reason, Payne found tension to be high in Mannheim, where a move was being made to desegregate the night spots. About a dozen black and white soldiers banded together and stopped in at bars normally reserved for one race or the other. "The expected fights didn't come off," reported Payne, "but the German proprietors were pretty nervous. Muttered one, 'Never know how to figure those Americans.'"

Her reporting also included accounts of life for the African American wives. "A Negro woman is a great object of curiosity," Payne wrote. "Negro men, whether in uniform or in civvies, seem to be accepted as a matter of course, but when a lady of color appears, it causes a great deal of elbow nudging, stares and excited conversation. Some are amused and snicker behind their hands. Others sit or stand and fasten their eyes on you in a marathon look with the same fascination of a strange species of fowl or animal."

One wife so hated this treatment that she sent her husband out to do the shopping. And then there was the petite brown-skinned wife of a sergeant that Payne encountered. When she would overhear the word *schwarz*, she would turn around and sweetly say, "*Guten Tag, mein lieben dumkopfs*" ("How do you do, my dear stupid ones"). But Payne insisted it was not German hostility, rather the national character of bluntness. "The Auslanders," said Payne, "have neither the finesse of the French nor the polite continental dignity of the Swiss." In fact, one black woman told Payne she encountered more genuine hostility and whispering from Southern American whites than among the Germans.

In the late afternoon of May 23, the Pan American Super 6 Clipper carrying Payne touched down at Chicago's Midway Airport. Clad in a polka-dotted dress and a white hat, and wearing round dark sunglasses, she paused at the base of the stairs to be photographed, flanked by two stewardesses. ETHEL PAYNE BACK AND GLAD OF IT, heralded the *Defender*.

CHAPTER 19

SOUTH AT THE CROSSROADS

THE JET LAG FROM HER WHIRLWIND TOUR OF THE GLOBE had hardly abated when on a June evening Payne went to Washington's Raleigh Hotel to bask in her success at home and abroad. The Capital Press Club, the black alternative to the National Press Club, had selected her as its "Newsman's Newswoman" of 1955. Bestowing the honor, complete with a three-foot-tall twenty-five-pound trophy, was the centerpiece of the club's annual gala dinner in the hotel on Pennsylvania Avenue, four blocks from the White House. Payne shared the stage with Vice-President Richard Nixon, who was being given a citation for his work with his committee on government contracts and employment, and Congressman Adam Clayton Powell, who delivered the main speech.

The soiree underlined Ethel Payne's growing public visibility. She had even become fodder for journalist Drew Pearson, whose syndicated muckraking column, Washington Merry-Go-Round, was feared by politicians and loved by newspaper readers. At a Howard University banquet in May, while Payne was still out of the country, Pearson claimed that the Eisenhower administration had instituted a "reign of terror and intimidation" against those raising embarrassing questions concerning race discrimination. Although he did not mention Payne by name in his talk, instead referring to her as "a Chicago *Defender* correspondent," Pearson said that press secretary Hagerty's private meeting with her was an attempt to "silence the press from asking legitimate questions on racial prejudice."

But in his column, also published while Payne was away, Pearson made no attempt to mask her identity. In fact, Pearson elaborated on his portrayal of Hagerty's intimidation campaign by claiming it had included the use of Payne's personal income tax returns. A furious Hagerty took the unusual step of holding his own press conference to rebut the charge. He admitted he had called Payne to his office for a meeting and had threatened her with the loss of her credentials. But Hagerty denied he engaged in the illegal action of getting copies of her tax records. "I don't normally criticize stories," he told reporters. "But when any columnist or anybody in the newspaper profession says I'm using tax returns, they are completely either deliberately lying or they are completely uninformed." The brouhaha made the *New York Times*, the *Washington Post*, the *Los Angeles Times*, among other mainstream newspapers, and page one of the *Defender*.

Besides writing front-page news for the *Defender*, Payne was making its front-page news.

THE HAGERTY MATTER DIED DOWN and Bandung turned into a distant memory. Payne threw herself back into her work, trying to keep up with the burgeoning number of civil rights developments in Washington and in the South. "While there was never a dull moment, there were plenty of times when I just sat and cried with weariness and frustration," Payne recalled. "My problem was that I wallowed in self guilt if I missed an important news break, never rationalizing that it was impossible for me to be on top of every story breaking."

The optimism Payne felt in May 1954 when the Supreme Court handed down its *Brown v. Board* ruling was fading. Under the headline IKE'S ANTI-BIAS RECORD ALL TALK, NO ACTION she offered a dour assessment of the administration she had previously praised.

Payne recounted in detail the key civil rights questions put to Eisenhower during her two years of attending his press conference. "The record," she wrote, "shows that although President Eisenhower has spoken out against using federal funds to promote and continue discrimination, no concrete steps have been taken to halt the practice."

Even the Supreme Court let Payne down. In May it had issued its much-anticipated order concerning how the nation would be required to desegregate its schools. Payne's front-page story did not mask her displeasure. Calling the court's plan that states should proceed in desegregating schools with "all deliberate speed" a "poor compromise," Payne made it clear that in her view the justices had capitulated to the South by failing to set a firm deadline.

In the midst of this gloom, events in the South caught Payne's attention. For more than two years she had tried to persuade the *Defender* to send her on a tour of the South on a larger scale than the one she took in 1953. Her editors remained uninterested. But suddenly the South turned into a Chicago story.

Emmett Till, a teenager from South Side Chicago, had gone to spend his summer with relatives in rural Mississippi. Familiar with segregation Chicago-style, Till was woefully unprepared for Mississippi's feudal system. One evening, dared by other boys, Till entered a store and either wolf-whistled or made some sort of comment to a young white woman who had been a local high school beauty queen. The story of his impudent behavior spread rapidly in the white community. Several nights later two men came to the house where Till was staying, dragged the boy to their car, and sped off into the darkness. Three days later his decomposing body was discovered in the Tallahatchie River.

Till's body was returned to Chicago in a sealed casket that his mother, Mamie Bradley, ordered opened for four days of viewing. The disfigured head shocked Chicago and—after *Jet* magazine published photographs of the mutilated corpse—blacks across the nation as well. (No major white newspaper published any of the photographs.) The

South, from which so many Chicago blacks had escaped, had come north.

The *Defender* opened its pages to coverage of every aspect of the funeral. As *Jet* had done, it too published the horrifying photographs of the dead boy. Few mourners had ever heard of the young man until they read about the crime. The marks of the barbed wire by which he was bound to the weight used to sink him in the river were still visible on his corpse. "The people saw them and grew angry," reported the *Defender*. "Most of them were thinking it is no crime for a boy to whistle at a pretty woman. They were thinking, 'My son might do it—or yours.'

"And thinking that, they suddenly felt 'Bo' Till belonged to them. And they came to see him. Many of them talked to him.

"They all swore they'd never forget him."

THE TWO WHITE MEN who had dragged Till from his great-uncle's house were put on trial before an all-white, all-male jury in a small backwater Mississippi town. Every lawyer in town donated his services and a pot of money was raised for their defense. Mamie Bradley, Congressman Charles Diggs Jr., and the national and black press headed south to attend the trial. The *Defender* editors refused to send Payne, saying they feared for her safety. "So I had to stay in Washington against my will," she said. "It's not that I am brave. My curiosity and an insatiable desire to be on the scene simply overpower any fear I may have."

Instead the *Defender* assigned L. Alex Wilson, the tall cerebral reporter who had discovered Payne's writing ability in Japan and now ran the Memphis *Tri-State Defender*, which Sengstacke had launched four years earlier. The trial was short and the two men were acquitted of murder. The only possible charge hanging over the two would be if another grand jury, this one in the county where Till's body had been found, rendered an indictment on kidnapping.

In Washington, Payne was left to pursue the federal angle on the story. First she covered attempts by civil rights leaders to get the Justice Department to act in the matter. The chief of its criminal division declined, saying the department had no jurisdiction over the crime. But he assured Roy Wilkins, Thurgood Marshall, Clarence Mitchell, Medgar Evers, and Ruby Hurley during an hour-and-forty-minute meeting that the department would pursue instances of murder and threats in Mississippi that related to voter intimidation.

Following the meeting, Wilkins told Payne that the federal government should not escape its responsibility to prevent further bloodshed in Mississippi by shifting the obligation to the state government. That, however, is exactly what the federal officials were doing, leaving the last remaining hope for justice in the hands of a Mississippi grand jury. While it pondered indicting two men for kidnapping, segregationists worked on the outside to make it easier for the jury to choose not to.

It had been believed that Emmett Till's father, Louis, had served and died as a private in World War II. Roy Wilkins planned on inserting remarks about the dead boy's father's service to his country in the speeches he was preparing for rallies. But on October 14, 1955, the *Jackson Daily News* published a copyrighted story entitled "Till's Dad Raped 2 Women, Murdered a Third in Italy," revealing that Louis Till had been tried, convicted, and hanged by a military tribunal for raping two Italian women and murdering a third in Italy during the waning days of the war. None other than General Dwight D. Eisenhower had signed the execution order. What more proof did one need, was the insinuation of the news trumpeted by the Southern newspapers: Black son was like black father, unable to restrain himself around white women.

Mamie Bradley had not previously known the details of the death of her husband, from whom she had been separated before his enlistment. The Army merely sent her a telegram notifying her of Louis's death that listed the cause as "due to willful misconduct." She wrote inquiries to everyone she could, even to the president, but to no avail. By 1955, Bradley had decided she would never learn the full story. "I never imagined I would find out like this," she said.

Payne immediately sought to identify the source of the story. Certainly the reporters had not just happened upon it. She started with Bradley's attorney William Henry Huff. An NAACP lawyer, Huff had been confronted about the story by reporters from the white press. It "may be true," he told them, "but it has no bearing on the case." But in actuality he knew how damaging the report was on the effort to get Till's killers indicted. When he talked with Payne, he told her that he believed Mississippi senators James Eastland and John Stennis, iconic defenders of segregation, were behind the leak.

Payne contacted the Army. Its spokesman denied it had released the records. After more digging, Payne learned from officials in the Judge Advocate General's Corps, the office that oversees military justice, that Senator Eastland had used his position as chair of the Senate Internal Security Subcommittee to get the information from them. But on the record, a spokesman for that office backpedaled rapidly when confronted by Payne. He said that it was "a rigid policy of the Army never to permit records to be shown, but questions of inquiry on cases are answered."

On October 19, Payne published her revelations in a front-page story titled ARMY GAVE TILL FACTS TO EASTLAND. Outraged that Eastland had been able to obtain the story of her husband's demise when she hadn't been able to in all her years of inquiries, Bradley was immensely grateful to Payne for disclosing the identities of the leakers.

A LITTLE OVER A MONTH LATER, in December 1955, Payne and other reporters got word of a new kind of civil rights protest. In Montgomery, Alabama, forty-two-year-old Rosa Parks, a black seamstress, had electrifyingly inspired the city's black community when she was arrested for refusing to give up her bus seat to a white passenger as required by city law. Three out of four bus riders in the city system were black, and for years they had endured onerous segregation laws that forced them to the back of the bus. Adding to the humiliation was that four black passengers could be made to stand in order to seat one white person, as no black was allowed to share a row with a white.

The arrest of Parks sparked a boycott of the bus company. In place of the buses, a vast network of car pools and taxis, offering reduced group fares, ferried the boycotters to work and shopping. Meanwhile, a hundred miles northwest of Montgomery, in Tuscaloosa, another woman was threatening the racial order of the South. Twenty-six-year-old Autherine Lucy, who held a BA in English, was enrolling in the University of Alabama's graduate library science program, having won a three-year court battle to be the first black student to win admission. Under the watchful eyes of police, Lucy's first day of classes passed without incident. But over succeeding days white protesters began to mass on campus. By the third day she could safely reach her classes only by car, and later she escaped an angry crowd of 2,000 by lying hidden in the backseat of a police squad car. Rather than face the mob, university trustees suspended Lucy "for her own safety."

Payne was convinced that an important new front in the civil rights struggle was opening in Alabama, but her previous pleas to Chicago to be sent south had been rebuffed. She remained miles from the action. On Monday, February 6, 1956, however, her luck changed. The *Defender's* ambitious publisher had turned the paper from a weekly into a daily, becoming after the *Atlanta World* the nation's second black daily newspaper. The paper would now need a lot more copy. At 7:00 PM Louis Martin called and told her to get to Tuscaloosa and cover the Lucy admission fight. The next morning Payne went to National Airport.

ON TUESDAY, FEBRUARY 7, Payne landed at the Birmingham, Alabama, airport. She learned that the main roads leading to Tuscaloosa were blocked to black lawyers, civil rights activists, and reporters. So instead Payne went into the city, where she found Lucy, who was staying with her brother-in-law and fending off anonymous threatening calls. Relatives stood guard with rifles and revolvers. "I'm not going to have her snatched from my care as they did the Till boy," said her brother-in-law. Lucy told Payne that she was shocked at the violence directed toward her. "If the outsiders would leave the students alone," she said, "I will definitely be able to make friends. I pride myself that I have always been able to make friends and to get along with people."

Publicly the students in Tuscaloosa expressed no interest in Lucy's offer of friendship. Gathering around a Confederate flag at night, they sang "Dixie" and chanted, "Hey, hey, ho, ho, Autherine's gotta go." Press cameras captured the protests, in particular sending down the wires a photograph of a white student stomping on top of a car full of terrified black passengers. "The picture," noted one observer, "gave the nation an accurate portrait of blacks engulfed in a sea of white rage."

The next morning, Payne and James Hicks, whom she had first met in Japan and who was now the executive editor of the *New York Amsterdam News*, rented a car and successfully made the drive to Tuscaloosa. There they met up with Emily Barrett, a reporter for the *Alabama Citizen*, a local black weekly, who had accompanied Lucy during her first days on campus. The three entered the University of Alabama campus. At the office of the public relations director, they asked permission to interview students. The officials turned down their request. The dean of women and the president also refused their requests for interviews.

"You are in real danger," warned the public relations director. "The mob is in control here. You are Northerners and considered outsiders here." Turning to Barrett and Payne, he added, "You women might be mistaken for Miss Lucy and trouble can start all over again." If they insisted on questioning students, the university would not be responsible for what might happen. The warnings issued by the public relations director may have been intended to scare Payne off, but at the same time, the danger was very real. Already Payne could see a small group of students gathering outside and looking into the office through the window.

Before escaping from the hostile campus, Payne did manage to talk to some students, including Leonard Wilson, one of the leaders of the demonstrations. Prior to becoming a student at the university, Wilson had gained attention by introducing a measure at the Youth Legislature during his senior year of high school that called for sending Negroes back to Africa. Obsessed with segregation, he spent an hour a day compiling a scrapbook of newspaper clippings.

"It is for the long-range benefit of this great institution that it remain an all-white school," Wilson told Payne. "Lest it fall from its present standards, keeping 'Bama white is the only solution satisfactory to the great majority of taxpayers of Alabama." Another student blamed the NAACP for putting Lucy's life at risk. None of the students with whom she talked supported Lucy's right to attend the university, but several were critical of the mob reaction.

The *Defender*'s editors topped Payne's dispatches with ETHEL PAYNE ADVISED TO QUIT CAMPUS and ETHEL SEES HATE IN STUDENT EYES.

HICKS AND PAYNE RETURNED to Birmingham and then turned south, driving the hundred miles to Montgomery. The protesters welcomed them. The bus boycott, now entering its tenth week, was holding firm. But Payne found that hostility on the part of whites was on the rise. In fact, in her first report from the site of the protest, she said organizers were promoting a voluntary curfew. They urged that black citizens remain in their homes on the night that Mississippi senator Eastland, whom Payne referred to as a "racebaiting senator," spoke to a rally of the White Citizens' Council.

As her first order of business, Payne sought out Ralph Abernathy

Sr. The outspoken young minister had been the first religious leader that Nixon approached at the start of the boycott. The protesters believed that a boycott would fail without support of the city's black ministers. In turn, Abernathy worked to include other ministers and contacted the Reverend Martin Luther King Jr., a twenty-six-year-old minister who had come to town the previous year and with whom he had become good friends. At their first meeting, organizers created the Montgomery Improvement Association (MIA) and selected King as president. In a short time, Abernathy and King were working as a team and becoming the public face of the campaign.

Only a few out-of-town reporters had preceded Payne and Hicks to Montgomery. Carl Rowan, the African American reporter for the *Minneapolis Tribune* whom Payne had first encountered in Bandung, and his colleague, a white reporter named Richard Kleeman, had stopped in the city while on a tour of the South to write a series of articles for their paper in the wake of the *Brown v. Board* decision. From Bandung to Montgomery, Rowan and Payne were increasingly chasing the same stories and prizes. On their own, the two had made civil rights their main beat. They and their editors also saw them as competitors. In fact, the month before, their bosses had entered each journalist's coverage of the Bandung conference in the Pulitzer Prize competition. Neither won.

Beyond attracting Rowan and Kleeman, the story of the bus boycott had not yet gained traction in the mainstream media. Most newspapers and magazines had relied so far on wire copy, and the stories had run in the back pages. Neither the *New York Times* nor the *Washington Post* had sent a reporter to the scene. The story still belonged to the black press.

CHAPTER 20

THE GLADIATOR
WEARS A REVERSE COLLAR

FOR ETHEL PAYNE, MONTGOMERY BROUGHT BACK MEMO-
ries of the 1941 March on Washington Movement. In fact,
Edgar D. Nixon, one of the veterans of the march whom
Payne knew, was a boycott organizer. But unlike her experience with
the fractious Chicago march organization, what she saw in Birmingham was quite different. "The most impressive thing about the boycott is the absolute unity of purpose," Payne told her readers. She
found that the MIA had built a superb organizational structure that
oversaw its finances, coordinated the alternative network of transportation, and possessed a steering committee that could respond
quickly when needed.

Payne shadowed Ralph Abernathy because Martin Luther King
was in Chicago. The second-in-command struck her as "a soft-spoken
rugged man with a pleasant smile." Over a series of days she watched
as he made his round of nighttime meetings around the city, where he
was greeted with cries of "Don't get weary, son, we're with you." After
the last evening meeting, Payne followed Abernathy home, where he
talked late into the night with her and a handful of reporters. Even at
this late hour his house was like a command center.

Payne left Montgomery and flew to Chicago. There, in the offices of the *Defender*, she took stock of what she had seen in Alabama. Whatever she wrote would be mostly new to her readers. The boycott had barely been covered in the white newspapers. Abernathy's and King's names had only begun to be mentioned. The *Defender*, like other black newspapers, had given increasing attention to the story. But even then, it only made it to the front page when it was connected to violence.

Payne was convinced there was more to the story than the boycott, though it was a new, exciting, and potentially potent weapon. But behind the protest's facade, she perceived that an important and fundamental change was taking place in the leadership of the civil rights struggle. The key leaders of the boycott—from Fred Gray, the group's lawyer, to its most visible commanders, Abernathy and King—were all men of the cloth.

"A NEW TYPE OF LEADER is emerging in the South," Payne wrote as she began her report under the headline THE SOUTH'S NEW HERO that appeared on February 15, weeks before the rest of the press would begin profiling the protest organizers. "He is neither an NAACP worker, nor a CIO political action field director. Instead, the gladiator going into battle wears a reverse collar, a flowing robe, and carries a Bible in his hand. This new, vocal, fearless, and forthright Moses who is leading the people out of the wilderness into the Promised Land is the Negro preacher."

Payne was onto something profound, perhaps even more significant than she realized. Since the Civil War, the black freedom struggle had been led in turn by educators and intellectuals such as Booker T. Washington and W. E. B. Du Bois, who were followed by labor leaders such as A. Philip Randolph and the Brotherhood of Sleeping Car Porters, and most recently by lawyers such as Thurgood Marshall and the NAACP. Now Payne perceived yet another change in leadership, perhaps the most important one yet.

Everywhere Payne looked in the South she saw the emergence of a new leadership. She told her readers about the Reverend Joseph A. DeLaine, who was fighting for the integration of South Carolina schools, and Reverend T. H. Jennings, who organized a bus boycott in Louisiana that inspired the one in Montgomery. "The Negro preacher is praying," Payne wrote, "but he is also fighting for the democratic way of life for his people that has so long been denied them."

Her reporting was even ahead of what others on the front lines could see. Marshall, for instance, failed to understand the significance of the boycott. He thought the action was premature because the NAACP would eventually prevail in court and the bus company's practices would be found to be an illegal form of discrimination. But what he and others failed to understand was that the daring actions of the Montgomery boycotters were galvanizing blacks nationwide. It was like rousing a sleeping giant. In Montgomery, according to Payne, every Negro minister was crossing all denominational lines to join the effort in a unity of purpose. "So the church," Payne said, "is leading the way in painful transition to a new social order."

In Chicago the editors were so impressed by Payne's reporting that the paper's lead editorial was devoted to her observations. "A seasoned reporter who has literally made the world her beat, Miss Payne has brought back from behind the 'color curtain' some heartening news in the battle that is raging for the second emancipation of the black man," read the editorial. "It is a fitting tribute to the courageous Negro clergyman."

Payne followed up her first report with a second one enlarging on her theme of a leadership transition. In South Carolina, for instance, Payne said a bishop was ordering his ministers to escort their members to voter registration sites and polling booths. "The courage and stout heartedness of these new Knights of the Cross have brought hope and inspiration to millions of discouraged people," she wrote. "For many, it has been the reaffirmation of confidence that in a time of need, true leadership will come forth to guide the people."

HER ARTICLES AND ANALYSIS complete, Payne returned to Alabama. In Montgomery she found the boycott was still holding strong, although tensions were high. Along with King's home, organizer Edgar Nixon's home had been bombed. Floodlights illuminated Nixon's property at night and a watchdog provided a warning should anyone approach. "But," she added, "it looks as if the boycott can go on and on and on."

The unity was such that Payne devoted an entire article to Jeannetta Reese, a black woman who was ostracized for giving in to white pressure by recanting the permission she gave Fred Gray to use her name in the lawsuit against the bus company. "What Jeannetta failed to recognize was that a phenomenal thing had happened in Montgomery," wrote Payne. "The bus boycott had brought about a unity of purpose and nobody was tattling to 'Mr. Charlie.'"*

From Montgomery, Payne went to Birmingham to catch up with Lucy and her lawyers. They were seeking to persuade a federal judge to have Lucy readmitted to the University of Alabama. At the federal courthouse, Payne found a tense and crowded scene. In keeping with custom, black and white spectators lined opposite sides of the hall while waiting for Judge Harlan Hobart Grooms, an Eisenhower appointee, to convene his court. In a few hours, Lucy got what she wanted. The university was ordered to readmit her in four days. "That means only one thing," she told Payne and others in the hall, "that I am going back to school."

---

* "Mr. Charlie" was a term frequently used in blues songs that referred to white men who are regarded as oppressors of blacks.

In the Masonic Hall offices of her Birmingham attorney Arthur D. Shores, Lucy sat with Payne, several other reporters, and Thurgood Marshall. She was exhausted and the situation was growing more dangerous. A university trustee put it plainly. "She will probably be killed," he said. Marshall offered to pay for Lucy to go anywhere she wished for a rest. Payne suggested she come with her to Chicago. James Hicks, however, won the honor for New York with a soliloquy praising the city's virtues from the Brooklyn Bridge to *Cat on a Hot Tin Roof.*

The decision made, Lucy and an entourage reduced to Hicks, Payne, and NAACP organizer Ruby Hurley retired to Payne's room at the A. G. Gaston Motel, where they relaxed over a steak dinner while the rest of the press corps scoured the city looking for Lucy. But Hicks couldn't rest. "Ethel and I have worked side by side on many a big story from Tokyo to Miami and I respect her as one of the most able gal reporters I know," he said. "And it gave me no comfort to have Miss Lucy sitting there in Ethel's room: I was afraid that if I went to bed I might wake up the next morning to find Ethel and Autherine in Chicago!" Ethel was not so underhanded or at least resisted the temptation, and Lucy went to Hurley's home for the night.

EARLY THE NEXT MORNING, Payne and Hicks met in a coffee shop. They both learned they should have stayed up the night before. "For as we sipped our coffee," said Hicks, "the radio announced that the crackers at Alabama University had 'permanently expelled' Autherine Lucy from school." Stunned, they dashed over to Shores's offices. "Everything was bedlam there," Hicks said. "The 'Bama bigots hadn't even given Shores the courtesy of telling him about it."

The university's rationale avoided race. They deemed the charges of conspiracy Lucy made in the courtroom to be slanderous and said that this reflected poorly on her fitness as a student.

(They would also eventually expel the anti-desegregation student leader Leonard Wilson.)

Lucy and her legal team rushed to the airport for a 10:50 Eastern Airlines flight to New York City. Hicks managed to snag the last ticket on the flight. The airline tipped off the press, and a cordon of police officers was required at LaGuardia Airport as if Lucy's arrival was that of a movie star. Payne managed to catch up with the group the following day at the New York offices of the NAACP, where Lucy faced a battery of reporters with Marshall and Roy Wilkins by her side. The glare of the publicity and the pressure of the case became too much for the twenty-nine-year-old, who had never been to New York, much less traveled a lot outside of Alabama. She collapsed into the arms of her two lawyers.

Regaining her composure, she told the reporters she agreed to come to New York to obtain medical help and rest from the strain she had been under since the case started. She had intended on returning to the campus and resuming her classes, but the expulsion order convinced her that staying away for the time being was the best course. Meanwhile she went shopping with Payne.

In the company of Marshall's secretary and a detective assigned to protect her, Lucy and Payne headed off by subway to Fifth Avenue the next day. "One of the most charming things about Autherine is her genuine modesty and the quaint habit she has of lapsing into some of the colloquialisms of the regions where she comes from," wrote Payne in her account of the shopping expedition. "As the train came roaring in, she commented in her Southern drawl, 'It makes a heap of noise for a spell, doesn't it?'"

Surfacing at Forty-Second Street, they went into Arnold Constable and other department stores. Lucy selected a dress, fawn-colored elbow-length gloves, and a beige hat of straw and crepe ruching. Payne refrained from providing sartorial advice. "Your scribe was neutral," she told her readers, "since shopping panics me." Back at the Marshalls' apartment, Lucy modeled her new outfit. "Ain't that a pip. Baby, you sure look good," said Thurgood Marshall.

PAYNE AND LUCY, in the company of the NAACP's public relations director, took the train to Washington. When they reached Washington's Union Station at 4:25 PM, the scene was a repeat of that at LaGuardia Airport. News photographers snapped pictures and their flashes attracted a crowd of autograph seekers, including twenty-five women from Sweet Briar College, in southern Virginia, returning from a weekend at Princeton University. Payne and the NAACP man guided Lucy, hatbox in hand from her shopping trip, out of the station and into the city.

The purpose of Lucy's trip to Washington was to attend a national assembly for civil rights convened by the NAACP. It was being held in the Mellon Auditorium, the largest government-owned meeting hall in the capital. Lucy, now a heroine of the struggle, was to be presented to the crowd during its first evening rally. It would be the high point of her struggle. She eventually decided not to pursue the court case further, and it would be another seven years before the first African American student would successfully enter the University of Alabama. Thirty Southern congressmen registered their displeasure at such use of a government facility. But the national leaders of the Republican and Democratic parties, both vying for the support of black voters, sent their emissaries to speak to the nearly 2,000 delegates. Senator Hugh Scott of Pennsylvania, one of the Republicans' most vigorous supporters of civil rights, debated Paul Butler, chairman of the Democratic National Committee.

Butler was already in trouble with his audience before arriving. Earlier in the year Payne had put the Democratic chairman on the front page of the *Defender* when he said that the "time is not ripe" to push any civil rights legislation through Congress. Talking to Payne and four other black reporters, he even claimed that he had consulted with Senator Hubert Humphrey, a champion of civil rights, and the Minnesotan was in agreement. Representatives Adam Clayton Powell and Charles Diggs publicly rebuked Butler and said his reluctance to push civil rights legislation would put the party in jeopardy of losing the black vote. And more damning, a Humphrey aide accused Butler of lying about his boss.

The three-day conference succeeded in helping promote civil rights as an issue for the fall elections, Payne concluded. But it also highlighted the split among Democrats. "There has always been a conservative—the polite term for the Dixiecrats—and a so-called liberal wing, composed mostly of Northerners who pay lip service to progressiveness in the human rights arena," Payne explained. But she was convinced that Northern liberals were finally willing to fight for this issue because the party was losing its electoral strongholds. "Chief among these," she said, "is the Negro vote which for more than twenty years was the exclusive property of Democrats."

AGAIN PAYNE MADE HER WAY back to Montgomery, reaching the city on the eve of a trial in which King and ninety or so organizers of the bus protest faced charges brought under an arcane 1929 state law prohibiting boycotts. On Sunday, March 18, 1956, she went to the Dexter Avenue Baptist Church. The day was beautiful. "Outwardly Montgomery was quiet," reported Payne. "But there was an uneasy calm over the city." At the Dexter Avenue Church she found King instructing his congregation, many of whom were among those indicted, to face their courtroom accusers without hate and "to tell the truth and know that we are right."

"Violence," King told the packed church, "carries the seeds of its own destruction. Every true Christian must be a fighting pacifist. Even if we didn't have tension in Montgomery, there would still be no peace. If Negroes continue to accept the old order, there will be peace without meaning. We don't want peace if it means keeping our mouths shut about injustice or accepting second class citizenship."

As she had done on her previous visits, Payne stayed in a private home. But she noticed that the trial had made Montgomery the destination of choice for the national press. Reporters from the *New York Times* and the *Washington Post* as well as *Time* and *Newsweek* and even the television networks were here. Not since the inauguration of Jefferson Davis as president of the Confederacy ninety-five years earlier had the dateline of Montgomery appeared in so many papers and magazines, noted one observer.

Dean Drug Store, a fifty-year-old establishment in downtown Montgomery, had served as a central meeting place for reporters since the start of the boycott. "First it was all the black correspondents who came down, and then the whites got in," Payne said. The presence of the white journalists strengthened the reporting coming out of Montgomery, Payne noted. "They would fill us in sometimes about what the white power structure was saying, and in turn, we'd give them little bits of information that they hadn't yet gotten access to." With the exception of those from the *Montgomery Advertiser*, Payne found an immense camaraderie among the reporters. "I think they were all universally sympathetic with the spirit of the movement and what had happened."

King, who was being tried first, presented himself before Judge Eugene W. Carter's courtroom, which was filled with a mostly black audience. Court officials worked hard to maintain strict racial segregation. Payne was greatly amused by their efforts. She shared with readers the dilemma they faced in seating a swarthy reporter from India. After conferring gravely over the matter, the officials seated him with the white reporters, even though he announced he would like to sit with the Negroes. "There was a great deal of laughter over this!" said Payne.

The prosecution got off to a poor start in its efforts to show when and how the boycott began. They made better headway using the subpoenaed MIA records. The financial trail certainly revealed the strength of the protest. In the first sixteen weeks of the boycott, the MIA had banked more than $30,000 that it used to pay the gasoline and oil expenses for the automobiles used in the car pool.

At the end of the day, Payne and other reporters crowded around King on the courthouse steps. Asked about the money, King said with a smile, "I have heard rumors about me using it to buy a Cadillac, which is absurd." He promised he would continue to drive his 1954 Pontiac for at least another five years. That night Payne followed the crowds to St. John AME Church. She found it so jammed with people eager to learn about the first day of the trial that a large segment of the crowd was forced to listen from the sidewalk as loudspeakers broadcast the speeches from inside.

THE TRIAL LASTED FOUR DAYS. Reporters keeping count found that Judge Carter overruled seventy-six objections made by the defense team. As the lawyers expected that the case would ultimately be decided on appeal, this poor treatment at the hands of the judge might serve them well later. On Thursday, the testimony complete, Judge Carter took only minutes to find King guilty, fining him $1,000 or 386 days in jail. The imposition of the sentence and the prosecution of the others were held in abeyance pending appeal. King exited the courthouse smiling as more than three hundred supporters greeted him outside. Responding to the cheers of "Behold the King" and "Long Live the King," the convicted reverend promised that the verdict would not lessen his ardor. "We will continue with the protest in the same spirit," he said, "with nonviolence, passive resistance, and using the weapon of love."

A few hours later, Payne landed an interview with King. At length he explained that the movement was, from its start, a spontaneous outgrowth of years of oppression. "It came from the people, and it is truly a people's movement," he told Payne. "One could say that this is really part of the worldwide revolt of subjugated peoples in their yearnings for the dignity that belongs to free men." Neither the conviction nor the violence directed at the movement would deter them, King promised. "These are the times that try men's souls," he said. "The eyes of the world are watching us, but we are not pursuing our course because of this. We are determined to carry through our fight because it is the only right and decent thing to do."

Montgomery had been exhilarating. "Somehow, I felt I was woven into the drama that was going on," Payne said. "This was something taking place for me and for all the people that I knew, and we were all drawn into this thing. It was like a historic battle being drawn out on a field, and you were part of it. You were not the audience, but you were part of it. You just felt drawn into it."

Upon her return north, Payne spoke to a gathering in Bloomington, Illinois. Combining her international reporting with her recent coverage of events in Alabama, Payne repeated a theme of hers since the 1941 March on Washington Movement: The lack of progress on race in the United States was hurting the nation overseas. Secretary of State John Foster Dulles ought to "unpack his bags and stay home."

In Chicago, Payne put the finishing touches on two immense projects. The first was a lengthy series called "The South at the Crossroads." It was not good reporting, the dozen full-page installments hurriedly written. The series offered not news but a readable and understandable explanation of the key events that had made headlines over the past two years. Payne analyzed the effect of the *Brown v. Board* ruling, recounted the Montgomery bus boycott that was still under way, profiled Martin Luther King, highlighted how the dominance of key congressional committees by white Southern Democrats was stymieing legislative progress on matters of civil rights, detailed the plight of Southern liberals, and attacked "gradualism" as a delaying tactic. "How many more Emmett Tills and Rev. George Lees," asked Payne, referring to two recent murders, "are needed before the federal government decides that something more than moderation must be used against cold-blooded killers?"

The pages of the *Defender* were not just consumed by Payne's exhaustive series but also featured Mamie Bradley's almost book-length memoir as exclusively told to Payne through a series of interviews. Bradley had not forgotten how Payne had helped when Senator Eastland dug up the information on her husband's demise and rewarded her with exclusive access.

In the midst of churning out all these words, Payne made time to attend Martin Luther King's speech in the Gothic Rockefeller Memorial Chapel on the campus of the University of Chicago, where she had once wanted to study. The speech exposed a 1,600-strong audience of white and black Chicagoans to the minister's inspiring speechmaking abilities that Payne had witnessed close up in Montgomery. The audience, she reported, sat spellbound.

Payne explained to her readers unfamiliar with the name of Mahatma Gandhi that King was fusing the techniques that had won India its independence with the principles of Christianity to win Negroes their freedom.

Scribbling on her reporter's pad, Payne took down King's closing words. "We must use as our weapons the love which transcends everything and can make you compassionate with those who hate you," King said, his voice resonating off the stone walls of the chapel. "If you can't run, walk; if you can't walk, crawl, but keeping moving forward."

CHAPTER 21

GHANA

I N THE FOUR YEARS SINCE ETHEL PAYNE AS A WET-BEHIND-the-ears reporter covered her first convention, she had developed into the *Defender*'s unquestioned star political reporter. As was now its habit whenever Payne traveled, the *Defender* announced her plans with fanfare, referring to her as its "globe-trotting reporter" and "a political expert and civil rights authority."

With the summer of 1956 came the quadrennial political conventions, but this year they hardly merited the attention of a skilled reporter. In San Francisco the Republicans predictably renominated Eisenhower, and in Chicago the Democrats settled again on Adlai Stevenson. But Payne was enraged at the Democrats for what she saw as a backroom deal that weakened the civil rights plank. Stevenson's strategy was to offend no one. To accommodate him, the party suppressed a battle over a stronger plank supported by his rival, New York governor Averell Harriman. "Instead of the International Amphitheatre being turned into a bloody battleground with the liberals riding the chargers as so eagerly expected by 100 million TV viewers, the showdown was mild as a tea party sponsored by the church missionary society," reported a sullen Payne.

Republican operatives discerned an opportunity in the discontent among African American members of the Democratic Party. Val

Washington, the black assistant to the National Republican Committee chairman, felt that Payne's frustration was an opening not to be missed. "She is thoroughly mad with the theory of 'moderation' that the Democrats are trying to sell to the Negroes," Washington wrote to Max Rabb in the White House. Washington knew Payne well. He had once worked for the black press, including a seven-year stint on the business side of the *Defender*, and had frequently helped Payne with her reporting since she had come to the capital. "There is no doubt in my mind," he said, "that she is going to do everything she can to help us in this campaign." To that end, Washington urged that Rabb reward Payne by obtaining State Department funding to send her to a conference of African writers in Paris in late September. The State Department, however, didn't buy into the idea, deciding instead "an acceptable delegation of American Negro intellectuals will be formed under private sponsorship."

The supposition that blacks could be lured back to the GOP was not without basis. Congressman Adam Clayton Powell threw in his lot with Eisenhower, telling voters that a candidate like Stevenson who had been endorsed by both Eleanor Roosevelt and Mississippi senator James Eastland "has to be either a hypocrite, a liar, a double-talker, or a double dealer." Both King and Abernathy said they would vote Republican. On election day, black voters in record numbers pulled the Republican lever, more than at any other time in the past quarter of a century. In the South, white voters gave Eisenhower Florida, Virginia, Texas, and Louisiana. "Montgomery, Ala.," reported Payne, "where Jefferson Davis marched through the streets on his inauguration as President of the Confederacy, went GOP."

In a front-page analysis called HOW IKE BROKE BACK OF SOUTH, Payne credited dissatisfaction with the Democrats for the surge in support among African Americans for the Republican Party. It was, in short, a protest against the Democratic-controlled machines in the South that stood as bulwarks against desegregation, she said. "From now on the Negro vote in the South will command more respect by both parties, particularly the GOP looking for a cadre which to build itself."

But as frustrated and angry as she was with the Democratic Party, Payne was not about to jump ship. Rather, from her vantage point in Washington and from her trips to the South, she remained convinced that black voters could push Democrats into action. "Negro Democrats disgusted with pussyfooting and compromising that led to disaster in many places are prepared to deliver an 'EITHER OR' ultimatum to party heads before Congress opens," Payne threatened in an end-of-the-year warning. "EITHER repudiate the Dixiecrats OR face a wholesale walkout from the party."

Despite Ethel Payne's journalistic ascension to the ranks of the premier black reporters, 1956 included a low moment. Richard Wright, whom she counted among her friends after the time they spent together in Bandung, betrayed her confidence. In *The Color Curtain*, his published account of the conference, he told the story of a visit to his quarters by a white woman. She had come to his room to ask frank questions about a black female journalist who was engaged in worrisome nighttime activities. Awakened one night, the woman told Wright, she discovered her roommate bent over a small blue flame. It seemed like she might be combing her hair, but maybe she was practicing voodoo?

Wright was puzzled until his visitor disclosed she had found an empty tin can marked "Sterno." Comprehending what the woman had witnessed, Wright told her that she had simply seen a black woman straightening her hair.

"But why would she straighten her hair? Her hair seems all right."

"Her hair is all right. But it's not straight. It's kinky. But she does not want you, a white woman, to see her when she straightens her hair. She would feel embarrassed—"

"Why?"

"Because you were born with straight hair, and she wants to look as much like you as possible . . ."

Slowly his guest comprehended. "Negroes have been made ashamed of being black," he continued. "And this woman, your roommate, is trying to make herself look as white as possible. Can you blame her? It's a tribute that she pays to the white race. It's her way of saying: 'Forgive me. I'm sorry that I'm black. I'm ashamed that my hair is not like yours. But you see that I'm doing all that I can to be like you.'"

"God in Heaven," said the woman, "why doesn't she forget her hair? She's pretty like she is!"

"She *can't* forget it. The feeling that she is black and evil has been driven into her very soul."

Readers would certainly have not known that Payne was the inspiration for the black woman portrayed in Wright's fictional tale. But by any measure it was a heartless use of an intimacy between the two to make a point about racial oppression. For the remainder of her life, Payne's hair remained a source of consternation. Eventually she found her solution, like many other black women of her era, in acquiring a collection of wigs. Once she began wearing wigs, Payne almost never permitted herself to be seen without one, sometimes even going to bed with a wig when she had an overnight guest.

IN JANUARY 1957, Eisenhower asked Vice-President Richard Nixon to represent the United States at the Ghanaian independence celebration in March. For Africans, the moment was significant. The Gold Coast British colony would become the first sub-Saharan African country to gain its independence. For African Americans, it was an electrifying development. Not only would this be a nation ruled by blacks, but Kwame Nkrumah, who would become Ghana's first prime minister, had gone to Lincoln University in Pennsylvania and modeled his politics on the ideas of Americans Marcus Garvey and W. E. B. Du Bois.

In addition to inviting Payne and other reporters to the independence ceremonies, the future rulers of Ghana extended invitations to numerous Americans, especially prominent African Americans, including Sengstacke, Payne's publisher. "The occasion has engendered so much excitement," Payne said, "that thousands of Americans of both races will make the long trek to Africa to participate in the rejoicing."

Ghanaians promised to provide housing, food, work space, and in-country transportation to the foreign press. To ensure the black press would witness a moment benefiting Nixon and Republicans, the State Department classified the trip as an "intergovernmental agency project," thereby offering Military Air Transport Service seats at a price half that of commercial airlines. It even permitted Sengstacke to bring his wife at the reduced rate.

While the potential political dividends to Nixon from coverage in the black press were considerable, the irony of his going halfway around the world to score political points while avoiding his own backyard was not entirely lost on some scribes. "Nixon expects to be the GOP candidate in 1960 and he has been for some time shooting for the crucial minorities in the pivotal States where elections are won and lost," noted columnist Doris Fleeson wrote. "He has yet, however, as has the president, to make a similar handshaking tour of the American South where the Negro segregation issue is boiling."

An estimated 10,000 people were on hand when Nixon and his entourage landed in Accra, the capital of Ghana. But the majority of the thirty-five American press representatives were nowhere to be found. On the final leg of the 4,924-mile journey, engine trouble had caused the press corps' DC-6B to turn back to Casablanca for repair. Payne, who had arrived on an earlier Pan Am flight, was one of the few Americans who watched as the crowds cheered for Nixon,

calling him a "Show Boy," a Ghanaian term of approval for a politician. When the bedraggled reporters finally reached Accra, Nixon
had a surprise in store for them. Equipping himself with a press
armband, notebook, and camera, he greeted the perspiring and furious reporters at the bottom of the plane's stairs with notebook and
pencil poised. "Anything to say, fellers?" he asked.

Later that night, at 1:30 AM, a plane bearing the final group of
Americans arrived. On board were Martin Luther King Jr., A. Philip
Randolph, Lester Granger of the Urban League, with whom Payne
had battled, Ralph Bunche, representing the UN general secretary,
Representative Adam Clayton Powell, and two dozen other notable
African Americans. "When the Pan American plane set down here,"
said Payne, "somebody aptly quipped had it crashed, the top Negro
leadership of the United States would have been lost." The group,
however, was in no mood for jokes. They felt slighted that no one had
been sent to greet the party.

As THE HOUR OF INDEPENDENCE neared for Ghana, Payne discovered the celebration accomplished something that civil rights leaders
in the United States had failed to do so far. Back in Washington,
Nixon had left unanswered King's letters inviting him to come to the
South and witness firsthand the "anti-Negro violence." In Accra, the
vice-president could not duck for cover.

At a university convocation, where Nixon presented an American
scholarship, he came face-to-face with King for the first time. "Nixon
shook hands warmly with Rev. King while Mrs. Nixon and Mrs. King
stood by chatting," said Payne, watching the two men. "The vice-
president said they had read the recent *Time* magazine article, in
which Rev. King was featured on the cover, and said he had enjoyed
it very much."

"Mr. Vice-President," King said, "I'm glad to meet you here, but
I want you to come to visit us down in Alabama, where we are seek-

ing the same kind of freedom the Gold Coast is celebrating." Nixon demurred, but he invited King to come and meet with him in Washington. Although it was less than he sought, King was elated with the invitation. He told Payne and her colleagues he hoped Nixon would serve as a conduit to bring the segregation problem to Eisenhower's attention. "We are not sure," King said, "the president actually knows of all the violence and the desperation of the situation."

American domestic politics, however, had to be put aside for another time and place. Under the agreement between the United Kingdom and the Gold Coast, Ghana would be granted its independence at midnight on March 5. When the ceremonies in the parliament concluded, the massive crowd of celebrants moved to the polo grounds to await the stroke of the clock. "It was so still that even the breeze from the sea was quiet as the upturned faces early hung on the words of Kwame Nkrumah, the man who had led them to freedom," Payne said. Speaking in Twi, the common language of Ghana, Nkrumah's voice quavered and broke with emotion, his arm rose in a clenched-fist salute, and he cried out "Ghana forever!" The crowd picked up the chant and rocked into the night to the rhythmic cry of "Freedom, freedom, freedom!"

In the days following, Payne joined the press plane that traipsed after Nixon as he visited several other African countries. Along with her was Howard K. Smith of CBS News, several well-known correspondents such as Peter Lisagor of the *Chicago Daily News* and John Scali of the Associated Press, as well as representatives of the black press such as *Jet* magazine's Simeon Booker, with whom Payne had become good friends in their time together in Washington.

THE STOPS IN THE VARIOUS NATIONS produced little in the way of news beyond the usual platitudes about frankness and cordiality pronounced by Nixon and whichever leader he met. Instead, Payne turned her interest toward what she saw outside the official schedule.

In Liberia, after the delegation visited industrial plants and plantations, Payne took note of the unclothed Liberians in roadside thatched huts. "A few yards from the president's palace are makeshift tin houses with no running water and chickens scratching in the yard." In Uganda, on a drive between Kampala and Entebbe, Payne was again struck by the contrast between the lush pastures filled with cows and the hard life of the Ugandans. "The thatched huts and barefoot Africans staggering under loads on their backs serve to remind you that this is Africa; the primitive clashing against the modern."

After visits to Sudan and Ethiopia, the group reached Rome for recuperation and refueling. There Payne obtained an interview with Nixon. She asked him if the domestic struggle over civil rights had international consequences when it came to Africa. "What happens in the U.S. in the matter of race relations can have a serious effect on the success or failure of our dealings in Africa as it proceeds towards independence and freedom," Nixon said. It would determine whether newly independent African nations would go communist. "Those who promote discrimination and prejudice in the U.S. are not only hurting our country at home, but internationally as well," he said.

If Nixon was surprised at a question of international affairs coming from a member of the black press, this line of questioning seemed natural to Payne. Attending the Bandung conference, circumnavigating the globe, and now touring Africa had cemented her conviction that the fight for civil rights had an international dimension. Forces outside the United States could be brought to aid the civil rights movement at home, and equally if not more important in her mind, the fight for black freedom in the United States was part of a larger international struggle.

BACK HOME PAYNE WAS ONCE MORE on the domestic civil rights beat. She caught up with Martin Luther King again in early April when he, Roy Wilkins, and A. Philip Randolph came to Washington to announce a Prayer Pilgrimage for Freedom to be held on the steps of the Lincoln Memorial on May 17. Wilkins explained that the rally would serve as a protest against the violence and intimidation to which blacks were subjected. Randolph quickly added it would not be a second March on Washington Movement like the one he had led in 1941. Instead it would be a spiritual demonstration in support of pending civil rights legislation and to commemorate the third anniversary of *Brown v. Board.*

As the date for the rally neared, Payne made the rounds of churches in the nation's capital and found parishioners transforming the houses of worship into hospitality centers in preparation of an anticipated 50,000 pilgrims. In the end, the number who made it to Washington was far smaller than organizers had hoped. Payne reported the crowd at 30,000, resisting the temptation to inflate the turnout. The largest contingents were 11,000 people from New York and some 8,000 from Southern states who came for the hours of prayers, sermons, and speeches interlaced with musical performances by Mahalia Jackson and two choirs, including an interracial one from Philadelphia. The crowd listened quietly and patiently—"most orderly crowd they had handled," said the police—until Howard University president Mordecai Johnson called for supporting desegregation efforts even at the risk of jail time. "The multitudes," said Payne, "went wild and the pace of enthusiasm for the entire afternoon was set."

When at last the venerated Randolph introduced King, the crowd erupted in a thunderous ovation. "Speaking in slow measured tones to the quiet spellbound group," Payne said, King explained it was not a day for rabble-rousing. Rather, there was "no place for misguided emotionalism" in dealing with the complexity and intransigency of the problem blacks faced.

Payne and other observers regarded King as the movement's undisputed leader. "Those who a few months ago thought of the young King as a brilliant comet shooting across the sky never to be seen again," Payne explained, "came away from the rally with a firmer conviction than ever of his mature, wise leadership when he pinpointed the whole basic struggle of the Negro in these simple phrases: 'Give us the ballot and we will quietly and nonviolently, without rancor or bitterness, implement the Supreme Court's decision of May 17, 1954. Give us the ballot and we will no long have to worry the federal government about our basic rights.'"

But, having been among Randolph's field soldiers in 1941, Payne couldn't resist reminding readers of the labor leader's role in the unfolding events. "Indirectly," Payne wrote, "the day was a tribute to the man who first began the agitation for full citizenship, 15 years ago in June, A. Philip Randolph who conceived the idea of a march on Washington."

THE SUNDAY AFTER THE PRAYER pilgrimage Payne went to the Nixons' home. It was the first time the Nixons had hosted a gathering in their new house in the exclusive Spring Valley neighborhood in Northwest Washington. To celebrate their purchase and score some political points, Nixon had invited reporters who had accompanied him on his trip to Ghana to tour the three-story house. In particular, the vice-president wanted it known that he and Pat had struck the restrictive covenant on the deed forbidding the sale of the house to anyone other than a Caucasian. Nixon told Payne he had been impressed by the prayer pilgrimage. This was good news, because while in Washington, King had sent Nixon a list of dates for the proposed meeting between the two that the vice-president had promised while in Ghana.

Payne continued to be impressed with Nixon's avowed commitment to civil rights, but not all of her colleagues in the black press were so smitten by the man. "Although he was probably in the company of Negroes more than any other member of the administration, Nixon never seemed really comfortable in that company," noted *Jet's*

Simeon Booker. In fact, this discomfort was awkwardly evident when Booker and his wife arrived at the Nixon house that night. Richard and Pat Nixon were overly effusive in their welcome and left Booker completely puzzled. The mystery was soon resolved when it turned out they had mistaken Booker for another black White House correspondent, the Republican sympathizer Louis Lautier.

Two days after her visit to the Nixon home, Payne reported that King would have his audience with the vice-president on June 13. In the company of Abernathy, King arrived at Nixon's office at 3:30 in the afternoon of the appointed day. Labor Secretary James P. Mitchell, who served as vice-chairman of Nixon's contract committee, joined them. The meeting, originally planned for one hour, stretched to two hours and forty-five minutes as Payne and other reporters cooled their heels in the corridor outside the office. When King and Abernathy emerged from the meeting, they were escorted quickly to an awaiting car, leaving behind a frustrated group of journalists.

Luckily for Payne, who needed some comment from the participants if she was going to file a piece about the meeting, King and Abernathy met with reporters later in the day at a Washington hotel. The two claimed the meeting had produced concessions. The administration pledged to push for the passage of a civil rights bill and Nixon also promised that King and other civil rights leaders would get a chance to meet with Eisenhower.

Nixon, in Payne's eyes, was the hero of the day. Unlike the Democrats who pledged support to civil rights, this Republican was taking tangible action.

CHAPTER 22

A TOOTHLESS ACT

WORK ON THE CIVIL RIGHTS BILL BEGAN IN EARNEST shortly after the King-Nixon meeting. For the first time since the nineteenth century, Congress gave serious consideration to legislation aimed at protecting the voting rights of African Americans, only 20 percent of whom were able to register as voters at the time, and at expanding the federal government's right to monitor civil rights.

The House of Representatives easily rejected amendments intended on watering down the measure; 167 Republicans joined with 118 Democrats to send the measure to the Senate, where the real battle lay.

Ethel Payne was optimistic. She predicted the bill would pass the Senate and provided her readers with a senator-by-senator tally showing thirty-seven Republican and twenty-two Democratic votes, for a total of fifty-nine, ten more than needed for passage. At some length she described the major stumbling blocks and the implications for the 1958 and 1960 elections. "It is no secret that both the Democrats and the Republicans would like to make political hay of civil rights," Payne wrote. "Perhaps," she added, "because civil rights has been for so long a football, falling just short of a touchdown, there is more skepticism on the part of the average person as to the Simon pure motives of those who so loudly espouse its cause."

From the press gallery Payne watched what she called "the long-awaited showdown" get under way. And showdown it was, presaging many future legislative battles over civil rights. Southern opponents used parliamentary skills developed over years in power to buy time and weaken the bill. In fact, on the very first day Payne watched a demonstration of their wiliness when Georgia senator Richard Russell first protested the inclusion of the bill to the Senate calendar on the basis of a printing error and then insisted the bill be referred to the Judiciary Committee.

Led by Southern Democratic senators Russell, James Eastland, Strom Thurmond, Sam Ervin, Herman Talmadge, John Stennis, Russell Long, and Harry F. Byrd, the opposition concentrated its fire on two sections of the legislation: Section III, which would expand the Justice Department's authority to enforce civil rights through civil and criminal proceedings, and Section IV, which would reserve to judges the power to determine the fate of civil rights law violators instead of a Southern jury. On this provision, the Southerners sought to amend the bill to include trial by jury for anyone who disobeyed a judge's order, such as in the case of a white official blocking blacks from voting. The innocuous-sounding amendment was a deadly alteration to the bill's enforcement powers because in the South a jury would be all white.

Payne sought to use her reporting to keep the heat on vacillating liberals, many of whom were now currying favor with the growing black vote. For instance, when Massachusetts Democratic senator John F. Kennedy voted with Southern senators to bottle the bill up in the Judiciary Committee, which was controlled by one of their own, Senator Eastland, and in favor of another parliamentary move aimed at slowing the bill's progress, Payne cornered the senator. "Kennedy," she reported, "insisted that the issue involved was over a matter of procedure and had nothing to do with his position on civil rights. 'I just felt it was a bad precedent to act in bypassing a Senate committee,' he said."

In the interview, which she claimed was an exclusive, Kennedy was visibly angry at having his civil rights credentials challenged. "I have no apologies to make for my action. I think my eleven-year record in the House and Senate is a demonstration of my position on civil rights, and this has not changed at all."

By the end of July, Payne reported with chagrin on the mortal wounds being inflicted on the bill. "When the smoke cleared away, the South had triumphantly succeeded in tearing out the entire Section III and then were free to rally forces for the next attack to append a trial by jury clause into the decimated bill."

IN EARLY AUGUST the bill faced what appeared to be its Appomattox. Majority leader Lyndon B. Johnson made his move, desperate to prevent the debate from splitting apart his party and endangering his leadership. Already his fingerprints were on the successful effort to strike Section III. He now brought the amendment concerning trial by jury to a vote on the floor. An angry Payne tried to expose Johnson's tactics, publicizing his work at getting recalcitrant colleagues to toe the line by enlisting help from the powerful head of the mine workers' union and logrolling on bills of parochial interest.

"Shock-haired Jack Kennedy," Payne said, "who is glassy-eyed from star gazing at 1960, toppled over like a ten pin in a bowling alley after his pal, Sen. George Smathers of Florida, and Lyndon Johnson put a fatherly arm around him and recounted some political facts of life to him." According to Payne, Kennedy was not alone in succumbing to Johnson's pressure tactics. Senator John Pastore, the first Italian American elected to the Senate, caved after getting assurances from Southern senators that they would vote to increase immigration quotas. "On Tuesday, if the vote had come, the amendment would have lost," Payne said. "But by Wednesday, the Johnson bulldozer was mowing down resistance like hay in a field."

To Payne the treachery seemed all the more painful after watching her political mentor Clarence Mitchell go without sleep and food. He haunted the corridors and cloakrooms of the Capitol in search of votes right up to the moment when Senator Thurmond made his epic effort to halt the final passage of the bill by launching what was to prove to be the longest filibuster ever in Senate history, twenty-four hours and eighteen minutes. Payne remained in the chamber until a little after midnight. As she departed, she spotted Mitchell still doggedly keeping watch, virtually alone, in the gallery across from the press seats. When she took her seat in the morning she looked across the Senate and saw that a haggard and red-eyed Mitchell was still there.

"I have watched him from the press gallery, sitting in the visitors' section of both houses, listening to abuse of the NAACP, the Negro people, and assaults upon the bill from the North and the South," Payne said months later, reflecting on the moment. "We all sat watching while Sen. Lyndon Johnson, the most astute maneuverer on the Hill, cracked his whip and marshaled his forces to cut the guts and heart out of the bill."

Thurmond's speechifying resistance was shut down and the watered-down bill was approved. In the end, all that was left of the measure was to establish a civil rights commission and grant the Justice Department limited power to file voting discrimination suits. As with the 1955 *Brown v. Board II* opinion, which set out a vague timeline for the desegregation of schools, the Civil Rights Act dismayed Payne. In contrast, the white press, except in the South, heralded its passage. The wire services called the bill's passage "history-making" because Congress had not approved a civil rights measure since 1875, and the *New York Times* hailed it as "incomparably the most significant domestic action of any Congress in this century."

Payne and civil rights leaders knew better. She warned her readers that what President Eisenhower would soon sign was "the battered, almost unrecognizable version of the civil rights bill" and that Congress had passed it only "after virtually all the teeth had been pulled from the original administration version."

In the *Defender* Payne eviscerated the Democrats, highlighting how liberals from the newly elected Frank Church to John F. Kennedy had "broken faith with Negro voters." In this moment Payne became the Democrats' Cassandra. "Now, the Northern and Western Democrats are splitting up and realigning themselves with the reactionary South, leaving only a small band of liberals standing alone." But as was true with the words of the mythological prophetess, Payne's predictions fell on deaf ears.

The Panglossian attitude displayed by the white press toward the act highlighted the segregation of the nation's press. It also reflected the sense among many whites that supporting civil rights was a benevolent gesture, whereas blacks viewed their struggle as an effort to obtain rights that were owed them. As a result, the mainstream media that had heralded *Brown v. Board* in 1954 and now praised the passage of the Civil Rights Act did so for their historic momentousness without focusing on the restrictive elements found in the details. White readers were thus left with an impression of steady judicial and legislative progress on race issues. But blacks, clued in to the limitations of these victories by the reporting of their newspapers, were not so sanguine. In many ways the white press was setting up its readers for bewilderment in the coming years when blacks expressed their frustration and rage at the lack of change.

AS THE CIVIL RIGHTS ACT made its way to a vacationing Eisenhower in Newport, Rhode Island, for a presidential signature, a rebellion in the hinterlands became national news. On the morning of Tuesday, September 4, 1957, nine black students prepared to enter the all-white Central High School in Little Rock, Arkansas, as part of a court-approved integration plan. As a precaution, civil rights activist Daisy Bates, who published the local black newspaper with her husband, and some ministers decided to bring the students to the school as a group. Unfortunately, there was no phone at the house of one of them.

So, clutching her notebook, fifteen-year-old Elizabeth Eckford set off for the school on her own, wearing round dark glasses and a freshly ironed white blouse and skirt with a black checkerboard pattern that she had made. Awaiting Eckford was a cordon of armed soldiers from the Arkansas National Guard that Governor Orval Faubus had ordered into place to bar the entry of the nine black students. All by herself, Eckford approached. "A nigger," yelled a member of the growing mob, "they're coming, here they come." Rebuffed by the soldiers in front of her and facing an angry crowd behind, Eckford turned and walked toward the municipal bus stop to return home. As she did, Hazel Bryan, a white student, heckled her. The press camera shutters clicked. The television news film rolled. The images of Eckford stoically walking away followed by Bryan, her face distorted in anger, were soon splashed on newspaper front pages and television screens worldwide.

The nine children were then kept home, lawyers for the NAACP returned to court, and a standstill ensued. Payne caught a flight to Little Rock. She wasn't the only reporter with the name of the erstwhile sleepy state capital on her plane ticket. Dozens of national newspaper, magazine, and broadcast network reporters poured into town. Among the black reporters who arrived were Payne's friends James Hicks and Alex Wilson—both of whom were getting used to finding their discovery in Japan turning up at major civil rights battlefields—and Carl Rowan. As none of the black reporters were welcome in Little Rock's motels, they found beds in private homes.

After landing at Adams Field, Little Rock's airport, which was named after an Arkansas National Guardsman who was killed in the line of duty twenty years earlier, Payne headed to the city's black business district. Much like Chicago's Black Belt, the vibrant and thriving Ninth Street was a city within a city, filled with black-owned barbershops and beauty parlors, funeral homes, insurance agencies, pharmacies, jewelers, and other enterprises. And it was also where one went to hear the likes of Count Basie at the Taborian Hall Dreamland nightclub or eat one's fill of pork chops with black-eyed peas and turnip greens at the Flamingo Hotel.

Here Payne found "sidewalk philosophers" who "spit tobacco and lambast 'Old Faubus'" and gladly shared their view that the governor had created an unnecessary crisis and castigated the state's Democratic Party. "Before Sept. 3, Little Rock was just the capital of Arkansas," Payne wrote in her first dispatch from the scene. "Now thanks to the foolhardiness of Gov. Faubus, it has become infamous as the seat of defiance of the federal government and it looks as though the governor will have to reap the wild wind of his own undoing."

AFTER A NIGHT'S REST in a private home, Payne received a dinner invitation from Lee Lorch, a white mathematics professor at the small black Philander Smith College in Little Rock. The two had met the previous year when Payne was traveling for her "South at the Crossroads" series. In fact, she had written two articles about Lorch, tracing his repeated firing from colleges as an example of the treatment accorded to whites who joined the civil rights movement. "Lee Lorch and his family had been hounded through four states from the North to South like refugees in displacement camps," Payne had told her readers. "And in the process of punishing Lee Lorch for his views, three proud institutions of learning have been made to grovel in the dust and bow the knee to bigotry."

Payne was particularly interested in reconnecting with the Lorches because on the day Eckford had faced the troops and the mob, it had been Grace Lorch who had stepped forward to protect the young student as she sat alone on the bench at the bus stop. Enduring catcalls, Lorch had remained with Eckford until she safely boarded a bus. She was also hankering for some decent food. "The restaurant situation for Negroes in Little Rock is worse than bad," she said.

Lee Lorch picked up Payne from the house where she was staying. As they drove through town, Lorch said it was the first time they had a guest over to their apartment overlooking the Capitol building and he cautioned Payne that something untoward might be said.

At the building they entered the elevator, operated by a young black woman. "I don't believe I ever got your name," Lorch said to the woman.

"Frankie," she replied.

"Oh, but you do have another name, don't you?"

"Sure, it's Frankie Coleman."

"Miss or Mrs.?"

"Mrs.," replied Coleman, at which point Lorch introduced Payne, calling the operator "Mrs. Coleman."

"Frankie, looked slightly nonplussed at this departure from southern tradition," said Payne, "but new gal of the South as she is, she didn't quibble over the fact that I was riding in the front elevator."

As soon as they reached the apartment, the telephone rang. The manager was calling because he understood that the Lorches were "entertaining a colored guest and this was in violation of the rules and when would he be vacating?" Lorch replied he knew nothing of the rule and "he was accustomed to entertaining his friends, whatever their pigmentation happened to be."

The following morning the Lorches received an eviction notice. "Right now," Payne reported to her readers, "Little Rock to me is about the crummiest corner on the map. When I got home, Henry Cabot Lodge was on TV sounding off at Russia and giving the commies hell. Well, he should be in Little Rock now and see what's going on."

PAYNE SPENT HER FINAL DAY in Little Rock with the nine students at the home of Arlevia and Hosanna Claire Mothershed, whose daughter Thelma was an eleventh grader. All of them were honors students in the Negro schools they had attended, which was why they had been selected for entry into Central High School. "It was refreshing to watch this group of bright uninhibited and unafraid students calmly discuss the situation which swirls around them in the angry bilious pattern of race prejudice," Payne said.

"It never crossed the minds of either the children or their parents that they should toss in the towel and go back to Horace Mann, the all-Negro school," Payne reported. "They all seem to realize that much more is at stake than just the issue of whether they will be permitted to attend a mixed school and they are fully aware of their responsibility in history."

Payne left Little Rock as the story shifted to a meeting between Governor Faubus and President Eisenhower engineered by Arkansas U.S. representative Brooks Hays. Although he had signed the 1956 Southern Manifesto denouncing *Brown v. Board*, Hays was valiantly trying to resolve the crisis in his district by bringing the two men together. His efforts to find a middle ground made him as many enemies among segregationists as among desegregationists. Rumors circulated that the governor would capitulate, and in Little Rock citizens remained glued to the radio. For his part, Eisenhower did not seem to expect much from the meeting. He simply hoped it wouldn't interfere with his vacation and made plans for a round of golf in the afternoon in Newport, Rhode Island.

Payne caught up with Faubus at the Sheraton Biltmore Hotel in

Providence, Rhode Island. "He was courtly and gracious," said Payne. "Almost as chivalrous as his friend, Congressman Brooks Hays, who accompanied him." Hays came over to Payne to shake her hand and tell her how nice it was to see her again. For his part, Faubus posed for photographers pointedly shaking hands with Wallace Terry Jr.,* a black student reporter for the *Daily Herald*, which was published by Brown University. A photograph of the two appeared on the front page of the following day's *New York Times*.

At his press conference in the hotel, Faubus spotted Payne— the only woman in attendance—and corrected his greeting to "ladies and gentlemen." Payne gained Faubus's attention a second time. Would he, asked Payne, lift his order banning black reporters from Central High School? There had been no intention to bar any reporter, Faubus replied. Rather, he asserted that the National Guard troops had been zealous in their efforts to prevent anyone from getting hurt. Payne told Faubus she was heading back to Little Rock. What assurance could he give that she would be allowed in the school? Faubus assured her that every courtesy and cooperation would be shown to all reporters alike. Payne doubted the governor's word.

Payne watched with delight when San Francisco African American disk jockey "Magnificent" Montague, who managed to sneak in among the reporters, agitated the otherwise unproductive press conference. Montague and some other staffers from KSAN had come east to deliver 4,000 telegrams and letters to the president,

---

* Terry would later become a reporter for the *Washington Post* and *Time*. He went to Vietnam in 1967 (the same year Payne would go) and became the first permanent African American correspondent assigned to cover the war. He later published the bestselling *Bloods: An Oral History of the Vietnam War by Black Veterans*. His *Missing Pages: Black Journalists of Modern America; An Oral History*, which was published posthumously, featured a chapter on Payne.

and the station was planning a rally on Sunday in support of the Little Rock Nine, at which Elizabeth Eckford was scheduled to appear. "Governor," said Montague, "that little girl says she's scared, but she wants to go back to school. Why don't you give the kids a chance to learn, let them go back to school Monday, and if there's any trouble, then call out the National Guard to protect them and not keep them out."

"Grimly," said Payne, "the governor replied: 'I did not come here to debate the question.'" But Montague was not done. When Faubus tried to make his way out of the crowded room, Montague cornered him. In what Payne described as an "injured tone," Faubus said to the disk jockey, "Why do you try to crucify me? I'm the most liberal governor in the South."

"Do you call pointing guns at children liberal?" Montague snapped.

THE NEXT MORNING EISENHOWER and Faubus met at Newport's naval base. The ambiguous statements issued by the two men following the parley did nothing to resolve the crisis. "Gov. Oval Faubus seems to have come off with a fatherly pat from President Eisenhower in exchange for a promise to try to be good," Payne said. "One thing is sure," Payne wrote in her front-page account, "the meeting of the president and the governor gave newsmen one of the roughest kinds of assignment to cover to come up with so little. It was a flop of a news story."

But Payne took a chance. Gathering what fragments of information she had, Payne predicted that Faubus would withdraw the troops upon his return to Little Rock. Apparently the president was of the same belief. Instead, on Monday the nation found that Faubus was sticking to his guns, and the soldiers remained in position guarding the white school from an incursion of nine black teenagers wanting nothing more than to hit the books.

What with the traveling, the long hours, and perhaps the wet weather in Rhode Island, Payne came down with a fever. She called Louis Martin in Chicago and the two agreed that instead of returning to Little Rock she ought to head back to Washington. Taking her place in Little Rock, Alex Wilson watched when a few days later a federal court ordered the removal of the Arkansas National Guard from the school. Without the troops present, the mob prevailed. Wilson was violently assaulted and the nine black students remained away. On September 24, President Eisenhower, still in Newport on vacation, ordered Army troops to Little Rock, marking the first time since Reconstruction that federal forces were being used to protect blacks in the South. Under the watch of the soldiers, the nine students entered the high school the following morning for their first full day of classes.

In Washington, a recovering Payne learned from her sources that the FBI was convinced Faubus not only encouraged violence during the standoff but also had plotted some of the disorderly activity that swirled around the school. In a front-page story, Payne claimed that the FBI report, coming on top of Faubus's unwillingness to back down during the Newport meeting, led the president to call out the troops.

As the Little Rock story died down, Payne engaged in some frivolity. Queen Elizabeth and her husband, Prince Phillip, arrived on a state visit, causing Washington to put off its concerns about race. In fact, Eisenhower postponed a meeting with black leaders set up by Adam Clayton Powell to accommodate the royal couple. Filing no less than five articles, Payne exhibited a schoolgirl's excitement, just as she had three years earlier when the Queen Mother had come. "The Queen's no frump as some bloke has intimated," Payne told her readers. "I wish I had her style and grace."

White House press secretary James Hagerty gave Payne a ticket to a football game between the Universities of Maryland and North Carolina, both of which had made some modest progress toward

integrating their student bodies. Pretending to cover the game for
the paper's sports department, Payne sent a lighthearted dispatch
back to Chicago. "Don't tell anybody that I don't know a forward
pass from a line drive, but I'll wager the family jewels that I know
when a touchdown is made."

CHAPTER 23

THE VICE-PRESIDENT
COMES CALLING

I F WHITE AMERICA BELIEVED THE CIVIL RIGHTS ACT OF 1957 was all the legal protection blacks needed in order to vote in the South, a subscription to the *Chicago Defender* would have set them straight. Unlike the mainstream press, Ethel Payne's newspaper made it its mission to document the violence and atrocities perpetrated on African Americans, especially those in the South willing to demand their equal rights. "I am just beginning to realize a grim truth," reported Payne from Birmingham, Alabama, less than two months after the president signed the act. "Living in the South today is about as uneasy and dangerous as it is along the Gaza Strip in the Middle East."

Payne had returned to Birmingham to cover the launching of a statewide voter registration drive, one of the first following the passage of the Civil Rights Act. Those counties in which African Americans outnumbered whites by as much as three to one were also the counties with the lowest black voter registration. In three of the counties there were no black voters registered at all.

Among her first calls was to Arthur Shores, the lawyer who had represented Autherine Lucy in her case against the University of Alabama and King in his trial in Montgomery. He invited her to his house for a Saturday-evening party. When Payne got there, she found his home to be like a fortress. Powerful floodlights lit the yards, a guard stood watch, and neighbors were keeping a round-the-clock vigil. Thirty minutes before she arrived, a bullet shot from a speeding car hit the window of the house. It did not shatter the plate glass but was found on the flagstone walkway. "Once again," Payne said, "as she has been for so many times before over a long period, Mrs. Shores was terribly upset, but she didn't let it interfere with her job as hostess."

The next morning the volunteers arrived for the two days of voter registration training. "Most of them," said Payne as she watched them come in, "were good plain folk showing the wear and tear of toil and living under almost indescribable oppression." Shores and another lawyer explained to the group that if they, or those they helped, were denied the right to register, complaints could be brought to the U.S. Department of Justice under the provisions of the new civil rights law. "But," Payne said, "the biggest question in the minds of the delegates, most of whose names must be kept anonymous to avoid reprisals, is how to overcome the fear and violence that come with attempting to get registered."

In Payne's eyes the year had not been a good one for civil rights. "The old saying that things sometimes get worse before they get better can be used to characterize the year 1957 in race relations in America," she wrote. "It was a time of both gains and losses. Mostly, the losses can be chalked up to failure to follow through on the psychological advantages of great decisions."

ON HER DEFENDER SALARY, Payne continued to have money troubles. Although she lived modestly, she had two weaknesses when it came to spending. First, she made up for her paper's frugality by frequently dipping into her own funds in the pursuit of a news story. Second, Payne was a spendthrift when it came to others. No matter how little was in her wallet, Payne was always the first to offer to pay for a meal, and she always brought presents back from her exotic journeys for her family and friends. Payne was like a fairy godmother, recalled one of her nieces. "Whenever she would return from one of many trips to faraway places it was a special treat for us," she said. "There were gifts for each one . . . She never forgot." She also never failed to donate to a cause when asked. Her monthly paycheck of $433 was quickly used up.

In September, she brought up the idea of picking up some part-time work from others with her publisher John Sengstacke, whose demands for loyalty made the subject of money a risky one to broach. "I might say I'm doing this because I feel I can talk to you quite frankly without being scared like I used to," she said. "Uh-huh, yes I was!"

She told him the political arm of the AFL-CIO had asked her to edit its newsletter. It was essentially the same work she had done for the CIO's political action committee that had gotten her in trouble earlier with Eisenhower's press secretary when he tried to muzzle her questioning of the president. This time, however, she would work through an advertising agency firm that handled public relations for labor. "Thus, there will be no chance of all the fiasco that occurred in 1955," she assured Sengstacke. "No bylines and no other identification. They are fully aware of the necessity for not jeopardizing my position with the papers." She gave her boss her word that taking on this extra task would not diminish the effort she put into her work with the *Defender*. "In fact," she said, "I'll be redoubling my efforts to do a good job."

Sengstacke agreed and Payne added $900 to her annual income for that year, a 15 percent increase.

PAYNE OPENED 1958 WITH a lengthy and favorable profile of Richard Nixon called "The Constant Campaigner." The vice-president was already campaigning so hard and effectively for the 1960 presidential race that the young Massachusetts senator John F. Kennedy predicted that Nixon would be the Republican nominee. During Nixon's trip to Africa, Payne told her readers, the vice-president was so enthusiastic in embracing a tribal chief for the cameras, particularly those from the black press, that a newsman quipped, "Well, this is the first time I've known an American presidential campaign to be run in far-off Africa."

Payne's assessment of Nixon focused primarily on his growing willingness to speak out against segregation, his work with the committee charged with eliminating discrimination in government hiring, and his role on civil rights issues on Capitol Hill. "When he made a recent speech in Asheville, N.C., attacking racial discrimination and calling for compliance at the community level, Western Union delivered advance copies of the speech to reporters' doors," reported Payne. It was the kind of coverage in the black press for which Nixon campaign managers dreamed.

Shortly after the article appeared, a staff member of the House Government Information Subcommittee sought Payne out. He wanted to know if she had any evidence that Eisenhower's press secretary James Hagerty had actually obtained copies of her tax returns as columnist Drew Pearson had alleged in 1955. Payne had no evidence to show that Hagerty had. She wrote to Hagerty to say she was sorry the matter had surfaced again. "As far as I'm concerned it's forgotten about," she said. "Personally, I think you deserve the Medal of Honor for endurance in a grueling occupation."

The truth of the matter, however, was that the administration remained hostile to the black press. "Coverage of Eisenhower's second term was a pathetic chore for a Negro reporter," recalled Simeon Booker, who stopped coming to press conferences since the president ceased calling on black reporters. "Four years of attending White House press conferences and observing the president's reaction to the wide range of questions put to him have convinced me that his greatest sensitivity is to queries on civil rights," Payne said. "The moment something in this area is posed, the Ike temper goes up and the defensive bristles become erect like porcupine quills."

In February, Ethel Payne, *Jet* magazine's Simeon Booker, and another reporter decided it would be fun to hold a reunion of the journalists who went to Africa with Nixon the previous year. Overseas trips by presidents and vice-presidents were still rare, and reporters often held anniversary get-togethers to remember the frequent engine troubles, bad accommodations, and indigestible food (at least for First World journalists), and share tales that were never reported.

"Where should we have the gathering?" asked Booker. "We want to do a little bopping and a little boozing."

"Well, let's have it at Ethel Payne's," said the third member of the group.

"I don't have anything in the apartment," said Payne, who had just moved into a five-story brick building on Belmont Road near Eighteenth Street.

"Well, that's fine," said her companions. "We can boogie on the floor."

So the gang of three set Saturday, March 1, as the date. At Booker's insistence, Payne sent a note to Nixon. "As March 1 approaches," she wrote, "there are nostalgic memories of taking off last year at this time on that never-to-be-forgotten 'safari' across Africa." Would the vice-president and his wife join the gathering?

The following Tuesday, Payne received a telephone call from Nixon's office. "The vice-president and Mrs. Nixon will be happy to attend the party," said the caller.

"Well, I panicked!" said Payne. "I just absolutely panicked."

Payne's new apartment, far roomier than her old haunts, was essentially unfurnished. Or at least she thought so. So she went to visit Hecht's, one of Washington's venerable department stores, and sought out the manager.

"I've got a problem," she told him.

"What's your problem?" he asked.

"The vice-president is coming to a party we're having on Saturday evening, and I don't have any money, and I don't know when I'm going to be able to pay for this, and I don't have any furniture."

The manager kindly consented to send a truckload of furniture, even dishes, on credit up to her new place. Payne's next-door neighbor got into the act and agreed to open her apartment and put together a spread of food. The group even procured a band for the building's foyer.

On the night of the party Richard and Pat Nixon arrived in high spirits. Protruding from his coat was a bottle of bourbon with a label that read "The President's Choice: Richard M. Nixon." He gave it to Payne, and in turn the group presented the vice-president with a commemorative leather pocket notebook and a white orchid corsage for his wife. To everyone's surprise, after the exchange of gifts and toasts, the Nixons stayed around for several hours. For Richard Nixon, the 1960 presidential campaign was under way and the room held influential African Americans. Not all became converts by his willingness to socialize with them. Booker, who cohosted the party, remained a skeptic. "Still, blacks simply didn't trust Nixon," he said. In his eight years in Washington, Booker noted, Nixon had failed to hire a single black person to work in his office despite urging employers to do so.

Several days later, the *Defender* reported in an article probably written by Payne herself that the paper's Washington correspondent went about her duties tired "but with her head in the clouds." Both Richard and Pat Nixon sent thank-you notes to Payne addressing her as "Ethel," citing their friendship and how impressed they had been by her collection of memorabilia from her travels around the world. Booker filed his report for *Jet*. It heralded Nixon's journey to Payne's place as "marking the first time a vice-president has socialized at the home of a Negro in Washington."

A FEW WEEKS AFTER the party, Payne fell ill again. But unlike in September, when a rest at home was sufficient, she was hospitalized at Washington's Providence Hospital on March 27. The doctors were concerned that there was a malignancy associated with her illness and took X-rays and conducted various tests. Finding none, and with Payne's health improving, the hospital sent her home in the middle of April. "After being in bed for two weeks and undergoing all the tests," Payne wrote soon after getting home, "I found myself really weak and I am just getting my sea legs back again."

She would need them. In the midst of her health ordeal, Payne's bosses in Chicago had dropped a bombshell. Louis Martin, her editor, informed her that after she had spent five years in Washington, they wanted her to come back to Chicago. The paper had begun subscribing to the UPI wire service, expanding its coverage of news from Washington and around the world. The publisher no longer thought it worth the expense of maintaining a correspondent in Washington.

Payne was stunned. She immediately appealed to Martin, recalling the circumstances in which he had sent her to Washington in the first place. "Do you remember back in 1953 when Ed Goodwin offered me 49 percent of the stock in the *Oklahoma Eagle* to come there and edit the paper and how you talked to me like a Dutch uncle?" Payne asked. "I still double [over] when I think of what you said about the grasshoppers and the stock consisting of a chair and a desk. It was your eloquent persuasion which made me settle on Washington. So it puzzled me when you said recently you couldn't understand why I like Washington so much because Chicago was the place for real opportunity."

At length, almost as if she were writing a legal brief, Payne spoke of the enhanced reputation of the paper since she had come to Washington. "A check of the *Congressional Record* would show that the *Defender* is more often quoted than any other Negro paper," she said. "This is not mere happenstance. It means that we have national respect."

On top of her good work, said Payne, she had come cheap. She had not received a raise in four years and supplemented her $5,200 to $5,400 annual salary from the *Defender* with freelance work. But her hometown offered no extra work of the sort she had been able to get in Washington. "Therefore to come back to Chicago now would mean a real financial hardship."

Payne consulted her Newspaper Guild contract with the *Defender*. It included a clause that prohibited transferring employees to work in another city without their consent and stated that employees should not be penalized for refusing to accept a transfer. Frostily addressing her note to "Mr. Martin," Payne declined the transfer.

The conflict was bizarre. For years the paper had touted Payne's presence in Washington, had used her name in advertisements, and, most tellingly, had built its headlines around her rather than the news. Now it was treating her callously.

John Sengstacke was taciturn as to his motives. A strong Eisenhower supporter, he may have grown discouraged with Payne's drift away from her positive coverage of the administration to her now-disparaging articles. If this was not the cause of Sengstacke's unhappiness with Payne in Washington, money was certainly an issue. Since going daily two years earlier, the hoped-for additional advertising and increase in circulation had not materialized; meanwhile, editorial costs had risen substantially to meet the need for more news copy. Sengstacke had also purchased a new building and a new press, which by his own admission that spring was an ill-timed decision, as the nation was wallowing in a recession. Cutting costs was an imperative.

However much she argued, Payne knew that Sengstacke's decision, for which Martin was only the messenger, was irreversible. In her entreaties, Payne revealed both her gratitude and affection for Martin. "If I have amounted to anything in the world of journalism, it has been because you have guided me and I have always had the greatest confidence in your advice, even though some times we may have irked each other. I should have qualified that to say I did most of the irking."

The answer to her appeal came swiftly. The *Defender* sent her a formal announcement that it was closing its Washington bureau. Payne was flummoxed. She turned to the guild for help. Unfortunately, the union couldn't do anything beyond determine that she would receive payment for severance and vacation time. Because she had refused to go back to Chicago and the Washington office was being closed, the paper "reluctantly considers that you have resigned," explained a guild officer.

In August, Sengstacke sent Payne a letter along with a check for $1,004.60, the balance due her. He added a postscript: "I know that you are and will always be a *Defender* booster."

CHAPTER 24

THE DOOR REMAINS CLOSED

I F THE *CHICAGO DEFENDER* NO LONGER WANTED HER IN Washington, Ethel Payne decided to find someone who did. She turned to organized labor. The CIO, which earlier had given Payne freelance work, had merged with the American Federation of Labor (AFL). The resulting labor behemoth found a place for her in its new ten-story modernist edifice on Sixteenth Street overlooking St. John's Church, known as "the Church of the Presidents."

In June 1958, less than a month after leaving the *Defender*, Payne was installed as the first black employee at the AFL-CIO's Committee on Political Education (COPE), which worked for the election of candidates friendly to the labor movement and tried to ensure their subsequent loyalty by monitoring and publicizing their voting records once in office. With a salary of $170 a week, 60 percent more than what she had earned at the paper, Payne became the highest-ranking African American women in organized labor.

Payne put her pen to work promoting the agenda of the labor movement, particularly among African Americans and women. She channeled her journalistic experience into producing two biweekly publications, one that went to the wives of union members and another for minority leaders in and out of the labor movement. She also prepared press releases for black newspapers.

But the union had hired more than a writer. In Payne, COPE found someone who could carry the union's message to previously impenetrable black organizations. Within a year, Payne logged more than 100,000 miles in travel attending such varied gatherings as the Imperial Court Daughters of Isis, an auxiliary to the Ancient Egyptian Arabic Order Nobles Mystic Shrine of North and South America and Its Jurisdictions, and the Improved Benevolent and Protective Order of the Elks of the World, both African American versions of the white fraternal orders better known as the Shriners and the Elks. Payne even attended the annual convention of black beauticians in Cleveland, which welcomed civil rights activists, especially a female one.

With the hike in salary Payne converted her membership in the NAACP, dating back more than twenty years, into a life membership. The $500 gift, however, went astray and it wasn't until months later that the organization acknowledged it. "No voluntary organization chooses to offend anyone," Roy Wilkins wrote in a contrite letter. "But if I had a choice, you would have been the last person to be accorded this treatment." A month later, wearing one of her distinctive feathered fascinator headbands, Payne went to the house of the Right Reverend Stephen Gill Spottswood, a member of the NAACP national board, to receive her life membership plaque.

After years of being on the outside of Washington, Payne was on the inside.

WORKING FOR A LABOR UNION removed any remaining fetters on Payne's partisanship. In early 1959, Clare B. Williams, the assistant chairman of the Republican National Committee, returned from a tour of the South and proclaimed that moderation, understanding, and time would be required to end segregation. "To say that I was indignant is an understatement," Payne wrote to Williams, making sure to send copies to the GOP's Val Washington and others.

"Seldom have I seen a more contemptuous attitude displayed in your quoted statements on the integration question." The word *moderation* has the connotation to black Americans of "never never," Payne said. "Worse still, you have committed the Republican Party to condoning lynchings, violence, and defiance of the law."

Payne also found herself freed from the conventional journalistic restraint on seeking personal favors from those one covers. Back in Chicago, her nephew James A. Johnson, who was a good student and ambitious, worried that his public school's rough-and-tumble student culture was endangering his dream of becoming a doctor. Payne's years on Capitol Hill and her network of contacts gave her an idea. During the 1957 Christmas holidays, Payne talked with Congressman Barratt O'Hara, an avuncular member of the Chicago delegation and a onetime newspaperman, about the possibility of nominating Johnson, who lived in his district, for a position as a Capitol page. If the plan worked, Johnson would come and live with Payne and attend the Capitol Page School, benefiting from its top-flight instruction. The idea excited her nephew, to whom Payne had been the "mysterious aunt who was always doing exciting stuff."

In the summer of 1958, Johnson had reached the minimum age of fourteen and O'Hara pushed ahead with the nomination for the congressional session beginning in January. O'Hara was under the impression that there had been black pages in the past. "I did not want to push the boy into an integration battle that might prove embarrassing," he said. He was mistaken. At the time, neither the Senate nor the House believed it had ever had a black page.

In a chamber in which everything from committee assignments to parking and stationery allotments was in the firm control of veteran Southern representatives, the nomination of a black youngster as a page remained out of the question in 1959. But the committee that made the decisions regarding pages was under the misapprehension that O'Hara and Representative Thomas O'Brien, the state's senior member of the congressional delegation, were sponsoring the same page candidate, a white teenage boy. The staff only glanced at O'Hara's letter before letting him know his nomination had been approved. Then the trouble began.

THINKING EVERYTHING WAS ALL SET, O'Hara's staff telephoned Payne several times to plan for Johnson's arrival and provide a list of the clothing—blue suit, white shirt, black tie—that the youngster would need when he reported for work. Payne called her sister and told her to put herself and her son on a plane.

Only when the two arrived did O'Hara and Payne learn that the chair of the patronage committee, a Democrat from Pennsylvania, had declared the young boy was not in line for a page position, nor would he get one. The Southern leadership of the House had put the kibosh on Johnson's nomination and was surprised and furious at O'Hara's gumption. Both O'Hara and Payne acted dumbfounded, although they had to have known of the potential roadblocks. While leaders claimed the denial was procedural in nature, no one was fooled. "Most Negroes are firmly convinced that Jimmy Johnson was knocked out by the Dixiecrats," wrote Louis Martin in his *Defender* column.

Meanwhile the press, white and black, glommed onto the story. The *Chicago Tribune*'s Washington correspondent persuaded Johnson to be interviewed on the steps of the Capitol, where he posed for an Associated Press photographer. "The Southern congressmen don't want me," Johnson said, almost in tears.

With the Page School's door apparently solidly locked shut, Payne enrolled Johnson in a Washington public school "while," she told reporters, "we continue to try for a page position." But none materialized. Instead, O'Hara and Payne came up with an alternative plan. According to the rules, one did not have to be a page, only an employee of Congress, to attend the Page School. So five members of the House agreed to each hire Johnson as a part-time messenger. By March, Johnson was attending the Page School; he dressed and worked like a page, but remained barred from the floor of the House.

With a partial victory achieved, Payne had a new concern. At age forty-seven, she suddenly found herself in charge of a youngster for the first time in her adult life. Fortunately she found help. The pastor in Johnson's Chicago church contacted his counterpart in a church in Payne's neighborhood. A meeting was arranged at which Payne and Johnson were introduced to the Davises, an African American family who were members of the mostly white congregation of the Augustana Lutheran Church. In fact, their teenage son Herman "Skip" Davis was the church's first black acolyte. The pastor explained to the Davis teenager that Johnson would soon be the first black page on Capitol Hill and that his aunt was one of the first black White House correspondents. "But as young kids fourteen years old," said Davis, "all you are thinking about is how we can have fun together."

The two boys immediately became fast friends and the Davis family relieved Payne of the worry about what to do with her nephew while keeping up with her busy schedule and travel. If the two were not at Payne's apartment they could be found in the Davises' house. "But we knew what rules were," recalled Davis, "and because Aunt Ethel traveled a lot, we never caused any problems at all out of respect for our parents and Aunt Ethel."

Johnson did well with his schoolwork. "He's faithful to the books. He's never allowed the frustrations to discourage him," Payne told *Ebony* magazine. "He should be made a page—just for one day—under suspension of House rules."

THE CONTROVERSY OVER Payne's nephew died down in the press, but its lingering effect had national policy implications. In late January 1960, civil rights legislation intended to plug some of the holes in the weak 1957 Civil Rights Act was bottled up in the House Rules Committee. Payne's friend Clarence Mitchell, the lobbyist for the NAACP, was searching for signatures, particularly Republican ones, for a discharge petition that would pry the bill out of the committee and send it to the floor for a vote.

Representative William H. Ayres, a Republican from Ohio, saw a golden opportunity to needle the Democrats, whose members were divided on civil rights issues. He informed the Democratic leadership that he would sign the petition "as soon as they do justice to little Jimmy Johnson" by giving him his promised job as a page. "If they can't keep their word to one Negro," he added mischievously, "how do they expect to handle the problems of eighteen million?"

Mitchell was beside himself. "I too believe that it is a national disgrace when Congress finds it impossible to give one little boy a job simply because of the color of skin," he told Ayres. But it wouldn't help Johnson or other victims of racial injustice if civil rights legislation remained held up in committee. "It amounts," Mitchell said, "to punishing those who need legislative protection of their civil rights because of unjust discrimination against one member of the racial group most effected by segregation."

Eventually the bill found its way to the floor and was passed. But as with the 1957 Civil Rights Act, which this one was intended to improve, the law was mostly a symbolic gesture that did little to strengthen the federal government's hand on matters of racial discrimination. Its passage, as well as that of the 1957 law, revealed that Southern lawmakers could no longer halt legislation abhorrent to them, but they could still gut the bills that endangered their beloved segregation.

TWO YEARS INTO HER NEW LIFE at the AFL-CIO, Payne found her job increasingly intolerable. The work was dull in comparison to her former life. Instead of being able to dash off to some trouble spot in the South, she now had to fill out travel requisitions weeks ahead of any trip. She had become a bureaucrat.

More odious to her was organized labor's dismal record on race in its own affairs. In Washington, for instance, black workers were barred by union rules from working on a major restoration project to the U.S. Capitol. Union president George Meany refused to fix this injustice. A. Philip Randolph, with whom Payne had worked side by side on the March on Washington Movement, sought to create the Negro American Labor Council to put pressure on the AFL-CIO to end segregated locals. For his actions, Randolph became a Meany target and was censured by the AFL-CIO's executive board. "Who the hell appointed you guardian of all the Negroes in America?" Meany yelled at Randolph during the union's annual convention.

"Now the letters are pouring into headquarters here in protest of this latest business," Payne told her mother. Inside the AFL-CIO headquarters, Meany's inaction in regard to the racist behavior of its member labor unions put the spotlight on Payne and the handful of black employees. "It means," said Payne, "that we have literally become 'sacred cows,' so afraid are they of offending us any further!" But Payne was trapped. With her lack of a college degree, she couldn't walk away from her high-salary job without some alternative, especially with her nephew living with her.

But that did not mean she had to remain loyal. She bit the hand that fed her when the AFL-CIO turned its attention to the 1960 election. It sought to strengthen its hand within the Democratic Party by winning coveted seats on the Democratic National Committee (DNC). In Washington, the AFL-CIO believed it had a lock on getting J. C. Turner, a prominent white Washington labor union official, onto the DNC. Payne, however, had a different plan.

She and several other women formed the Metropolitan Women's

Democratic Club to, in Payne's words, "give the girls a chance to flex their muscles in the political action field." The club was an affront to traditional political organizers. Women were counted on to work in politics but not to take on leadership roles.

Payne was elected the club's first president. For its initial foray into the political arena, the women decided to work to elect to the DNC underdog Frank D. Reeves, a Canadian-born black NAACP attorney. With their help, Reeves pulled off an upset, denying the AFL-CIO its seat on the DNC and becoming the first African American on the party's governing board.

The Metropolitan Women's Democratic Club and other similar organizations connected career-minded women, particularly black women. At the time, women were expected to find fulfillment in domesticity, not activism. In these sororal organizations they could be appreciated for who they were. Payne valued the support all the more because she remained alone in life. She had not married and had not sustained any serious relationship with a man. Her success and stridency was off-putting to African American men. But club friends, such as Arabella Denniston, Mary McLeod Bethune's former right-hand person, provided important companionship. The two single women played the board game Scrabble, often into the wee hours of the morning, fighting furiously over words. "She'd grab her dictionary," recalled Payne, "and I'd say, 'Your dictionary is no damn good!' So I'd bring my own dictionary. We used to have a lot of fun."

Payne was soon at odds again with her bosses over their support of the leading Democratic Party candidates for the nomination, John F. Kennedy, Lyndon Baines Johnson, Stuart Symington, and Adlai Stevenson. Payne knew from firsthand experience on Capitol Hill that even Richard Nixon, the likely Republican nominee, had a better civil rights record than any of the Democratic contenders. In particular, Payne retained serious reservations about Kennedy. "My doubts grew out of the senator's switching positions in a crucial test on a civil rights vote in 1957."

In July Payne went to Los Angeles for the Democratic National Convention. It was the first time she had sat with the party activists rather than in the press box at a convention. The morning after Kennedy secured the nomination on the first ballot, rumors circulated that he was going to pick Lyndon Johnson as his vice-president. Seeing a South that was growing hostile to the Democratic Party, Kennedy wanted a Southerner, especially one who could secure the electorally rich state of Texas. Payne, like many other blacks, was leery of the choice. She was willing to forgive Kennedy's transgressions in the fight over the 1957 Civil Rights Act, but she still blamed Johnson for the evisceration of the act.

Kennedy, as predicted, picked Johnson. Payne and every black delegate, elected official, and party activist at the convention received a telegram inviting them to a meeting at the Biltmore Hotel. Chicago congressman William Dawson, who had given the seconding speech for the Johnson nomination, and Reeves, who had seconded the Kennedy nomination, greeted the group. But Payne observed that the crowd remained skeptical, even sullen. After some delay Kennedy arrived, accompanied by Johnson. "There was muted applause and some grim-faced onlookers kept their arms significantly folded," Payne said.

Johnson told the gathering that he understood how African Americans felt about him but pledged that if they were elected, he and Kennedy would not disappoint them. "I'll do more for you in four years than anyone else has done for you in one hundred years," Johnson said. Payne looked at Reeves. He had, she said, "the satisfied look of the broker who has delivered for his client."

In the fall the Kennedy-Johnson ticket prevailed by the smallest of margins made possible in part by winning 70 percent of the black vote. Not long after, Payne's nephew came back to the apartment carrying a large package. Johnson proceeded to take down some pictures on one wall and put in their place a large picture of John and Jackie Kennedy. "That's our leader," he said to his aunt.

THE YEAR 1961 SPARKED hope among many African Americans. In Walter Mosley's novel *Black Betty*, Easy Rawlins considered the prospects of the year: "About our new young Irish President and Martin Luther King; about how the world was changing and a black man in America had a chance to be a man for the first time in hundreds of years."

For Payne the year brought hope that she might be able to leave the AFL-CIO. She did not want to give up her life in the capital. "I'm now in my eighth year of life in Washington, and still fascinated by the panorama of politics and its accompaniment of rumors, intrigue, cynicism, frustrations, and pomp and circumstance," she told her family.

After the new president took office, Payne's name showed up on a list of rumored appointments. It was thought she might be given the assistant directorship of the Labor Department's Women's Bureau. The invitation never materialized. The lack of a college degree took her out of consideration. "Contrary to all those speculations you may have read about my going into the administration," she wrote to her family, "I'm right here at the AFL-CIO and as the kids would say: 'Nothing is shaking.'"

On Monday, June 12, 1961, Payne, her sister Avis and Avis's husband James, as well as other relatives, gathered to watch as James Johnson and thirteen other boys graduated from the Capitol Page School. "You have been privileged to serve in one of freedom's greatest institutions—the Congress of the United States," Vice-President Johnson told the students. Then, almost as if he were addressing Payne's nephew, he said, "You know the frailties of its members, but you know the vastly greater strengths of the institution." When the time came for James A. Johnson to receive his diploma, the audience stood on its feet applauding, providing him with a send-off to a college education, medical school, and a naval career culminating in the post of rear admiral.

"Although his family is disappointed that he did not realize his dream of being accepted as a page on the House floor," said Payne, "he had made so many friends and well-wishers that it has been a great experience.

"He thinks philosophically that he has paved the way for Congress to relax its resistance and in the future, some other colored boy will get the opportunity to break the iron curtain and become a page."

A YEAR INTO THE KENNEDY administration, on January 26, 1962, COPE fired Payne. No public reason was given. Some press accounts attributed the termination to an economy move. "Ranks of the AFL-CIO's staff employees and some labor circles are wondering out loud why it happened," reported the *Pittsburgh Courier*. When she was asked, Payne refused to comment beyond confirming she had been let go.

The speculation was that Payne's independent political streak had become too much for union leaders. From the beginning her fidelity to the labor movement's alliance with the Democratic Party had been suspect because of the widely publicized visit to her home by then vice-president and 1960 Republican presidential nominee Richard Nixon. Payne's support for insurgent candidate Frank Reeves had certainly not helped.

At first it was thought that Payne might become deputy director of the newly created Agency for International Development. Instead, Payne accepted an offer from the Democratic National Committee to become the deputy field director. Margaret Price, the director of women's activities for the party, hired Payne to recruit and organize black women. "The appointment is the first move of the Dems to develop a striking force among Negro women," noted *Jet* magazine.

In September, the White House dispatched Payne, along with presidential aides Hobart Taylor Jr., special counsel to the Commission on Equal Employment Opportunity, and Andrew Hatcher, the first black person to serve in the White House Press Office, to the annual meeting of the Improved Benevolent and Protective Order of Elks of the World, the largest black fraternal organization, in Detroit. The goal of the White House emissaries was to win support for Kennedy's Medicare bill. But the Elks' Grand Exalted Ruler, who was a Republican, declined to lend his organization's support to the controversial legislation. However, before Payne left Detroit, he permitted her to argue in favor of Medicare in a closed session. In doing so, she became the first woman to speak before the group. The audience did not buy Payne's message, but she received a standing ovation.

CHAPTER 25

WE SHALL OVERCOME

WHILE IN BIRMINGHAM, ALABAMA, TO WORK ON A voter registration drive in May 1963, Payne reconnected with her former colleagues from the press. In the years since she had first gone to the South while working for the *Defender*, many black and white reporters had gotten to know each other well, pursuing together what they called the "deseg beat." But like a kid outside a candy shop window, Ethel Payne could only look into the world she had left.

One night she was holed up with a group of her journalism friends at the A. G. Gaston Motel, where Martin Luther King and other movement leaders camped when in town. Confined to their rooms by a heavy downpour, the reporters heard a loud knock. Opening the door, they found *New York Post* reporter Murray Kempton dripping wet with a bulky package tucked under his raincoat.

"You all can't have any of this," Kempton exclaimed to the African Americans in the room, "this is white folks' whiskey." He had discovered that segregation was so rigid in Birmingham, the liquor store had a barrier running down its center. On one side there were brands of liquor for white customers, and on the other side, brands for blacks. Years later when Payne regaled a college audience with this tale, she added with a laugh, "The cash register was in the middle and it didn't discriminate."

The year 1963, however, was a low moment for the civil rights movement. What had once worked no longer did. In Birmingham, the jailing of Martin Luther King had attracted national attention to the campaign he was leading to desegregate downtown commerce but the effort was faltering. In a stroke of brilliance, however, organizers turned to the city's African American students. Pouring out of the city's public school, the students marched peacefully into the downtown. When the police turned high-pressure fire hoses and police dogs on them, the images of the young students under attack filled the front pages of newspapers and TV evening newscasts, triggering national outrage. By mid-May the city caved in and released all who had been arrested, and merchants agreed to desegregate downtown stores.

The Birmingham success reenergized national civil rights leaders. In late May 1963, on behalf of three leading civil rights organizations, A. Philip Randolph called for a March on Washington in August to draw attention to the lack of progress in reaching the movement's goals in the centennial year of the Emancipation Proclamation. King quickly agreed to join the march, as did other leading activists and organizations. Feeling the pressure, President Kennedy called for new and stronger civil rights legislation that would use the power of the federal government to open all public establishments and expand the right to vote. Of those likely to favor civil rights, only Payne's former employer, the AFL-CIO, refused to lend its support to the march.

THE SCOPE AND SIGNIFICANCE of the march grew as the August date approached. Two weekends before the appointed date, sitting in her Washington apartment, Payne opened her old wooden file cabinet, the one she had been trying to clean up for years. From it she pulled a scrapbook with clippings and letters from the early 1940s, when she had worked on the earlier March on Washington

Movement led by Randolph. "It seems impossible that it was 22 years ago when the dream of a March on Washington was first born," Payne wrote in a guest appearance in the *Defender*, her first byline in the paper in five years. "But there was the record in the pages of a scrapbook, the leaves so brittle that they crumble at the slightest touch." On page after page she had pasted flyers, articles, and editorials from the *Defender*, and—most precious to her—letters from Randolph.

"Now 22 years later," she wrote, "the man whose dream of a March on Washington was deferred by a promise while a whole new generation of Americans grew up, will at long last lead his legions numbering more than 200,000 across the Potomac and up to the Shrine of the Great Emancipator to demand payment in full on the promissory note." Payne listed the names of those with whom she had worked in Chicago and reminisced. "We worked and worked. We walked and talked, distributing thousands of leaflets," she said. "Yes, those were the good old days—they weren't really good days. It just felt good to be part of the flowing stream of Negro consciousness."

In the two decades since, the country and Payne had undergone an astounding transformation. In 1941 she had been unable to obtained decent work because of her race; now she held a well-paying job because of it. The civil rights movement, in which she served as an activist and for which she had functioned as a chronicler, had not just opened the door to the Democratic Party's national office but had put African Americans to work at its desks.

The changing political climate also elevated Payne's status. In her job at the Democratic National Committee, as well as when she had worked for the AFL-CIO, she was always introduced as the *former* reporter who had challenged the president and been on the front lines of the battles. Her reputation put her on guest lists. In January, for instance, she had been among the dignitaries invited by Attorney General Robert Kennedy to an exhibit marking the centennial of the Emancipation Act, and in June the president asked her to attend a White House meeting of leaders from women's organizations to discuss civil rights. When a newspaper referred to her as "one of the top national figures in Washington," it was not for the work she currently was doing but for what she had done in the past as a reporter.

But at age fifty-two, Payne was hardly ready to be put out to pasture. She remained eager to be active. "Before I order my rocking chair, I've got some stirring and turning to do," she told her family. "Causes and crusades are my life blood and I hope to be a part of moving civil rights out of the talking stage into reality."

WHEN MORE THAN 200,000 DEMONSTRATORS converged on the Lincoln Memorial on August 28, 1963, Payne joined her old colleagues in the press seats despite lacking press credentials. She couldn't help but notice the immense scope of this march in comparison to the smaller Prayer Pilgrimage for Freedom she covered six years earlier. Washington would have to pay attention now.

A. Philip Randolph welcomed the crowd as its members found places to stand, trees to lean against, bits of memorial walls to sit on. His place of honor brought back memories of when Payne had worked for him in the 1941 effort to organize a Washington march. Sadly to her mind, now, like then, women continued to be given a backseat. Bayard Rustin paid tribute to black female activists, but their absence from the list of scheduled speakers highlighted their continuing exclusion from leadership posts.

As the program neared its conclusion, Martin Luther King rose to deliver a speech intended to serve as the centerpiece of the rally. He had only just finished it early that morning, before the sun rose. Payne and the reporters were given mimeographed copies.

As King began to read, the crowd fell silent. The audience reaction was palpable from where he stood on the stairs of the monument. Seized by the moment, he put aside his script and instead extemporaneously talked about a dream, a theme he had been using in recent speeches. "I say to you today, my friends," said King, "that in spite of the difficulties and frustrations of the moment, I still have a dream."

The reporters sitting around Payne couldn't follow the copy of the speech they had been given. It was not on the page. In words that would be carved on monuments and recited by schoolchildren for generations, King spoke of his vision. "I have a dream that my four children will one day live in a nation where they will not be judged by the color of their skin but by the content of their character." King's eloquent plea moved civil rights veterans and even hardened reporters. "I saw white and black veteran reporters seated near me with tears in their eyes, streaming down their cheeks," said Payne. "I had tears, too."

A few days later, while staying at the Sheraton East Hotel in New York, Payne took out a piece of the hotel's stationery and wrote to Randolph. "Dear Phil," she began. "We are still glowing from the great experience of the March last Wednesday. Remembering 1941 and 1942, I can say I'm glad that at long last your dream did come true."

BECAUSE SHE HELD A POST on the Democratic National Committee, Payne's name continued to show up on lists of potential administration minority appointments. She also became one of the most frequently invited speakers at Democratic Party events. Building on the momentum of the march, the committee intensified its voter registration efforts. Payne, along with two others, was assigned to boost the number of black voters in New York, Chicago, Indianapolis, and other metropolitan areas.

Payne sought to do more than increase black voting. She was also frustrated by the low turnout of women. Wherever she spoke, she urged women to vote. "Too many feel like the woman who told me that her husband does the voting in their family," Payne told a reporter in Denver, Colorado.

It was so different being on the inside as a party functionary, rather than being on the outside as a reporter. Her life centered on the Democratic Party. For instance, in February, President Kennedy had held a reception to celebrate the centennial of Lincoln's Emancipation Proclamation. The guest list for the gala read like a who's who of American blacks, although Martin Luther King and A. Philip Randolph pointedly stayed away to protest the failure of the administration to move forward on promised civil rights actions. Payne chose party loyalty over fidelity to King and Randolph. After the reception, Representative Carl B. Stokes, in his first term in office, and other activists retired to Payne's apartment to talk about the 1964 elections. They talked late into the night and decided to try to persuade the party to hold a series of grassroots gatherings around the country leading to a summit to placate black impatience with the lack of progress.

Like most everything, their plans went into limbo on November 22, when President Kennedy went to Dallas, Texas, on a political fence-mending trip and returned in a coffin. Despite the president's slowness in pushing Congress to move on civil rights legislation, his other actions—such as meeting with the March on Washington organizers to pose in the Oval Office—had scored points for him with African Americans. They, like much of the country, were enamored with the Kennedy mystique. "He was a glamorous, charming man, and he was disarming," said Payne. "He had a way with it."

Now Texan Lyndon Baines Johnson, the man whom Payne blamed for the gutting of the 1957 Civil Rights Act, ascended to the presidency. To her surprise, as well as to that of many in the movement, Johnson pledged to keep the promise he made to the black delegates and activists at the convention three years earlier. He resumed Kennedy's previously unsuccessful efforts to get a strengthened civil rights bill out of Congress. "No memorial oration or eulogy could more eloquently honor President Kennedy's memory than the earliest possible passage of the civil rights bill for which he fought so long," Johnson said in his first address to Congress shortly after Kennedy's death.

He got his way. Despite their strong presence in leadership positions in the House, Southern Democrats were powerless to thwart the bill's progress. In the Senate, however, arcane rules and apportionment of votes by states rather than by population gave recalcitrant Southerners an advantage they did not possess in the House. It was there they planned their last stand.

Georgia senator Richard Russell led the charge against the bill with eighteen other Southern senators, a group that included Senator Strom Thurmond, who in 1957 had conducted the longest filibuster ever. Two decades earlier, Senator Russell had pledged to "resist to the bitter end any measure or any movement which would have a tendency to bring about social equality and intermingling and amalgamation of the races in our states."

Payne knew firsthand what an opponent he could be from her days as a cub reporter at the 1952 Democratic Convention, when she scored an interview with him, to her day-by-day coverage of the 1957 fight. But this time there was nothing the segregationist could do. The verbal ramparts they built in the Senate held for fifty-four days until a bipartisan group of senators brought it down with a compromise bill to the floor that, unlike in 1957, retained tough enforcement provisions.

On July 2, 1964, Lawrence F. O'Brien Jr., President Johnson's political point man, prepared a memorandum for his boss listing the names of those who were expected at the White House that evening when the bill would be signed into law on national television. He grouped the invitees by such classifications as "Executive Branch" and "House of Representatives" and "Religious Leaders." Among representatives for "Negro Groups" were the familiar names of Martin Luther King, Whitney Young, A. Philip Randolph, and others. On the last page of the list given to the president was a group called

Ethel Payne sits for an early portrait in 1911 or 1912.

Ethel stands in the snow with her older brother, Lemuel, in front of the family's South Side, Chicago, Throop Street home.

In the 1940s, Payne (on the right) became increasingly active in Chicago's civil rights movement. She recruited members for the NAACP and in 1941 worked with A. Philip Randolph's March on Washington Movement as a key organizer in Chicago.

Payne sails to Japan in 1948 to work as a hostess in an army service club. On the back of this snapshot, she wrote, "1st day at sea, notice my sea legs."

On an army base in Japan between 1948 and 1951, Payne enthusiastically takes to her job of creating entertainment for the black servicemen, including arranging birthday parties. (*Courtesy of the Moorland-Spingarn Research Center*)

Payne leads a group of soldiers out for a night's entertainment in Tokyo. "We hired 25 rickshaws and did the town up," she wrote. (*Courtesy of the Moorland-Spingarn Research Center*)

Payne sits down to interview Illinois governor Adlai Stevenson shortly after becoming a reporter for the *Chicago Defender* in 1951.

Payne joins Illinois Democratic senator Paul Douglas at a Capital Press Club dinner in Washington in the 1950s.

With other reporters, Payne interviews Roy Wilkins, the executive secretary of the NAACP, in the mid-1950s. The journalist on the far right is Louis Lautier, the first black reporter accredited to the White House press corps.

As Payne's reporting grew to be an important component of the *Defender*, the paper advertised its association with her. (*Courtesy of the* Chicago Defender)

Vice-President Richard Nixon gives thought to a question from Payne when he, along with his wife, Pat, came to Payne's Washington apartment for a party in 1958 reuniting the reporters that covered the vice-president's trip to Ghana the previous year. (*Courtesy of James A. Johnson*)

The Nixons gladly pose for photographs during the 1958 party. In this one, Payne and her nephew Joseph Sample stand by the vice-president and his wife.

As a reporter with an interest in world affairs, Payne frequented embassy functions in Washington like this one at the Embassy of Ghana, a country whose independence celebrations she had covered in 1957.

Payne's nephew James A. Johnson was denied a post as a Capitol page in 1959 because of his race. He was able to attend and two years later graduated from the Capitol Page School when five members of the House each agreed to hire him as a part-time messenger. (*Courtesy of the Moorland-Spingarn Research Center*)

THIS
ENTRANCE
CLOSED

Payne and President John F. Kennedy enjoy a light moment in the Rose Garden in 1962.

Payne watches President Lyndon B. Johnson deliver a talk to a visiting group of civil rights leaders in 1965.

While Payne had severely criticized Lyndon Johnson when he was the senate majority leader, she became a strong supporter of his when he succeeded in obtaining passage of important civil rights legislation as president.

Payne interviews a soldier from Chesapeake, Virginia, during her three-month reporting tour in 1967. She was the first black journalist to report on the war from Vietnam. (*Courtesy of the Moorland-Spingarn Research Center*)

Payne stands with U.S. representative Shirley Chisholm in 1972 when the politician became the first black candidate to seek a major-party nomination for president.

President Jimmy Carter greets Payne at the White House. In the course of her work, Payne met every man who served as president from Eisenhower to Reagan.

In 1973, Payne gathers with a group of American journalists that were among the first to be invited inside China since the communist takeover in 1949. The woman staring off in the distance is Susan Sontag, the New York intellectual who was then a contributing editor to the new magazine *Ms.*

Payne takes to the streets of Shanghai wearing her fake leopard-skin coat.

By the 1970s, when this photo was taken, Payne had become an icon in the black press and was widely sought as a speaker.

Payne demonstrates her polite demeanor encountering President Nixon's secretary of state, Henry Kissinger. In the spring of 1976, Payne accompanied the peripatetic Kissinger on a 26,000-mile tour of Africa.

Beginning as a young woman, Payne favored hats of all sorts. In this photograph from the early 1960s, she sports one of the most colorful ones from her extensive collection.

Payne calls on Daisy Bates in Little Rock, Arkansas, in 1981. Payne had become friends with Bates when she covered the 1957 Little Rock school desegregation battle in which the activist had played a leading role.

At a 1982 gala dinner in her honor, Payne is reunited with Alice Dunnigan who, as a reporter for the Associated Negro Press (ANP), had been the first African American female journalist accredited by Congress and the White House.

Payne found a lot to criticize about President Ronald Reagan's administration but put her differences aside in social moments because of her unerring sense of civility.

Payne and presidential candidate Jesse Jackson chat during his 1984 bid for the White House.

In ill health and using a cane, journalist Max Robinson accompanies Payne to a Washington event in June 1988. Robinson was the first African American network news anchor. He died of AIDS that December.

Payne traveled to South Africa in May 1990 to interview Nelson Mandela following his release from twenty-seven years in prison

Ethel Payne: "First Lady of the Black Press"

Payne stands by a photograph of herself at a younger age, part of a special exhibit celebrating her life at the Anacostia Library in Washington, DC, a few months prior to her death.

"Other." The second of those names was that of Ethel Payne, mistakenly listed as "Mrs."

Payne put on her striped skirt and jacket and made her way to the White House in the late afternoon sun. She returned that night to her apartment bearing a pen that had made the act a law.

THE FOLLOWING SPRING, the civil rights movement made it clear that its legislative business was not done. On Sunday, March 7, 1965, protesters in Alabama seeking to draw attention to the state's insistent use of Br'er Rabbit–like trickery to keep blacks off the rolls of registered voters began a march from Selma to the state capital in Montgomery. State police used deadly force to halt the march as it crossed the Edmund Pettus Bridge, only hundreds of yards into its planned fifty-mile journey.

A week later, President Johnson came to Capitol Hill to address a joint session of Congress. Payne secured a seat. She did not want to miss this moment. As a voting rights organizer for the Democratic Party, she was anxious to see what the president was willing to do to back up his stated intentions of following up the 1964 Civil Rights Act with a federal voting rights law. The violence that met the group drew national attention to their cause and was forcing his hand. When Johnson rose to the dais on the floor of the House, more than seventy million Americans tuned in on their televisions to see what he had to say. In the gallery above, Payne listened in amazement.

In sonorous tones and in his distinct drawl, Johnson spoke in almost religious terms of the right to vote, making almost no reference to the Constitution or laws. Rather, he focused on an elusive idea of the "American Promise" and represented it in a narrative in which the time had come to grant the final act of freedom to its black citizens. "As a man whose roots go deeply into Southern soil, I know how agonizing racial feelings are," Johnson said. "I know how difficult it is to reshape the attitudes and the structure of our society."

All who listened knew the speech was unlike any the president had given before. They witnessed a rare moment in politics where quiet eloquence silenced noisy opposition. The events in Selma, Johnson said, were part of a movement that reached into every part of the nation. African Americans were securing for themselves the freedom they had long been denied. "Their cause must be our cause too. Because it's not just Negroes, but really it's all of us who must overcome the crippling legacy of bigotry and injustice." Then, pausing and leaning forward, Johnson repeated the words of the movement's anthem, "And we shall overcome."

Payne could not find words to describe her feelings at the end of his speech. Two days later, in her office, she sat at her typewriter. "I would like every schoolchild in American to have a copy of this speech," she wrote the president. It ranks in importance, she said, with Lincoln's Gettysburg Address and the Emancipation Proclamation. "I am proud and grateful for your leadership and I pledge to give my best efforts for the implementation of your program."

Taking her pledge to heart, Payne flew to Selma to join the third attempt to make the march to Montgomery, but this time with the backing of a federal judge, who enjoined the police from stopping the marchers, and federal troops summoned by the president. Nonetheless, it was like stepping into the lion's den. "You could just feel the hatred," Payne said. "It was just like an enveloping cloak around you."

At the spot where the earlier marches had been halted, hundreds of angry white Southerners, infuriated by the presence of federal troops, watched as 3,000 marchers crested the Edmund Pettus Bridge and descended toward them while army helicopters hovered above. Held back by a line of soldiers with bayonet-tipped rifles, the angry whites waved Confederate flags and racist placards. "I'll never forget the faces, the contorted faces of housewives, standing out and screaming like they were just lunatics from the asylum, you know, just screaming such terrible epithets and hatred," said Payne. They called out "Nigger, nigger, nigger!" and "Go to hell," and cursed President Johnson. "The reaction of the people was so vitriolic," Payne said. "You never realized how deep human hatred can be. And that was the way it was all along the march."

Another life was taken. Klan members murdered a thirty-nine-year-old Detroit mother of five, Viola Liuzzo, for having given a ride to a young black protester. "This was a madness, just a total madness," Payne said. "This was a time when all—it was a purging of the white South, all the venom that came out, and perhaps it was good, because it was just boiling over, and it was such an excess. It was a preparation for later acceptance of what they knew was inevitable."

The police attack on the marchers and the ultimate success of the march impressed Capitol Hill. The Senate minority leader, Republican Everett Dirksen, joined the majority leader, Democrat Mike Mansfield, in supporting a bill like that demanded by the marchers in Selma. By August a bill was on the president's desk granting the federal government immense judicial powers to end Southern methods of keeping their black citizens from the voting booth.

A Johnson aide was dispatched to deliver to Payne one of the pens the president used in signing the Voting Rights Act. Aside from Martin Luther King, she became one of the very few people who were not lawmakers to have a pen from the signing of both the 1964 Civil Rights Act and the 1965 Voting Rights Act, the two most seminally important legislative victories of the civil rights movement. She put both pens on display in her apartment.

THE DNC CHRISTMAS PARTY that year held a surprise for its employees. Despite the huge election victory the previous year, the party was broke. In fact, it was $2.5 million in debt. Of the eighty-five

DNC employees, forty would lose their jobs. Payne's job hung in the balance. "Is it possible that the Democrats are wiling to drift back to the nearly lily-white participating level the party had prior to Miss Payne's arrival three and a half years ago?" asked Rosemarie Brooks, in her weekly Washington Round-Up column.

Payne deftly skirted the axe by taking a leave of absence to serve as a consultant to the Social Security Administration. Of the 19 million Americans eligible for the new Medicare program, almost 3.5 million had not signed up for the low-cost supplementary portions of the program. The administration put Payne on a twenty-two-city road trip to speak in churches and to civic groups to reach those who had not yet signed up before the annual deadline on March 31.

Payne returned to the DNC in time for an April conference of volunteers put on by the Democratic Party's women's division headed by Price. The gathering reflected the mood of women across the country. They were growing restless. It had been three years since the publication of Betty Friedan's *Feminine Mystique*. Friedan, Shirley Chisholm, and Pauli Murray were making plans to meet in Washington with other women to launch the National Organization for Women.

Payne could see the frustration among the women she worked with in the Democratic Party, particularly black women. Letters such as one from the president of the National Beauty Culturists' League, an African American organization of cosmetologists, made it clear women felt unappreciated. "I see no future for the Negro women of the South," wrote Katie E. Whickam, who was the first woman officer of the Southern Christian Leadership Conference. "We are forced to believe now that we are not wanted for anything but to get out and get the votes during the campaigns."

Unrest among the troops contributed to an already anxious atmosphere at the DNC in the summer of 1966. After his landslide victory over Barry Goldwater, President Johnson had steadily lost favor with the public as the war in Vietnam escalated. The midterm elections, always challenging for the political party that holds the White House, loomed ominously that fall. It was time for the DNC to dispatch its troops from Washington. Party officials decided to send Payne to Texas, where more than 400,000 black voters could conceivably be lured to the polls in the wake of the recent ratification of the Twenty-Fourth Amendment, repealing the poll tax.

THE ELECTION IN THE LONE STAR STATE was a high-stakes personal grudge match. After Johnson's election to vice-president, the Democratic governor appointed a fellow party member to fill the Senate seat. But in the ensuing special election, seventy-one candidates created a plethora of choices. The diminutive Republican John Tower, a college professor from Wichita Falls, emerged on top and went on to win the runoff when he was paired against a conservative Democrat who gave Texas liberals no reason to come out and vote.

Now, five years later, Tower was running for reelection. The Democratic establishment from President Johnson on down to Texas governor John Connally wanted to restore the normal order of things and pinned their hopes on Waggoner Carr, an established Democrat with a conservative record. Under normal conditions, simply being the Democratic candidate would have been enough to put Carr in the Senate. But times had changed, and Tower avoided being identified with the extreme conservatism of Goldwater. In fact, his only liability was his party label. "If Tower were running under the Democratic symbol," noted pollster Louis Harris, "he would have little difficulty winning a second term."

On August 28, Payne flew to Texas, charged by the party to get out the black vote. She crisscrossed the state in commercial and private planes for six weeks straight. "You should see me," she told friends, "crawling in and out of a Piper Cub." But no matter how hard Payne exhorted black voters to support the Democrats' standard-bearer, it was an impossible task. "On the surface," Payne said, "it would seem that job should be simple, just to get people to go to the polls and vote that man out." But infighting destroyed any hope of party unity. "The liberals are mad at everybody and some Democrats instead of Republicans get confused and slug at other Democrats and so it's a real can of worms, I'll tell you," she reported.

Moreover, her candidate was weak on minority issues and Tower's campaign skillfully tapped into the state's anti-North and anti-liberalism vein, further complicating Payne's efforts. The *Informer and Texas Freeman*, the oldest black newspaper published west of the Mississippi, broke the code of black newspapers and attacked Payne, one of their own, someone who had been an icon of the black press. Noting that she was a "big shot Democratic official from Washington via Chicago" working in tandem with another outsider, George L. P. Weaver of the AFL-CIO, the paper said "Texas Negroes resent this intrusion and interference."

"It will be smart," continued the columnist, "and the exercise of good judgment and wisdom by Texas Negroes to repulse, resent, and repel these outsiders who think Texas Negroes are so dumb and stupid to slit their own throats by voting for Carr simply because these Negro big shots or any other Democratic big shots ask that they do."

On Election Day, an exhausted Payne settled into a room at the Sheraton-Lincoln Hotel in Houston, where the Beatles had stayed the summer before. There was nothing left to do but wait. "There's a worried air because this is a close election—this morning's polls showed the candidates 49–49," Payne wrote, finally finding time to send a letter to her family and friends.

Tower won handily, with almost 57 percent of the vote. But the election still yielded dividends for black Texans. For the first time in modern times, African Americans held legislative office, two men had won seats in the statehouse, and a young woman named Barbara Jordan was going to the State Senate. "I'm leaving Texas," said Payne, "with a pack full of memories and high hopes for the future."

BUT THE END OF the campaign season left Payne jobless. It had been eight years since she had left the *Defender*. Now, for the second time in her exile from journalism, she was without employment. A few weeks later, the phone rang in Payne's Washington apartment. It was her old publisher, John Sengstacke. "How would you like to go to Vietnam?" he asked.

PART THREE

CHAPTER 26

SOUL BROTHERS IN VIETNAM

FTER AN ABSENCE OF MORE THAN EIGHT YEARS, ETHEL Payne was back on the front page of the *Chicago Defender*. DAILY DEFENDER TO HAVE ITS OWN "MAN" IN VIET NAM, read the headline announcing Payne's new assignment. "The facts behind the hardships and dangers Negro GIs are encountering at Christmas time in the Viet Nam jungles and in Saigon will be brought to *Daily Defender* readers firsthand by a woman correspondent," heralded the article. While Payne would not be the first woman to cover the war, the assignment made her the first black reporter to do so.

The publisher told *Defender* readers that he was dispatching Payne to the war because he knew "that Negro mothers, wives and other kin are overly anxious about them during the holiday season." Payne, he said, was to report on the activities of Negro soldiers and send messages back home from them. Asked about the dangers of the assignment, Payne admitted that her family and friends were worried. "But if colored soldiers and other military men can face it, I can too."

Even before agreeing to a salary for her return to the fold, Payne began planning for her tour. She booked a flight on Pan American out of San Francisco that would reach Saigon on Christmas Eve. "I don't mind going Economy," Payne told Sengstacke, "except that you are limited to forty pounds as against sixty-five pounds first class and frankly I don't know if I can make it, especially with a typewriter which is pretty necessary I am told." In either case, the airfare was not cheap, but she assured him that once she reached Saigon, the military would provide her with all her transportation and cover a lot of her expenses.

In consultation with Pentagon press officials, it was decided she would visit the main base camps of each branch of the military and make a side trip to Korea to interview General Benjamin O. Davis Jr., the first African American Air Force general, whose father had been the first African American Army general. Robert Komer, the president's aide in charge of the American efforts to gain the allegiance of the South Vietnamese population, briefed Payne. Komer, she said, "is particularly anxious to have more stories on the pacification mission which would explain more about why we are in Vietnam." *Pacification*, the military's euphemism for its efforts to weaken the insurgent Viet Cong by cutting off its access to the population, was coming back into fashion. The administration figured it could use some favorable press.

AHEAD OF THE WHITE PRESS on matters of civil rights, the black press had been woefully behind on the Vietnam War story. Foreign news was thought by *Defender* editors to be of little interest to their readers. Sengstacke said he had no need for foreign correspondents. "I think we've got enough issues to fight right here in this country."

But with each passing year, ignoring the war became harder for the black press. African Americans made up a disproportionate number of the draftees. "Knock on any door and you will probably find a family that has a son, nephew or cousin in Vietnam," a priest said about his Chicago parish. Blacks also supported the war at a higher rate than whites and looked favorably upon military service. In fact, in 1966, two-thirds of black servicemen reenlisted, a rate twice that of whites. Certainly military pay, housing, and the promise of a more meritocratic life appealed to many young African Americans. "Denied the rights and opportunities to advance at home," Payne said, "they flock to the Armed Forces in search of a 'better shake' than they can get in civilian life."

On the other hand, Vietnam was a risky story. By 1966 the nation was becoming polarized, and black publishers feared earning the wrath of a president who had delivered the Civil Rights and Voting Rights Acts. Not only were the editorial pages devoid of commentary on the war, but also the news side stayed clear of anything beyond routine items from the war front. That state of affairs prevailed until a sound of disquiet could be heard from among African Americans.

The White House also heard the same rumblings, especially after March 1965, when Martin Luther King told reporters that the war was "accomplishing nothing" and that he advocated a negotiated settlement. Louis Martin, Payne's old editor, was then working as a Democratic National Committee official. He was worried about the potential collapse of support for the war among African Americans. Martin found a solution in the mail one day. In a letter marked "confidential," Simeon Booker filled him in on the reporting trip he had just taken to Vietnam for *Jet* magazine. "A lot of guys here thought I was a fool to make such a risky trip," he wrote to Martin, "but really I feel that as a Negro reporter, Vietnam is [as] important to our U.S. future as civil rights.

"For the first time, perhaps, the U.S. has fielded a truly democratic team in Vietnam," Booker continued. "I feel with such a wonderful project of democracy in action and the first confrontation with commies—democracy using country tools of propaganda, work projects, and affection to halt the cave in of a nation—should get far more play in our Negro press."

Martin forwarded a copy of Booker's letter to Bill Moyers, who had just been appointed Johnson's press secretary, and to three oth-

ers in the White House. "Since Dr. Martin Luther King and a few
of the civil rights leaders are trying to get into the Vietnam act, I
think the information in the attached letter from Simeon Booker,
who just returned from Vietnam, might be helpful," Martin wrote in
the accompanying memo.

"The central point," Martin said, "is that Negroes should know
what Negroes are doing and how well they are doing it in Vietnam.
This could be a source of great pride to American Negroes and at the
same time strengthen their support of the policies of the administration." Moyers took out his pen, marked the corner of Martin's memo
with "This is interesting," and passed it on to Art Sylvester, the Pentagon's press chief.

Sylvester agreed that an effort should be made to get experienced
correspondents to cover the war. "This would be the best of all possible solutions for the Negro media, as well as any other group with a
special interest." To that end he recommended that Martin and others "use every appropriate opportunity to urge major media and news
agencies to assign mature and experienced correspondents to Vietnam to give them thorough firsthand coverage of the major United
States/Government of Vietnam effort there."

It wasn't long before Martin's old boss at the *Defender* was on the
phone to Payne.

AFTER TWENTY HOURS OF FLIGHT, which included three break-
fasts as the Pan Am jet chased the sun across the Pacific sky, Payne's
plane made its descent to Saigon's Tan Son Nhat airport just before
midday on December 24. "From the air," Payne thought, "this
country has a picture book look, green fields, peasants working
with bullocks and water buffaloes." But when the plane touched
down, Payne spotted tanks, helicopters, gun carriages, camouflaged
emplacements, and barbed wire. This was necessary security. A few
weeks earlier a Viet Cong unit had come close enough to the air-

field to lob shells at it. "Your first reaction is a sinking feeling at the pit of your stomach," she said. "For one brief moment you want to chicken out and climb right back in that plane and fly off to the safety of your own turf."

A representative from the U.S. embassy met Payne's plane. In the sweltering heat they drove into Saigon. "This is a fascinating Oriental city—incredibly alive and teeming and filthy," she said upon getting her first view of Saigon. The car deposited Payne at the Hotel Excelsior, which would serve as her base for the next several weeks. Situated on Nguyen Hue Street (the Street of Flowers), the Excelsior resembled a concrete apartment building with narrow balconies looking down on the crowded street. It was unlike the ten-story-tall Caravelle Hotel, with its high-ceilinged rooms, where American correspondents usually lodged. But rooms were in short supply. Author John Steinbeck, who had come to write war dispatches for *Newsday*, had resorted to a bribe to get a room in the Caravelle the previous month.

Print and broadcast reporters were increasingly making Saigon a destination. What had been a modest war three years earlier, involving only 15,000 American advisers and $500 million in aid, had grown into a major conflict with more than 400,000 American troops on the ground and billions of dollars in annual war expenditures. Back home the names of provinces such as Tay Ninh, Binh Dinh, Quang Ngai, and Dinh Tuong, cities such as Da Nang, Nah Trang, and Hue, and places such as the Mekong Delta were all becoming familiar to Americans whose nightly news filled television screens with scenes of war.

Early the following morning, Payne went to the Caravelle Hotel to gather with other reporters and photographers for a ride to a Christmas show being put on by Bob Hope. The famous comedian and movie star was in his twenty-fourth year of bringing entertainment shows to American troops. While waiting for transportation, Payne spotted John Steinbeck and his wife, Elaine, among those milling around on the steps of the hotel. Their son was stationed in Vietnam.

John Steinbeck got into a flag officer's car and was driven off to join General Westmoreland on a tour of a Saigon outpost. Left behind, Elaine Steinbeck joined Payne and the other reporters on a beat-up bus and the group headed north to Di An.

A CHRISTMASTIME TRUCE had begun, but as a precaution three armed soldiers on a jeep with a mounted gun escorted the bus. Rain during the night had turned the road into pasty red mud. After an hour of slow travel they reached Di An, the headquarters of the 1st Infantry Division. Here Payne met her first black soldier in the field, "a handsome Negro officer." The two chatted at length. "I was to hear again and again his view that this war is different from any other because old color lines have been erased," Payne said. "We're in this together," the soldier told Payne, "and the only thing that matters is the job to be done."

After a briefing by the general in charge, Payne's group went outside to the Christmas show. Clad in military green, soldiers packed the field before them in the heat under a cloudless sky. Wounded soldiers in blue pajamas sat on wheelchairs or lay on gurneys, having been delivered by ambulances. "The 20,000 young men, a mosaic in black and white, were joshing one another and waiting like kids for Santa Claus," she said. Bob Hope, along with comedian Phyllis Diller, with her trademark Medusa-like hairdo, triggered waves of laughter, and singer and former beauty queen Anita Bryant enlisted the men in singing "The Battle Hymn of the Republic" and "Silent Night." "I didn't know whether it was sweat or tears I was wiping away," Payne said.

At one point during the program, Hope was upstaged. High above, beyond the helicopters and fighter plans on patrol, a commercial jet leaving Vietnam streaked across the sky. "Suddenly Miss World, Bob Hope, Phyllis Diller, and the rest of the entertainment mighties faded into second spot as 20,000 pairs of eyes peered heavenward and we heard the chant, 'Going home, boy, that's where I want to be.'" The mass homesickness lasted only a few seconds and the show resumed. "But for that instant when the silver bird flew by," said Payne, "they were kids longing for home and families."

As she left, black and white men perched on parked tanks wished her a Merry Christmas. "God bless you all," said Payne, holding back further tears. The group found the bus mired in mud and the men put aside their C rations, which served as their Christmas dinner, to push the vehicle free. An hour later, on the same road, Viet Cong snipers killed three American soldiers and wounded eight.

By the time Payne reached the hotel, it was too late to have dinner at the military mess hall. She took out a package of dried prunes and opened a packet of peanut butter crackers. This would be her Christmas dinner. "And I cried and cried while I was banging out my first story."

Recalling her impressions upon landing, driving into the city, and entering a war zone, Payne typed, "Happiness in Viet Nam is soaking your feet at night while you're banging out your story and nibbling on dried prunes and wishing you could get up and go to the tap and get some nice cold clear water to drink; but remembering that you just better not. If you don't want to end up with a war-torn stomach."

THE MILITARY PUBLIC RELATIONS staff was eager to take Payne on one of its well-rehearsed tours. The staff was intent on doing everything within its power to uphold the government's contention that the war was being won and to sustain the public's support back home. A journalist who had preceded Payne by a few months felt that reporters were often "overwhelmed by the help and hospitality they received from the American propaganda machine." Payne put it more simply: "The Pentagon was very anxious for me to get some favorable stories."

Among her first stops was a visit to the USS *Enterprise*, the Navy's nuclear-powered aircraft carrier, floating in the Gulf of Tonkin. To reach the ship, Payne caught a plane in Da Nang, 550 miles north of Saigon, for the hour flight out to sea. Once on board, Payne marveled at the floating city that held 5,200 personnel, squadrons of planes and helicopters, and a cavernous maintenance facility below deck. "I was the first woman correspondent to come on board," Payne wrote home, "the captain ordered the royal treatment for me—plush quarters and all."

As was true for each visit to the various military installations, Ethel Payne's interest remained only with African American soldiers. "I was there to see how black troops were faring," Payne said. "So this was an important angle—I think the most important thing that I saw and that I reported on all through the war." For her dispatches Payne settled on a style reminiscent of World War II correspondent Ernie Pyle, who focused on the lives of the soldiers and sent back dispatches written as letters rather than as news stories.

Payne also used her reporting as a means to address the complaints of the servicemen. For instance, she heard sailors gripe about the lack of mail from home. "Just wandering the deck of the mighty United States carrier Enterprise, you pick up the names and addresses of all kinds of young men who find mail call a bit too lean," she wrote in a dispatch. In her typical manner, she then published the names and addresses of dozens of lonely Navy men pining for letters.

Back on dry land, she found servicemen feeling desolate from the lack of American-style entertainment. Only a small number of the troops were able to attend something like Bob Hope's show, and the entertainer was having an increasingly hard time recruiting stars because they were not in sympathy with the war. "Some of the fellows are pretty bitter," reported Payne. A mud-caked marine told her, "We're over here doing a job to protect them, and they haven't even got enough interest to walk through and shake hands. Who do they think they're kidding about that wrong war stuff?"

Payne decided to take a survey of the servicemen with whom she talked about what kinds of entertainers they wanted to see. In order of preference, the men selected Nancy Wilson, Sammy Davis Jr., Anita Bryant, Patti Page, Ramsey Lewis, the Supremes, Lena Horne, Ella Fitzgerald, and Harry Belafonte. "A note to the State Department," added Payne. "It's a long, lonely war, and as a matter of morale, couldn't you cut some red tape and get some more warm bodies, preferably feminine, over here to relieve the monotony?"

Saigon hardly offered the men much. Payne found the city depressing, dirty, and lacking in suitable company for the young black soldiers, who were of an age that they could have been her children. "Loneliness over here is an occupational disease, along with malaria and dysentery." The fraternizing between soldiers and Vietnamese women reminded Payne of her years in Japan. She also found self-segregation of the kind she saw when she stopped in Germany during her 1955 round-the-world trip. The Khanh Hoi neighborhood had been nicknamed "Soulsville" by the black soldiers, who claimed it as their turf even though they were not barred from other places. "It's just more comfortable," a private first class from Alabama told her, "and besides, ain't it got a railroad track down the street just like back home."

While Vietnamese and Cambodian women willing to fraternize were in plentiful supply, including the prostitutes in Loop Alley, whose services cost a dollar, the black soldiers Payne encountered were desperate for the company of black women. "When a colored girl from the states makes an occasional visit here, she is greeted with joyful whoops by the GIs, who just want to touch her skin."

EVERY REPORTER WHO DID A TOUR of Vietnam eventually spent time in Da Nang. Payne was no exception. The city, situated on the South China Sea north of Saigon, was the home of the war's busiest air base, actually one of the world's busiest airports for a while. In

1967, the city was also the base of operations for major units of the Army and Marines. "This is where the heavy casualties have been made and the field hospitals are full," Payne wrote incautiously to a sister.

For Payne's tour of Da Nang, her military handlers had arranged a trip to Tuy Loan, a small hamlet about five miles from the base that was regarded as a model of pacification. Under a gray sky above and muddy roads beneath, marines in a light truck picked up Payne from her base quarters. At the gate, the guards warned that the road ahead was being cleared of enemy combatants and it might be best to wait. Payne's driver checked his watch and concluded that the road would be clear by the time they reached it. The marines in the back of the truck took up their positions, rifles at the ready.

As they drove along, thoughts raced through Payne's mind. "Well, old girl," she said to herself, "you wanted to see the war and this is it; but why didn't you make out your will and tell the family where the insurance policies are?" She looked at the blue haze on the mountain and the green of the rice paddies they passed. "Wish my knees would quit shaking and that fluttery feeling around my heart would go away," she thought. "What's that behind the bushes on the right? I wonder if the V.C. got us if they would be kind to a colored lady?"

"Are you okay?" asked one of the marines, who put his hand on her shoulder.

"Just fine," replied Payne.

"Don't you worry, ma'am," he said. "The marines never let a lady down."

At last, after dodging nothing more dangerous than a bullock-drawn cart and a group of barefoot peasants, they reached Tuy Loan. Greeting her was Lance Corporal Lorenzo Forest, a nineteen-year-old black marine from Memphis who, along with an integrated group of nine other marines, had been living in the village for several months. Forest took Payne on a tour, explaining along the way that they had been working on civil projects ranging from installing new sewer lines to building a makeshift hospital. To furnish it with light and heat, the men had cut wooden barrels in half, sunk them into the ground, and filled them with manure and night soil treated with a chemical. The fumes from the mixture were used to generate power.

Payne was charmed by Forest and his work. She described him to readers as "one of the extraordinary persons who gives you the feeling that despite the mistakes, the political and military blundering and the agony of conflict, somehow, there is a real purpose here, a communication which transcends the evils of hate and the barriers of language and custom."

Forest and the others told her about the need for medicine and supplies at the hospital. As when the loneliness among sailors prompted her to publish a list of men in need of pen pals, Payne now convinced her editors in Chicago to publish an "Open Letter" to readers. "Dear Folks at Home," she wrote. "Sometimes the war in Vietnam seems very far away and incomprehensible . . . To the men who are involved there is no doubt about their purpose. They only wish you could see for yourself so that you could have a better understanding." She then listed items in short supply from toothbrushes to baseball equipment and urged that readers send them to an FPO address in San Francisco.

IN ITS EFFORT TO ENSURE a favorable portrayal of the war in the press, the military had no lack of similar projects to show Payne. She was introduced to black doctors tending the wounded at the Third Field Hospital, nicknamed "the Walter Reed of Vietnam"; a Tuskegee graduate with a degree in agronomy who was working to curry favor with farmers of Dinh Tuong province by helping expand the productivity of the rice paddies; and an integrated military medical team who were treating leprosy, tuberculosis, and other diseases found among the inhabitants of Pleiku, a strategically important town in the central highlands inhabited by an ethnic minority known as the Montagnards, or Degar.

The military hit pay dirt in their efforts to gain favorable coverage when they took Payne to Hill 10 southwest of Da Nang. There she spent time with the members of the 1st Platoon of Lima Company, who had been holding the hill for ten weeks to deny the enemy a route to the air base. "Looking at all these fresh young faces and seeing the comradeship of Negroes and whites together, all Americans, I wondered if the American people back home can really comprehend and appreciate what is going on here, if they realize that this is more than just guns and blood being spilled against a cunning adversary," she wrote in her dispatch.

"It is the battle," she continued, "to restore human dignity, to know that in this family of man, there is a responsibility as brothers, regardless of skin color or language and custom." The squad leader told her how the Vietnamese, particularly the children, appreciated any help or kind gesture from the troops. "It came to me that the way to understand what is going on here is to become involved. After all, it's our war too."

As the days of her departure from Vietnam neared, Payne boarded a helicopter for a trip to Song Be, the site of an earlier major battle near the Cambodian border. When the helicopter cleared the air corridor out of Saigon, a message came over the radio that her trip would be cut short so as to return to Saigon by 4:30 that afternoon. Her request for a much-sought-after interview with General William C. Westmoreland, the commander of the U.S. forces, had been granted.

That afternoon Payne was escorted through a maze of passages in the highly fortified command center to a waiting room outside Westmoreland's office. She passed the time examining a photographic map of Saigon on the wall until the office door flew open and in walked the general, apologizing for having kept her waiting. "He is the epitome of the professional soldier in bearing and decorum," Payne said, "but he has a warm courtliness which puts visitors at ease."

Westmoreland and Payne sat down, and she handed him a typed list of questions she had brought with her. With military precision and curtness, Westmoreland proceeded to answer them one by one.

How do you find the performance of Negro soldiers? "I have a great admiration for the Negro troops," replied the general. Are there special discipline problems with Negro troops? "I deal with American troops, and race, color, or creed is no consequence to me." Are Negroes court-martialed at a higher rate than whites? Don't know, but an aide can get you the answer. What about decorations? Can you give an estimate of the number of awards given to Negro soldiers? Don't know, but will ask an aide. And so it went until the general reached the end of her list.

The interview ran on page one. The Pentagon's military war might have been going badly, but on this day its public relations machine scored a victory.

CHAPTER 27

PLAYING INTO THEIR HANDS

E THEL PAYNE HAD GONE TO VIETNAM TO SPEND TIME with black soldiers and report on how they were faring. Race, not war, was on her mind at each stop. At the end of nine weeks in Vietnam, after meeting hundreds of servicemen, Payne decided that most black soldiers preferred to push to the back of their minds civil rights and other issues, including the war itself. "Like every other soldier on the line, the immediate and overriding concern is how to stay alive," Payne wrote in a long report called "How Negro Troops See War." Soldier after soldier told her that American segregationist practices did not follow them across the ocean. "When you are in combat, you're equal in everything," a black soldier outside Da Nang told her. "You live together. You sleep together. You eat the same things. You fight the same way. You stink the same way."

Reflecting on her brother Lemuel's service in the Army during World War II and her own experience with the military in Japan, Payne deemed this the first war in which American troops were entirely integrated. "Gone are the days of separate units and the special categories of service reserved for Negro soldiers," she said. "Gone, too, is the type of individual who resigned himself to the system." In his place, according to Payne, are more aggressive, militant, and confident black soldiers.

This was not to say there was no discrimination. In her visits to the various camps, she ran across tales of racism and prejudice and did not hesitate to write about them. The most common incidents of bigotry were assaults and name-calling, particularly between urban black soldiers and Southern whites. When she visited Cam Ranh Bay Air Base, north of Saigon along the coast, she encountered a group of black soldiers brooding over a notice on a bulletin board. It offered a reward for information regarding a series of recent assaults. In describing the attacks, the assailants were described as "unknown negro soldiers."

The black soldiers were indignant over the one-sided nature of the notice, claiming nothing had been done when they had been assaulted. They were irate about the potential of the notice to encourage false reports against them and were insulted by the use of *Negro* with a lowercase *n*. Sparing no detail, Payne published a lengthy account of the racist behavior and discontent among the soldiers. "We get threats in the barracks, on the job and at the EM [Enlisted Men's] club," one soldier told Payne. "They put lynch ropes on our bunks and write warnings in the latrines, but if we even look like we want to go after them, the company commander threatens us with Article 15."*

Payne sought out the base's white commanding officer, Brigadier General Mahlon Eugene Gates. An earnest, affable fellow, he introduced himself with his old family nickname of "Ink." Gates was surprised when Payne told him the use of the word *Negro* in lowercase was considered derogatory. He listened attentively when Payne discussed the larger complaints about the notice and invited her to offer suggestions. Not being one to be demure on such an occasion, Payne told him to identify and isolate the troublemakers, train unit leaders and commanders on dealing in a more equitable manner with the troops, and use the chaplains to counsel the soldiers.

---

* Article 15 was the term used to describe confining a soldier to barracks and giving him extra duty for two weeks.

Despite this incident, Payne believed the experience of serving in a more integrated setting would spark change back in the United States. "After the searing experience of being in Vietnam in a war of unparalleled cruelty, Negro soldiers are coming home to claim their share of democracy," she wrote. White soldiers, who endured the same baptism of fire, will return convinced that prejudice is wrong. "But with or without help, Negroes will demand a better deal from America."

"In general," Payne wrote her mother from Bangkok after leaving Vietnam, "integration has been very successful in the military service, much faster than at home, but human beings are still fallible and every once in a while it crops up."

LEAVING VIETNAM, Payne was grateful she had survived. Though she did not come near actual combat and had felt danger only on a dusty road outing with marines, she was leaving a war zone. On the day before she left, Bernard Fall, a highly respected correspondent, historian, political scientist, and expert on Indochina, was killed after stepping on a land mine. "I felt the experience personally," Payne wrote her mother, "since we had become quite friendly and just a week ago while we were at dinner, he was so happy because he was bringing his family to Hong Kong and buying a house there to stay two years while he worked on more books about the Far East."

But, unlike Fall, who was widely known for his critical reporting on the conduct of the war, Payne did not question the American war policy or the effectiveness of its military operations. She had not gone to Vietnam to cover a war. If she had, she might well have become a critic like her colleagues Frances FitzGerald and Martha Gellhorn, who arrived in Vietnam around the same time. Instead, following her instructions from her publisher and by her own choosing, Payne had focused her coverage on race. By doing so, she wrote about the war's one good story and played into the hands of Moyers, Martin, and others in the administration eager for favorable coverage in the black press to retain the support of African Americans for the war and the president.

"I didn't really understand the politics of the war," Payne admitted two decades later. "I think I was—maybe I was a little brainwashed myself because I didn't concentrate on that, and I should have. I was so busy concentrating on how well the black troops were doing, that maybe I overlooked that.

"I've always regretted to this day that I didn't do what I felt was an adequate job in reporting on the immorality of the war."

She paused in South Korea for the promised interview with General Benjamin O. Davis Jr., the only black general in the American armed forces. They met in a small brick building in the midst of a sea of Quonset huts that served as the military headquarters of the United Nations Command. In a wide-ranging interview, Payne brought up General Westmoreland's comparison of the service of black and white troops. "Gen. Westmoreland said that during the Korean Conflict, Negro troops did well, but not as well as their Caucasian colleagues. With progress in race relations, he thinks they are now doing as well as all other soldiers," Payne told Davis.

Westmoreland's patronizing comment about the service of black troops offended Davis but he replied carefully, reflecting his years of working around white commanding officers. "I don't think there's any question about their outstanding performance in Vietnam, regardless of whether they are Negroes or not," said Davis, his voice rising. In World War II and Korea, black soldiers fought under—selecting the right words—"an unnecessary burden." The burden—his way of referring to segregation in the military—had been removed, he said. "We have a real fine operation in which every man can prove himself, and this is the way it should be."

Making one last stop before returning to the United States, Payne revisited the country that had once been her home for three years. "Rip Van Winkle awakening from his 20-year sleep could not have been more amazed than I at the changes I found in Japan after 16 years." As she rode in from the airport, nothing seemed familiar. "The freeways stretching like strips of spun-ribbon taffy could have been Washington, D.C., or any other American city." When Payne asked her young cabbie about the Dai-ichi Hotel, General MacArthur's headquarters, in front of which she had stood on her last day in Japan, he thought she was talking about a hotel. When they passed it, she saw it now served as an insurance building.

There was, however, one unchanged aspect of life in Japan that saddened Payne. The tan babies, children of black American soldiers and Japanese women—some of whom had reached adulthood—continued to face discrimination. "They are scorned as outcasts and inferiors," she wrote.

She boarded a flight back to the United States. Sixteen years earlier she had crossed the Pacific by plane to come to work for the *Defender*. Once again she was making a similar journey to begin a second chapter in her life as a reporter for the storied paper. Yet, resuming the beat that she had given herself—that of civil rights—she knew that these many years later the movement remained a long way from its goals.

CHAPTER 28

THE POOR PEOPLE'S CAMPAIGN

U PON HER RETURN FROM VIETNAM IN MARCH, ETHEL Payne wasted no time in resuming her old duties as the *Chicago Defender*'s Washington correspondent. Once again she rushed about covering goings-on in Congress and at the White House, attending Commission on Civil Rights meetings, churning out profiles of high-ranking blacks, particularly women, and restarting her column So This Is Washington after an interlude one week short of nine years.

As a member of the press, Payne regained entrée to Washington social life, especially now that once again, in contrast to the previous decade, Negroes were in demand among the liberal power brokers. For instance, Payne found herself on the list for a diplomatic white-tie dinner and was seated at a table with Soviet ambassador Anatoly Dobrynin. "Well," said Payne, "that called for the full treatment—nails, hair, etc," she said. "All gussied up in a high style wig, floating chiffon and a stand-up girdle with sittin' down shoes."

Her new apartment, into which she had just moved, doubled as an office. Its $165 rent was a godsend, as her *Defender* salary of $785 a month was a considerable cut in pay from what she had earned at the Democratic Party. Less spacious than her last place on Belmont Road, the new flat on Sixteenth Street nonetheless was cleaner, safer, more convenient, and filled with light. (In this, her fifteenth year in Washington, she still retained her voting address in Chicago.)

"During the day and night, while I'm working, it gets cluttered with papers spread all out," said Payne, "but when company comes I pile it all in a rolling file which can be whisked under the map ledge in the hallway." She kept a radio on at all hours and made frequent dashes by cab to Capitol Hill or the White House, where she was once again obtaining accreditation as a correspondent, this time for Sengstacke Publications, which now included the *Memphis Defender*, the *Pittsburgh Courier*, and the *Detroit Chronicle*, in addition to the original *Chicago Defender*. This enlarged publishing empire expanded Payne's readership.

IN EARLY JUNE, Payne joined 750 men in black tie and women in gowns for chicken and sweet potatoes at the twenty-fourth annual gathering of the Capital Press Club in the Sheraton-Park Hotel. Payne was one of three reporters whom the club was honoring that night with its Journalist of the Year Award for her reporting from Vietnam. It was the second time the club had given her the prize. The last time it had been for her reporting on the Bandung conference eleven years earlier.

The club had scored a coup and landed Martin Luther King as its dinner speaker. There had been considerable debate among club leaders about King's appearance since he had come out against the Vietnam War. Many of his movement colleagues, including the NAACP, were rushing to disassociate themselves from his efforts to connect the civil rights and peace movements. His allies in the white press deserted him as well. The *New York Times* said that by fusing race and peace King had done a disservice to both movements. The *Washington Post* said that his stance had diminished his usefulness to his cause and country.

Even the *Defender* joined the chorus of critics. First, it did so by reprinting Payne's account of how soldiers viewed the war on the front page a week after King's speech. In her article, she reported that 99 percent of the men she interviewed while in Vietnam supported the war. Eleven days later, the editorial page made the *Defender's* views clear. Saying that King "had been swept along by the prevailing tide of hysteria against the war in Vietnam," the paper predicted that "he will be a shepherd without flock."

"He knew he was under siege for his views," observed Payne, who sat not far from him at the club dinner. When he took to the lectern, King began by recalling the halcyon days of the movement in the 1950s and early 1960s and its great legislative victories in 1964 and 1965. "Now we are moving into a transition period, moving from one phase of the revolution to another," he said. "We are in a struggle for genuine equality." The early gains, such as opening hotels, transportation, and restaurants, were won at a "bargain rate," King continued. Finding jobs for Negroes and eradicating the slums lay ahead. "The audience," said Payne, "was so quiet one could have heard a mouse running over velvet."

In a slow and rhythmic cadence, King continued. "There must be a radical redistribution of economic power." Whenever the government funds a poverty project in Mississippi, it is labeled creeping socialism. "In this country there is socialism for the rich," King said. "Only the poor are cast out into the unproductive world of free enterprise."

"By this time," said Payne, "the audience had come alive and the applause was at steady intervals, but a hush fell again as Dr. King approached the third phase of his speech on the subject of war." Without mincing words, King repeated his opposition to the war and claimed that women and children had been brutalized while others had been victims of napalm. These charges, Payne noted in her account of the speech, were unsubstantiated and "indicative of the weak spot in the King logic." It was clear that, just back from her carefully managed tour of Vietnam, Payne was not ready to join the critics of war even if they now included King.

But King was not done with confronting his own critics. "To those who say, why don't you stick to civil rights and leave the peace issue alone, I say, I refuse to be limited or segregated in my moral concern." The applause was deafening, reported Payne. In her eyes King, the dissenter, had won over the crowd and, at least on this point, her as well. "When he finished there was a standing ovation and it was clear to the hawks and the doves that 'the conscience of America' had spoken clear and firmly."

LESS IMPRESSED WITH THE GENUINENESS of King's stance on the war was Payne's rival Carl Rowan, who along with her had pursued the same trail of stories in the civil rights battlegrounds of Montgomery and Little Rock. He published an attack in the widely circulated *Reader's Digest* claiming that King had been transformed by communist influence and his growing sense of self-importance. As a result, King had alienated important elements of the civil rights movement and become persona non grata to the president, Rowan concluded.

It was indeed true that a rift had opened between King and Johnson. The war was also causing discord between the White House and other African Americans who had previously supported the president. Several months later, Payne was at a luncheon put on by Lady Bird Johnson as a forum for a discussion about urban crime and violence. The singer and actress Eartha Kitt—then regularly referred to by the press as a "sex kitten"—used the moment to directly criticize the war policy of the hostess's husband. Shouting angrily at the First Lady, Kitt said that youths were rebelling because they were "snatched off to be shot in Vietnam."

Lady Bird Johnson grew pale but Kitt continued her tirade. Others in the room grew silent. "The sisters of color who were present became immobilized like so many ebony statues," said Payne. "It was like Watts in conflagration in the White House." The press loved the moment, and Kitt's assault made the front page of newspapers everywhere and received scolding editorials from many quarters. Despite a growing admiration for and friendship with the First Lady, Payne wrote a long and evenhanded account of the conflict that concluded Kitt had been provoked by behind-the-scenes machinations that thwarted her plans to use a visit to Washington to support several antipoverty efforts on Capitol Hill.

KING'S FALLING-OUT with the Johnson administration was not the civil rights leader's sole problem. His Southern Christian Leadership Conference (SCLC), formed following the Montgomery bus boycott, was losing members and hemorrhaging money. He faced a leadership challenge among young followers from Stokely Carmichael, who controlled the Student Nonviolent Coordinating Committee (SNCC) and had replaced the slogan of "Freedom Now" with "Black Power."

Payne pursued the story of King's transformation and struggles to win back leadership of the civil rights movement. From Cleveland, Ohio, she reported on his denunciation of the emerging radicals. "He did not name anyone specifically," said Payne, "but it was clear that his attack was aimed at black-power advocate Stokely Carmichael and his followers." The new leaders were inciting people to riot while remaining as bystanders, according to King. "When I urge people to march, in nonviolent peaceful protest, for their rights, I make sure that I am at the head of the line, leading them, and not skulking behind."

In August 1967, Payne traveled to Atlanta for a convention in honor of the SCLC's tenth anniversary. There King confronted his restless delegates by proposing a campaign of massive civil disobedience as an alternative to rioting. Specifically, he called for poor people to come to Washington for a sit-in. Payne was skeptical of King's plans. "Neither are the suspicious hostile ghetto youth, the fifteen- to twenty-five-year-olds who give vent to their rage by smashing store windows and hurling Molotov cocktails, convinced that King's way is the answer to their frustration," she reported. "To them it seems, nonviolence is Whitey's way of keeping things quiet in order to continue exploiting black people."

Three years after the passage of the 1964 Civil Rights Act and two years after the 1965 Voting Rights Act, it seemed to young African Americans that they faced a future not much better than that of their parents. Black power offered a new and promising call for change. "King," Payne said, "knows that he is in a race against time to defuse the ticking bombs of impatience in the big cities." The urban disorders and the controversy over black power were causing many to think that the civil rights movement was coming to a close. The *Nation*, one of the stalwarts of the movement among the white press, believed it was "nearing the end." Everywhere Payne looked she saw evidence that the unity she had chronicled since 1955 was crumbling. The previous month she had reported on a mini-revolt at the NAACP convention in Boston challenging the rule of the organization's old guard. In Newark, New Jersey, Payne had chronicled the National Conference on Black Power.

It was a somber moment for Payne. She told her readers the Newark gathering signaled that "the point of no return was reached in the crisis of race in America." Even though the meeting was held in the Cathedral House, a facility of the Episcopal Diocese of Newark, delegates attacked religion as "a hobble to black independence." Even though Payne no longer attended church, she was nonetheless shocked. "But such is the temper of the times that yesterday's crusaders are as old and out of date as whalebone corsets," she wrote. "The word Negro is out and black is in and the machete knife of black impatience is hacking through the hundreds of accepted mores." From Boston to Atlanta, Payne found the movement in disarray.

"The use of the word 'disarray' gets at me," said James Nabrit Jr., who after announcing his resignation as president of Howard University sat down for a long interview with Payne. "We have always had infighting among individuals and organizations," he said. "There is not a Negro or a white person who can say, with accuracy, what a Negro should do or not do. We can't sit down and pick one Negro to lead."

THE DISUNITY DID NOT STEM from a lack of effort on the part of the old guard. Payne was convinced that King was trying to move the SCLC forward rather than resist change. He obtained consent at the August conference to organize Afro-American unity meetings, put on identity workshops, and promote community economic development programs. The move toward Afro-American unity, Payne reported, was an enormous shift from King's philosophy of interracial cooperation. "It means that the Nobel Peace Prize winner is taking a bold step to grab the initiative in the black revolution from the more extreme black power advocates."

Over the fall, Payne found that official Washington was growing nervous with what it saw. The previous almost deferential tone of the civil rights leaders was turning hostile, and King, who had been considered by many in the capital to be a moderating force, now spoke in heated tones. "We have found throughout our experience that timid supplication for justice will not solve the problem," he told an interviewer. "We have got to confront the power structure massively."

Senator John McClellan, an Arkansas Democrat who chaired the special Senate subcommittee that investigated crime and civil disorder, met with Payne and a few other colleagues of hers. He wanted to send a message through the black press to the organizers of the planned poor people's march. What King is planning to do, McClellan said, may violate the law. "This borders on tyranny and insurrection," the senator said. "These people ought to be advised before they start the march that they will be stopped."

King's planned protest, however, was gaining traction. In January 1968, Carmichael—no longer with SNCC—convened a closed meeting with almost a hundred civil rights leaders at New School of Afro-American Thought on Fourteenth Street in Washington. Payne, along with other reporters, was kept at bay, standing in the freezing cold until midnight before giving up and deciding to piece together an account the next day from her sources. What she found was encouraging news for King. The group had not attacked the old guard. Instead they appealed for a united front.

A few weeks later Payne further learned that Carmichael would join the protest if certain conditions were met, such as a pledge from King that he would hold out for actual congressional action rather than promises. She found a more conciliatory black power advocate. "Stokely Carmichael is sincerely dedicated to Black Unity, or least he projects this image," reported Payne. "In an effort to win more grassroots support he has stopped his public rabble-rousing and temporarily the sound of 'honkey' and 'uncle tom' has gone into the freezer."

As she had done with civil rights legislation while a reporter in the 1950s, Payne assiduously pursued the story of the Poor People's Campaign. Like King, she was frustrated by the lack of progress following the legislative and judicial victories of the movement and was encouraged by the prospect of shaking up government. "All that talk about putting up shacks among the cherry trees has official Washington shuddering and the promoters of the Annual Cherry Blossom Festival horrified at the thought even of violating the tranquility of the sacred limbs," Payne wrote as plans for the protest took shape.

She followed the story behind the scenes, reporting that King and Carmichael were holding secret meetings and that an appeal from the White House to call off the march had been dismissed. Even at the SCLC, said Payne, changes were being implemented for the new mission. "Our policy and goal," said the organization's new manager, "is to organize the SCLC to the point where it can be an organized movement and not simply a movement organization."

Carmichael lived up to his side of the bargain and continued to refrain from his incendiary vocabulary of the past. At a press conference to announce the aims of the new Black United Front and its support for the poor people's march, Payne kept her eyes on the man. "Stokely Carmichael was massively present, but passively silent," she wrote.

By mid-March, Payne had learned all the details of the planned springtime mobilization. It called for King to kick off the protest by being arrested for holding a sit-in at a government office with about a hundred followers on April 22. Afterward, caravans of buses would begin their trek to Washington loaded with poor people from all parts of the country. A campsite, with kitchens and toilets, would be erected somewhere in the nation's capital to house the protesters, who would stay for at least two months. They would call the site the New City of Hope.

CHAPTER 29

RESURRECTION CITY

ARTIN LUTHER KING'S TALK OF BRINGING A NEW protest to Washington frightened national leaders, much as A. Philip Randolph had twenty-seven years earlier when he called on black Americans to march on the capital. White elites were befuddled. From their reading of white newspapers and viewing of mainstream television news, many had presumed the need for protest was over now that black citizens had been generously granted the civil rights so long denied to them. And as far as poor people in general were concerned, had not Johnson's War on Poverty generously come to their aid?

Ethel Payne watched with eagerness and hope. If King's planned protest came off, it would directly challenge the nation's power structure in ways that had not been done before. He wanted to bring together the downtrodden and disinherited members of society across all racial and ethnic lines to force a confrontation over the biggest societal division of all—that which kept the poor in poverty. Despite ennobling and historic legislation as well as lofty federal programs, the nation would soon confront evidence that it had failed to overcome racism and poverty. "People ought to come to Washington, sit down if necessary in the middle of the street and say, 'We are here; we are poor; we don't have any money; you have made us this way,'" wrote King. "'And we've come to stay until you do something about it.'"

There remained only one holdout from the growing unity. Speaking at the National Press Club on April 3, Roy Wilkins, the NAACP's executive secretary, said his organization would not join in. There would be a great danger of violence because King might not be able to control the marchers, Wilkins said. Payne was furious. She had her own complaints about King. In fact, Payne was one of several black reporters who knew about King's extramarital relationships but kept quiet. But Wilkins's speech criticizing King was for her a violation of a long-held rule among African Americans. "Never under any circumstances could you have got me to stand up in front of an audience of white people—hard nosed, some bigoted newsmen—and downgrade him," she wrote privately to friends.

ON THE DAY WILKINS LOBBED his criticism at King, the civil rights leader was eight hundred miles away from Washington in Memphis, Tennessee. He had come to the city in support of striking sanitation workers. At a packed church meeting, with a thunderstorm raging outside, King spoke of the threats on his life. "Like anybody, I would like to live a long life," he said. "Longevity has its place. But I'm not concerned about that now. I just want to do God's will. And He's allowed me to go up to the mountain. And I've looked over. And I've *seen* the Promised Land. I may not get there with you. But I want you to know tonight, that we, as a people, will get to the Promised Land! And so I'm happy, tonight. I'm not worried about anything. I'm not fearing any man. My eyes have seen the glory of the coming of the Lord!"

Less than twenty hours later King lay dead on the second-floor balcony of the Lorraine Motel, struck by a single bullet fired from a Remington rifle whose trigger was pulled by an assassin who had been on his trail across the country and escaped capture.

The anger in black neighborhoods could not be contained. By midnight rioting broke out in Washington and dozens of other cities. The next day confrontations between rioters and police in the capital grew so intense that President Johnson brought in federal troops to restore calm. "It was almost like the sacking of Rome by the barbarians here," said Payne. "For four days we were literally under siege or rather the curfew and the restrictions made it seem like that."

Despite her allusion to Visigoths, Payne was not unsympathetic to the rioters. "These were the have-nots of the city—those who have dwelled in the shadows of the Capitol for so long and who have been ignored by Congress," she said privately. When the rampage was over, Payne wandered out, armed with her press pass, to look over the damage at the epicenter of the riot, where buildings were still smoldering. She found that "first to go were the notorious credit houses and discount places which have been robbing the people for years." Except for the Salvation Army, whose destruction she chalked up to a mistake, those businesses with signs of "Soul Brother" or "Soul Business" had been spared. These included the office of her doctor Edward C. Mazique, a famed African American physician who was friends with civil rights leaders, on whose window was scrawled "Soul Doctor," and Reverend Walter Fauntroy's New Bethel Baptist Church. In contrast, the white-owned grocery store at the corner was a pile of ashes and twisted metal.

Back in her apartment, Payne was deluged with calls from readers, activists, and mentees wanting to talk and get direction. "Nowadays it's a different world with the accent on youth, and this should be so," she said when telling friends about the calls. Payne felt the only thing she could do was repeat advice she had given for years. "So I go back to the old premise that women united can change things, not with pretty theories and polite tea parties, but by coming to grips with the heart of the problem." Specifically, Payne told callers, there were three women best suited for the task. They were Coretta Scott King, Jacqueline Kennedy, and Myrlie Evers, all three widows from assassinations. "Together they can have a powerful impact on the conscience of America."

Payne decided not to go to Atlanta for the funeral. She kept her reasons private. But it was not for any loss in admiration for the slain leader. She had stuck with him even after he turned against the war while she had not. She noticed, with satisfaction, that Roy Wilkins—who had withheld his support of the Poor People's Campaign—stayed away as well. Watching the funeral on television, she was glad of her decision. "The spectacle at Atlanta of so many politicians jostling for position at the funeral, some of whom had only lately condemned Martin Luther King's tactics, was appalling," she said.

RALPH ABERNATHY, whom Payne had first met during the early weeks of the 1955 Montgomery bus boycott, assumed the leadership of the SCLC, beating out Jesse Jackson, the youngest member of King's entourage. He vowed to complete King's planned Poor People's Campaign. As the first vanguard of the poor reached the capital in early May, Payne wrote: "Martin Luther King Jr. has achieved in death what eluded him in life—a coalition of the poor people of America." Senators Russell Long and Robert Byrd, evangelists of segregation, fumed but were powerless to stop high government officials in the executive branch from putting out the welcome map for the marchers' representatives, all of whom were running late. "It was the first time," Payne wrote, "that it could be accurately said that the government of the United States waited for the poor people."

But experience restrained Payne's enthusiasm. She knew from her years of covering Congress that it was unlikely to simply yield to the protesters' demands. "But right now with the charred ruins of the cities, the ghost of Martin Luther King, and the strains of 'We Shall Overcome' pervading the atmosphere," Payne wrote, "the jumpy legislators don't want to offend the downtrodden who have come to collect the promissory note of King's dream." On his list had been demands for full employment, a guaranteed minimum income, $30 billion for anti-poverty programs, and the annual construction of 500,000 affordable residences.

At the start, the marchers won their first concession from the government. It agreed to permit them to use a fifteen-acre strip of land parallel to the reflecting pool near the Lincoln Memorial. Below the massive memorial to the emancipator and stretching out on America's most famous lawn, organizers set out to build a city to host representatives of its poorest segments. The encampment was named Resurrection City.

At first, Payne thought she saw a high level of organization. Architecture students from Xaverian College created prefabricated structures of plywood that were erected, forming small neighborhoods. Important health information was collected from each resident and an elaborate system of identification, including identity cards, was put into operation.

Caravans of buses, even a mule train, departed from different points around the country such as Selma, Alabama, and Marks, Mississippi, loaded with poor whites, blacks, Hispanics, and Native Americans, headed toward Washington. But when the buses reached their destination, Resurrection City was not yet ready to receive them. After several days, reports began to circulate of low morale and sickness. Payne, along with reporters from the *Washington Star* and the *Times* of London, met with Reverend James Bevel, an SCLC leader. He said that only a few had abandoned the encampment but admitted the Poor People's Campaign was having financial trouble. "We are live theater," Bevel told Payne. "Just as some Broadway productions have to close down temporarily for lack of funds, this is our situation, but we don't expect to have to do this."

Payne was skeptical of Bevel's claims. She went to St. Augustine Catholic Church, where priests and nuns were trying to house and feed marchers for whom no provisions had been made. Among them were eighty members of the Blackstone Rangers, one of the most famous gangs from Payne's hometown of Chicago and adherents of the black power movement in the city. When told they would have to build their own shanties, the Rangers drifted off into the city. Rumors spread they were seeking to connect with other gangs and spark violence. "It turned out," said Payne, "that they were on a sightseeing tour."

In the church's cafeteria, Payne found a young priest from Chicago. "I'm cheesed off," he said while halfheartedly stabbing food on his plate. "Nobody wants to listen and face facts. Here you have 387 people with no plan and no direction." Nearby, in the corner, a group of white protesters from Milwaukee and Madison, Wisconsin, sat forlornly awaiting instructions or help from organizers.

City church leaders told organizers that they could no longer cope with the deluge of marchers while the construction continued on the six hundred shanties being erected on the mall. The press was beginning to report on the chaos, but the SCLC leadership kept the cameras at bay. "We've had it," said a CBS news employee after waiting for more than an hour to speak with a protest coordinator. "Most of us are in sympathy with your cause, but we're fed up with your uncooperative attitude."

"Well," replied the coordinator, "you're going to slant the news anyway."

Andrew Young, who was now second in command of the SCLC, repudiated the statement, but the damage was done. And Payne found the hostility to the white media was also repeated when well-known cartoonist Bill Mauldin followed a caravan from Chicago with the intention of drawing cartoons, as he had done in World War II, in support of the cause. Marshals informed him there was a ban on the news media. "Hell," he said, "don't they know I'm for them?"

Sympathetic to the marchers, Payne published a warning. "Leaders of the Poor People's Campaign have scoffed at stories of disorganization and dissension as manifestations of a biased press," she wrote. "But as the march was going into its third week, it becomes the unavoidable truth that unless some sense of responsible direction and coordination is given to the campaign, and very soon, it is doomed to collapse and Martin Luther King's dream of the promised land will fade like a desert image."

FREQUENT HEAVY RAIN, with more than two inches coming down over two days alone, turned Resurrection City into a soggy mess. Payne rechristened the camp Mud City. But touring the camp, she found residents to be coping stoically. One tent dweller told her that if such obstacles as rain bothered residents, they would never make it to the promised land.

Payne's doctor, Edward Mazique, established the Health Services Coordinating Committee with seven organizations of progressively minded doctors, dentists, and nurses. It aimed to provide medical care for acute conditions and emergencies, provide physical exams to residents, some of whom had never seen a doctor, and improve the well-being of the protesters by providing health education. He recruited Payne to serve as the group's public relations director.

One day Payne toured the camp with Mazique. He was embroiled in a fight with the city's health department, who did not like his makeshift group's interference with their work. Without disclosing her role with Mazique's group, Payne reported on the fight for control over medical services to the encampment and the complaints of the black doctors. "They said that what was at stake," wrote Payne, "was the philosophy of empathy with the poor which was being established with the presence of middle-class doctors and dentists who were giving time and service voluntarily in a very critical area."

John Conyers Jr., a black congressman from Detroit serving his second term, also spent the day touring the site. He wanted the city to cut its red tape and give permission to lay pipes that would drain the showers into the Tidal Basin. A plumber complained to Payne that official Washington was more concerned with the health of the Tidal Basin than with that of the residents in the camp.

Conditions were indeed Spartan. "When you enter the city," said Payne, "the worst side of the camp is where the big trucks have chewed up all the grass, so that the rains made the ground a sea of mud." She noticed that the higher, drier ground was staked out by young militants such as the Milwaukee Commandos, which had been created as a peacekeeping force during civil rights protests in that city, and a New Jersey black power group. "The language is the tough cool talk of the city," she said. "The girls are as rough as the boys."

Compounding the troubles was disharmony between protesters. Reies López Tijerina, a Hispanic leader famous for his fight on behalf of land-grant heirs in New Mexico, charged that the campaign was black dominated and neglected the issues of Native Americans and Hispanics. Abernathy quickly promised to add land rights and fishing treaties to the list of protest demands. "The rift points up the confusion and failure to develop an all-inclusive strategy by the leadership," concluded Payne.

As organizers struggled with crises brought on by inadequate shelter and provisions, the more important efforts to make political headway were also faltering. Payne found that this failure was due in great part less to the camp's administrative problems than to the campaign's internecine leadership squabbles. Abernathy was no Martin Luther King, and the protesters did not respond to his lackluster style. In contrast Jesse Jackson, who now led the SCLC Operation Breadbasket, suddenly emerged as a potential leader after conducting protests around the city. Payne was moonstruck. She compared his looks, augmented by having let his hair grow out into curly ringlets, to Michelangelo's *David*. "When he strides into a tense situation as occurred during the arrest of eighteen demonstrators outside the House Office Building last week," Payne told her readers, "he raises a clenched fist and shouts 'Soul Power' and the crowd goes wild."

But within days, Payne reported on Jackson's ouster from the leadership as the power struggle within the civil rights movement played out. Taking his place was Hosea Williams, for whom Payne had little regard, calling him bombastic and a trouble seeker. However, she found a glimmer of hope in Bayard Rustin, the brains behind the 1963 March on Washington, who had been brought in to fashion a manifesto, and in Sterling Tucker, director of Washington's Urban League, who was to organize the final demonstration set for June 19.

Rustin put together a seven-point list of demands, calling for jobs, an increase in financial and food assistance, and other specific policy changes. Tucker said he would model the demonstration on the March on Washington, culminating on the steps of the Lincoln Memorial. But once again, Payne's rising expectations were quelled. Bayard Rustin, whom she considered the only person capable of putting together the protest, quit after he was publicly denounced and humiliated by Hosea Williams, who told Payne he was "the real boss of this show."

With Rustin gone, Jackson banished to Chicago, and the camp a waterlogged shambles, Payne felt the protest encampment's end was near. "The pilfering and licentiousness has spread throughout and even the most warmhearted sympathizers now feel that it is time for them to leave."

IN THE MIDST OF the disorder and leadership fights, Robert F. Kennedy, the one national politician in whom most encampment residents placed their trust, was shot by a gunman hours after winning the California presidential primary. Hundreds knelt in the mud of Martin Luther King Plaza in Resurrection City, praying for his recovery. He died the following day, and the hearse bearing his body stopped at the encampment on its cross-country journey to Arlington Cemetery.

The encampment's population fell below 1,000 and leaders valiantly continued to make plans for the culminating protest march. On June 19, somewhere between 50,000 and 100,000 people rallied in front of the Lincoln Memorial as SCLC leaders and politicians spoke. To Payne's pleasure, women took center stage, unlike at the march five years earlier. Coretta Scott King led off speeches by Dorothy Height, president of the National Council of Negro Women; Martha Grass, who spoke on behalf of Native American participants; and Peggy Terry, of the JOIN Community Council of Chicago.

"They expressed the concern and hopes of millions of their sex about the problems of poverty and racial injustice," reported Payne in a front-page story headlined WOMEN SET THE TONE OF THE POOR MARCH. King called for a "campaign of conscience" to be led by women and said that women had a moral obligation to oppose the war. "The white woman," Payne wrote, summing up the speakers, "fights for equality with the white man, but the black woman must fight for equality for herself and the black man."

Talking to sources in Atlanta, Payne learned that Coretta Scott King's remarks, which she had highlighted in her coverage, had a secondary meaning that had escaped her at the time. King was upset by the behavior of SCLC leaders staying at their makeshift headquarters in the Pitts Motor Hotel in Washington. "The carousing till all hours with women of questionable character trooping in and out affronted the wife of the slain leader," said Payne.

Thus Coretta Scott King's call for a "campaign of conscience," said Payne, was "a quiet countermove to the demoralized leadership of the Poor People's Campaign." Having experienced men's demeaning treatment of women in the movement as early as 1941 when she worked for A. Philip Randolph and his March on Washington Movement, Payne knew firsthand what King was saying and confronting. "The emergence of women as leaders," wrote Payne, "has again raised an old familiar bug-a-boo among Negro males, the resentment of female dominance."

THREE DAYS LATER, Payne was sitting in the upstairs lounge of Billy Simpson's restaurant with Willard Murray Jr., a California activist who worked for Los Angeles mayor Sam Yorty. The spot was a popular hangout for notable African Americans in government and entertainment, and its owner was a supporter of both the civil rights and the antiwar movement. Simpson announced that police were moving in on Resurrection City with plans to close it down. Teargas canisters had been set off and the last remaining residents were fleeing.

Payne and Murray caught a taxi and headed downtown. As the two neared Resurrection City, the wind carried the smell of teargas toward them. "All of us were choking with our eyes streaming." Police barricades caused the taxi to detour toward Memorial Bridge to reach the camp. Payne found about two hundred police officers massed in front, women with small babies walking in a daze, and youths with transistor radios muttering threats. Moving to city hall, Payne encountered Abernathy meeting with SCLC leaders and representatives of other groups as Roger Wilkins from the Justice Department arrived.

The police remained at bay and calm was restored. "A young buck grabbed a gas mask from a policeman and ran back into the city," Payne said. "No one attempted to follow him. It was plain that the police did not want to escalate the hostility, since sixteen hours remained before the permit would expire." But it was the beginning of the end. Within several days the hangers-on left, the last ones departing when a thousand police officers cleared the camp.

Payne came across a woman from Mississippi who had endured seven weeks of heat, rain, and mud. Now she wept as she gathered her belongings to return to a life of sharecropping with her husband in Marks, Mississippi. "Drifting like eider down borne by the wind," wrote Payne, "the poor went off in all directions, their tattered banners discarded and their hopes still marooned on a lonely isle of poverty."

After six weeks, the section of the National Mall by the reflecting pool that had teemed with thousands lodged in shanties and tents was empty and quiet except for the sound of the occasional group of policemen on patrol. Martin Luther King's final campaign was over. Like the piles of debris, his Poor People's Campaign was in shambles. "Resurrection City is no more," wrote Payne. "Maybe the dream was only a mirage."

CHAPTER 30

NIXON REDUX

A RRIVING IN MIAMI IN THE MID-AUGUST HEAT TO COVER the 1968 Republican Party convention, Ethel Payne might have rightfully thought that Resurrection City had not died two months earlier but simply moved. Veterans of the Poor People's Campaign, dressed in denim overalls, work shirts, and straw hats, occupied the lobby of the swanky Fontainebleau Hotel. Leading them was Ralph Abernathy, sporting a Brooks Brothers suit. "True to his promise that 'poor people no longer will be unseen, unheard and unrepresented,'" Payne reported that Abernathy aimed to make sure Republicans were confronted with the needs of the poor.

"If nothing else," said Payne, "the whole episode gave the convention the electric charge it was lacking to really get turned on. The sedate ladies from the Women's Division who were selling tickets to a Wednesday brunch for the leading GOP feminists sat in a state of shock at the carryings on."

To the relief of the ladies, the protesters soon vacated the hotel. Payne watched from across the street as the bedraggled group spilled out. She also spotted a yacht making its way down the bay, loaded with Rockefeller delegates and festooned with balloons. "The poor people," wrote Payne, "their tattered banners waving, moved on, inevitable and inexorable—a reminder that 'the problem' was not only there, but was sitting in the midst of the many splendored palaces of Collins Ave."

In the Miami Beach Convention Center, a phoenix-like Richard Nixon, long thought politically dead, locked up his second nomination for president. Eight years earlier, when Payne had been distrustful of candidate John F. Kennedy for his conduct in the 1957 Senate consideration of the Civil Rights Act, Nixon had not been the anathema represented by his new incarnation. The old Nixon was one she had known well. But the man who once pushed for the Civil Rights Act, went to Africa, met with Martin Luther King, and came to her house with a bottle of bourbon was now unrecognizable, wrapped in the rhetorical shroud of his law-and-order campaign. Suggesting that government was soft on crime and police were unduly restricted in their work, Nixon's law-and-order rhetoric appealed to white Southerners who harkened to a life before all the "troubles," as they might refer to the civil rights struggle. Blacks, on the other hand, were leery, concerned that talk of reducing crime was aimed at them.

From Miami it was on to Chicago for the Democratic National Convention. The small protests the Republicans faced were nothing in comparison to what awaited Democrats. Their party was in complete disarray. President Johnson had startlingly withdrawn from the race after faring poorly in the New Hampshire primaries, and Robert F. Kennedy had been assassinated. "The Democratic Convention, which a year ago was rated the most likely to be routine, promised to provide the most suspenseful event of the year," wrote Payne.

In assessing the field, Payne concluded the nomination would go to Hubert Humphrey. In Chicago, where the police fought protesters on the streets and bedlam reigned inside the International Amphitheatre, Humphrey was indeed selected on the first ballot. Payne voiced her doubts of the Minnesotan's prospects on the fall ballot. "Today's generation doesn't remember 1948," she wrote, referring to the period when Humphrey stood up at great political risk for a civil rights plank.

"It is not impressed with the reminder of what happened then. To the reckless and disenchanted younger voters, to the disillusioned black voters today, Hubert Humphrey is regarded as a puppet of Lyndon Johnson, who in turn is denounced as a warmonger, as he strikes out now on the campaign trail."

But the convention did, in Payne's view, have some positive moments. There were a record number of black delegates. The integrated delegation from Mississippi that had been barred from the 1964 convention was seated. And for the first time, the names of two African Americans were put into nomination at a major political party. Channing Emery Phillips was nominated for president and Julian Bond for vice-president. (Bond, however, pointed out that at twenty-eight he was below the constitutional requirement that he be thirty-five years old.) "Whatever else may be said about the disastrous effects of the Democratic Convention, black political power came on strong," wrote Payne.

IN THE FALL CAMPAIGN, Payne wrote almost every week about Humphrey and rarely, if ever, mentioned Nixon, except when there were unflattering reports. As Election Day neared, Payne joined the Humphrey campaign plane. Between San Jose, California, and Las Vegas, Nevada, she talked with the candidate. In her report, she highlighted Humphrey's excoriation of Nixon on the issue of race and the Republicans' failure to rebuke George Wallace, a third-party candidate whose campaign rested on appealing to disaffected white segregationists. Her old friend Nixon couldn't catch a break with her. But on election night Nixon prevailed, and eight years of a Democratic White House friendly to the civil rights movement came to an end.

In December the four hundred or more black appointees in the Johnson administration began packing their belongings and saying their farewells. In the presidency that had brought about the Civil Rights Act and the Voting Rights Act, African Americans had been appointed in record numbers to government posts. Their futures, however, were less secure than those of departing white officials. "While such well-known personages with the Kennedy-Johnson administrations such as Pierre Salinger, Bill Moyers, Theodore Sorensen, Mike Feldman and Joe Califano have left government service for six-figure jobs," Payne told readers, "black members in the super grad categories have only a minuscule chance of landing fat incomes in private industry."

On December 17, Payne joined a large crowd, which included 150 black White House appointees, at the resplendent Federal City Club to mark the end of the era and to say farewell to President Johnson. On behalf of the black appointees, Supreme Court justice Thurgood Marshall presented to the president a mahogany and silver desk set containing an exact replica of the first voter registration certificate issued to an Alabama black voter following the passage of the 1965 Voting Rights Act.

Johnson was moved, noted Payne, and paid tribute individually to many of the figures in the audience, including Louis Martin, who as an editor of the *Defender* had first hired Payne in 1951 and now, as an official of the Democratic Party taking his leave, was heading back to the paper in Chicago. The Washington civil rights guard, to whom Payne was a valued ally, was leaving, and in their place was a new crew, for whom Ethel Payne's name on a telephone call slip—let alone that of the *Chicago Defender*—would mean little.

AT FIRST PRESIDENT NIXON seemed to make an effort to court the black press. Its newspaper and magazine publishers were invited to a White House stag black-tie event given in honor of Whitney Young Jr., head of the National Urban League, who was thought to be in line for a cabinet post. The appointment, if it came, would be significant. Only one other African American had served in a presidential cabinet, and this happened during a Democratic administration.

The appointment didn't materialize, although rumors circulated that Nixon had actually offered it to Young. In her reporting, Payne painted an administration hardly sympathetic to African Americans. She filed pieces on Young's complaint that blacks were not getting jobs in the new administration, Clifford L. Alexander Jr.'s resignation as chair of the Equal Employment Opportunity Commission (EEOC), and Ralph Abernathy's meeting with Nixon, after which he said the president was more interested in the poor of Vietnam than the poor of the United States.

On the other hand, occasionally she saw hints of the old Nixon. For instance, on April 29, Nixon presented Duke Ellington with the Medal of Freedom and put on a gala for the jazz artist's seventieth birthday. The lavish soiree in the East Room went past midnight as many of America's most famous musicians held a jam session. The president joined in the music-making at the piano. "It was nice to discover," said Payne, "that the president wasn't a two-headed monster, but a fellow who could be jolly and human and could play 'Happy Birthday to You' in the key of G."

When members of the National Newspaper Publishers Association, the renamed trade organization of the black press, were invited to meet with President Nixon, Payne sat in for her publisher. Prior to their meeting with Nixon, Daniel P. Moynihan addressed the group in the Indian Treaty Room of the Executive Office Building where years before Payne had challenged Eisenhower during his press conferences. The professorial presidential adviser was the author of *The Negro Family: The Case for National Action*, a report that for three years had rankled many African Americans because of its conclusion that poverty in their ranks was due to lack of families with both a father and a mother present. Moynihan made no effort to make converts among the publishers, according to Payne. "He continues to be a thorn in the side to most blacks and manages to arouse hostility by the pompous manner in which he speaks." When he completed his speech one publisher demanded to know what he was talking about. "Whereupon," Payne said, "Moynihan asked loftily, 'Were you listening?'"

At 5:00 PM the group was ushered into the Cabinet Room, where Nixon and a number of aides awaited their arrival. The president was cordial and listened carefully as the group's spokesman explained their concerns about the lack of black appointments in the administration and the dearth of money in the budget for jobs programs. Nixon promised to meet with the publishers again.

Weeks later, from the third row in the press briefing room, Payne watched and listened as Nixon misstated the size of the African American population, cutting it in half, returned to his law-and-order campaign rhetoric, widely regarded as coded reassurance to segregationists, and pronounced that he had full confidence in FBI director J. Edgar Hoover despite recent revelations that the Bureau had tapped the phones used by the late Martin Luther King.

The Richard Nixon of 1957 whom Payne had respected was gone. In his place was the new Nixon, who found a political advantage in the increasing division between affluent whites and poor blacks. "This polarization, predicted by the Kerner Report,* had been developing quietly under a semi-official veil at a rather lighting-like pace during the past six months since President Nixon took office," Payne wrote.

IN APRIL, ONE DAY SHORT of her eighty-eighth birthday, Payne's mother had died in a Chicago nursing home where she had resided for the past seven months. In her daughter Ethel's ledger, Bessie got credit for having instilled in her a strong code of ethics, inspiring ambition, and steering her to a career in writing. With her mother's

---

* The name given to the report issued by the National Advisory Commission on Civil Disorders, chaired by Governor Otto Kerner Jr. and charged with investigating the causes of the 1967 race riots.

death, Ethel's family was reduced to her two surviving sisters from the original brood of six siblings. Approaching fifty-eight, Payne began to face the sense of mortality that confronts most people as one ages. Within a few years, after the death of yet another friend, Payne would write, "One can be philosophical in accepting death as part of life; nevertheless, the passing of old friends and relatives diminishes one in many ways."

Payne and her two sisters created the William and Bessie Payne Memorial Scholarship in memory of their parents and as a tribute to their belief in the importance of education. In August, Payne put on a gathering to present a $250 check to Mamie Harriday, a shy, slight young woman with big black eyes, who was attending Lincoln University in Jefferson City, Missouri. Thirty friends came, including journalist Sarah McClendon, the cantankerous reporter who had been getting under the skin of presidents since Truman was in office, and Ofield Dukes, who had just opened his public relations firm, with Motown Records as his first client.

When it came time to present the check, the person with the responsibility for the envelope couldn't find it. Payne had to substitute a blank piece of paper. "At least five people told me afterwards that they were prepared to stay all night to find that check as they weren't going to have it said that with all those colored people, wouldn't you know this would happen." The check was found.

Meanwhile *Defender* publisher Sengstacke was once again mulling over the idea of bringing Payne back to Chicago to work out of the office rather than in Washington. It was a reprise of the plan that had led to Payne leaving the paper in 1958. When he raised the subject, Payne bristled. "After sixteen years in Washington," she said, "my roots are here and it is difficult to pull up."

Payne told Sengstacke and Louis Martin, who had resumed his post as the *Defender*'s editor, that she had been away too long and become too oriented to national reporting to work effectively at the paper in Chicago. But more important, the paper needed her in

Washington. The wire services do not provide the kind of coverage that relates to the interest of black Americans, she wrote. In fact, she continued, they ought to be thinking about creating a larger consolidated Washington bureau to represent the black press. The administration ignored black reporters at press conferences and has failed to live up to the policy promises made during the May meeting with black publishers. "Both of these separate incidents reflect the general lack of respect for the black press and our failure to marshal the strength to command it."

Sengstacke withdrew his idea of bringing Payne home, but only for the time being.

PAYNE'S FRUSTRATION with the Nixon administration came to a boiling point in March 1972. She was certain that Nixon purposely avoided her and her colleagues in the black press. The Congressional Black Caucus, which feuded steadily with the president, invited Payne to testify at a hearing on the mass media and the black community. She used the moment to describe three years of stonewalling by Nixon and his press staff. "He has given preferential treatment to individual reports or select small groups, granting them exclusive interviews," Payne said at the widely covered hearings. "No such privilege has ever been given a black or minority reporter, nor has the opportunity to question him during a formal press conference arisen."

Almost immediately following her testimony, Payne got on a plane for Gary, Indiana, for the first National Black Political Convention. The gathering, which included just about every black elected official and activist in the country, including radicals and Muslims, was organized like a convention with delegates. But unlike meetings of the two major political parties, it sought to agree only on an agenda rather than on a candidate.

The *Defender* gave the gathering a billing equal to the quadrennial political conventions, including running a two-page spread of photographs. In her first report from Gary, Payne said the convention "could be likened to a fast race horse at the post, restless, impatient, pulling at the bit and challenging its rider to run with it or get off its back." Gary mayor Richard Hatcher, whose 1968 swearing in as the first elected black mayor of a major metropolitan city Payne had attended, opened the gathering with a speech that she found to be a "ringing challenge to the older order of things."

"We reject the role of advisor to the parties' governing circles," Hatcher said. "Advisors are impotent. We are strong." Instead, Hatcher claimed, as did the following speakers, they wanted to foster a black political unity. "If we are to support any political party, the price will now run high . . . very high," he said. The anti-party sentiment was high, according to Payne. "Perhaps the most significant remark came not from a dashiki-clad black militant but from a modestly suited 'establishment member' who said 'to hell with both parties.' It was a theme taken up by Jesse Jackson. In his speech, which brought the convention to its feet, he warned the Democrats and Republicans 'cut us in or we'll cut out.'"

THE 1972 POLITICAL CONVENTIONS played themselves out as they had in 1968. The Democratic gathering in Miami was almost as chaotic as the last time the party had met. Payne found black delegates divided on whether to support Shirley Chisholm, the first African American woman in Congress and now a candidate for president, or switch to the front-runner George McGovern, or stick with the old standby Hubert Humphrey. In the end, when McGovern won the nomination with 1,729 delegates, Chisholm retained only 152 delegates.

As she had felt with the 1968 convention, Payne believed "blacks came out of this convention with greater bargaining power than they had as delegates." In fact, Payne believed that the activism of blacks at the Democratic Convention might spur on blacks in the Republican Party. It ended up being wishful thinking. When Payne returned to Miami Beach for the Republican Convention she found that black delegates had made no progress and were divided even about selecting a strategy to get a black member onto the party's national committee.

That autumn Nixon won his landslide reelection over McGovern, but 90 percent of black voters remained in the Democratic fold. In Payne's view, the loyalty paid off. "Despite the debacle of the McGovern defeat, blacks have gained considerably more political power nationally," she wrote, detailing the increase in black members in the U.S. House of Representatives.

Still, the tone of Washington, set by the White House, was frosty if not hostile to African Americans. The change that Nixon had brought to the capital was never more evident than in December, when Payne was among a thousand people invited to a two-day symposium at the LBJ Presidential Library, which had recently been completed in Austin, Texas. Former chief justice Earl Warren, the architect of the *Brown v. Board* decision, gave the keynote address. But all eyes were on the former president when he reached the speaker's platform. To do so, he was defying the orders of his doctors, who were worried about his weak heart. Payne watched as Johnson popped a nitroglycerin capsule into his mouth. "Lady Bird strained forward in her front-row seat and Luci's hand flew to her mouth, suppressing a gasp of concern," said Payne. "Nevertheless, his performance was as great as the most famous Shakespearean actor."

Johnson lamented that he hadn't "done enough" for the cause of equal rights, repeated the peroration of his famous 1965 speech to Congress, "We shall overcome!" and called for a renewed thrust for civil rights. "It was a signal to the bench," wrote Payne, "the coach has signaled Congress, the administration and the country that the struggle for equal opportunity is not over."

CHAPTER 31

AFRICA BOUND

As Washington prepared for the changeover in administrations, Ethel Payne received an invitation that put her on the path of fulfilling a lifelong dream of widening the scope of her reporting to beyond the shores of the United States. Since her days as a student in Chicago, Payne had believed there was a connection between the struggle for freedom at home and that abroad. Whenever she could, she would drive the point home to her readers. But with the exception of two trips in the 1950s, one to Bandung and the other to Ghana, she had done it from Washington. Now this would change. To readers, the byline of Ethel Payne and a foreign dateline, particularly one in Africa, would become inextricably linked.

This began innocently enough with a request from Lillian Wiggins, who worked for the *Afro-American*, that Payne accompany her to a meeting with Nigerian ambassador Joe Iyalla. It was not a social call. The ambassador wanted help from the two reporters. Iyalla's native country, the largest black nation in Africa, was in its second year of a civil war that had started after a 1966 coup attempt broke the fragile postcolonial unity among hundreds of tribes thrown together into one nation by European mapmakers. Essentially the Igbo tribe, which lived primarily in the southeastern portion of the nation, had declared its homeland an independent state named Biafra. The Nigerian government launched a military attack to bring the region back under its control.

Although a military underdog, the renegade state was winning the public relations war and gained sympathetic support from the public and politicians in many European nations as well as in the United States, especially after the rebels circulated photographs of children with distended stomachs who were starving as a result of a government blockade.

An immensely frustrated Iyalla told Payne and Wiggins that his government's side of the story was not being told in the press. "He felt," Payne said, "that they just weren't getting a break." He invited the two women to visit Nigeria as his government's guests to report on the war.

In late January 1970, Wiggins and Payne left Washington. After a layover in London, where they were ferried about in a Rolls-Royce with a white chauffeur, and lodged in the Royal Garden Hotel courtesy of the diplomatic representative to England known as the high commissioner for Nigeria, the women flew 4,200 miles south to Lagos, the capital of Nigeria, on the Atlantic Coast of Africa.

Unlike life in war-torn Vietnam, the situation in Lagos seemed quite normal to Payne. "Except for a few minor inconveniences, one would scarcely know there was a war going on here," she said in her first dispatch. "Nobody from the vendor on the street corner to the residents of the palatial homes on Victoria Island or Ikoyi is really suffering."

But as far as Ethel Payne was concerned, she had not traveled halfway around the world to report on a war from the safe confines of the capital city. She pressed her hosts to send her closer to the fighting. The government agreed to fly Payne and Wiggins to Port Harcourt, which had been recaptured by the most notorious of its military commanders, a soldier with the moniker of the Black Scorpion. Colonel Benjamin Adekunle's nickname was only a small part of the lore surrounding him, as Payne soon learned. "He is wily and a master in guerrilla tactics as well as espionage," Payne said. Once he disguised himself as a fisherman to rescue his wife and children marooned on an island under siege by rebels. "Three times the rebel radio has reported him killed," said Payne, "and he is constantly the target of would-be assassins."

Excited by the prospect of meeting this wartime legend, Payne and Wiggins climbed into a small plane. On board they found their press party had grown to three, as they were introduced to Winston Churchill, the grandson of the wartime British prime minister. A member of the Conservative Party and a supporter of Biafra, he had come to Nigeria on assignment for the *Times* of London.

UPON LANDING IN PORT HARCOURT, the three reporters were immediately taken by car to Colonel Adekunle's house, traversing no fewer than five checkpoints before reaching it. The colonel, in white slacks and a maroon pullover, greeted them in his living room. While chain-smoking cigarettes and offering his guests drinks from a well-stocked bar, Adekunle pored over maps and barked out orders. When he snapped his fingers, his staff began showing *The Outsider*, an American film in which Tony Curtis portrayed Ira Hayes, the Native American who was among the Marines who raised the flag at Iwo Jima and later died as an alcoholic.

"Adekunle's particular reason for running this film was to make a point to Churchill on the white man's bias," said Payne. The plan did not displease her. She found Churchill to be argumentative and pompous. "Oh, he was so arrogant, so brash," she recalled. "He came over with a fixed idea, and it was almost like it was British colonialism reasserting itself." Churchill had the same effect on Adekunle. "It wasn't long before he came smack up against the leash of the colonel's temper who damned the 'bloody British baaastards' to hell," observed Payne.

The following morning, the reporters were taken by dusty roads into the bush country to visit government brigades and tour a Red Cross refugee camp. A troop commander showed them two young boys who he claimed were rebel spies because they bore special markings on their toes. Their interrogator, apparently the only one who spoke the captives' language, was but a child of fourteen. He had been given a job as a military gofer upon the death of his father, who was killed in action. "War is hard on women and children," Payne wrote in an article about the boys, "especially when they become the pawns and the victims of conquest."

After two days in the field, Wiggins, Payne, and Churchill returned to Port Harcourt covered in dust and exhausted. But the two women's dreams of a bath and rest were thwarted when they reached the Presidential Hotel. An army captain who was waiting for them told them to get into his lorry and go directly to the officers' club, where Colonel Adekunle was waiting for them. When they disembarked, two women in traditional Nigerian garb escorted Payne and Wiggins upstairs and instructed them to disrobe. "At this point," said Payne, "I was beginning to wonder if we were being prepared for the sacrificial offering!"

It was nothing of the sort. The colonel did not want Payne and Wiggins to come into his club garbed in Western attire. In a matter of a few minutes, the two women were wrapped in skirts, helped into exquisite cloth blouses, and topped with large turbans. "Well," said Payne, "we walked downstairs and there was a whole company of officers, with the colonel in the middle, all who arose and applauded." The band struck up a tune and Wiggins and Payne were ushered onto the floor for a dance.

Later that night the reporters retired to the colonel's house for another movie. Soon Churchill and Adekunle were arguing about the role of the Red Cross. The evening came to an abrupt halt, said Payne, when the Brit "made the mistake of saying something about nobody wanting to come out to this stinking country." Within twenty-four hours, Churchill was told he was no longer welcome in the region and he flew back to London. Adekunle apologized to the women for the display of his temper and took them back to Lagos in his private jet, where they caught a flight back to the United States.

THE ARDUOUS TRIP to Nigeria was only the first of a dozen such journeys to Africa for Payne. A year later, she returned to the continent to cover Richard Nixon's secretary of state, William Rogers. His fifteen-day, ten-nation trip would mark the first time ever a secretary of state had toured Africa.

Payne raised the $2,500 she needed for the trip by apportioning the cost to the five members of the National Newspaper Publishers Association. Each of its five members—the Sengstacke publications, the *Cleveland Call & Post*, the *Philadelphia Tribune*, the *Afro-American*, and the *Michigan Chronicle*—paid $500 to cover her expenses. Sengstacke increased his contribution to $600 to cover incidental expenses. "Bless you love," Payne wrote back. "You're the greatest." This was a different tune than the one she had been singing the month before.

The group traveled across Africa at a rapid pace, sometimes spending only twenty-four hours in one country. Nothing of substance transpired beyond the novelty of having an American secretary of state come by for a visit. As soon as she was back in her Washington apartment at her IBM Selectric typewriter, Payne used what she learned in her travels to churn out a lengthy article and a commentary. In the article published in the widely circulated weekend edition of the *Defender*, she provided readers with a crash course on the economy, education, and health needs of African nations and a description of what black Africans wanted from the United States and how Africans felt about American blacks. The commentary offered a dim view of the Nixon administration's policy toward Africa. Rogers's policy statement, produced following the trip, fell short of any expectation that it might contain new commitments of aid and an increase in sanctions on white supremacist countries. It was clear to Payne that neither the concerns of African Americans nor those of Africans were on Richard Nixon's mind.

Unbeknownst to her, the White House tape recordings proved her correct. National Security Advisor Henry Kissinger was jealous of the good press Rogers had received on his trip and shared his annoyance with the president. "Henry," the tape caught Nixon saying, "let's leave the niggers to Bill and we'll take care of the rest of the world."

WHEN CONGO PRESIDENT Joseph-Desiré Mobutu came to Washington soon after Rogers's African tour, Payne was among those invited to the White House for a state dinner. It was not her first encounter with the African ruler. During the trip with Rogers, Payne and her colleagues had floated up the Congo River in President Mobutu's luxurious steamer, eating a meal of beef and asparagus flown in from France. After the White House meal, the guests retired to the East Room to hear pianist André Watts perform. Following custom, members of the press were permitted to mingle with the guests. Payne took a seat behind Supreme Court justice Thurgood Marshall, who had just returned to work after being ill. Pat Nixon made a point of coming over to greet Payne. Her husband, the president, was now rumored to be planning a trip to Africa in the next year. "It's easier for him to show interest in Africa than it is to take care of urgent problems about blacks here," Payne wrote to her sister Thelma Gray.

Payne soon torpedoed the administration's efforts to appear African-friendly when one of Nixon's cabinet members handed her the necessary ammunition. Maurice Stans, Nixon's commerce secretary who also served as head of the administration's Office of Minority Business Enterprise, had gone to Chad on a three-week safari. Upon his return he got professional help to edit and narrate his homemade

movie of the trip. After showing it to his neighbors, he put on screen-
ings at the Commerce Department and at the Women's National Press
Club, where Payne was in the audience. That's where the trouble
began.

The film showed Stans and his traveling companion acting like
British colonists addressing the natives as "boys" and snatching coins
from necklaces on women. More revolting to Payne was a segment
of the movie in which a group of whites uncovered an ancient burial
ground while the natives hung back, refusing to participate in what
they deemed a desecrating act. "After the whites had unearthed the
tomb," said Payne, "it was Stans who displayed the bones and skull
and a few artifacts." The spectators, which included a grimly silent
Ghanaian ambassador, were taken aback. James Pope, U.S. Information Agency African press section chief, rebuked Stans for using the
term *boy* and called the film "an Amos 'n' Andy Show."

Payne rushed an account of the incident into the *Defender*, pro-
voking a firestorm that she further fanned by writing a widely quoted
letter to the secretary. Working damage control, Stans's assistant sent
a lengthy and feisty rebuttal to Payne's bosses in Chicago. In turn,
Payne took issue with the assistant's claims. In the end, Stans agreed
to shelve the film and not show it, at least while he remained in government.

THE FOLLOWING YEAR, on March 11, 1971, Whitney Young, the longtime head of the National Urban League, who had been rumored to
be in line for a cabinet post in the Nixon administration, went out for
a swim off a stretch of Nigerian beach with former attorney general
Ramsey Clark, his wife, and friends. Young, Clark, along with John
Lewis and Jesse Jackson, had traveled to Lagos to attend a conference
on Afro-American affairs.

Ten minutes after Young left the shore, his compatriots noticed that he looked like he was in trouble, raising his arms above the water but not his head. Suddenly a wave submerged him. His friends rushed to his aid, but it was too late. The forty-nine-year-old leader had drowned.

To bring Young's body home, President Nixon dispatched a plane, under the command of Brigadier General Daniel "Chappie" James Jr., who was the highest-ranking black officer in the Air Force. For the journey, the White House selected Payne, Simeon Booker, and photographer Maurice Sorrell, both with *Jet* magazine, and several Urban League and government officials, including presidential assistant Donald Rumsfeld. Three Southern white pilots and a black navigator guided the plane the 5,400 miles to Lagos. "To Whitney Young," said Booker, "it would have been a planeload of examples of the kind of equality for which he had struggled."

Landing in Lagos, as she had numerous previous times, Payne found her way quickly to Young's sister. The sister had the difficult task of going through her brother's personal belongings. In a suit pocket she came across a well-worn copy of Joe Darion's lyrics to *Man of La Mancha*. Across the top, Whitney Young had penned, "I challenge you to leave this room with the spirit of our founding fathers spurred by Joe Darion's lyrics." At Lagos's Cathedral Church of Christ, Payne joined a congregation of three hundred that included a head of state and many prominent members of the American civil rights movement. In what Payne described as the service's high point, Bayard Rustin broke off from his eulogy and sang an old song once sung at funerals by Alabama slaves called "Death Ain't Nothing but a Robber."

When it was his turn, the Reverend Jesse Jackson recalled urging Young to accept President Nixon's offer of a cabinet post. "He told me that he wanted the cabinet job and that he knew he could have done a good job," Jackson said. "But he didn't accept it because he thought that the 'brothers' just would not have understood." The Air Force jet carrying Young's casket returned to New York. Just before landing at Kennedy Airport, where a large crowd waited, Payne listened as Jackson told the passengers, "I don't want to see any of you all going off this plane carrying those souvenirs you picked up in Africa and wearing those funny hats. I want you to button up and be dignified and humble!"

After services in New York City's Riverside Church, Nixon flew to Lexington, Kentucky, which Young had designated as his final resting place. Payne was again among those selected to accompany the body. On the flight south, Nixon and his wife walked the length of the plane and talked with each passenger on board. "At my age," said Pat Nixon, who had turned sixty-nine a few days earlier, "it seems one is always going to funerals." Speaking to Payne and other reporters on the flight, the First Lady said she was pleased her husband planned on recounting at the burial how he had offered Young a place in his cabinet. "I was there," she said, "when he made the offer and I know that he really wanted him on the team."

At the grave site in Greenwood Cemetery, where a chain-link fence still stood that once separated the white graves from the black ones, Nixon won points from Payne and other black observers. "President Nixon's attendance at the burial service in Greenwood and his presence marked the first time that a U.S. president had shown such respect for a black man and such concern for a black family in grief," Simeon Booker wrote in *Ebony* magazine, which devoted more than a dozen pages to photographs of Young and his funeral services.

No more than five months later Nixon again called on Payne for funeral duty. This time it was the death of President William Tubman, the longtime ruler of Liberia. Recent racial remarks by the gaff-prone vice-president Spiro Agnew ruled him out as a leader of the funeral delegation. Instead Nixon designated White House counselor Robert Finch, who had actually been Nixon's first choice for vice-president. Congressman Charles Diggs and the NAACP's Roy Wilkins also joined the group. Wilkins was making his first trip to

Africa, and Payne reported that the last piece of advice given to him was "Don't go near the water."

ETHEL PAYNE WAS FRANTICALLY PACKING for yet another trip to Africa in the summer of 1972 when Maurice Robinson, a CBS producer, reached her by telephone. He was producing a new radio program called *Spectrum,* which featured short commentaries by an assortment of pundits from the liberal Nicholas von Hoffman to the conservative James J. Kilpatrick. Robinson called Payne after lunching with Mildred Roxborough, a friend of Payne's who worked for the NAACP. Robinson told Roxborough that he thought the show could benefit from the addition of a black woman. "I've got just the right person for you," Roxborough replied.

Robinson asked Payne if she would be willing to substitute for four weeks for columnist Shana Alexander while she took a leave. Payne jumped at the offer and agreed to squeeze in a stop at CBS's Washington bureau to take a voice test before leaving the country.

Robinson liked the sample of her voice and caught up with Payne again, this time by paging her at Dulles Airport, where she was awaiting her flight to Zaire. He told her he would be in touch. When her plane reached Kinshasa, an aide from the U.S. embassy brought Payne a telegram from CBS offering her the slot on the show, which now also included a weekly appearance on the televised *CBS Morning News* with John Hart. She would be paid $100 per broadcast; at twice a month it would boost her income by 25 percent. But more important, if she were to get the job, Payne would become the first African American female radio and television commentator on a national network.

Upon her return to the United States, Payne met with Robinson in New York. CBS put her up in a hotel while she recorded her first two-and-a-half-minute commentaries. For the first one she prepared a piece, stemming from her journey to Zaire, about negritude, a movement in

Africa that rejected Western ideas and stressed pride in being black. "Basically," she said, "it's a philosophy of exploring your inner self and your inner roots, and coming to be comfortable, so that you have a sense of pride and a sense of projection of that particular kind of ethnic identity."

Robinson was pleased with her early efforts. But he detected caution on her part. "I think anyone with a heavy news background, such as yours, will take a while to realize the complete freedom he (or she) has on *Spectrum*—to talk about *anything* on which you have an opinion—and the greater the variety the better." Payne followed his advice and soon listeners heard her ruminate caustically about noisy children on planes, charitably about George Wallace after an assassination attempt left him crippled, and nostalgically about Hubert Humphrey.

In 1972, with the exception of Belva Davis, a television reporter on the West Coast, and Carole Simpson, who could be seen on television news in Chicago, almost all broadcast news jobs were closed to African Americans, particularly female black reporters. When Payne took to the air she was an immediate source of pride for many listeners and viewers. John Raye, a black reporter with a Seattle television station who would go on to become the city's first African-American evening news anchor, remembered turning on his set one morning and seeing Payne deliver her commentary. "My gosh, this is something," he said he thought at the time. "Back in those days you very rarely saw black people on television."

The Zaire trip during which Payne received the invitation to join CBS had been, like the Nigerian tour three years earlier, made on the dime of those who would benefit from her news coverage. The Congo had recently changed its name to Zaire by order of its strong-arm ruler, Joseph-Desiré Mobutu. Courtesy of the Press Association of Zaire, Payne flew to Kinshasa in the summer of 1972 for the meeting of the First Ordinary Congress of the Popular Revolution Movement. In stark contrast to the party politics that Payne covered in the United States, the Mouvement Populaire de la Révolution (MPR) was the only legally permitted party in the nation. Its convoluted election rules and doctrines were dissimilar only in name to one-party rule in communist nations, with the result of a long, uninterrupted, and autocratic rule by President Mobutu, who had recently changed his name to Mobutu Sese Seko Kuku Ngbendu wa Za Banga,* or Mobutu Sese Seko for short.

Payne was completely taken by Mobutu and the congress. "It was black power in French and Lingala, sleek and lean and exotic," she reported in gushing tones. Convinced of Mobutu's good intentions, Payne compared him to Adam Clayton Powell in his sense of timing and described his use of power as having led the country safely out of a bloody past of rebellions fomented by interfering outside powers. Payne went as far as reporting that the MPR was created "to give people a method of becoming involved in political action for the job of nation building. It is participation African style."

If nothing else, Payne's dispatches rewarded Zaire's government's generosity by producing a round of flattering stories about Mobutu's rule in the *Defender* and other black newspapers. "Tribal feuding has given way to the fervency of authenticité [official state ideology] as defined by Mobutu. The army remains the backbone of the administration, but it is disciplined to serve, rather than rule," said Payne.

Payne was certainly not alone in her praise for Mobutu at the time. His rule had indeed brought stability to his land. "Ask any Zairian whether he or she disagrees with some of his measures or not and he or she will end up saying that 'Mobutu brought us peace. We don't want any more wars.'" Mobutu also used the Cold War to his advantage,

---

* His new name meant "the all-powerful warrior who, because of his endurance and inflexible will to win, will go from conquest to conquest leaving fire in his wake," according to the *Encyclopedia of War Crimes and Genocide* (New York: Infobase Publishing, 2009).

disguising his repressive tactics as fighting Communists and earning the loyalty of the American government, flattering reports by George H. W. Bush, then ambassador to the United Nations, and toasts by President Nixon at a White House dinner.

But in the end, Payne could not bring herself to publicly criticize a black African leader any more than she could have with embattled civil rights leaders in the 1950s and 1960s. In her mind, to do so would have undercut the movement. Payne believed her duty still lay with the larger freedom struggle, in which, to her way of thinking, journalism was a tool of advancement.

CHAPTER 32

CHINA

T HE DUST HAD HARDLY SETTLED ON ETHEL PAYNE'S suitcase when she had to pull it down from the closet again. On the first Thursday of 1973, she had been awakened by a phone call from California. The man on the line identified himself as Thomas B. Manton. Born in Burma, the son of American missionaries, Manton ran the China-American Relations Society. Manton wanted to know if Payne would be interested in joining a group of reporters leaving soon for China. "That is like a hungry person being asked if he or she would like a choice steak," Payne said.

Only a handful of Western journalists had been inside China since the communist takeover in 1949. When Nixon went in February 1972, he brought with him more than a hundred reporters, but only one female print reporter and no one from the black press. In the eleven months since, the country still remained mostly off-limits to the American press. "For a journalist," said Payne, "the thought of going to China is like a tantalizing prospect of the world's greatest assignment."

However, because Manton's group was leaving in a week, Payne would have to scramble to complete the paperwork, obtain vaccinations, and reorganize her schedule to accommodate the unexpected three-week absence from Washington. The lack of advance notice was because Payne had been a last-minute addition. When Manton submitted the names of seven editors, authors, reporters, and one publisher to the Chinese embassy in Canada, which was handling the details of the trip, as the Chinese did not yet have an embassy in Washington, he was asked if there were any African Americans on the list. There weren't. The search for a suitable candidate led Manton to call Payne. "Who says black ain't beautiful? And lucky!" said Payne.

On January 12, Payne caught up with the other seven members of the delegation in San Francisco. There was one other woman, Susan Sontag, a New York intellectual who was a contributing editor to *Ms.* magazine, the first issue of which was appearing on newsstands that month.

After landing in Hong Kong, the group traveled briefly by train to the Frontier Closed Area, land that China maintained as a buffer between it and the British colony. There the group debarked and walked across the Lo Wu covered footbridge, which had been the scene of famous repatriations, similar to the border crossing in Berlin known as Checkpoint Charlie. On the other side, they completed customs formalities under a huge mural of a beaming Chairman Mao Zedong. "Flanking the chairman on either side were two black Africans in native garb," noted Payne.

Now inside China, a five-member team, who also served as interpreters, acted as chaperones. "Shepherding eight undisciplined Americans around the country for twenty-six days is an exercise in endurance," Payne said sympathetically. But soon she and her colleagues chafed at the constrictions put on their movement. Writing in her diary, Sontag said group members complained that they felt herded about and deprived of their freedom of movement by an endless series of official welcomes involving white tablecloths, tea, fruit, cigarettes, introductions, and speeches at communes, railway stations, schools, factories, and museums. "Americans prefer to be voyeurs," she wrote. "Chinese insist we are guests."

Almost every day the group toured factories, textile mills, schools, universities, government bureaus, and hospitals, at one of which they watched doctors use acupuncture as a form of anesthesia for an operation. With no choice of itinerary, the group was shown only what served to demonstrate the success of the revolution. Typical of their visits was a stop at the Number 1 Northwest Cotton Textile Mill, situated in a suburb of Xi'an. In comparison to American industrial plants, the twenty-year-old factory was more like a community than a place of employment. Dormitories housed thousands of unmarried women in their twenties, many of them bunking four to a room, with squat toilets down the hall. The workers with families lived in three-room houses with outdoor plumbing. The plant operated kindergartens and elementary schools, as well as twenty-four-hour-a-day child care, for the 3,200 children.

During a visit to a unit of the People's Liberation Army, a two-hour drive from Canton, the director of the corps's political division touted the lack of overt distinctions in rank among the soldiers, the friendship between the soldiers and the local population, and the willingness of the soldiers to help peasants in the busy seasons. One soldier earnestly proclaimed that he and his compatriots saw it as an opportunity to help the people. Payne shed her usual reporter's guard. "Instead of being a tax burden to the people, the People's Liberation Army not only feeds itself but is so integrated with the civilian population that it helps sustain it."

Over the next few weeks, the significance of the mural Payne spotted on her entry to China grew apparent as her hosts used every possible occasion to point out China's close ties to Third World nations, something she had first witnessed in Bandung two decades earlier. Officials explained that the government's limited foreign aid budget was devoted to African independence movements in Namibia, Zimbabwe, Angola, and Mozambique. "There is deep consciousness here of China's leadership role in the Third World," Payne reported. "This is reflected in the treatment of her own minorities."

Payne found further proof of the government's commitment to minorities when she and her colleagues were taken on a tour of the Central Institute for Nationalities in Beijing, where a cadre of leaders from the nation's fifty-four identified minorities were given leadership training. Once again, Payne reported unquestioningly on what she was told. "China places emphasis on autonomy and retaining the cultural tradition of these groups," Payne wrote, adding that there was even an official policy to encourage more births among minorities. "This is quite in contrast to the U.S. attitude," she concluded.

PAYNE WAS DAZZLED and astonished at every turn. Unlike in the United States, where her race singled her out in a negative fashion, it was a calling card in China. "Every opportunity the people get, they tell me through an interpreter of their warm regard for black Americans," she wrote to her sister Thelma Gray. "Many places have posters showing friendships between black Americans and Chinese."

In Shanghai, Payne's blackness stopped Chinese in their tracks. In her fake leopard-skin jacket, vinyl boots, and dark glasses, she went out for a walk down the busy Zhongshan Road that runs along the Huangpu River, where ships docked. In minutes traffic was backed up and hundreds of pedestrians began following her. "A black woman in China is a rare apparition," Payne concluded. "I guess there have been so few that it is a sensation." But she appreciated the honest curiosity of the Chinese. "None of the sidelong glances, the nudges and furtive giggling behind hands that I used to get in Japan. These people just come up and stare in innocent wonderment."

Reg Murphy, an *Atlanta Constitution* editor who was a member of the delegation, figured that in the land of the Mao jackets, the crowd had mistaken Payne for an African empress. Murphy hustled his colleagues to gain a position ahead of where she walked. As she came past, the reporters began a slow and solemn salaam. "The crowd of Chinese following Miss Payne turned big-eyed in wonder," Murphy said. "Their suspicions had been confirmed: This was the potentate of some rich country visiting the land of militant equality." Payne nodded her head at her court and swept past. "Only when the troupe was back in their cars did she finally lose control and laugh until great tears rolled down her cheeks," Murphy said.*

In addition to their curiosity about her looks, the trustworthiness of the Chinese she met enthralled Payne. Once, for instance, when she was leaving the Minzu Hotel in Beijing, a member of the hotel staff caught up with her and handed her a worn-down yellow pencil she had left in the room. "Such scrupulous accounting of personal items happens wherever you travel in China," Payne observed. "One American relates how he tried in vain to discard a pair of worn socks, only to have them follow him from city to city."

As it had been for other Western reporters getting their first look behind the Bamboo Curtain, it was all a marvel for Payne. After all, here was a country that less than a quarter of a century ago had been destitute after three decades of revolutionary warfare. Quite unlike its communist neighbor the Soviet Union, it had transformed itself into a seeming paradise where workers were promised an "iron rice bowl" of lifetime employment, housing, health care, pension plans, and education for their children.

"You can't help but be impressed," Payne wrote to her family from her hotel in Xi'an. "There are so many things our American system could take note of." Child care was the best she had seen. Everyone,

---

* A year after the trip to China, Murphy was the victim of a highly publicized kidnapping in which he was ransomed for $700,000. Murphy was able to identify his kidnapper, who was sent to prison.

including the elderly, had a place in society. "I am finding that is the most orderly society in the world—never mind the ideology," she said. "The point is that they have built a stable society where no one goes hungry or uncared for."

For their work as tour guides, the Chinese government officials obtained news coverage of the sort American politicians could only dream. But Payne was hardly alone in dropping her journalistic caution. "The total effect of this hostmanship," said *New York Times* reporter Fox Butterfield, who had accompanied Nixon, "is like a powerful tranquilizer, enough to make otherwise rational and intelligent people suspend disbelief."

IT MAY HAVE BEEN the fact that Payne toured a communist nation from which most Americans were barred, or merely a coincidence, but the Federal Bureau of Investigation became interested in Payne.

On April 11, 1973, the acting director of the FBI, Louis Patrick Gray III, was sent a memo from the New York City field office stating that the agency should take a look at Ethel Payne. "A confidential source who has furnished reliable information in the past" was alleging subversive behavior on her part, the memo said. It requested that the Washington field office identify Payne "and conduct appropriate investigation." They warned, "Extreme care should be exercised in utilizing this information. It must be suitably paraphrased in any communication and, if disseminated outside the bureau, it should be classified at least 'confidential'—no foreign dissemination."

Payne, of course, was not the only American in the crosshairs of FBI investigators at the time. Among its many domestic surveillance activities, the FBI ran a Ghetto Informant Program that had grown beyond its original goal of recruiting informants to even include visiting "Afro-American-type bookstores" to see what kind of militant literature was sold. The FBI targeted black lawmakers as well, such as Representative Ron Dellums, whose office phones were wiretapped, and Representative Ralph Metcalfe Sr., who had been spotted at meet-ings attended by militant black leaders. And even though the FBI had shut down its most notorious program, COINTELPRO, which had infiltrated an endless array of political organizations, the bureau's spy-ing activities continued to include journalists such as Pulitzer Prize winner David Halberstam. No one, it seemed, was beyond the inter-est of FBI field agents.

The investigation of Payne came under the purview of two under-cover operations then being run by the FBI. Her file, at least those portions that have not been redacted, show the investigators were worried she might be a "key black extremist" of "black nationalists." One presumes none of the FBI memo writers read the *Defender.*

In June, the Washington agents reported to their superiors that the subject of their investigations was indeed a bona fide member of the press, was a past president of the Capital Press Club "composed of approximately 100 black news representatives in WDC," and was scheduled to be a moderator at an upcoming National Urban League convention. Hardly the activities of a subversive. Wisely, the agency called off its investigators.

---

* A Freedom of Information request obtained a copy of Payne's FBI file. It was so extensively redacted that most of the information it contained is still being kept classified more than two decades after her death. The author filed successive appeals for two years. The final appeal was denied in May 2014. However, in doing so, the FBI provided a new copy of the contested file. Several sections previously redacted were now visible, intentionally or not. For more, see "US Government Secrecy Making Historical Research Difficult" by James McGrath Morris, Al Jazeera America, October 23, 2013.

CHAPTER 33

YOU CAN'T GO HOME AGAIN

As the summer of 1973 approached, Ethel Payne reluctantly gave in to John Sengstacke's repeated requests that she move back to Chicago and serve as associate editor of the paper. "I hope that it will work out all right," she told her sister Thelma Gray. "I am not enthusiastic, but when I weigh all the options, I've elected to go." Leaving Washington was hard. "After twenty years of covering the national and international scene," she said, "the accumulation of books, papers, memorabilia of all sorts and just plain junk, the order of packing up baffled even the movers!"

Members of Washington's black elite, such as the former chairman of the Equal Employment Opportunity Commission Clifford Alexander, public relations guru Ofield Dukes, and Washington television anchor Max Robinson, put together a farewell party for Payne at the National Press Club. The selection of the venue was a moment to savor. When Payne had first arrived in Washington, the club had barred blacks and women from membership.

Payne put the best face possible on her exit, promising to be "popping in and out of Washington frequently." She warned readers, "Fasten your seat belts, folks, it's going to be a swinging ride. Seriously, I hope to be able to give some input to the kind of fighting journalism upon which the *Chicago Defender* was founded."

By early August, Payne was unpacking her 5,400 pounds of

belongings in a luxurious two-bedroom apartment in a high-rise building on Lincoln Park West overlooking Lake Michigan on which the *Defender* paid the rent as an inducement for her return to the city. The upscale North Side neighborhood, only beginning to be integrated, was a social and economic distance from her native Englewood on the city's South Side. But the move to Chicago not only took Payne away from her active life in national politics, it also sped up her transformation into an icon.

Instead of writing stories about Capitol Hill, she now penned speeches for dinner gatherings. Rather than raising questions at White House press conferences, she was receiving awards for those she had asked in the past. In rapid succession she was solicited to contribute a chapter to a book about black journalism, invited to join a magazine's advisory board, inducted as an honorary member of Delta Sigma Theta sorority, selected for the Ida B. Wells Media Woman of the Year Award, requested to give commencement addresses, and asked by Howard University to donate her papers to its archive.

One day on the street below her apartment, Payne was reminded of her growing stature. Shirley Small-Rougeau was walking with a friend after taking their children to the zoo. As a black civil rights activist in the South, Small-Rougeau had read Payne's work in the *Defender* and admired her courage and tenacity. The two women spotted Payne on the street carrying her groceries, and Small-Rougeau's companion, who knew Payne personally, offered to introduce her. "I felt like I was meeting the president of the United States," recalled Small-Rougeau.

"When I finally regained my composure," she continued, "I started babbling about Daisy Bates, Ella Baker, Fannie Lou Hamer, and all the other folks from the movement that we knew in common. She looked at me and was probably thinking, 'Who is this silly child from Hicksville?' However, she was such a lady, she would never have said that to me verbally."

Payne felt the change from her days as a reporter covering important civil rights fights to becoming the reporter who had been there. When she was selected for a tribute from the Women's Scholarship Association, Payne lamented in wistful tones the end of an era using words that could well have been applied to herself: "The great coalitions that formed the peaceful protest movement that have added such dignity to the cause of human freedom have come apart and are but past phases of history."

However, she was hardly idle. If she wasn't in San Diego delivering a speech at a meeting of the National Council of Negro Women, she could be found talking before the Studies of Afro American Life and History conference in Atlanta. She developed an inventory of dinner-speaker jokes and polished a repertoire of journalism tales drawn from covering the Bandung conference to following Nixon to Ghana, from challenging President Eisenhower in White House press conferences to meeting Martin Luther King. While she had a desk chair in the *Defender's* office, it seemed almost as if her preferred seat was one in an airplane.

AFTER AN ABSENCE from Chicago of more than twenty-five years, Payne was unnerved by the crime in her hometown, particularly black-on-black crime. "It seemed that everyone was living in fear— fear of being mugged, raped, robbed or killed," Payne said. "Homes were not homes. They were fortresses with locks and bars. Gone were the days when we used to sit on front porches and exchange pleasantries with neighbors."

Statistically speaking, Payne was right. In a typical year in the 1960s, Chicago averaged 400 murders. "The death toll in the city by the lake topped 800 in 1970 and 1971," reported the *Chicago Tribune*. "And in 1973, the city hit a cruel new record of 864 homicides." Following two particularly heinous murders committed by teenage black youths, Payne offered a plan of action that she called a "March on

Crime." To unveil it, she spoke at a meeting of the Chicago alumni chapter of Delta Sigma Theta, the sorority into which she had recently been inducted, and used her position at the *Defender* to put her plan on the front page.

"Super Fly and Tricky Dick* are about all that the kids see in examples of making it big," Payne said. "This country is ready for some mass exorcism to drive out the evil that has fallen upon us, beginning with a purge at the top." Her actual suggestions, however, were more modest. They included developing a pact of cooperation between the police and the community, creating a neighborhood alert system, urging those who walked at night to do so in groups, launching an education campaign that would include stickers ("We support the war on crime by doing our part"), and sponsoring essay contests for schoolchildren.

Payne was entering tricky territory. Since President Nixon's call for "law and order," African Americans had grown suspicious of efforts at crime control. It struck many of them as a cover for increasing repression. "Used this way, 'law and order' means that Afro-Americans should get back in their place," said a writer in *Crisis*. Even Whitney Young, one who would never be grouped with extremists, had voiced concern. "Shrill calls for law and order," he said, "have resulted in greater oppression and denial of justice."

Payne wisely enlisted the help of Cardiss Collins, who was serving her first year in a House of Representatives seat that had been held by her husband until his death in a plane crash, and Connie Seals, the executive director of the Illinois Commission on Human Relations.

---

* *Super Fly* was a 1972 film directed by Gordon Parks Jr., one of the earlier blaxploitation films, with music by Curtis Mayfield. "Tricky Dick" was a pejorative nickname for Richard Nixon. Payne was highly critical of most movie portrayals of blacks. "The white cinema structure taps on the desires of blacks to relate to black heroes," she wrote. "In this identification I say, 'right on,' but in the creation of superniggers for this identification process, I say cinemas should cease and desist" (*ChDe*, 3/9/1974, 8).

With the two allies, her effort could not be linked to the right wing's odious law-and-order campaign.

ON SUNDAY EVENING, February 24, 1974, more than forty women, many representing community groups, came to the *Defender* offices for an organizational meeting. Collins and Seals were selected as co-chairs and Payne agreed to serve as coordinator. A week later the *Defender* included an application form to join the "war on crime," and the paper promised to publish the name of each reader who joined. Within months, thousands had joined and eventually the group landed nearly $90,000 in grant money from the state.

"This could not have happened ten years ago," Payne told Reg Murphy, the *Atlanta Constitution* journalist with whom she had traveled in China. The success of her organization, Payne said, reflected the changing mood in the black community; it no longer believed that calls for law and order were racist. "As long as the black community felt it was being singled out by racist white folks, there was no hope of forming an effective coalition," Murphy wrote. "Now there is hope, and one of the heroines of the struggle is Ethel Payne, a woman of strength and poise."

Despite her crime-fighting efforts, Payne's heart was not in Chicago. The mail reminded her of the past and increased her sense that she had left the center of the action. Letters came from Coretta Scott King, thanking her for writing about the new King Center; from Lee Lorch, who had reread her coverage of Little Rock ("[Your words] made me think again of the warmth and kindness you showed us"); from Daniel "Chappie" James, the first black four-star Air Force general ("Just wanted you to know we still love you and miss you very much"); from Lady Bird Johnson, thanking her for a radio commentary reminiscing about LBJ; and from Hubert Humphrey, who had bumped into her on one of her trips ("It was like old times").

Given the chance, Payne headed to the airport. In short succession she went off to Mexico for the first World Conference on Women, part of the United Nations Decade of Women, where she ran into Betty Friedan, and then to Nairobi for another meeting of the World Council of Churches.

IN THE SPRING OF 1976, the peripatetic secretary of state Henry Kissinger prepared to embark on a 26,000-mile tour of Africa. A list of potential reporters was put together for a press pool to accompany the secretary. As the departure date neared, someone looking over the list noticed that it lacked any black journalists, as had happened with the press delegation chosen for the 1973 trip to China. According to Payne, Kissinger suggested she be included. "You know that woman who gives me hell on CBS?" said Kissinger. "Let's ask her." In addition, an invitation was rushed to Charles Sanders, the managing editor of *Ebony* magazine.

To pay for travel costs as a member of the press pool, Payne turned once again to the National Newspaper Publishers Association. Carlton Goodlett, its president, was excited by the prospect of Payne's representing the member newspapers and told his editors that he considered Payne's inclusion in the press pool a "unique breakthrough for the black media." For a long time, Goodlett and other editors in the black press had chafed in their exclusion from State Department matters. Of course, his enthusiasm also reflected his need to persuade member papers to carry a prorated share of Payne's $5,300 travel costs.

The strategy worked and she received a pledge of funding. To supplement her funds, Payne had worked out a deal to file reports for the Mutual Black Network, a four-year-old venture of the Mutual Broadcasting System for African American radio stations. Payne had not considered how her bosses at CBS might react to her plans. When they learned of her deal with the Mutual Black Network, they sent word to Payne and Kissinger's staff, already en route to

Africa, that her contract strictly prohibited her from doing work for other networks.

An undersecretary took up the matter with CBS. He requested that a high-ranking State Department official in Washington contact CBS bureau chief Sanford Socolow. "Please explain to Socolow that important factor in making selection of news organizations to be represented on trip was fact that Ethel Payne was to be black pool media reporter for both press and Mutual Black Network," read the cable to Washington. Reluctantly CBS, who had its own reporter on the trip, agreed to permit Payne to do up to three broadcast reports for the black radio network.

The problem resolved, Payne filed both radio and print dispatches as the delegation continued on its cross-continent dash, stopping in Zaire, Liberia, and Kenya before escaping the continent for a rest stop in Paris. The close quarters gave Payne uncommon access to Kissinger. She found the secretary to be gregarious and inquisitive, frequently asking her questions when he learned she was on her eighth African trip and had been to all the countries on the itinerary. In turn, Kissinger read Payne's dispatches and—like a savvy politician—complimented her on her work.

AT ITS VARIOUS STOPS, the small delegation was frequently included in official dinners and receptions, unlike when Kissinger's entourage traveled through more developed nations. On board Mobutu's yacht, on which Payne had been with Secretary of State Rogers six years earlier, the group ate wild boar with manioc leaves washed down by French wine, and later at Jomo Kenyatta's dinner table, they almost sampled impala. That delicacy was withheld after the State Department sent a telegraphic warning regarding Kissinger's culinary preferences. "You should find suitable substitute for impala, Secretary not a fan of venison at all and finds the prospect of eating impala saddening."

At one point Kissinger fell ill after one of these repasts. Hearing this, the press pool became suspicious. "We remembered," said NBC television's diplomatic correspondent Richard Valeriani, "that it was under the cover of gastroenteritis that Kissinger had slipped secretly into China in 1971, and now we wondered if he were off in the bush meeting with Ian Smith or one of the guerrilla leaders still fighting in Angola against the Cubans." But instead of fretting about the possibility, the reporters instead headed off on a tour of Kinshasa's open-air ivory market led by Payne. There she acquired a delicate carved figure with a cracked crown. "An old man assured me in halting English that it was the careless slip of the apprentice knife, but the face was by the master carver," she said. "What else could one do with such a beguiling performer?"

Payne questioned Kissinger's sincerity. She was convinced his vanity was such that he could not believe a part of the world was beyond his diplomatic skills and would not ignore South Africa. Above the Atlantic on the flight home from Paris, Kissinger granted an audience to Payne and Sanders. They did their best to throw specific questions at him, but most of his answers were full of generalities regarding policy and platitudes about the leaders he had met while in Africa. Only once did a query get under the skin of the normally unflappable secretary of state. When asked why he had not taken any black State Department officials with him on the trip, Kissinger bristled. Pointing out that he did at least include an African American ambassador, Kissinger said, "I think it is an insult to blacks to do things for them just because they are black."

The same issue trapped Kissinger again a couple of months later. Conversations with Payne during the trip had convinced him to become the first secretary of state to speak before the National Urban League convention. The decision apparently did not sit well with President Gerald Ford's aides. When his assistant Richard Cheney and campaign manager Stuart Spencer learned of Kissinger's plans, they worried it would upset their delicate negotiations with Southern

Republican delegates needed to secure Ford's hotly contested nomination bid.

Kissinger nonetheless went ahead and flew to Boston to speak at the convention. After delivering his speech, he took questions from Payne and other reporters. Once again defending the lack of African Americans in the State Department, Kissinger suggested he couldn't find enough qualified blacks. "The requirements for entry into the State Department are generally more complicated than they are for other agencies," he said. "It serves nobody's purpose to appoint black personnel unless they can meet all the qualifications." His comments were met with boos and hisses for having referred to "qualifications" three times. "That was like setting off a blast of dynamite," said Payne. "Kissinger seemed unaware that the word carried for blacks a coded message, implying inferiority which barred them from hiring and upgrading on a par with whites." When he got back to Washington, President Ford complimented Kissinger on his speech. "The mistake I made," Kissinger replied, "was to take questions."

IT WAS A HEADY SUMMER. After traveling to Africa for the second time in the company of a U.S. secretary of state, Payne's request for a private interview with Jimmy Carter, following his nomination as the Democratic candidate for president, was rapidly approved. Less than a month after the convention, Payne was in Plains, Georgia, waiting outside of Carter's house while he finished meeting with California governor Jerry Brown, who had finished third in the race for the nomination.

Payne began by asking Carter about his plans to reach black voters. The presidential aspirant said that in the past blacks had not turned out to vote because they felt it didn't matter who was elected. "Quite often candidates have avoided direct relations with blacks and other minorities," Carter continued. "I've done just the opposite." The interview continued, touching on law enforcement and crime, topics now of great interest to Payne, and education. The interview not only ran in the *Defender* and other black newspapers but was reprinted as well in the *Atlanta Constitution*. Payne left Plains happy. "He talked such a good game that I came away enthusiastic," she said. Yet by October her ardor had weakened. "It's getting late," she wrote, "and there are barely four weeks left in the campaign. I have yet to see any meaningful implementation of those fine commitments."

In the midst of the campaign, Payne found time for yet another sudden trip to Africa as a guest of Senegal president Léopold Senghor for a weeklong celebration of his seventieth birthday. "I was so excited that I am going half prepared (broke all my nice sculptured nails), but that's life." The whirlwind trip took on an added challenge when United Airlines lost her luggage and she had to find suitable clothes in Dakar.

Next it was back to Asia. Payne accepted an all-expenses-paid trip to Taiwan, which, since Mainland China had reestablished diplomatic ties with the United States, was no longer being called China but rather the Republic of China. She and eleven other female journalists were treated like foreign dignitaries and lodged in Taipei's Grand Hotel, a fourteen-story palace-like structure with red columns and topped with a gold-tiled roof. They were, in Payne's words, "dined and wined and yes, propagandized in a manner only Genghis Khan could have matched."

After the journey to Asia, Payne went to Washington for two months. The U.S. Information Agency had hired her to serve on its selection board, which reviewed the personnel files of career officers and made recommendations for promotions. However, Sengstacke viewed this assignment as another sign of her disloyalty, especially as Payne had not informed him personally that she would be in Washington. Since he had brought Payne back to Chicago, Sengstacke had become increasingly convinced that Payne was using the paper as a platform for her own agenda of speechmaking, travel, and activism instead of using her skills to benefit the paper.

"Ethel, we have had a pleasant relationship over the years, and when I requested you to leave Washington and come to Chicago, I stated that we needed your expertise in the home office," Sengstacke told Payne. "Your other activities have kept you busy and out of Chicago and the help we need from your knowledge at the *Daily Defender* has not materialized." Concluding Payne wasn't going to increase her work, Sengstacke decided that the paper would keep her column but cut her salary in half, wryly asking if that was okay with her.

Unapologetic, Payne challenged his assessment of her work. Her articles on national and international news and her work with the anticrime coalition had done a lot for the paper, she argued. As for her salary issue, Sengstacke had hit a raw nerve. "I think you will concede that my salary was never sufficient to meet the basic requirements of living; therefore, I have been subsidizing myself and the paper for a very long time. You, yourself, did praise my work. Do you really want to arbitrarily cut it off?"

For her part, Payne was unconvinced that her frequent absences were the source of the friction between the two. Rather, she believed that each other's prideful nature combined with Sengstacke's cold demeanor made them incompatible. "For all the years I have known you, there has been a Berlin Wall of ice between us most of the time, and it is this which has led me to avoid you as much as possible. On those occasions when you were relaxed enough to laugh and banter, it has been a real joy," Payne told him. "Maybe I should spit fire and say, 'Now look here, John Sengstacke. I see it this way.' You might have thrown me out on my ear, but at least there would have been communication.

"I would like to declare a truce in this cold war long enough to sit down with you, not with your glowering at me across the desk, but maybe for coffee or a drink. I may even have you over for dinner from my poor larder and I promise not to poison you," Payne said. "Let's have a little human rights and that's as far as I'm going in being sweet and kind. After being kicked out."

"Respectfully and maybe even tenderly," she closed her letter.

But they were both too stubborn to compromise. For the second time in the twenty-seven years since Payne first walked into the *Defender* offices on Indiana Avenue as a cub reporter upon her return from Japan, her byline was absent from the newspaper's pages.

CHAPTER 34

FINDING A NEW ROLE

S IXTY-SEVEN-YEAR-OLD ETHEL PAYNE FACED A DISMAL future as 1978 began. Not only had her ties to the *Defender*, an association that had sustained her public identity for almost a quarter of a century, been severed, but also CBS had decided not to renew her contract for her broadcast commentaries. It was, as the network periodically decided, time for new voices and faces. But she was spiritually unwilling and financially unable to retire.

As had happened at other low points in her life, it was a telephone call that offered her a lifeline. An official with the Ford Foundation explained that she had been recommended for a new research program. He told her that the foundation was providing money to George Washington University in Washington, DC, for a variety of research projects and wondered if she might have an idea for one. "So immediately my mind went to the status of black colleges," Payne said.

The foundation liked the idea for an assessment of historically black schools and provided sufficient funds to enable Payne to travel to fifteen colleges, to attend meetings of national education organizations, and to pay herself a salary. Working on this project with her usual zeal, Payne wrapped up the report within the year. She concluded that black colleges still played a major role in closing an achievement gap between white and black students but warned that the schools should insist on retaining their traditional cultural identity now that they admitted white students. "Just as blacks who are enrolled in predominately white institutions are expected to adapt to the ways of the dominant culture, so whites who attend historically black institutions need to have the opportunity to learn from black culture," she wrote. "Pluralism does not preclude the sharing of ethnic traditions."

Delta Sigma Theta published the report as a short book entitled *Black Colleges: Roots, Reward, Renewal,* and it was circulated among black educators, funders, and civil rights leaders. Benjamin Hooks, the executive director of the NAACP, told others it was "an excellent analysis of a very sensitive and complex subject." For a South Side Chicago kid without a college degree, it was a nice moment. But like many such reports, it did little to alter the challenges faced by historically black colleges.

The report done and the grant exhausted, the mail brought no encouraging options. The LBJ Presidential Library turned down Payne's application for one of its grants. Her friend Eddie N. Williams, head of the black-oriented Joint Center for Political and Economic Studies in Washington, kindly told her that she could make a substantial contribution to his organization's work. "At the moment, however, your interests and our ability to meet them do not match up." He even warned that part-time employment at the center was unlikely should she come back to Washington. *Harper's* magazine, the *New York Times*, and the *Chronicle of Education* were not interested in her proposed articles. Even the University of the District of Columbia passed over her application for the post of "Writer/Editor #78-65." Adding insult to injury, it did so using a form letter.

It was dispiriting and frightening, but she persevered. She did receive an offer, one for very little money, to continue her *Defender* column From Where I Sit under a new name, Behind the Scenes, in the *Afro-American* and the *Miami Times*, as well as in a small chain of California weeklies. "And that and my Social Security was enough to, you know, tide me over," she said. "It wasn't that much, but it was enough to tide me over."

THREE ALLIES IN WASHINGTON finally came to her rescue: Louis Martin, who was finishing a stint working at the Carter White House; Doris Saunders, an old *Defender* reporter who was heading up the Census Advisory Committee on the Black Population; and John Raye, the black television newscaster who had been encouraged in his professional pursuits when he saw Payne on television in the 1970s. Raye now worked for the U.S. Census Bureau, which was making an effort to bolster the participation of minorities in the once-a-decade count of the population under orders from the president. He told Payne about an opening for a writer and spokesperson in his office. With his help and Martin and Saunders's support, Payne landed the job and headed back to Washington after an absence of seven years.

In her new post, Payne put her writing skills and editorial contacts to use for the department. Back in Washington, Payne settled into a third-floor flat in the Rittenhouse apartment building, a multistory edifice looming above Rock Creek Park with four wings jutting off at odd angles from its center portion. Her two-bedroom apartment overlooked the complex's pool and was well suited to her needs. She converted one bedroom into her office, placing her trusty Selectric typewriter on a table next to her desk. Soon the office was so cluttered with newspapers, government reports, and books that her old friend Catherine Brown, whom she had known since the 1950s, nicknamed it "the CIA room." On the window were a half dozen potted plants that Payne—as well as her house sitters— doused with water in which Payne placed her used eggshells to reduce the acidity of the soil. The remainder of the apartment was soon decorated with memorabilia such as tribal statues, carvings, her collection of dolls from twenty-nine countries, and photographs of Payne with presidents.

She reconnected with her friends, picking up her old Washington social life as if she had not been gone for seven years. An invitation to a dinner party at Payne's apartment became much sought after. For Payne, a meal at her place was a way to bring interesting people to the table. Many well-known people host dinners so they can hold court, but this was not so with Payne. She was the opposite. Her dinner parties were a chance to let others shine.

She chose her guests carefully and from a wide array of people. "Lord only knows who you were going to meet," said one guest. Normally no more than six people were invited, all selected with an eye to creating great conversation. Food was, of course, important. Southern food, lots of greens, sweet potatoes, and the like were often on the menu along with nice wines. "You put Betty Crocker, Aunt Jemima, Maxim's, and the Tour d'Argent all to shame!" wrote one person in a thank-you note.

AT 2:05 IN THE morning on May 29, 1980, Vernon Jordan, who took over as head of the Urban League after the drowning of Whitney Young, was returning to the Marriott Inn in Fort Wayne, Indiana, in the company of Martha Coleman, a younger white woman who had attended his speech that evening and given him coffee at her house afterward. As he got out of Coleman's Pontiac Grand Prix, an assailant hidden in the darkness shot Jordan in the back, using a high-powered rifle. The wound was serious. As he received medical care in a nearby hospital, the police searched for the shooter, who they believed was motivated by a domestic dispute involving Jordan's companion. But as it was the first assassination attempt on a major civil rights leader in a dozen years, the media descended upon Fort Wayne. Not far behind were President Jimmy Carter, Senator Edward

Kennedy, and Benjamin Hooks. The police finally determined that the shooter was a racist serial murderer who, when he finally confessed, admitted he had been angered by seeing Jordan with a white woman.*

Payne had known Jordan for years as a journalist and frequently had participated in Urban League conferences. In fact, when she left Washington in 1973, Jordan took the time to tell her how much he regretted her departure. "As you move on to your new assignment in Chicago, you leave behind a record of truly outstanding service to millions of readers," he wrote.

Now Payne was not feeling so charitable about him. What was Jordan, a married man, doing out so late at night with a white woman? "If Jordan has a good answer to all the unanswered questions I am sure everything will be forgotten," Payne told the *Chicago Tribune*. "Surely, he owes his constituency an explanation. It must be remembered that black men who align themselves with white women strike a very sensitive emotional nerve with black women. It's part of the whole pattern of rejection of us by black men, and it's not taken lightly."

"There's one thing that's a sore point with many black women," Payne later said, "and that is the trend of black men who have become prominent, who have made it, and who have risen through the ranks, and then the first thing they do is either marry a white woman or live with a white woman."

This was not a new note coming from Payne. Matters of the heart remained sensitive for her as she approached her seventies without a partner. She had found that her professional success had been an insurmountable barrier for many black men. "You know, black women have a particular problem," she told a reporter a few years later. "Some

---

* The would-be assassin was acquitted by a jury but was later found guilty for multiple other murders. He then confessed to having stalked and shot Jordan.

black women have succeeded beyond males to some extent. And that has created some friction because black males sometimes—not often, but sometimes—see black women in competition with them."

"The truth is that black women want to be loved and respected by their own men," Payne had written two years earlier. "They need to be wanted. If they lash out in fury, it is because there is so much pain from within." Counting her fiancé in the 1940s, Payne had lasting relationships with no more than three men. "We understood each other and were good company, and that was it," she said of the men she dated. "But I knew, you know, that there was no percentage in my getting fluttery, you know, because in the first place, I don't think they were interested to that extent."

From his hospital bed, Jordan read what Payne said about him. "As deeply hurtful as her comments were—the most important people in my life, my daughter, my wife, and my mother, were black women—I knew that this was just insane," he said. "It was nevertheless an issue I had to deal with when I began to give interviews after leaving the hospital."

When he was released, one of his first public appearances was before a group of black women attending an Urban League fashion fair. He was asked to make a few brief remarks. When he was introduced, the women gave him a standing ovation. "As I walked across the stage, I thought to myself, 'Where are you, Ethel Payne?'"

THE VERNON AFFAIR was soon eclipsed by the news of the election in which the incumbent president Jimmy Carter faced Ronald Reagan, who after several attempts had finally secured the Republican nomination. Payne picked up an assignment to write an assessment of Carter's chances for *Dollars & Sense*, a magazine edited by Payne's friend Barbara Reynolds.

When they first met in the mid-1970s, Reynolds, a *Chicago Tribune* reporter, had been at work on a biography of Jesse Jackson, with whom she had been a close friend. "The more I dug, the more an unflattering portrait of Jackson emerged," recalled Reynolds. The result, when it was published, brought the wrath of Jackson supporters down on her. "I was accused of using a white ghostwriter to destroy Jackson," Reynolds said. "I was accused of being his lover, who turned mean after he spurned me." Books disappeared from store shelves despite having been on the city's bestseller list, television bookings were canceled, and death threats prompted police protection. Payne came to the book's launch. She had never forgotten Payne's gesture, and now as a magazine editor was able to assign to her occasional articles for $400, money Payne could certainly use.

Payne predicted in the article that Carter could win reelection if he took a number of steps, including paying attention to the black vote. "To do this," she wrote, "he will have to knock some staff heads together and make them understand that arrogance and insensitivity towards blacks, no matter how inconsequential they may seem, will only add to the president's problems."

Payne's optimism, however, was founded more on hope than reality. By fall, like most observers, she knew that Carter's chances of earning another term in the White House were slim. The result, predictable as it was, terrified her. "Along towards midnight of November 4, the emotional reaction among blacks across the country to the landslide victory of Ronald Reagan came close to a massive breakdown," she said. In her own case, the election caused her to wake up in the middle of the night from a dream in which the Ku Klux Klan, the Moral Majority, and the Christian Voice—the latter two being conservative groups that triumphed in 1980—were conducting a purge of undesirable blacks.

IN AUGUST, PAYNE TURNED SEVENTY. "The numeral seventy scarcely perturbs me," she said. "I am blessed with good health and energy enough to continue my normal peripatetic style of living." She even found inspiration in the current occupant of the White House, whose policies she held in contempt. "Thanks to Ronald Reagan, seventy no longer carries with it the stigma of being ancient."

Like the president who had gone from Hollywood to the White House, Payne embarked on a professional transformation. In May 1981, the Fisk University board of trustees adopted a resolution to create a chair in journalism for Payne. The germ of the idea took seed the previous year when Payne's friend Barbara Reynolds visited Fisk University president Walter J. Leonard. He was eager to create more opportunities for women on his campus and to provide his students with inspirational models of strong, successful women.

Leonard and Reynolds developed a scheme of creating a chair, to be funded by a proposed endowment of $300,000, which would bring Payne to the campus in Nashville to strengthen the study of journalism and recent history. "When such names as Adam Clayton Powell, Roy Wilkins, Whitney Young, and Mary McLeod Bethune draw blank looks from high school kids, we're in trouble," Reynolds said.

Payne's friends John Raye and Shirley Small-Rougeau joined Reynolds in the cause. Raye put together a forty-five-minute documentary on Payne's life called *Portrait of a Queen: The Legacy of Ethel Lois Payne*. Small-Rougeau took on the planning of a tribute dinner for June in Washington to raise $30,000 toward the endowment and provide Fisk president Leonard with an event at which to announce the endowed chair that Payne would be the first to hold. Billed with the unwieldy long title of "A Tribute to Ethel L. Payne on Her Selection as the First Recipient of the Ida B. Wells Chair in Journalism and Mass Communication at Fisk University," the dinner took place at Washington's Capital Hilton.

"They came from all points of the country—relatives and friends some six hundred strong to demonstrate their faith in an idea," said a gratified Payne, who basked in the adoration. Comedian Dick Gregory told a reporter at the dinner, "I feel her energy, honesty, and integrity. She represents the lives of all black women, and the beauty of this night is that no one has to tell any lies."

As she was escorted around the room in the company of a prominent television news anchor, Payne paused before a table at which sat Robert L. Woodson, an African American community development leader whose conservative views made him unpopular among many in the civil rights movement. "Would you come and see me sometime?" Payne asked Woodson. Believing that Payne was only being polite, Woodson was noncommittal. "No," replied Payne, "I'm serious."

"The very fact that she made the appointment in such a public place and she said it in front of a television anchor says a lot," recalled Woodson. "There were some people who were shocked." Several days later, Woodson did go to Payne's apartment for breakfast and a vigorous discussion of his ideas, including his opposition to busing. Payne never debated him and only asked questions. "It was refreshing that someone of her age and experience was not full of herself," Woodson said. "She truly thought of herself as a vessel that sought to be filled."

After the screening of Raye's film, organizers put on a version of *This Is Your Life*, an immensely popular television show from the 1950s and 1960s that took a surprised guest through his or her life by means of cameo appearances by friends, family, and professional acquaintances. Ten speakers in all—including her sister Alice Samples, her former boss Louis Martin, former colleague in the White House press corps Alice Dunnigan, and Organization of African Unity ambassador to the United Nations Oumarou Youssoufou—recounted tales of Payne's life in politics, journalism, family, foreign affairs, and civil rights.

"Come fall, when I report to the Fisk campus to take up my duties," said Payne after the soiree, "I shall be remembering the love and support of so many relations and friends who made this dream possible."

CHAPTER 35

ON HER OWN AFRICAN MISSION

B UT BEFORE SETTING OFF FOR HER NEW LIFE IN NASH-
ville in the fall of 1982, Ethel Payne had yet another African
journey to make. By this point she had been to Africa ten
times. Everything African interested her, from the struggles of the
newly independent nations to the fight to end apartheid in South
Africa and Rhodesia. She followed all the news she could get about
African countries and made friends with all of their legations in
Washington. But over the years, what she had actually seen of the
continent was more often than not a blur that came while traveling in
a tightly guarded press corps following an American political leader.
On other visits, she had been the guest of African potentates and
had been offered only flattering views of the country. While she had
briefly escaped her handlers in both situations, she had never taken a
trip of her own design. That was about to change.

She had been staggered by the growing plight of African refugees.
Looking into it, Payne found that 5 million of the 17 million refugees
in the world were in Africa, 700,000 in Somalia alone. The hardened
reporter decided that she needed to return to Africa, but this time on
a journey of mercy.

In March, Payne contacted C. Payne Lucas, a returning Peace
Corps volunteer who headed the multimillion-dollar black-run Africare organization, which he had launched twelve years earlier. Payne,

who had known Lucas since the 1960s, had been an ardent early supporter of the nonprofit. Only a few years after its founding in 1970, she began urging her readers to contribute. "We were struggling in those days and Ethel Payne played a major role in getting our story told," recalled Lucas. And Payne continued to find ways to report on Africare. "Ethel never moved on, she came back time and time again."

Payne told Lucas that Africare should send someone with journalism experience to inspect African refugee camps, in particular those in Somalia, Sudan, and Zimbabwe. If the attention of media on the plight of African refugees could be increased, then Payne believed the amount of aid might also improve. She recommended herself for the task.

Lucas bought into the idea, and the United Methodist Church agreed to pay Payne's travel costs. For additional funds, Africare turned to supporter Vesharn Scales, a successful Maryland builder who had benefited from the new government minority set-aside procurement programs, including the construction of the subway in the nation's capital. He provided the money for his wife, Patricia, who was active with Africare, to join the mission along with Juanita Miller, who would serve as videographer.

Payne, the veteran African traveler, gave Scales instructions. Start taking your malaria medicine now before leaving; don't drink the water there, not even to brush your teeth; bring baby powder for chafing, a wide-brim hat that can be folded up, and as little jewelry as possible. "Things do have a way of disappearing and there is no recourse against theft."

An overnight flight from Rome brought Payne and her two companions to Mogadishu, Somalia. To inspect their first camp in Jalalaqsi, the group elected to travel by Land Rover rather than taking a small United Nations plane that flew only when weather permitted, "We made the five-hour journey over rough roads, arriving with our spinal columns still intact!" said Payne. Despite having traveled extensively in Africa and Asia, Payne admitted she was unprepared for what she faced when she got out of the car at their destination. "No matter how much one has seen through the eyes of the camera or read about the refugee camps, the sight of human misery is a shock."

"Sprouting like mushrooms in the dry, dusty surroundings were row upon row of makeshift huts—put together with twigs and branches covered with tarpaulin," she said. "Here was the habitat of the world's most neglected, the wanderers fleeing from circumstances beyond either their control or comprehension." In minutes Payne and her companions were engulfed in a sea of malnourished children, women who looked years beyond their age carrying infants, and old men and women staring through sunken eyes at the Americans. It was only the first of such sights.

The Somali government did its best to limit what Payne and her group could see. A couple of days later, for instance, the Americans tried to inspect a refugee camp near Qoryooley. But an official thwarted their plans by bringing them instead to his office in time to witness a demonstration by refugees in support of the government. Payne's suspicion about the genuineness of the demonstration was heightened when she noticed that the women were better dressed than the refugees she had seen at Jalalaqsi and many wore gold bracelets and earrings. Meanwhile, on a nearby road, refugees frustrated with the Somalia government were forming their own counterprotest. The Africare guide grew uncomfortable and loaded the group back into the Land Rover to return to Mogadishu. Crossing a bridge on the way out of the area, Payne looked out the window and saw the carcass of a hippopotamus with carrion posed nearby and waiting. It was as if the wildlife was mounting a tableau vivant of the human desperation in the camps.

The trip was unlike any Payne had made to Africa. Before this journey Payne the ardent advocate for Africa had seen the continent mostly from the vantage of conference halls, Western hotels, presidential palaces, and the protective bubble of a traveling American government official. She had no worries this time about offending some less-than-honorable African leader or organization who had paid her way. She was free to use her journalistic skills on an unfettered mission of mercy.

FOR FIVE DAYS, Payne visited those camps she could reach, meeting with doctors, relief officials, and three African American women working among the refugees. "As black Americans, the three of us were both a novelty and a curiosity," Payne said. On their last day in Somalia, Payne, Scales, and Miller were admitted to the well-guarded presidential compound for a meeting with President Mohamed Siad Barre, who had seized power in a 1969 coup. In the years since, he had accumulated one of the worst human rights records on the continent. Remaining on her best behavior, she listened silently to Barre defend his creation of one of the largest militaries in Africa, claiming the forays into his nation by Russian-backed Ethiopians on Somalia's western border posed a continuing danger.

The visit to Somalia concluded, the group flew south to Nairobi, Kenya, and then north to Sudan. "In five days, we had been introduced to another world, another way of life, as gray as the storm clouds that we encountered on our arrival, yet as hauntingly beautiful as the sun that broke through on our departure," Payne said.

They landed at Khartoum's airport at the peak of Ramadan. With temperatures nearing 120 degrees, the group went straight to the air-conditioned Meridien Hotel. The following morning, despite the oppressive heat, Payne headed off for a meeting with the commissioner of refugees. Power was out throughout downtown Khartoum and she had to scale five flights of stairs. The commissioner greeted her with hot tea, which she accepted while he and his assistant did not drink in observation of their fast.

Sudan consisted of more camp inspections similar to those they had made in Somalia. Next it was off to Zambia. It was Payne's third visit to the country, the two previous occasions with Secretaries of State Rogers and Kissinger. In the company of a Peace Corps member, an Episcopalian pastor on leave from a Washington, DC, church, and the Zambian commissioner of refugees, Payne found herself once again in a Land Rover bouncing its way across a barren landscape. Their destination was the Meheba refugee camp, which the United Nations had opened in 1971 for refugees fleeing the war in Angola. It took three days to make the 500-mile trek to the camp, which was near the borders of Zambia, Angola, and Zaire.

The camp now held 10,500 settlers in an area approximately that of a good-sized county in the United States. Most were still refugees from Angola, and many had been there for ten years. They feared for their lives if they returned to Angola and were unwilling to risk living under Mobutu's rule in Zaire. "The life of refugees is one long struggle for survival and a semblance of security," Payne wrote to her family. "By their standards, the people on welfare in the states live like kings."

At the end of her daylong tour of the camps, as the Land Rover passed by houses lit by fires cooking evening meals, Payne was absorbed in reflection. "Chickens, pigs, a goat here and there and children, including babies carried on their mothers' backs, and of course, the elders, reminders of Alex Haley's visit to the ancestral home of Juffure where 'Roots' began," she wrote. "This was Africa!"

CHAPTER 36

PROFESSOR PAYNE

U PON HER RETURN TO THE UNITED STATES, PAYNE HAD only a brief respite before packing her bags and heading to Nashville to take up her duties as a professor of journalism at Fisk University. "Outwardly, I am cool," she told her readers. "Inside, I am churning with mixed emotions and anxiety and elation."

Yet she was fully prepared for what lay ahead. The year before, at the urging of her friend Doris Saunders, who had chaired the Census Advisory Committee on the Black Population and now was a member of the fledgling journalism program at Jackson State University, Payne accepted a one-semester teaching appointment at the century-old historically black university in Mississippi.

In January 1981, as Reagan prepared to move into the White House, Payne left her Census Bureau job, which had been only a temporary posting, and packed her bags and headed south to Jackson, Mississippi. "It is a rediscovery of the black experience in America, and a veritable gold mine of literati, past and present," Payne wrote to her family. She also delighted in the Southern politeness of her students with their "Yes, ma'am," and "No, ma'am," confessing "that the sounds are strange to my urban ears."

Payne was assigned to teach three courses: editorial writing, semantics and journalism style, and advanced reporting. Prepped by Saunders about Payne's accomplishments, students eagerly signed up for her classes. They were amply rewarded by their decision. Payne, who had never taught before, inspired the students by providing lessons laced with stories from her life. "It opened my mind and eyes that there was more beyond being in school," recalled Gillie Haynes, one of her students in the advanced reporting class.

Payne took a shine to Haynes and the pair went out to dinner several times, including to a nearby mall, where the worldly Payne introduced Haynes to her first spinach salad. "She never made you feel uncomfortable or out of place or that you didn't deserve to be there," said Haynes. Payne made time for Haynes and other students and encouraged them to pursue careers despite the dominance of whites in the media. The advice she gave Haynes was similar to that she had given other young African American women she had inspired. "She told me," said Haynes, "to always carry myself like I was supposed to be where I was."

In class, Haynes was so moved by Payne's account of covering Little Rock in 1957 that she took on the idea of creating a Daisy Bates Day on campus and inviting the civil rights activist to receive an award from the students in the Jackson State Department of Mass Communications. Bates, however, was unable to make the trip, so in May, after commencement, Haynes and Payne traveled together to Little Rock to make the presentation in Bates's home.

Haynes was not the only student that Payne befriended and inspired that spring. Rita Bibbs first heard through her Delta Sigma Theta sorority that Payne was coming to teach. "We were so excited," she recalled. Entering her class, Bibbs was also nervous about whether she and the other students could live up to the expectations of a world-traveling correspondent. Instead, she encountered a warm, supportive teacher. "She always made you feel smart," said Bibbs.

At the end of the spring, Payne obtained an internship for Bibbs

at Delta Sigma Theta's Washington offices and provided her lodging by insisting she house-sit her apartment. Bibbs arrived in Washington when Payne had already left on a trip. But the front desk of
the Rittenhouse apartment building had been given instructions to
let the young woman in. Payne's note referred to Bibbs as her niece,
denoting that she had joined a coterie that held a special place in
Payne's heart.

Haynes and Bibbs had both experienced Payne's willingness
to help young black women take a step up. Payne was ceaseless in
her efforts, having come up the ranks when there were virtually
no women to provide a hand up. Jennifer Smaldone, for instance,
was working for a nonprofit Chicago organization on whose board
Payne served several years earlier. Payne heard about a job opening
at WBBM radio and urged Smaldone to apply while working behind
the scenes to smooth the way. After she got the job, Smaldone would
look up from her desk only to find Payne stopping in. "Be quality," she
would say, urging Smaldone to serve in turn as an example for other
young black women.

A YEAR AND A HALF LATER, heading to her named professorship at
Fisk, Payne steeled herself for her first task. The university had asked
her to deliver the address at the fall convocation marking the beginning of the school year. "That is a real challenge," she said. "What
does one say to young blacks entering academia with their dreams
and expectations, but who will be confronted with more complex
problems than their counterparts of the seventies?" The answer was
a feisty exhortation to work for change. She recounted an imaginary
conversation among Martin Luther King, Roy Wilkins, Malcolm X,
Whitney Young, and other departed figures from her years of covering the civil rights movement. Her script reflected her increasing
frustration with the Reagan conservative electoral triumph, which
in her mind had set the clock back when it came to issues of race.

"Gentlemen," said Malcolm X in Payne's version of the heavenly conversation, "forgive me, but I seem to hear the same rhetoric that got us in trouble when we were in the real world. . . . "

"You thought you could talk reason with the Man and he would be fair with you, so you put blinders on your eyes," continued the imaginary Malcolm X. "Yes, you forgot what Frederick Douglass said, 'Power concedes nothing without a demand. It never has and it never will.'" Ever the internationalist, Payne reflected on her world travels. She spoke of the millions of displaced people who wander in flight from poverty, famine, persecution, and wars not of their making. "They are our brothers and sisters, and no matter how great our own problems are, theirs are even greater," she said. "Black Americans have a role to play in the survival of these people because their suffering is ours."

Speech concluded, journalist, activist, and world traveler Payne became Professor Payne. After years of chasing stories and meeting deadlines, she found academic life blissful. Settling into a townhouse apartment close to campus, she took up her duties. They were vague. Her primary responsibility was organizing a seminar on the great issues of the day. With funding from the Philip Morris tobacco company, Payne brought more than forty journalists, officials, foreign dignitaries, and activists to the campus, all drawn from her famous Rolodex.

Leonard worked hard to make Payne feel welcomed on the campus. Using well-honed diplomatic skills, he assuaged the fears of established professors with advanced degrees about the presence of a noncredentialed professor. Payne's seminar worked to her advantage because it did not conflict with established courses and brought eminent figures to Fisk. The professors, said Leonard, "began to look at her as a person who was supporting and making them a little bit larger on the landscape."

The seminar series, open to upperclassmen, centered on topics of race, criminal justice, American foreign policy, and the media. The latter brought the largest number of speakers to campus, including Paul Delaney of the *New York Times*; Renee Poussaint and Maureen Bunyan, both successful black television newscasters in Washington; and Jacqueline Trescott of the *Washington Post*. The point was to broaden the students' minds. "Understanding the implications behind the extended debate within the membership of OPEC and the price of gasoline at your local service station is as important as mastering computer science," Payne told the students.

PAYNE'S POST AT FISK also gave her the freedom to continue accepting paying speaking engagements and to travel. Early in 1983, Payne became riveted by political developments in her hometown. Two-term congressman Harold Washington was making South Siders believe that one of their own might win the mayorship. In a six-way primary that pitched him against incumbent mayor Jane Byrne and Richard M. Daley, the scion of the deceased mayor, among others, Washington did the unthinkable by winning the largest share of votes. "Blacks have long talked about the lack of political empowerment and now we seem to have made a breakthrough," Payne told a press conference in Omaha, where she was to give a speech. "It's the beginning of change, but we haven't reached the goal."

Normally winning a primary in the overwhelmingly Democratic Chicago was all one needed to gain office. But droves of white Democrats threatened to support the white Republican candidate. Washington, however, warded off the strong effort to prevent his election and in April won the mayorship by a little more than 3 percent of the vote. Payne joined thousands of supporters on April 29 in the Navy Pier Auditorium of Chicago to witness the inauguration of Chicago's first black mayor. "For me," said Payne, "it was quite an emotional experience, something I never dreamed of seeing in my lifetime."

Back on campus, politics of another sort was riling the atmosphere.

"Every day there is a new crisis—either financial or campus politics and feuds," Payne wrote to a family member. "I'm trying to keep my head clear as well as stay above the din." She didn't succeed. In April, she devoted her syndicated column to an account of the latest turn in the dispute between Leonard and his opponents in the faculty and student body. Specifically, Payne complained about the behavior of student journalists on the staff of the *Fisk Forum*, the university's paper, and the writers of an anonymously published *New Fisk Herald*. In her version of events, the *Forum*'s negative reporting had fostered a threatening climate of distrust on the campus. She also suggested that the anonymous publication, which bore a striking similarity in typography to the *Forum*, suspiciously benefited from flattering and extensive coverage in the school newspaper.

Her column was too much for Bruce Tucker, the newspaper's faculty adviser. He delivered to her a three-page single-spaced letter accusing her of being wrong about her facts and in her accusations. He was particularly angry at her for having singled out the work of one freshman in her column. "To bring your eminence and the weight of a nationally syndicated column to bear on a college freshman is grossly out of scale. We are educators. Our job is to enlighten, encourage, and sometimes gently correct our students—not to try to crush them."

Sparing no words, Tucker ended his missive. "In sum," he wrote, "you have caricatured for a national audience Fisk's outstanding newspaper; you've misrepresented its contents; you've recklessly and groundlessly insinuated that it's abetted an anonymous and scurrilous publication; you've held a college freshman up to a national ridicule he certainly does not deserve; and you've damaged me professionally."

A week later, Payne curtly acknowledged receipt of Tucker's letter. "It is not now and never has been my intention to inflict harm on anyone," she wrote. "Criticism may seem harsh at times, but I believe that it is the healthiest component in a democracy."

As the spring semester neared its completion, Payne was not inclined to accept the offer to remain another year. "Unless some stringent commitments are made I will not be back," she wrote to a family member. Academic politics, it turned out, could be as bruising as politics in Washington.

CHAPTER 37

HYMIETOWN

T O ETHEL PAYNE'S JOY, THE PRESIDENTIAL CANDIDACY
of Jesse Jackson was gaining traction since his announcement in the fall of 1983 that he would become the second
African American, after Shirley Chisholm, to make a serious bid for
the Democratic nomination. Payne, who had first met Jackson during the 1960s and had once described him in print as looking like
Michelangelo's *David*, raised more than $1,000 for his campaign from
her friends.

In late January 1984, her candidate sat down for breakfast at Washington National Airport with Milton Coleman, a forty-six-year-old
seasoned black reporter from the *Washington Post* who was covering
the presidential campaign. "Let's talk black talk," Jackson said, invoking a phrase he used when he wanted to say something to a reporter
without being identified as the source. "I don't know what Jackson
says to white reporters when he wants to talk on background," Coleman said. "But with me and other blacks, he has placed it in the racial
context: 'Let's talk black talk.'"

What Jackson said, however, created an uproar. Discussing what
he saw as the preoccupation of Jews with Israel, he used the derogatory terms *Hymie* and *Hymietown*. Coleman found he was not alone
in having heard these words from Jackson, and in February he shared

details of the conversation with another *Post* reporter who was working on a piece about Jackson and foreign policy.

In the thirty-seventh and thirty-eighth paragraphs of the published story, the reporter mentioned that Jackson had used the terms, followed by a denial from the candidate. No one much noticed it until several days later when the paper published an editorial calling on Jackson to explain his choice of words. For a week Jackson stonewalled as the issue dominated the coverage of his campaign. Finally the contrite candidate spoke at a synagogue in New Hampshire and sought forgiveness for his insensitivity. The episode left Coleman, as the one who had revealed Jackson's slurs, in the middle of a firestorm of controversy made worse when the often incendiary Nation of Islam minister Louis Farrakhan issued what seemed to many like a thinly veiled death threat. Coleman stood convicted of the crime of betraying his race.

In her apartment Payne took to the keys of her IBM Selectric and poured out her anger in a column unlike anything she had written before. In the past, Martin and other editors at the *Defender* had blue-penciled Payne's copy on occasion. But now her self-syndicated columns went directly from her typewriter to the reader, and her venom was unrestrained.

Comparing Coleman to a slave informer in the antebellum South, she questioned his motives. The way she saw it, Jackson had been beguiled into thinking he could "let his hair down with the brother." In doing so, the candidate had overlooked "the fact that Coleman was programmed to record every nuance, every phrase, every move that might be used in revealing the flaws in the superstar and report it back to his superiors in the citadel of power at the *Washington Post*."

Payne suggested Coleman might even be part of a larger plot to thwart Jackson's campaign. "It was no longer just an aberration on the body politic," she wrote. "It had become serious and the warning signs were posted—stop him before the whole thing gets out of hand."

She even invoked the famous Janet Cooke affair, when a black reporter working under Coleman had faked a Pulitzer Prize–winning story about an eight-year-old drug addict, triggering a vain search for the boy while generating paper sales. "The stigma of being involved in a seamy scheme of promoting sordidness at the price of truth left him with a serious credibility gap in the black Washington community," she said. "That is why many doubted him as the sole witness to the 'Hymie slur.'"

She didn't stop there. Even acknowledging, although using quotation marks around the word *confession*, that Jackson had admitted his use of the words, Payne accused Milton of racial betrayal of the deepest kind. "The question of Milton Coleman and the Judas factor remains," she wrote.

FOR PAYNE, COLEMAN HAD VIOLATED her lifelong creed: One did not blindly follow the dicta of journalism if they conflict with loyalty to her race, particularly on issues relating to civil rights. "For black journalists, particularly me, I think it made us know that we could not stand aside and be so-called objective witnesses," she said. "We were absolutely unable to make the distinction between what is 'objective journalism.' So I adopted a code of trying to be fair, but I could not divorce myself from the heart of the problem, because I was part of the problem."

But even fairness became hard for Payne when she thought black figures did a disservice to their struggle for equality. She expected resistance from whites but did not tolerate behavior among blacks whom she viewed as impeding the movement. In 1955, Payne had written approvingly when a Montgomery black woman was ostracized for not supporting the bus boycott, and in 1968 she faulted NAACP leader Roy Wilkins for questioning King's leadership in front of a white audience.

Three years before attacking Coleman, Payne had lambasted Tony Brown, the host of the popular PBS talk show *Tony Brown's*

Journal, which focused on African Americans, and Chuck Stone, a former *Chicago Defender* editor once nicknamed "the angry man of the Negro press." Their crime in her eyes was their participation in a right-wing Black Alternatives Conference at the Fairmont Hotel in San Francisco, supported by Edwin Meese III, a white conservative about to become President Reagan's attorney general. Among the leading figures at the gathering were Thomas Sowell, the most visible conservative intellectual, and his follower the future Supreme Court justice Clarence Thomas. "While politics makes strange bedfellows," Payne wrote of Brown and Stone and their participation in what she deemed an odious meeting with the enemy, "it included newsmen as participants in the game rather than as critics of politicians."

Payne's fight with Coleman also reflected the generation gap that existed between young black reporters and those, like Payne, who had been pioneers. "She was a creature of her generation," Coleman said, looking back on the incident many years later. "It was hard for her to understand why someone who is black who is reporting on Washington could behave differently than she thought she needed to behave, to remain happy not betraying the race. I respect that because she was from a different generation."

Her anger also stemmed from angst. In her seventies, Payne found the world was leaving her behind. Whereas she had once had the most recognizable byline in the black American press, she was now reduced to mailing her column to those black newspapers with older readers who still found value in an Ethel Payne commentary. But a shrinking readership put these few remaining newspapers on life support and caused Payne to endure the financial humiliation of collecting on late payments. There simply wasn't much left of the black press. In the last decade the number of black newspapers being published had fallen by 22 percent and circulation had plummeted by 33 percent.

"Ethel and the black press successfully put themselves out of business by advocating a wider participation in society," said Ernest Green, a friend of Payne's who had been among the nine black Little Rock students in 1957 and later served in the Carter administration. He recalled that when he worked for Carter, Payne would come by his office regularly. But she had a hard time getting the Labor Department's media people to regard her as an important reporter now that the black press circulation was falling and the white press was reporting on minority issues.

The civil rights movement had made it impossible for the white press to continue to ignore the black community. "At first many white publications simply plagiarized articles from black newspapers, but eventually they found it necessary to hire more black journalists than the token few that some had on their staffs," said Calvin W. Rolark, publisher of the *Washington Informer*. "Thus began the raid on black newspapers."

Not only did the best black media staffers migrate to the mainstream media but so did advertisers. Younger black readers, particularly those for whom the civil rights movement was a moment in history, considered the black press stodgy, boring, and irrelevant to their lives. Falling circulation and dropping ad revenues in a publication foretold that the golden days of the black press were over.

A black journalist with talent was an object of desire in the better-paying, better-read white media. But not Payne. Her writing style belonged to an era gone by. The new world of black journalism found Payne's style quaint and old-fashioned. *Essence*, a successful magazine for black women, asked Payne to write a personal article about how she remained active at her age. But the slow-paced reminiscences of her family life and the strength it had provided her seemed sadly out-of-date to the editors. Audrey Edwards, the magazine's editor, offered to take another look at a revised article but added that "editors here are not as excited about the piece as they were originally."

Even work from publications that once had been sympathetic

to the movement dried up with conservative electoral victories. For instance, President Reagan's Commission on Civil Rights staff appointee Linda Chavez killed a Payne article slated for its quarterly journal, leaving it to her assistant to deliver the news. "You have assumed unwarranted authority in unilaterally dismissing something after the fact," Payne snapped back at the hapless aide. "I do not take this incident lightly. Too much has gone into the long, hard struggle for equality of opportunity and human dignity to sit idly by and watch the demise of the agency at the hands of insensitive and callous individuals who have abrogated their public responsibility."

But no one was listening. Payne remained widely admired and the subject of flattering articles, but she had become a relic of another era.

CHAPTER 38

AGITATE, AGITATE, AGITATE

I N THE COLD RAIN ON JANUARY 4, 1985, ETHEL PAYNE grabbed her cane and left her Washington apartment and headed to the South African embassy on Massachusetts Avenue in the company of a university professor three decades her junior. The embassy had been the site of frequent demonstrations since November, when three activists were arrested for a sit-in protest. Across the country, anti-apartheid forces had been increasingly gaining strength, inspiring protests along with a movement to force institutions, such as universities and colleges, to divest economically from South Africa.

For Payne, ending apartheid was the one major battle left in the black freedom struggle across the globe. She did not want to be left on the sidelines. Over the years she had been an active member of TransAfrica, a black foreign policy advocacy group at the center of the anti-apartheid fight in the United States, and had donated money to the African National Congress, the banned South African political party led by Nelson Mandela. Since her earliest days as the *Chicago Defender*'s Washington correspondent, she had worked assiduously to connect her readers to the international dimensions of civil rights, and in particular to the horrors in South Africa. In 1955, for instance, she took the Navy to task for ordering four hundred blacks serving on the USS *Midway* to follow South African segregation laws while on shore leave in Cape Town, South Africa.

During her years as a reporter Payne retained an ambition that her journalism could help bridge the gap between Africans and African Americans. In the decades since her first trip to Africa in 1957, she had reported from more than a dozen emerging African nations. "Nothing is more ambiguous than the kinship between U.S. blacks and their 'brothers and sisters' in Africa," she wrote upon returning from one of her many trips. "We have a deep emotional attachment to the motherland, but scandalously little true knowledge about the diversity of that vast continent and its people."

South Africa, however, remained a nut she couldn't crack. Her efforts to obtain a visa had been rebuffed while she was working for the *Defender*. She had highlighted the nation's refusal to admit her in a CBS *Spectrum* commentary. If South Africa "really wants to convince the world that it does mean to change, then let it free itself from fear by opening the doors to everyone," Payne said. But now, as an independent columnist, Payne was planning to do something she could not do as a reporter. With a simple knock on the embassy door, Payne and her companion were admitted. "We managed to penetrate that symbol of apartheid," Payne told friends, "even though a tight wall of security surrounds it." If they believed a slow-moving seventy-three-year-old woman and her companion meant no trouble, the embassy staff members quickly learned their mistake. The pair immediately began to harangue the staff, insisting on the release of political prisoners held in South Africa and for an end to apartheid.

The embassy called the Secret Service, which provided protection to the foreign legations. After an hour, the two women were escorted out in handcuffs and taken away in a police car to face charges of unlawful entry, a misdemeanor under DC law. They spent a few hours incarcerated until lawyers from the Free South Africa movement arranged for their release. Payne kept the plastic handcuffs the police had used on her. As it had been with her 1947 arrest by Chicago police to protest the mistreatment of a group of black men, the handcuffs were jewelry of honor.

FEBRUARY BROUGHT BACK other memories when Payne got in touch with the subject of one of her earliest Washington news stories. Annie Lee Moss, the Army clerk who had figured prominently in the McCarthy hearings that Payne had covered, was spending a quiet Sunday evening at home reading, her television being out of commission, when her niece called. "Aunt Annie, did you know that you're on television?" asked the niece. "Well, it's somebody playing you." It turned out that CBS was airing the miniseries *Robert Kennedy and His Times*, based on Arthur Schlesinger Jr.'s book by the same name. The producers had not contacted or consulted with Moss. "For Mrs. Moss it was a painful reminder of an ordeal that virtually destroyed her life," Payne wrote in her column.

But Payne hardly had time to waste on nostalgia. Her fifteen-year-old Selectric typewriter might have ceased working—"suffering from old age and overuse, I guess"—but not Payne. She spent much of the remainder of the year on the move, traveling to Nairobi, Kenya, for the Third World Conference on Women ("Practically every woman in Washington as well as the rest of the country is trying to go to Nairobi for the end of the UN Decade for Women"); East Lansing, Michigan, for a conference on "The Black Woman Writer and the Diaspora"; Atlanta, for the National Congress of Black Women; Miami, to write a series of articles; and Dallas, Texas, for a convention of her cherished Delta Sigma Theta sorority. There she substituted as a speaker for Shirley Chisholm. "I assured the audience that I shared their disappointment because I had neither the fire nor the figure of the former gentle lady from New York," Payne said.

In the fall, her friends at the Capital Press Club honored her again, as they had on several occasions in the 1950s when the club thrived as

an alternative to the segregated National Press Club. At its dinner in
the JW Marriott Hotel in which the club presented its Pioneer Award
to television actor and comedian Bill Cosby, it recognized Payne with
its International Award. In accepting the prize, Payne chose to speak
about Woodbury Clift, the son of columnist Eleanor Clift, who had
won an essay contest sponsored by Africare, on whose board Payne had
just been elected. "Young Mr. Clift sees the world as a very sick society
bent upon self-destruction," said Payne. "Tonight I accept this award
for Woodbury Clift and for all those who are engaged in the task
of assuring that his generation and others will be able to enter the
twenty-first century free of the fears that through the neglect of our
individual obligations we pass along."

SOUTH AFRICA CROSSED her path again in 1986. Since her appointment to the Africare board, she had become a diligent and atten-
tive member at its meetings. The organization, which had projects
in many African nations, was struggling with how to deal with the
pariah nation of South Africa.

The topic came up at a September meeting of the executive committee, chaired by Episcopal bishop John T. Walker, who had just
returned from South Africa the day before. Kevin Lowther, the longtime Africare employee who had met Payne during her 1982 tour of
refugee camps, addressed the committee members. He wanted the
organization to look at how it might be able to work in South Africa
and Namibia, a neighboring nation ruled by South Africa, so that it
would be in a position to work even more productively when apartheid ended.

Payne was the first to speak up. She asked if pursuing this idea
would mean that Africare would have any involvement with the government there. Lowther explained that while the government would
have to grant visas, there would be no need for additional contact
with the regime. The issuance of visas, however, was a considerable

power, said Walker, noting that on his last trip his visa was valid for only five days, and the five days was underlined.

Further complicating any entry by Africare into South Africa was, first, its own firm policy of working only in those nations in which the government invited the organization and, second, South Africa's creation of homelands to contain its black population. But, Lowther told the board, several nongovernmental organizations (NGOs) were operating in the homelands, and one of them, Operation Hunger, would be willing to work with Africare. "I was struck by the amount of self-initiative that the people in the homelands displayed," Lowther told the board members. "This speaks very positively for the long-term future of the country."

Several months later the full board met. Lowther had returned from a trip to South Africa and summarized for the board members a lengthy report he had prepared reviewing the pros and cons of working with indigenous NGOs in South Africa and Namibia. "Bishop Walker stopped us all in our tracks," Lowther said, "by announcing, very clearly, that if the board agreed to pursue the South Africa–Namibia option, he would resign from the board." He related how he had come under criticism for supporting the involvement of American colleges and universities in South Africa now that the anti-apartheid movement was gaining steam. If Africare's action went against this tide, he would have to spend yet more time defending that decision. "No board member believed that Bishop Walker was bluffing," said Lowther. "That ended the discussion."

OUTSIDE OF HER ROLE at Africare, Payne was enlisted in another effort relating to South Africa. In the years of Nelson Mandela's long imprisonment, his wife, Winnie Mandela, emerged as one of the most internationally visible opponents of apartheid. Since 1982, Payne had championed Winnie Mandela by sending out letters to enlist supporters to free her from detention and permit her to travel. In

1987, leaders of Delta Sigma Theta decided to try to induct Winnie Mandela as a means of raising the awareness of South Africa among American blacks. They turned to Payne for assistance.

Payne drafted a letter to Mandela and consigned it along with ones from Hortense Canady, the sorority's president, and Coretta Scott King, to a contact she had at the State Department, with the assurances that they would be delivered by private means. A short time later, a friend called and asked Payne if she could clear her schedule to meet with two South Africans who were in Washington for a brief visit. "I made the quickest chicken casserole on record, " Payne said. Over lunch the visitors related tales of life under apartheid. As the meal neared its conclusion, they let it be known they were carrying some personal messages to Winnie Mandela, who was to greet them at the airport upon their return. The letters turned out to be the ones Payne had given to her State Department contact.

In January, Payne received word that the invitation had reached Winnie Mandela. One of her contacts spent four hours with Mandela in her Soweto home. "As you know, she shuns promoting herself or being promoted," Payne reported to Canady. "She did say, however, that she realizes the need to have more communication with U.S. blacks, and she is pondering the best way to do this."

Payne recommended to the Delta leadership that if Mandela accepted, she be made an honorary Delta in absentia. The suggestion was followed, and several months later, in a quiet ceremony at Washington's Howard University Inn, Mandela was inducted, with Payne standing in for her. "The coup is credited to journalist Ethel Payne," reported *Jet* magazine.

Despite the honors given to Mandela by Delta Sigma Theta, her image was in need of repair. First, she had come under fire for what seemed to be an endorsement of the brutal practice of necklacing, the name given to the burning of opponents alive with tires and gasoline. Second, the *Washington Post* and other American newspapers were passing on press accounts from South Africa about the lavish home Winnie Mandela was building in Soweto, one of the black homelands.

Payne rushed to Mandela's aid. She stayed clear of the necklacing charges and instead took up the less significant charges of her luxurious home indulgences. Suggesting that the *Post* article, done by seasoned correspondent William Claiborne, was a salvo in a larger attack on the credibility of apartheid opponents, Payne used her weekly column to question the veracity of the piece. "There are many discrepancies," said Payne, "which suggest that Claiborne did not check his facts, but relied on government propaganda or sources allied to white conservative thinking." Her own contacts in South Africa reported that Mandela still lived in a smaller house with her extended family and that construction of the larger house had stalled for a lack of funds.

Nothing would weaken Payne's devotion to Winnie Mandela. "I don't have words to convey to you all our caring and concern for you and all our brothers and sisters who so valiantly endure the pain in the struggle for freedom," Payne wrote to Mandela, addressing her now as "Sister Winnie" because of her induction into Delta Sigma Theta. "We too are in the struggle."

IN HER DEFENSE OF Winnie Mandela, Payne called her the "Grand Lady of South Africa." The honorific of *Grand* could have been easily applied to herself. In fact, at seventy-five Payne was now regularly introduced as "the First Lady of the Black Press." While she still cranked out a weekly column, it was her past accomplishments that kept her a visible Washingtonian. For instance, the White House was glad to have her photographed seated at the cabinet table with President Ronald Reagan, housing secretary Samuel Pierce, and Robert Woodson, to whom Payne had been kind at the 1982 dinner in her honor.

"I hate to talk about myself in these terms," Payne said in 1987.

"But I think you know that I've become a celebrity. I have to deal with that celebrity status. I am so much in demand as a sort of an icon." At a lunch given by George Haley, brother of the famous author, Payne was introduced as "the mother of journalism."

"I was so embarrassed," said Payne. "But that's the way everybody— everybody started clapping, you know. You know, all this recognition, all this fame. That's been the thing that I guess I've become. I guess now I'm a role model."

Kathleen Currie, an oral historian and journalist, came calling that summer. She had been hired by the Washington Press Club Foundation for an oral history project that aimed to collect the remembrances of more than fifty women journalists.

Sitting in a comfortable chair in her office, sometimes putting her arthritic leg on a footstool, Payne patiently answered Currie's many questions about her youth, her career, and her views on journalism. During seven sessions over a period of four months, Payne recounted it all, offering many tales now well polished from her many speeches about her career. However, she frequently looked for ways to explain her motivation as a journalist and, in the end, fell back on an admonition of Frederick Douglass, which Payne quoted frequently—"Agitate, agitate, agitate."

The Miller Brewing Company commissioned Bryan McFarlane to do a dozen paintings of contemporary and historical black journalists for a traveling exhibit and its annual calendar. "I just couldn't believe they had picked me to be part of this exhibit," said Payne when looking over the list, which included John B. Russwurm, who created the first black newspaper, Ida B. Wells Barnett, the journalist who famously chronicled lynchings, and William Raspberry, the *Washington Post* columnist.

The exhibit made its second stop on a national tour at the DuSable Museum of African American History in Chicago. In conjunction with a reception, Payne spoke at several of Chicago's elementary schools and at Medill School of Journalism, where she had taken nighttime writing classes almost fifty years earlier. Then she returned to the *Defender* office for a reunion. Seeing John Sengstacke, Payne said to him, "You're the one who really started all of this, John."

It was an easier thing to say, now that the two had patched up their relationship the previous year when Sengstacke was inducted into the Black Press Hall of Fame. Payne attended the ceremonies in Baltimore and spoke on a panel. In her remarks she paid tribute to Sengstacke for having hired her and having given her the chance to see the world. She looked to the back of the hall and spotted him sitting there. "There's John Sengstacke back there, and I want him to stand up, because I want to acknowledge what he has done for me."

Afterward, Sengstacke came up and gave Payne a hug. "Can we talk?" he asked.

"Sure," replied Payne. The two then sat in the auditorium seats and looked at each other for a long time.

"You know," said Sengstacke, breaking the silence, "there's a lot gone by. Let's let the past be past."

"John, you know, I've never held on to it. I've never held any prejudice."

ALTHOUGH PAYNE WAS VENERATED, daily life presented difficult challenges for her. Her high blood pressure exacerbated by her weight was worrisome. Arthritis, particularly painful in one leg, and uncertain balance required the use of a cane. The lack of money also remained a continual vexation, although she gave no outward sign. When she visited friends in New England, Payne asked the hostess if she would wrap up the leftover Cornish hen from the dinner for the train ride to Washington. Later that night, the hostess's husband remarked that he surmised their famous guest was struggling financially.

But Payne's generosity never faltered. When her sisters Thelma Gray and Avis Johnson sent her some money, Payne used it to take her niece Patricia Boyd, who was on dialysis, and her daughter to the Kennedy Center to see Rex Harrison and Claudette Colbert in a revival of *Aren't We All?* by Frederick Lonsdale. "After I have taken care of current bills," Payne wrote her sisters, "I will be on 'Lean Cuisine.'"

"Times were hard for her, but even then she was so willing to share whatever she had with the rest of us who were struggling to make ends meet," said Shirley Small-Rougeau, the activist Payne had met on the streets of Chicago. The two became fast friends when Small-Rougeau moved to Washington when her husband Weldon Rougeau became chief of the Congressional Black Caucus Foundation.

What Payne lacked in money, she made up for in the richness of friends and a devoted group of caregivers. In addition to Small-Rougeau, there was the recently married Rita Bibbs-Booth, the Jackson State University student whom Payne had brought to Washington; Catherine Brown, who as a teenager in the 1950s had met Payne when she visited her mother; John Raye, who had been inspired by Payne's television commentaries; Herman "Skip" Davis, with whom Payne's nephew had played; and Barbara Reynolds, the Chicago reporter, among others.

"We, our little group of friends, included her in all that we did, even going out to the jazz and blues clubs, organizational and family events, weddings, dinners and whatever," said Small-Rougeau. "She was our mentor and griot on everything we did back then." The women took turns ferrying Payne, who had never gotten a driver's license, to and fro. "We took delight in pleasing her," Bibbs-Booth said. "She touched the lives of so many of us, and for me changed my life, so it was a small thing to do." Payne also inspired young rising television newswomen such as Renee Poussaint and J. C. Hayward. One of them sent her cleaning lady over to Payne's apartment as a birthday present.

When Payne turned seventy-five years old, Small-Rougeau and Bettye Collier-Thomas, who was director of the Bethune Museum, put together a birthday bash for her at the Hyatt Regency in Bethesda, Maryland. Payne's sisters Thelma Gray and Avis Johnson flew in for the occasion. The gang gave her a Magnavox VideoWriter. Using it would have to wait for a course of instruction from Bibbs-Booth. Until then, she stuck to her two-finger typing on the repaired and much-treasured Selectric.

CHAPTER 39

FORGOTTEN

I N LATE SEPTEMBER 1987 ETHEL PAYNE, IN THE COMPANY of Afreda Madison, a longtime correspondent who worked for Black Media, Inc., arrived at the Washington Hilton for the annual Congressional Black Caucus dinner, a $300-a-plate event that was among Washington's premier social gatherings. The evening's program was of great interest to Payne. The scheduled dinner speaker was Marian Wright Edelman, who headed up the Children's Defense Fund. Neither woman had tickets but both had been promised admission by the staff director.

After waiting for more than an hour in the pressroom for the promised tickets, Payne and Madison made their way downstairs to the ballroom and walked past the area where television crews had set up their cameras. Behind the press area there were no seats, so the two women sat on empty seats in front. At seventy-six and walking often with the aid of a cane, Payne had to have a seat. But when the crowds filed in and the program was about to start, two security guards came up to Payne and Madison. They would have to give up their seats and stand in the back or they "would be locked up."

There were no other empty seats by this time. Payne picked up her cane and made her way back to the lobby. Madison at first refused to leave but eventually consented to exit through a pantry door. When the *Afro-American* got wind of what had happened to the two women, the Black Caucus had a public relations nightmare on its hands. "It makes my stomach turn to think that two women who have done so much to promote the Black Caucus, who have paid so many dues in their struggle to rise to the top of their profession, could be insulted in this way," wrote *Washington Post* columnist Courtland Milloy. He blamed the profusion of corporate money and the caucus's growing dependence on the funds. "It is a classic case of black people losing control, and their purpose, because money has become more important than the people that are supposed to be served."

Payne told caucus officials that in her thirty-six years in Washington she had never been threatened with being locked up while gathering news, although she proudly pointed out she had been arrested for her protest at the South African embassy. "The harsh manner displayed by security on Saturday is reminiscent of the Afrikaner way of handling protesters of apartheid," Payne told U.S. representative Mervyn Dymally, the chair of the Black Caucus. "The euphoria I took away from the spiritual uplifting at the Saturday-morning prayer breakfast was shattered by the Saturday-evening ugliness."

Dymally was quick to apologize. In fact, he had posted a letter to Payne before receiving hers. He placed the blame on the temporary personnel hired for the event. "Needless to say," he wrote to Payne, "there are far too many young people today who are not aware of the history of our struggle and the people who made their jobs possible."

THE 1988 PRESIDENTIAL CAMPAIGN fired up Payne. It was the seventh campaign she had watched with a journalist's eye. She chastised the Democratic Party over its treatment of Jesse Jackson in one of her now occasionally published syndicated columns. As Massachusetts governor Michael Dukakis closed in on the Democratic nomination, Payne said everyone could see that leaders were shutting Jackson out of party affairs before the convention. The consequence would be dire, predicted Payne. If the party deserts its loyal black voters, they will stay home in the fall.

Attending the convention in Atlanta, Payne reported on the latest political gossip. At the lunch counter in Paschal's restaurant, one of the city's most famous soul food restaurants, she listened as Dukakis's treatment of Jackson was discussed. "That Greek is going to need a lot of olive oil," said one patron, "before he can convince black folks that he's for real about Jesse." Back in the convention hall she talked with Hosea Williams, the longtime activist. He told Payne he had forgiven Jackson for his claim to being the last person to hold Martin Luther King in his arms when he had not been. "I told Coretta it's time to forget. We need to support Jesse. She looked at me and said, 'Hozee, he's the same Jesse. He hasn't change a bit.'"

But the forty-seven-year-old Jackson was the new face of what remained of the civil rights movement. Williams was sixty-two. So was Ralph Abernathy. Coretta Scott King was sixty-one. Roy Wilkins, Clarence Mitchell, and A. Philip Randolph had all died. The movement that Payne had chronicled was now being taught as history in classrooms.

Payne was keenly aware of the passage of time. There were now only three of the six Payne children still alive. At a family gathering in San Diego she presented to her nephew David Payne Johnson the carved ivory figure with the crack she had bought in Kinshasa during the trip to Africa with Kissinger while the secretary of state lay ill in bed. "I am the last direct descendant to bear the name Payne," she said, explaining that she hoped he would then pass on his middle name and the carved figurine to future generations. A year later, Payne shared with Johnson her growing recognition of her age. "At seventy-seven years," she said, "one becomes more aware of limitations of the life span."

But the cane-toting Payne remained a reporter to the last. Mayor Marion Barry, once a well-known and militant civil rights leader, was in his third term as mayor of Washington, DC. The city government was in shambles and the murder rate had reached record levels. Under investigation for his connections to a drug suspect, Barry continued to vehemently deny his not-yet-publicly-known addiction to cocaine. He agreed to speak to the Capital Press Club, perhaps believing he would avoid the kind of questioning he had been receiving from the white media. "Mr. Mayor," asked Payne, who had known Barry for decades, "if you had it to do over again, what mistakes would you acknowledge?"

Barry replied that he had no errors to admit. Instead he asked Payne for her opinion of him. The question was a mistake. "I think," she said, "you have a whole pile of stuff to contend with." An uncomfortable silence descended on the room and the mayor smiled uneasily.

IN THE FALL OF 1989 Payne applied to the South African embassy for a visa to travel to Namibia, hoping perhaps they would not remember her arrest in 1985. Forty years after witnessing the first sub-Saharan nation win its colonial independence, Payne wanted to be on the ground again in Africa for the launching of the continent's newest independent nation. In November, Namibia, which had long been ruled by South Africa, was scheduled to hold elections for what would become its parliament upon achieving its independence in the spring.

"It will be history-making and high adventure for me if things work out successfully," Payne wrote to a friend. She figured she would need $4,000 for the airfare and accommodations, and a month before her planned trip she had already obtained a pledge of $1,200 from the United Methodist Church. The black newspapers that remained her clients endorsed the idea but could provide no funds. Payne also kept her plans under wraps in case anything she said in print might anger the South African officials.

In the end she managed to raise the money and the South African embassy granted her a visa to join some 1,200 other journalists converging on Namibia. In early November, Payne was in Windhoek, Namibia, on the eve of the vote. For the twelfth time, Payne filed reports with an African dateline for the few remaining black newspapers than ran her column. It was no easy feat. At seventy-eight, downing pills for her high blood pressure and navigating about with a cane, she had to endure hours under the blazing African sun to get her story. Outside a cemetery, the burial site of the white Namibian Anton Lubowski, who had been killed while supporting the main liberation movement, Payne witnessed a massive election-eve rally.

Thirty years earlier, Payne had stood in a Ghanaian field and heard the chant of "Freedom, freedom, freedom" echo into the night as that nation celebrated its independence. On this day, as Namibia neared a similar moment, Payne was again on a field in Africa. "Patriotic songs and shouted slogans and the signatory dances of the liberation movement went on for more than three hours until the exhausted participants wended their way home to prepare to rise at dawn for the first of the four days allocated for voting."

She remained for three weeks, filing stories for the black newspapers still carrying her column, which for the past two years had included Louis Farrakhan's the *Final Call*. But it, like many of her client newspapers, was slow in paying and sometimes didn't pay at all. Her longtime relationship with the *Afro-American* newspapers hit a shoal. The previous year her weekly commentary was cut to biweekly and its size reduced by half. Other articles she submitted were published but not paid for because the newspaper seemed to be under the impression that Payne had submitted the articles gratis. "I don't have that luxury as a single senior citizen whose livelihood depends on earned income," Payne told the president of the newspapers.

Yet Payne would not utter a public word about her maltreatment at the hands of the black press that had sustained her for four decades and provided her with a platform and a window on the world. "We defend our newspapers so protectively from criticism the same way we do for black colleges and black churches as part of our heritage," Payne wrote at the time. "We gloss over the warts."

AFRICA BECKONED ONE last time in the spring. In February 1990 the South African government had released Nelson Mandela from prison after a twenty-seven-year detention. Soon after, there was talk of a June visit to the United States. Delta Sigma Theta wanted to make sure that Winnie Mandela included its Miami Beach convention in the itinerary if the trip were to materialize. As it had done several years ago when the organization wanted to recruit Winnie Mandela as an honorary member, it turned once again to Payne for help. Would she be willing to travel to South Africa and meet with the Mandelas?

The trip was set for May, a month before the Mandelas' scheduled visit to the United States. "A palpable elation suffused her spirit as the trip's logistics began to materialize," recalled Joseph Dumas, a young journalist whom Payne was mentoring at the time. Fatima Meer, an Indian-born South African anti-apartheid activist with whom Payne had corresponded over the years, made all the arrangements. She had been imprisoned with Winnie Mandela in 1976 and had just published Nelson Mandela's biography.

At ten on the morning of May 24, Payne arrived at the Mandelas' new house in the Orlando East section of Soweto. Payne spotted the armed security officers from the ANC guarding the perimeter and got her first look at the controversial house whose construction she had defended two years earlier. Three stories tall, with four bedrooms, it was, in Payne's words, "tastefully furnished, but not lavish."

In the living room, Payne drank coffee with Winnie Mandela, whom she met for the first time after years of correspondence. Still clad in his pajamas, Nelson Mandela greeted Payne. The two sat down and he answered her questions for thirty-five minutes, twenty more than the fifteen-minute audience that had been promised. Payne asked about the ongoing negotiations with the government and resistance among white South Africans. Despite his imprisonment, Mandela remained conciliatory in freedom. "The majority of whites want to see a peaceful change," Mandela told her. "Whites have nothing to fear from sharing power with all the people of South Africa." Payne was amazed at Mandela's attitude. "Ethel could not understand why Mandela was not angry," said C. Payne Lucas of Africare, who saw Payne upon her return to the United States.

The interview completed, Payne, dressed in a colorful floral outfit with a long strand of pearls, stood for a photo next to the much taller Mandela, in his red bathrobe tied closed with a cord. When she returned to the United States, Payne told her friends that lots of reporters had interviewed Mandela since his release but she was the only one to have done so while he was in his bathrobe.

A month later the Mandelas made a triumphant tour of the United States. A reporter with a Philadelphia paper asked Payne what she thought of it all. "I don't want to get too carried away," she said, "but I think Nelson Mandela is probably the best thing that's happened to us since Martin Luther King."

At the end of the year, Rodger Streitmatter, an American University professor of journalism, began assembling an exhibit chronicling Payne's life for the public library in Anacostia, a neighborhood where Frederick Douglass had once made his home. He selected two dozen photographs and an assortment of artifacts. When the exhibit opened in January 1991, the *Washington Post*, referring to Payne as the Black Press Corps' "unsung heroine," ran a photograph of Payne holding up an enlarged picture of herself as a six-year-old. It had been taken in 1918 when Chicago, like many cities, was hit by the influenza epidemic. "My mother suddenly realized that I might pass away, I might die, so she said she was very disturbed because she didn't have any photograph of me," recalled Payne. "So there was a photography shop up on Sixty-Third Street, about five blocks away, so they bundled me up and rushed me up there to have that picture taken, so my mother would have something in case I passed."

In April, Payne left her apartment on a personal mission. Two years earlier she had confessed to her nephew a need that had grown within her with each passing year. "In the time which is left to me," she told him, "I need to work faster and harder to leave something of value to you and the coming generations." The idea that had taken hold of her was to launch a kind of think tank staffed by young idealists to work on the most important issues of the day. Calling it her "magnificent obsession," she went to see James A. Joseph, president of the Council on Foundations, a national association of foundations and corporations.

Payne brought with her a prepared proposal for the Twenty-First Century Fellows Program, which would comprise a mix of black, white, Hispanic, and Asian students. Despite what she saw as a reemergence of racial tension and a growth in hate groups, "our very existence compels us to accept our interdependence," Payne told Joseph. "No one should understand that better than the young men and women who will be leaders of tomorrow."

On May 23, Dean Mills, the dean of the School of Journalism at the University of Missouri in Columbia, put his signature on a letter to be mailed to Payne. The members of the faculty of the nation's oldest school of journalism, which would not have admitted her on account of race when she was of college age, had voted to award Payne the Missouri Honor Medal for Distinguished Service in Journalism. "We hope you will be able to join us on November 8 at our Honor Medal banquet to accept the medal," he wrote.

As his invitation was making its way through the post, Payne's presence was hoped for at another event. John Rougeau, the youngest son of Payne's devoted friend Shirley Small-Rougeau, was among the 1,519 students slated to receive undergraduate degrees at Brown University on Saturday, May 25. In addition to inviting Payne to the commencement, Small-Rougeau had also arranged for them to travel to New York City to meet law professor Derrick Bell, who had famously been dismissed by Harvard University for refusing to end a two-year protest over the university's failure to hire and promote minority females.

Upon reflection, Payne and Small-Rougeau concluded it would be too much to take in both the graduation in Providence and a visit to New York City in one trip. Instead they decided Payne would forgo the graduation and they would travel to New York City by train a week later. "She was feeling a little 'poorly' when I left but was sure she would be 'bright eyed and bushy tailed' when I returned," said Small-Rougeau.

On Monday, Payne stopped in at the apartment of her Rittenhouse neighbors Jesse and Jackie Jackson. He had just been sworn in as the "shadow senator" for the District of Columbia, an elected post with no powers that was created as part of an effort to win statehood for the city. He was not in, but she spoke briefly with Jackie and their son Yusef. The following morning, the *Washington Post* lay uncollected at Payne's apartment door. Wednesday, a second paper joined the first. On Thursday, a neighbor seeing the growing pile of newspapers alerted the building's front desk.

Meanwhile Small-Rougeau and her son John had returned to Washington. She received a call from the front desk of the Rittenhouse. "Cold chills ran down my spine even though the caller had told me nothing yet," said Small-Rougeau. "When I asked if Ethel was all right, she told me no, that she had been found dead in her apartment. I fell to the floor in total shock."

Small-Rougeau went to the building and let herself in with the key Payne had given her. "There she was, lying on the floor looking so small; her robe and gown in disarray and her cup still half filled with her morning coffee; her toast untouched."

"All the years, the many projects, the people that we knew, the funny stories that she told, and her favorite saying of having a 'window seat on the world' raced through my head as I stood frozen in disbelief. I gently covered her and sat stroking her forehead with tears covering my face."

CHAPTER 40

CITIZEN OF THE WORLD

THEL LOIS PAYNE HAD DIED OF A HEART ATTACK, eleven weeks shy of her eightieth birthday. The news was reported in both the white and black press of the United States and as far away as South Africa. In addition to publishing an obituary, the *Washington Post* devoted an entire editorial to her passing. "Her voice was low, but her questions were piercing, and her reports on the world were cherished by millions of readers," the paper said. Recalling the remarks of a Howard University professor, the *Post* said, "Had Ethel Payne not been black, she certainly would have been one of the most recognized journalists in American society. . . .

"Those of us," the editorial concluded, "who did know Ethel Payne's work and enjoyed her friendship will miss the good company of a pro whose insight and graceful writing served to bridge so many worlds."

As a reporter, Payne had unswervingly remained faithful to the black press even when it decided it no longer needed her services. She was convinced to the end that, as during the civil rights struggles of the 1950s and early 1960s, the black press had an activist's role to play. In fact, she never gave up on the idea. "Somehow the black press has forgotten how to agitate for the purposes for which it was founded," she complained a decade later. And ten years after that, she told a student, "The black press can be a formidable instrument for change, if it just realizes its potential, its responsibility, its historical past, and if it lives up to that credo, because the fight is far from over."

On Capitol Hill, California representative Ron Dellums told his colleagues that when he was a young man, Payne's reporting had exposed him to a world beyond the confines of the Bay Area. Jesse Jackson asked congregants to pause and pray for Payne at a church where he was appearing in Gary, Indiana. Hundreds turned out at the funeral home to pay their final respects. Delta members Rita Biggs-Booth and Shirley Small-Rougeau prepared a sorority Omega Omega Service for their departed sister. Small-Rougeau was given the honor of pinning white lilies on Payne's garment.

Small-Rougeau and Payne's other friends and family wanted to organize a service at the Washington National Cathedral, which sits high on a hill overlooking the city and had been the frequent site of presidential funeral services. But John Walker, the chair of Africare's board, who knew Payne well, was no longer the bishop, and it seemed unlikely his successor would be amenable to the idea. Stymied in finding a suitable location, the group was relieved when James M. Christian, a loyal friend, provided a solution. He served as chairman of the board of the Zion Baptist Church, on the corner of Sixteenth Street and Blagden Avenue, the northern tip of what old-time Washingtonians referred to as the Gold Coast, where the city's black elite made its home.

The service began at 10:00 AM on Wednesday, June 5, when Reverend Donald Vails, a noted gospel choir director, played an organ prelude and Reverend Carlton W. Veazey welcomed the large crowd. This was followed by readings from the Old and New Testament, including 1 Corinthians, chapter 13, with its heartening adage: "And now abide faith, hope, love, these three; but the greatest of these is love."

Payne's nephew James A. Johnson, who had come to live with her in 1959 when he attended the congressional Page School, and her great-niece, Felicity Boyd, represented the fourth and fifth generations of the family and provided remembrances. Tributes were offered by television news anchor Maureen Bunyan, Frances Murphy, whose family owned the long-published *Afro-American* newspapers, and U.S. representative William Gray III.

Then, from the choir loft, Christian sang. He had chosen to perform the hymn "Take My Hand, Precious Lord." It was Martin Luther King's favorite and was sung at his funeral as well as that of Lyndon Baines Johnson. "I chose the song because I felt it captured Ethel's struggle and the fact that she was now at peace," said Christian, to whom Payne had been an adopted grandmother. He was, however, unaware of another connection he held with Payne. Christian, who had been singing solos since he was in high school, had been a member of the Howard University choir. It was the exclusion of that very choir from a 1954 Republican event that had led Payne to ask her first question at a presidential press conference and discover her power as a member of the White House press corps.

It fell to James A. Joseph, with whom Payne had recently shared her plans for the Twenty-First Century Fellows program, to provide the eulogy. "It is thus my task to say a word about the meaning of this extraordinary life, the message of this extraordinary woman, and the mission of those who must now pick up the torch and carry on," Joseph said.

"She used her skills not to acquire power for herself but to activate power in others," he continued. "At a time in which our world seemed to be fragmenting into 'we' and 'they' groups, Ethel was searching for the social glue of civil society, affirming the connectedness of humanity. She made the case in all sectors of our society that the fear of difference is a fear of the future.

"In her own work, she was not simply reporting the news," he said. "She was stretching the horizon of the heart, widening the circle of community, seeking to transform the laissez-faire notion of live and let live into a moral imperative of live and help live.

"People in Africa, Asia, and elsewhere have lost an authentic citizen of the world."

SEVERAL WEEKS LATER, VOICE of America broadcaster Maimouna Mills came to Payne's Rittenhouse apartment to meet with Ethel's sister Avis Johnson. Mills interviewed her for the VOA's Africa broadcast department. The now-silent flat overflowed with mementos and awards. "We tried to catalog them," said Johnson of the awards, "and our last count was more than eighty, and they represent all kinds of organizations, not necessarily newspapers or journalists, but community groups, national groups, that respected the fact that she was out there on the cutting edge."

Johnson recounted for Mills the influence of their parents and grandparents, the high points of her sister's career, her world travels, and the excitement she had felt returning from her meeting with the Mandelas a year earlier. "She has left a wonderful legacy," Johnson said. "There are people all across the world who have been touched through her interest and her work who I feel will want to carry on some of the things that she dreamed should happen."

Indeed, two years later the National Association of Black Journalists undertook such an effort when it launched the Ethel L. Payne Fellowship to fund reporting projects in Africa. Wayne J. Dawkins, a longtime member of the NABJ and author of its history, described the creation of the fellowship as a big move for the organization. The NABJ had regularly complained about lack of coverage of Africa in the American media, he said. "The fellowship was a way of stepping out on our own and not just waiting for the largesse of the newspapers and networks to do something."

The first two recipients were Karen Lange, a *Chapel Hill Herald* reporter, and Michelle Singletary of the *Washington Post*. For a decade, before the fellowship ceased to be able to raise sufficient funds to operate, the NABJ sent more than a dozen young reporters to Africa to pursue stories of their choosing. Typical of the group was Tracey Scruggs Yearwood, a CNN producer who now works as a producer for Oprah Winfrey. She used the money in 1997 to support a television documentary on grassroots women's movements in South Africa's post-apartheid era. Fred Harvey, a longtime journalist, used his fellowship to go to Sierra Leone to pursue his passionate study of African influence in the food, speech, and religious practices in his native South Carolina. The recipients were engaged in the kind of reporting that would have thrilled Payne.

In September 2002, the U.S. Postal Service selected Payne to be among four journalists it would honor on 37-cent commemorative postage stamps. The other three were Nellie Bly, Marguerite Higgins, and Ida M. Tarbell. Designer Fred Otnes created a collage featuring a black-and-white photograph combined with memorabilia for each of the women. For the Payne stamp he chose a black-and white photograph of Payne surrounded on one side by the nameplate of the *Chicago Defender* and the headline of the article she wrote about the Montgomery bus boycott.

The fellowship no longer has funds and the postage stamp remains visible only in the collections of philatelists. Payne's papers are scattered among three libraries and two museums. The Newseum in Washington maintains a display about Payne's career in its News History Gallery. But more than two decades after her death, only the rarest of visitors would recognize her name. As is true of much of the civil rights struggle, much is forgotten.

Civil rights activist Julian Bond has spent many years in the classrooms of American University and the University of Virginia. His time with students confirms what studies have shown about the dismal lack of knowledge of the civil rights era. His students, for instance, could not identify George Wallace, although one hazarded a guess that he might have been a CBS news reporter. Worse, the entire grassroots movement has been replaced by a popular classroom fable, according to Bond, that goes, "There used to be segregation until Martin Luther King came along, that he marched and protested, that he was killed, and that then everything was all right."

A decade before her death Payne intuited that the great movement she had chronicled was fading from public memory. On a Sunday in February 1983, Payne spoke to the congregation at St. John AME Church in Nashville. "Ours was a generation which spanned the time when black bodies were on the line," she said, "and as we struggled to send our children to college, we forgot to tell them about our past."

IN 1987, WHEN PAYNE SAT DOWN to record her oral history, she told Kathleen Currie that she had led a charmed life.

"Why do you say 'charmed'?" asked Currie.

"Because," replied Payne, "I've been able to be such an eyewitness to so many profound things and so many changes, and I've lived through it and I've witnessed. I've had a box seat on history, and that's a rare thing."

ACKNOWLEDGMENTS

IN AUGUST 1964, WHEN THE WATTS NEIGHBORHOOD OF LOS Angeles erupted into one of the city's worst race riots, the Associated Press dispatched a twenty-seven-year-old white reporter to the scene. A recent graduate of Columbia University's School of Journalism, Andrew Jaffe took out his reporter's pad to write down his observations and record his interviews in hopes of putting together the story. It was then that a young black resident of Watts said something that stuck with Jaffe long after the fires in Watts were out.

"You can never tell our story," the youngster said, "because you're not black."

I've thought frequently about this moment in Jaffe's life while writing this biography about Ethel Payne. She was black. I'm white. She was a female. I'm male. She grew up in modest, at times poor circumstances. I grew up in privilege. Who am I to tell her story? I wondered.

I found my answer in two places: First, I found acceptance and support among family and friends of Payne, who never questioned why I should be the one to write her story. Their encouragement and support was of critical importance.

Second, Payne's own approach to writing encouraged me. She never forgot or hid the perspective she brought to her work. She never pretended to be anything other than who she was. As a black person writing about racism, segregation, and the civil rights movement—all matters that deeply affected her life—she said it was impossible to be objective. Instead she adopted a rigid code of fairness. Above all, she believed that journalism—or any form of writing, for that matter—liberates and empowers one to be able to write empathetically about people, events, and ideas outside of one's own experience. I share that belief.

WHILE THE ACT OF WRITING is a solitary affair, researching and preparing a book is quite the opposite. I have an enormous cast to thank, and I beg forgiveness should I fail to properly acknowledge someone who rendered me assistance.

From the world of libraries and archives, I am indebted to Diana Lachatanere and the staff of the Manuscript, Archives, and Rare Book Division at the Schomburg Center for Research in Black Culture, New York, NY; Joellen El Bashir and Ida Jones at the Moorland-Spingarn Research Center, Howard University, Washington, DC; and the excellent staff of the Manuscript Division of the Library of Congress, Washington, DC.

Among the many in other libraries and archives who provided a hand were: Valoise Armstrong, Eisenhower Presidential Library; Monica Blank, Rockefeller Archive; Mary Marshall Clark, Butler Library, Columbia University, New York, NY; Eric Cuellar, Lyndon B. Johnson Library; Karen J. Fishman, Library of Congress; Valerie Harris, University of Illinois Chicago Library, Chicago, IL; Larry Hughes, National Archives, College Park, MD; Bill Kemp, McLean County Museum of History, Bloomington, IL; Jessica McTague, Geneva History Center, Geneva, IL; John Reinhardt, Illinois State Archives, Springfield, IL; Kathy Struss, Dwight D. Eisenhower Presidential Library; Annie Tummino, Civil Rights Archive, Queens College Libraries, CUNY, Queens, NY.

Individuals to whom I owe thanks include: Jinx C. Broussard, Louisiana State University, Baton Rouge, LA; Sandy Cochran, Albuquerque, NM; CM! Winters Palacio, City College of Chicago; Chris Martin, West Virginia University; Janelle Hartman, Communication

Workers of America, Washington, DC; Sig Gissler, Pulitzer Prizes, Graduate School of Journalism, Columbia University, New York, NY; Jonathan Marshall, Medill School of Journalism, Chicago, IL; Alan Mather, Lindblom Math & Science Academy, Chicago, IL; Ethan Michaeli, We the People Media, Chicago, IL; Donald Ritchie, Historian of the United States Senate, Washington, DC; Hugh Wilford, California State University Long Beach, Long Beach, CA.

At the St. John AME Church, West Englewood in Chicago, which the Payne family used to attend, I was welcomed by Mildred B. Hays and Gwen Roberts.

Melvin Cray permitted me to use a portion of his taped interview with Ethel Payne in 1984 for the Dollie Robinson documentary, Media Genesis Productions, LLC.

Among those who shared remembrances of Payne were Simeon S. Booker, James Christian, Milton Coleman, Ernest Green, Gillie Haynes, Vernon Jordan, Walter J. Leonard, C. Payne Lucas, Robert McClory, Reverend Richard L. Tolliver, and Robert Woodson.

Additionally Ethel Payne's friends Rita A. Bibbs-Booth, Catherine Z. Brown, Bettye Collier-Thomas, Skip Davis, Joseph Dumas, Vivian Lee, Grayson Mitchell, Barbara Reynolds, Shirley Small-Rougeau, Jennifer Smaldone, Kevin Lowther, and John Raye never tired of my questions.

Several researchers lent a hand. They included William R. Cron, Ann Arbor, MI; Molly Kennedy, Springfield, IL; and Jonathan Scott, Smyrna, GA.

I owe a special thanks to Dr. James A. Johnson, Ethel Payne's nephew whose battle with the House of Representatives to attend the Page School is detailed in this book. He opened his home to me and shared many valuable documents, photos, and audio tapes.

Jamal Watson was also very kind in sharing material he had accumulated in his research on Ethel Payne.

Members of the 2013 Media & Civil Rights History conference kindly commented on a paper I delivered there about Payne's journalism. The following people graciously consented to answer my email queries or be interviewed for this book, sometimes more than once: Sylvia Hill, Eleanor Clift, Woodbury Clift, Robert Farrell, Gillie Haynes, Grayson Mitchell, and Juanita D. Miller.

The *Chicago Defender* provided permission for me to quote extensively from the many articles Payne wrote. The Washington Press Club Foundation also kindly provided permission to use its Ethel Payne oral history transcripts, part of a remarkable oral history project called Women in Journalism begun by the National Women's Press Club.

I would be ungrateful not to mention the support from E/TL&DS and its president, J. Revell Carr. This is the second book project of mine honored by the organization. Also the wonderful members of my writers group in Albuquerque greatly improved my prologue.

Author David Stewart and I continued a long-standing practice of reading each other's manuscripts when in draft form. David's thoughtful comments played an immense role in shaping this book.

This book would not have come to pass had it not been for two believers: the remarkably talented editor Dawn Davis, who acquired the work when she ran Amistad, and my agent, Alan Nevins. Editor Tracy Sherrod and assistant Kathleen Baumer worked hard and brought it to fruition.

I was saved from embarrassing mistakes and many a dangling modifier thanks to the diligent copyediting and fact-checking performed by Nancy Inglis.

Finally, I owe an enormous debt of gratitude to Patty McGrath Morris, my wife of thirty-three years, who was my steady partner in every step of this adventure to chronicle Ethel Payne's life and gave me honest and valuable editorial suggestions.

SELECTED BIBLIOGRAPHY

For reasons of space, the publications listed in this bibliography do not include all works used in the preparation of this book, rather only those that contributed substantially and may be of relevance to those pursuing similar research. Newspapers, magazines, and journals used in assembling this book are listed solely in the endnotes.

Booker, Simeon. *Shocking the Conscience: A Reporter's Account of the Civil Rights Movement.* Jackson, MS: University Press of Mississippi, 2013.

Bowers, William T., et al., *Black Soldier, White Army: The 24th Infantry Regiment in Korea.* Honolulu: University Press of the Pacific, 2005.

Branch, Taylor. *At Canaan's Edge: America in the King Years, 1965–68.* New York: Simon & Schuster, 2006.

———. *Parting the Waters: America in the King Years, 1954–63.* New York: Simon & Schuster, 1988.

Bushnell, Scott M. *Hard News, Heartfelt Opinions: A History of the "Fort Wayne Journal Gazette."* Bloomington: Indiana University Press, 2007.

Chicago Commission on Race Relations. *The Negro in Chicago: A Study of Race Relations and a Race Riot.* Chicago: University of Chicago Press, 1922.

Clark, E. Culpepper. *The Schoolhouse Door: Segregation's Last Stand at the University of Alabama.* New York: Oxford University Press, 1993.

Daley, Christopher B. *Covering America: A Narrative History of a Nation's Journalism*. Amherst: University of Massachusetts Press, 2012.

Ehrenhalt, Alan. *The Lost City: The Forgotten Virtues of Community in America*. New York: Basic Books, 1995.

Eldridge, Lawrence Allen. *Chronicles of a Two-Front War: Civil Rights and Vietnam in the African American Press*. Columbia: University of Missouri Press, 2012.

Faber, Michael. *The Unfinished Quest of Richard Wright*. Urbana: University of Illinois Press, 1993.

Farmer, James. *Lay Bare the Heart: An Autobiography of the Civil Rights Movement*. Fort Worth, TX: TCU Press, 1985.

Fleming, Cynthia. *Yes We Did?: From King's Dream to Obama's Promise*. Lexington: University Press of Kentucky, 2009.

Gaffen, Fred. *Cross-Border Warriors: Canadians in American Forces, Americans in Canadian Forces*. Toronto: Dunburn Press, 1995.

Garrow, David. *Bearing the Cross: Martin Luther King, Jr., and the Southern Christian Leadership Conference*. New York: William Morrow, 1986.

Giddings, Paula. *In Search of Sisterhood: Delta Sigma Theta and the Challenge of the Black Sorority Movement*. New York: William Morrow & Co., 1988.

Green, Michael Cullen. *Black Yanks in the Pacific: Race in the Making of American Military Empire After World War II*. Ithaca, NY: Cornell University Press, 2010.

Grossman, James R. *Land of Hope: Chicago, Black Southerners, and the Great Migration*. Chicago: University of Chicago Press, 1989.

Guzman, Jessie Parkhurst. *Negro Year Book: A Review of Events Affecting Negro Life, 1941–1946*. Alabama: Dept. of Records and Research, Tuskegee Institute, 1947.

Halberstam, David. *The Fifties*. New York: Villard Books, 1993.

Hansberry, Lorraine. *A Raisin in the Sun: Thirtieth Anniversary Edition*. New York: Samuel French, Inc., 1958.

Hills, Ruth Edmonds, ed. *The Black Women Oral History Project*. Westport, CT: Meckler, 1991.

Hoffman, Joyce. *On Their Own: Women Journalists and the American Experience in Vietnam*. New York: Da Capo, 2008.

Houck, Davis W., and Matthew A. Grindy. *Emmett Till and the Mississippi Press*. Jackson: University Press of Mississippi, 2008.

Irons, Peter. *Jim Crow's Children: The Broken Promise of the Brown Decision*. New York: Penguin Books, 2004.

Joseph, Peniel E. *Stokely: A Life*. New York: Basic Books, 2014.

Kersten, Andrew Edmund. *A. Philip Randolph: A Life in the Vanguard*. Lanham, MD: Rowan & Littlefield, 2007.

Kluger, Richard. *Simple Justice: The History of* Brown v. Board of Education *and Black America's Struggle for Equality*. New York: Knopf, 1976.

Knightley, Phillip. *The First Casualty: From the Crimea to Vietnam; The War Correspondent as Hero, Propagandist, and Myth Maker*. New York: Harcourt Brace Jovanovich, 1976.

LaBrie, Henry G. *Perspectives of the Black Press*. Kennebunkport, ME: Mercer House Press, 1974.

Margolick, David. *Elizabeth and Hazel: Two Women of Little Rock*. New Haven, CT: Yale University Press, 2011.

Massey, Douglas S., and Nancy A. Denton. *American Apartheid: Segregation and the Making of the Underclass*. Cambridge, MA: Harvard University Press, 1993.

McWirter, Cameron. *Red Summer: The Summer of 1919 and the Awakening of Black America*. New York: Henry Holt, 2011.

Murrow, Edward R., and Fred W. Friendly. *See It Now*. New York: Simon & Schuster, 1955.

Newkirk, Pamela. *Within the Veil: Black Journalists, White Media*. New York University Press, 2000.

Newton, Jim. *Justice for All: Earl Warren and the Nation He Made*. New York: Riverhead, 2006.

Ottley, Roi. *The Lonely Warrior: The Life and Times of Robert S. Abbott*. Chicago: Henry Regnery Co., 1955.

Pacyga, Dominic A. *Chicago: A Biography.* Chicago: University of Chicago Press, 2009.

Pfeffer, Paula F. *A. Philip Randolph, Pioneer of the Civil Rights Movement.* Baton Rouge: Louisiana State University Press, 1990.

Poinsett, Alex. *Walking with Presidents: Louis Martin and the Rise of Black Political Power.* Lanham, MD: Madison Books, 1997.

Pomeroy, Charles, ed. *Foreign Correspondents in Japan: Covering a Half-Century of Upheavals; From 1945 to the Present.* Rutland, VT: Tuttle Publishing, 1998.

Reed, Christopher Robert. *The Depression Comes to the South Side: Protest and Politics in the Black Metropolis.* Bloomington: Indiana University Press, 2011.

Ridlon, Florence. *A Black Physician's Struggle for Civil Rights: Edward C. Mazique, MD.* Albuquerque: University of New Mexico Press, 2005.

Ritchie, Donald A. *Reporting from Washington: The History of the Washington Press Corps.* New York: Oxford University Press, 2005.

Robert, Gene, and Hank Klibanoff. *The Race Beat: The Press, the Civil Rights Struggle, and the Awakening of a Nation.* New York: Knopf, 2006.

Rowan, Carl. *Breaking Barriers: A Memoir.* New York: Harper Perennial, 1992.

———. *The Pitiful and the Proud.* New York: Random House, 1956.

Rowley, Hazel. *Richard Wright: The Life and Times.* Chicago: University of Chicago Press, 2001.

Spear, Alan H. *Black Chicago: The Making of a Negro Ghetto, 1890–1920.* Chicago: University of Chicago Press, 1967.

Streitmatter, Rodger, *Raising Her Voice: African-American Women Journalists Who Changed History.* Lexington: University Press of Kentucky, 1994.

Sullivan, Gerald E., ed. *The Story of Englewood, 1835–1923.* Chicago: Foster & McDonnell, 1924.

Swarns, Rachel. *American Tapestry: The Story of the Black, White, and Multiracial Ancestors of Michelle Obama.* New York: Amistad, 2013.

Taylor, Cynthia. *A. Philip Randolph: The Religious Journey of an African American Labor Leader*. New York: New York University Press, 2006.

Taylor, Quintard. *In Search of the Racial Frontier: African Americans in the American West, 1528–1990*. New York: Norton, 1991.

Tuttle, William, Jr. *Race Riot: Chicago in the Red Summer of 1919*. New York: Athenaeum, 1977.

Tye, Larry. *Rising from the Rails: Pullman Porters and the Making of the Black Middle Class*. New York: Henry Holt, 2004.

Walker, Margaret. *Richard Wright: Daemonic Genius*. New York: Harper Paperback, 2001.

Waters, Enoch P. *American Diary: A Personal History of the Black Press*. Chicago: Path Press, 1987.

Wilkerson, Isabel. *The Warmth of Other Suns: The Epic Story of America's Great Migration*. New York: Vintage Books, 2010.

Wilford, Hugh. *The Mighty Wurlitzer: How the CIA Played America*. Cambridge, MA: Harvard University Press, 2008.

Williams, Juan. *Thurgood Marshall: American Revolutionary*. New York: Times Books, 1998.

Wright, Richard. *Black Boy*. New York: Harper Perennial, 1993.

———. *The Color Curtain: A Report on the Bandung Conference*. New York: World Publishing Co., 1956.

———. *Native Son*. New York: Harper & Brothers, 1940.

DISSERTATIONS

Finley, Keith M. *Southern Opposition to Civil Rights in the United States Senate: A Tactical and Ideological Analysis, 1938–1965*. PhD diss., Louisiana State University, 2003.

Layfield, Denise Sue. *Chasing the Dream: A Collection and Synthesis of Oral Histories of Eight Journalists Who Covered the Civil Rights Movement*. Master's thesis, University of Georgia, 1986.

Lucander, David. *It Is a New Kind of Militancy: March on Washington*

Movement, 1941–1946. PhD diss., University of Massachusetts Amherst, 2010.

Sherrod, Pamela Jetaun. *Ethel L. Payne: Coverage of Civil Rights as a Washington Correspondent, 1954–1958.* Master's thesis, Michigan State University, 1979.

Zasimczuk, Ivan A. *Maxwell M. Rabb: A Hidden Hand of the Eisenhower Administration in Civil Rights and Race Relations.* Master's thesis, University of California, Davis, 1997.

A NOTE ON SOURCES

To conserve space, I eschewed listing article titles and used abbreviations for frequently cited sources and a numeric dating system. A guide to abbreviations appears below. So for instance,

Ethel L. Payne to Louis E. Martin, January 28, 1953, Ethel L. Payne Papers Box 5, Folder 2, Manuscript Room of the Library of Congress, Washington, DC.

appears here as:

ELP to LEM, 1/28/1953, ELPLOC, B5F2

The reference citation is linked to the text at the point at which I begin using the source. So quotations in subsequent paragraphs stem from the same source unless otherwise noted.

Several of the collections of Ethel Payne's papers remain unprocessed, so the box numbers used here may change over time. However, the endnotes contain enough information to permit researchers to find the item at a later date. I am also always glad to communicate with other writers and researchers, should you have any questions.

ARCHIVAL COLLECTIONS OR REPOSITORIES

ACWP   Rev. Addie and Rev. Claude Wyatt Papers, Chicago Public Library Vivian G. Harsh Research Collection of Afro-American History and Literature

ALPACM   Ethel Payne Papers, Anacostia Community Museum, Washington, DC

APP   The American Presidency Project (www.presidency.ncsb
               .edu) at the University of California, Santa Barbara

APRPLOC   A. Philip Randolph Papers, Manuscript Room Library of
               Congress, Washington, DC

A-SFP   Abbott-Sengstacke Family Papers, 1847–1997, Vivian G.
               Harsh Research Collection of Afro-American History and
               Literature, Chicago Public Library, Chicago, IL

DDEPL   Dwight David Eisenhower Presidential Library, Abilene,
               KS

ELPCHM   Ethel L. Payne Papers, Chicago History Museum, Chi-
               cago, IL

ELPJAJ   Ethel L. Payne Papers privately held by Dr. James A.
               Johnson

ELPLOC   Ethel L. Payne Papers, Manuscript Room, Library of
               Congress, Washington, DC

ELPMSRC   Ethel L. Payne Papers, Moorland-Spingarn Research
               Center, Howard University, Washington, DC

ELPSCRBC   Ethel L. Payne Papers, Schomburg Center for Research
               in Black Culture, New York, NY

GMMA   George Meany Memorial Archives, National Labor Col-
               lege, Silver Spring, MD

GRFPL   Gerald R. Ford Presidential Library, Ann Arbor, MI

HSTPL   Harry S. Truman Presidential Library, Independence,
               MO

ISA   Illinois State Archives, Springfield, IL

IRC   Files of the Interracial Commission, Illinois State
               Archives, Springfield, IL

JAJP   James A. Johnson collection of Ethel L. Payne papers in
               private possession

LBJPL   LBJ Presidential Library, Austin, TX

LMLOC   Louis Martin Papers, Manuscript Room of the Library of
               Congress, Washington, DC

MBPP   Margaret Bayne Price Papers, Michigan Historical Collections, Bentley Historical Library, University of Michigan, Ann Arbor, MI

NAACP   National Association for the Advancement of Colored People Collection, Manuscript Room of the Library of Congress, Washington, DC

NARA   Nelson A. Rockefeller Personal Files, Washington, DC, Rockefeller Archives, Sleepy Hollow, NY

PMWP   Philip M. Weightman Papers, Tamiment Library, Wagner Archives, Elmer Holmes Bobst Library, New York University, New York, NY

RMNPL   Richard M. Nixon Presidential Library, Yorba Linda, CA

SSP   Susan Sontag Papers, Library Special Collections, University of California Los Angeles, Los Angeles, CA

WEBDBP   W. E. B. Du Bois Papers, Special Collections and University Archives, University of Massachusetts Amherst Libraries, Amherst, MA

FREQUENTLY CITED PERSONAL NAMES

APR   A. Philip Randolph

ARJ   Avis Ruth Johnson (sister)

BP   Bessie Payne (mother)

ELP   Ethel L. Payne

EPW   Enoch P. Waters

JHS   John H. Sengstacke

LEM   Louis E. Martin

MMR   Maxwell M. Rabb

RMN   Richard M. Nixon

TG   Thelma Gray (sister)

FREQUENTLY CITED NEWSPAPERS

AfAm	*Afro-American*
AmNe	*Amsterdam News*
AtWo	*Atlanta Daily World*
ChDe	*Chicago Defender* (weekly)
ChMe	*Chicago Metro News*
ChTr	*Chicago Tribune*
DaDe	*Chicago Defender* (daily)
LAT	*Los Angeles Times*
MiTi	*Miami Times*
NYT	*New York Times*
PiCo	*Pittsburgh Courier*
WaIn	*Washington Informer*
WaPo	*Washington Post*
WaSt	*Washington Evening Star*

NOTES

1 **Resting on the table:** NYT, 7/3/1964, 1.

3 **Despite a storied history:** Enoch P. Waters, *American Diary: A Personal History of the Black Press* (Chicago: Path Press, 1987), 141.

3 **Until the civil rights movement:** *ChDe*, 10/28/1911, 1.

4 **But the Chicago Defender:** Vernon Jarrett (The HistoryMakers A2000.028), interview by Julieanna Richardson, 6/27/2000, The HistoryMakers Digital Archive. Session 1, tape 5, story 3.

4 **His speech concluded:** Accounts varyingly report that Johnson used seventy-five or seventy-nine pens.

9 **A train ticket:** The arrivals of both William Payne and Bessie Austin are dated using family records. For more on the Great Migration, see Isabel Wilkerson, *The Warmth of Other Suns: The Epic Story of America's Great Migration* (New York: Vintage Books, 2010).

9 **Well used to hard labor:** Bessie Payne, "The Story of the Life of George Washington Austin, 1847–1935" and marriage date found on family tree. City directories confirm the family's account of William's employment as a cooper. See also *DaDe*, 4/23/1909, 3.

10 **At first the Paynes:** The first houses they lived in were on Loomis Boulevard and Ada Street. ELP noted the location of her birth in an outline she prepared for an autobiography she contemplated writing, ELPLC B19F4. I was, however, unable to locate a birth certificate in the Cook County records; *ChDe*, 7/13/1912, 4. The house was on Eberhart Avenue. ELP wrote on the back of her aunt's photo that she had been the one to name her.

10 **William had left:** Larry Tye, *Rising from the Rails: Pullman Porters*

and the Making of the Black Middle Class (New York: Henry Holt, 2004), 68, 75–79. William Payne is listed in several newspaper accounts as working on the New York Central Line to Toledo, OH. See, for instance, *ChDe*, 4/7/1917, 3.

11 **Earning a Pullman salary and tips:** In 1910, only 6.4 percent of African Americans were in owner-occupied housing in Chicago, according to Quintard Taylor, *In Search of the Racial Frontier: African Americans in the American West, 1528–1990* (New York: Norton, 1991), 233; see also W. J. Collins and R. A. Margo, "Race and Home Ownership: A Century-Long View," *Explorations in Economic History* 37 (2001), 68–92; Thelma E. Gray, "The Subject is 6210 Throop Street," ELPLC B8F1.

11 **Although strict with:** ELP, "Wiliam and Bessie Payne—Who They Were," copy in author's files.

11 **The family's love:** *PiCo*, 5/10/1975, 5; Thelma Gray repeated the family story at a 1982 testimonial dinner.

12 **Bessie kept the home:** Thelma Gray, "Mom"; ELP, "Shades in Black and White," ELPMSRC B1657, Educational Papers. ELP tells of castor oil and gingersnaps in a speech to the Association for the Study of Negro American Life and History, 10/21/1973, ELPSCRBC B9.

12 **Bessie's family had:** ELPOH 3; ELP to Bessie Davenport, 7/29/1983, ELPLOC B5F1. In recounting this story to her old friend, Davenport, Payne added, "Fortunately, her [Bessie's] special bond with the Lord carried me through and made me a better citizen and contributing member of society."

12 **Bessie's parents:** ELP, "Laughing with Life," ELPLOC B40F1.

12 **Ethel, her older sisters:** *ChDe*, 5/25/1918, 7.

13 **Ethel's sister Alma:** ELP, "William and Bessie Payne: Who They Were," and Thelma E. Gray, "Alma Josephine"; ELPOH, 7.

13 **In particular, Ethel:** ELPOH, 7; Dunbar's poem later provided the poet Maya Angelou with the title for her autobiography.

14 **Ethel and her siblings:** Mayme Austin Mitcham, "Early Events in the Life of Mrs. Josephine Taylor Austin."

14 **Bessie's father, George:** Bessie Payne, "The Story of the Life of George Washington Austin, 1947–1935."

14 **But tall tales:** ELP, "Laughing with Life," ELPLOC B40F1.

15 **Ethel began her:** Thelma E. Gray, "The Subject is 6210 Throop Street," ELPLC B8F1. At Copernicus, twelve of the seventy-five members of the graduating eighth grade in 1913 were African American. "Copernicus is noted as being one of the best grade schools in the city," reported a black newspaper. "Its discipline is good, it has a high class of teachers, and is therefore more liberal in its general views." *ChDe,* 6/28/1913, 2.

15 **Accompanying Ethel to:** Thelma E. Gray, "Lemuel Payne."

16 **Each day's walk:** Chicago Commission on Race Relations, *The Negro in Chicago: A Study of Race Relations and a Race Riot* (Chicago: University of Chicago Press, 1922), 439–440.

16 **At school and at home:** ELP autobiographical outline, ELPLOC B19F4; ELPOH, 4–5.

17 **On Sunday August 27, 1919:** ELP, "Shades in Black and White," ELPMSRC Box 1657, Educational Papers; Denise Sue Layfield, *Chasing the Dream: A Collection and Synthesis of Oral Histories of Eight Journalists Who Covered the Civil Rights Movement* (master's thesis, University of Georgia, 1986), 128–129; Cameron McWirter, *Red Summer: The Summer of 1919 and the Awakening of Black America* (New York: Henry Holt, 2011), 127–148.

18 **By nightfall a race war:** William M. Tuttle, Jr. *Race Riot: Chicago in the Red Summer of 1919* (New York: Athenaeum, 1977), 32–33.

18 **South Side became:** Tuttle, *Race Riot,* 50.

18 **The Payne family huddled:** *ChTr,* 7/31/1919. 1.

19 **All but a few:** *ChTr,* 8/1/1919, 2.

19 **Finally, on the third night:** ELP, "Shades in Black and White," ELPMSRC Box 1657, Educational Papers; Layfield, *Chasing the Dream,* 128–129.

20 **When calm did come:** 1920 and 1930 U.S. Census figures for Throop Street. For instance, African Americans had made up 15 percent of the residents in the Washington Park Community, right

in the middle of South Side, before the riots. Within a decade they made up 92 percent of its population. See Dominic A. Pacyga, *Chicago: A Biography* (Chicago: University of Chicago Press, 2009), 255; ELPOH, 1. The neighborhood was bounded by 63rd Street on the south, 59th on the north, Loomis Boulevard on the west, and Aberdeen Street on the east; Alan H. Spear, *Black Chicago: The Making of a Negro Ghetto, 1890–1920* (Chicago: University of Chicago Press, 1967), 12.

20 *Excluded from Chicago:* The phrase is credited to historian Earl Lewis; Timuel Black interviewed in *DuSable to Obama: Chicago's Black Metropolis* DVD, produced by Barbara E. Allen and Daniel Andries (Windows to the World Communications, 2010).

21 *An African American newspaper:* ELPOH, 50.

21 *Taking a page:* ChDe, 3/30/1930, A1; Typical headlines included LOY LYNCHED BY MOB FOR STEALING COW THAT RETURNED LATER, ChDe, 1/30/1915, and TWENTY-THOUSAND SOUTHERNERS BURN BOY AT STAKE, 5/19/1916.

22 *Within a decade:* James R. Grossman, *Land of Hope: Chicago, Black Southerners, and the Great Migration* (Chicago: University of Chicago Press, 1989), 79, 87. Most reports of the *Defender's* circulation were unreliable. The number used here is derived from a number of sources.

22 *The Defender was:* Mr. Ward, "Bound for the Promised Land," ChDe, 11/11/1916, 12.

23 *As Ethal Paine neared:* Robert Lindblom Technical High School Building: Preliminary Summary of Information submitted to the Commission on Chicago Landmarks, December 2008, 17.

23 *Lindblom's facilities:* ELPOH, 7.

24 *It was not much easier:* Negro in Chicago, 242, 441; Gerald E. Sullivan, ed. *The Story of Englewood, 1835–1923* (1924), 69; *The Negro in Chicago*, 108; ELPOH, 7. A census of the photographs in the Lindblom yearbooks from 1926 to 1930 reveal no African American employees and only three to four black students per grade.

24 *Ethel Payne followed:* The transcript for Payne at the Chicago

Training School lists her high school classes: copy in author's possession; ELPOH, 7.

24 *Miss Dixon's English:* Charles A. Fenton, *The Apprenticeship of Ernest Hemingway: The Early Years* (New York: Farrar, Straus & Young, 1954), 8.

25 *Payne fell under Dixon's spell:* ELPOH, 23–24.

25 *One day as English class began:* Dixon was indeed one of Hemingway's two favorite English teachers.

26 *One month after:* Death certificate, 6005226 1926–02–21, Cook County, IL.

26 *Thelma, the second-oldest:* Gray, "The Subject Is My Father," ELPLC B8F1.

26 *On the evening:* ELPOH, 6.

26 *The following month:* Gray, "Historically Speaking," ELPLC B7F8.

27 *In the fall of 1929:* Margaret H. Dixon, "To My Graduating Class," *The Eagle*, January 1930.

28 *The 1930s did not:* Christopher Robert Reed, *The Depression Comes to the South Side: Protest and Politics in the Black Metropolis, 1930–1933* (Bloomington: Indiana University Press), 12.

28 *Like canaries in a coal mine:* ChDe, 3/22/1930, 13.

28 *The Payne family:* Lyman B. Burbank, "Chicago Public Schools and the Depression Years of 1928–1937," *Journal of the Illinois State Historical Society* 64 (Winter), 367.

29 *But no matter how:* ELP, "Wiliam and Bessie Payne—Who They Were," ELPOH, 8.

29 *Bessie's indomitable spirit:* ELPLOC B28F6.

29 *As for herself:* ELPOH, 5; Gray, "My Parents as I Knew Them," ELPLOC B28F6.

30 *At night the family:* "She did not think herself a genius by any means," Alcott said of Jo, "but when the writing fit came on, she gave herself up to it with entire abandon, and led a blissful life, unconscious of want, care, or bad weather, while she sat safe and happy in an imaginary world, full of friends almost as real and dear to her as any in the

flesh." Louisa May Alcott, *Little Women* (New York: Signet, 2004), 246. ELP, "Wiliam and Bessie Payne—Who They Were," and ELP Convocation Speech at Fisk University, 9/12/1983, ELPLOC B28F6.

30 ***In the midst of the hard times:*** ELPOH, 8.

30 ***The odds, however:*** ChDe, 3/29/1930; ELPOH, 9.

31 ***When she began at Crane:*** American Interracial Peace Committee press release January 1930, WEBDBP; *ChDe*, 1/18/1930, 10.

31 ***Payne decided to enter:*** *ChDe*, 7/19/1930, A1. I tried to locate the winning essays, but none of the archives related to the competition retained copies.

31 ***Despite this success:*** ELP to Du Bois, 11/12/1931, WEBDBP.

31 ***The Great Depression:*** Christopher Robert Reed, *The Depression Comes to the South Side: Protest and Politics in the Black Metropolis* (Bloomington: Indiana University Press, 2011), 134–135.

32 ***In the fall of 1930:*** AmNe, 10/8/1930, 2; Quoted in Roi Ottley, *The Lonely Warrior: The Life and Times of Robert S. Abbott* (Chicago: Regnery, 1955), 294. Other magazines that came out of Chicago around this time included *Half-Century, American Life, Reflexus,* and *Bronzeman.*

32 **Abbott's Monthly** *put out:* Craig H. Werner and Sandra Shannon, "Foundations of African American Modernism, 1910–1950," *Cambridge History of African American Literature* (Cambridge: Cambridge University Press, 2011), 259; *ChDe*, 8/9/1930, 13. In describing their plans, the magazine's editors announced they were seeking "short or long stories of the fiction type, success stories of individuals, human-interest stories of the confession class, sketches from artists and material in general for magazine purposes."

32 ***Well-crafted and clever:*** ELP, "Driftwood," *Abbott's Monthly,* Vol. 1, No. 3, December 1930, 46–78.

35 ***In November 1931:*** ELP to Du Bois, 11/12/1931, WEBDBP.

35 ***Payne left Crane:*** College transcript provided by Garrett–Evangelical Theological Seminary, copy in possession of author.

36 ***In her spare time:*** ChDe, 4/16/1932, 12.

36 ***Payne's success with Abbott's Monthly:*** Hazel Rowley, *Richard*

Wright: The Life and Times (Chicago: University of Chicago Press, 2001), 63. Wright was never paid for the story.

36 **In the spring of 1934:** Dana Lee Roberts, *American Women in Mission: A Social History of Their Thought and Practice* (Macon, GA: Mercer University Press, 1997), 155; John Thomas McFarland and Benjamin Severance Winchester, editors, *The Encyclopedia of Sunday Schools and Religious Education,* Vol. 1 (London: Thomas Nelson & Sons, 1916), 212. The school charged no tuition and was open "to any young man or woman of ability, determination, and consecration," according to the *Methodist Year Book 1921* (New York: Methodist Book Concern, 1921), 67.

37 **On the evening of June 15, 1934:** 1934 Yearbook on file at the Garrett–Evangelical Theological Seminary; Chicago Commission, *The Negro in Chicago,* 325.

37 **Instead Payne used:** Anne Meis Knupfer, "'To Become Good, Self-Supporting Women': The State Industrial School for Delinquent Girls at Geneva, Illinois, 1900–1935," *Journal of the History of Sexuality,* Vol. 9, No. 4 (Oct. 2000), 421; ELPOH, 11.

37 **When Payne arrived:** Descriptions taken from various sources, including Herman M. Adler, *Cook County and the Mentally Handicapped* (New York: National Committee for Mental Hygiene, 1918), 56–58.

37 **Payne was hired:** Ruth M. Lunn, "My Years of Service for the State of Illinois," *News Notes,* Illinois State Training School for Girls, February 1971.

38 **Payne's wards were:** Michael A. Rembis, *Defining Deviance: Sex, Science, and Delinquent Girls, 1890–1960* (Urbana: University of Illinois Press, 2011), 96–97, 103–104.

38 **The job was exhausting:** ELPOH 10–11.

38 **But after a year and a half:** Personal Bio Folder, ELPMSRC B1667; Wright, *Native Son,* 20.

39 **The aspiration to be:** Educational Papers, ELPMSRC B1657.

40 **Monotonously stamping lending:** Pamela Jetaun Sherrod, *Ethel L. Payne: Coverage of Civil Rights as a Washington Correspondent,*

1954–1958 (master's thesis, Michigan State University, 1979), 20–21; First Annual Report of the Illinois Inter-Racial Commission for the period August 1943 to December 1944, 53.

40 **Preparations for war:** *ChDe* 1/11/1941, 8; 8/31/1940, 7; and 2/22/1941, 8.

41 **Over six feet tall:** *ChDe,* 2/8/1941, 14. James Farmer described Randolph this way, "A. Philip Randolph was a Great Dane—the majesty, the gentleness, the noble head, the supreme dignity, the grace of movement." James Farmer, *Lay Bare the Heart: An Autobiography of the Civil Rights Movement* (Fort Worth, TX: TCU Press, 1985), 156.

41 **The planned protest:** *AtWo,* 6/18/1941, 1.

42 **To the president:** *PiCo,* 1/25/1941, 13.

42 **Twenty-nine-year-old Payne:** ELPOH, 14.

42 **She was an active:** *Crisis,* July 1940, 205 and December 1941, 391; Payne became a NAACP PANCA, the name given to those who enlisted more than twenty members. The name was created by transposing the letters in NAACP; *ChTr,* 8/25/1946, 8.

43 **Nor was she sheepish:** *ChTr,* 2/14/1937, 16.

43 **Hammering away at:** *ChTr,* 2/15/1942, SW1.

44 **The prickly personalities:** Cynthia Taylor in *A. Philip Randolph: The Religious Journey of an African American Labor Leader* (New York: New York University Press, 2006) noted the friction but felt it was mostly between the women and Burton. "Phil is extremely attractive to women, which results in his getting some of them to work like Trojans in the causes which he heads. But his work schedule scarcely gives him time to pay attention to 'em, which often causes injured feelings." Morris Milgram to Daniel James, 1/16/1949, APRPLOC. Neva Ryan told Payne that she would refuse to sit in on the meeting with Randolph, claiming that Payne was to blame for the delays. "I practically forced Ethel to call the meeting of the Planning Committee when you were here," she wrote in a complaining note to Randolph. "I further informed her that if she did not start things moving that I would take over."

44 *In the end:* A copy of the brochure may be found in ELPLOC B4F1.

44 *Armed with the flyer:* Neva Ryan to APR, 4/27/1942, APRLOC MOWM Correspondence Folder.

45 *As the day of the rally neared:* ELP, instructions for blackout, APRLOC B36, MOWM Circulars Folder.

45 *The work paid off:* ChTr, 6/27/1942, 20; PiCo, 7/4/1942, 14; ChDe, 7/4/1942, 1.

46 *The news coverage:* ChTr, 6/27/1942, 20.

46 *The rally took in:* ELP to AR, 7/3/1942, APRLOC MOWM Correspondence Folder; APR to ELP, 7/7/1942, APRLOC MOWM Correspondence Folder.

46 *The rally over:* PiCo, 81/1942, 11.

47 *She took the lesson:* ELP to A. Philip Randolph, 12/16/1941, APRLC MOWM Correspondence Folder.

47 *With rest, Payne:* AmNe, 9/26/1942, 5 and 10/24/1942, 3; APR to ELP, 10/8/1941, APRLC MOWM Correspondence Folder.

47 *In 1943:* ELP to APR, 6/5/1943, APRLC MOWM Correspondence Folder.

48 *Once again rebellion:* Paula F. Pfeffer, A. *Philip Randolph, Pioneer of the Civil Rights Movement* (Baton Rouge: Louisiana State University Press, 1990), 301. According to Pfeffer, Randolph remained sexist. In 1963 women reporters complained they were confined to the National Press Club balcony for a pre-march speech. "What's wrong with the balcony?" asked Randolph. To which the women replied, "What's wrong with the back of the bus?"

48 *She picked up:* ELP to APR, May 24, 1943, APRLC MOWM Correspondence Folder.

48 *Payne had reasons:* Quoted in David Lucander, *It Is a New Kind of Militancy: March on Washington Movement, 1941–1946* (PhD dissertation, University of Massachusetts Amherst, 2010), 69.

49 *The riots in Detroit:* ChDe, 7/10/1943, 1; AfAm, 7/10/1943, 1.

50 *During the meeting:* Merl E. Reed, "The FBI, MOWM, and

Core 1941–1947," *Journal of Black Studies*, Vol. 21, No. 4 (June 1991), 467–468; Luncander, *It Is a New Kind of Militancy*, 67–68.

50 **The concern was real**: ChDe, 7/31/1943, 14; ChDe, 7/17/1943, 3; ChDe, 7/24/1943, 2.

51 **Governor Green was**: ChTr, 8/1/1943, 14; ChDe, 8/14/1943, 20.

51 **"I hereby appoint"**: Gov. Green to ELP, 7/31/1943, ISA.

52 **In September 1943**: NYT, 9/19/1943, 18; AtWo, 9/13/1943, 1; ChDe, 9/27/1943, 12.

52 **In one of its**: Commission Minutes 10/1/1943, IRC; ChDe, 10/9/1943, 6.

53 **Payne's impatience for**: ChDe, 10/9/1943, 6.

53 **When members turned**: Commission Minutes, 11/3/1943, IRC.

54 **Frustrated, Payne nonetheless**: Commission Minutes, 11/3/1943, IRC.

54 **In Washington on**: ELP to APR, 1/24/1944, ELPLOC B4F1.

55 **Payne retreated to**: APR to Francis Biddle, 1/28/1944, ELPLOC B4F1.

55 **The failure to get**: ELP to APR, 9/2/1945, ELPLOC B4F1.

56 **The war's end**: ELP to APR, 9/2/1945, ELPLOC B4F1.

56 **As desired as it was**: ChDe, 8/18/1947.

57 **On a hot August day**: According to ELP, there were ten of them who were arrested, including her sister and infant son. When the court case came up, the judge dismissed the charges and scolded the police for "bad judgment." See short autobiography, ELP-SCRBC B37; Personal Bio Folder, ELPMSRC, B1667.

58 **In 1948**: ChTr, 12/8/1947, 5; ChDe, 3/27/1948, 5.

58 **During World War II**: ELP to APR, 9/2/1945, ELPLOC B4F1.

59 **In March Payne**: ELPOH, 17.

60 **Her mother's consent**: Fragment of ELP ltr to BP (June 1948 but undated); Scrapbook Folder. ELPMSC, Box 1160.

60 **Japan put a pause**: Payne never revealed much about her romantic life. Her first beau's name was Bernie Eskridge, with whom she played hooky from church. "At age 12 years old, Bernie Eskridge and I fell madly in love. I used to slip out of the house and go with him on his paper route. It busted up when he gave the 25-center

valentine he had bought for me to Dorothy Wimbly," said Payne (*ChDe*, 1/19/1974, 5). According to an essay she wrote for a class in 1940, Payne also dated a teacher for a while. ELP ltr to Bessie Davenport, 7/29/1983, ELPLOC, B5F1; ELPOH, 17–18. Paul is discussed in several of ELP's letters from Japan, which is how we know his first name.

60 **Setting off by train:** ELP ltr to unidentified sister, 6/10/1948, ELPJAJ.

61 **On June 15:** Fragment of ELP ltr to Bessie Payne, (June 1948 but undated); Scrapbook Folder. ELPMSRC, Box 1160.

61 **After nearly two weeks:** ELP ltr to unidentified sister 6/10/1948, ELPJAJ; ELPOH 19.

62 **Payne was assigned:** ELP ltr to Thelma 10/4/1948, ELPJAJ.

62 **"There were rules":** Vivian Lee to author, 6/25/2012. Lee and her family remained friends with Payne all her life. Lee called her "Aunt Penny," a nickname Payne got while serving in Japan.

62 **Being kept apart:** Charley Cherokee, National Grapevine column, *ChDe*, 3/1/1947, 15.

63 **Black soldiers:** *AfAm*, 6/1/1946, 7; Fred Gaffen, *Cross-Border Warriors: Canadians in American Forces, Americans in Canadian Forces* (Toronto: Dunburn Press, 1995), 160; Michael Cullen Green, *Black Yanks in the Pacific: Race in the Making of American Military Empire after World War II* (Ithaca, NY: Cornell University Press, 2010), 102.

63 **Even so:** Green, *Black Yanks in the Pacific*, 107.

63 **At the Seaview:** ELP ltr to unidentified aunt and uncle, 3/9/1949 ELPSCBC Box 5; ELP ltr to RJ 8/23/1948 ELPJAJ; *AfAm*, 11/11/1950, 6; *Pacific Stars & Stripes*, 5/28/1949, 6; Vivian Lee interview with author, 7/17/2012.

64 **On a Saturday:** Bruce M. Tyler, "Behind the Lines—Marguerite Davis," *Louisville Magazine*, Nov. 2006.

64 **Davis wanted to:** Yukiko Koshiro, *Trans-Pacific Racisms and the U.S. Occupation of Japan* (New York: Columbia University Press, 1999), 161–163.

65 **Military law freed:** Sey Nishimura, "Promoting Health in

American-Occupied Japan: Resistance to Allied Public Health Measures, 1945–1952," *Public Health*, August 2009, 99 (8) 1364–1375.

65 **But Payne was:** ELP ltr to ARJ, 8/23/1948, ELPJAJ.

66 **As her first:** ELP ltr to TG 1/9/1949, ELPSCRBC B5.

66 **As her second:** ELP ltr to JT, 4/17/1949, ELPSCRBC B5; ELP to unidentified aunt and uncle, 3/9/1949 ELPSCRBN B5.

67 **At Nara Park:** Japan typescript, ELPMSRC, Box 1160; ELP undated ltr to TG, ELPJAJ.

68 **She attended the war tribunals:** ELPOH, 20 and 30.

68 **At the end of:** ChDe, 1/21/1950, 9.

68 **Soon, however, the holiday:** She met with the head of UNESCO in Japan and wrangled an invitation to dinner at the home of Komakichi Matsuoka, a socialist leader and trade unionist. "Mr. Matsuoka," she said, "gave some very pertinent facts on the economic situation which I can use when I sit down to write." Japan typescript, ELPMSRC, B1660; ELP ltr to TG, 3/28/1950, ELP-JAJ.

69 **Payne's superiors remained:** Club Director-Tokyo, ELPMSRC, B1657.

69 **The occupation forces:** ELP to TG date unclear August/September 1950, ELPJAJ. The original letter says, "of volunteer [unreadable word] are doing all they can . . ." To make the quotation grammatically correct I made the missing word *volunteers.*

70 **The burdens of war:** Green, *Black Yanks in the Pacific,* 59.

71 **One of Ethel Payne's:** Charles Pomeroy, editor, *Foreign Correspondents in Japan: Covering a Half-Century of Upheavals; From 1945 to the Present* (Rutland, VT: Tuttle Publishing, 1998), 16.

71 **Hicks was impressed:** AfAm, 11/11/1950, 6.

72 **But what really:** Green, *Black Yanks in the Pacific,* 63.

72 **"By tradition":** ChDe, 11/11/1950, 13.

73 **By the standards:** AfAm, 9/2/1950, A5.

73 **Like Payne:** Robert H. Giles et al., *Profiles in Journalist Courage* (New York: Transaction Publishers, 2001), 70–71.

73 **Payne and Wilson:** *ChDe*, 12/2/1950, 10

73 **Wilson filed a report:** ELPOH, 31.

74 **When Wilson was:** *ChDe*, 6/6/1991, 20.

74 **About a month:** ELP, short autobiography, ELPSRBC, Box 37.

75 **"To get back to":** *ChDe*, 11/18/1950, 1.

75 **The identical headline:** *ChDe*, 11/25/1950, 12.

76 **"If there was":** Jessie Parkhurst Guzman, *Negro Year Book: A Review of Events Affecting Negro Life, 1941–1946*. Alabama: Dept. of Records and Research, Tuskegee Institute. 1947, 386.

76 **MacArthur's aides:** The lawyer was Leon I. Greenberg, whom she retained for $100, a considerable sum for her. (Expense account, ELPMSRC, Box 1657.) Greenberg served as a defense counsel at the Japanese war crimes trials, which Payne had attended.

76 **In the early months:** *ChDe*, 4/28/1951, 1.

77 **Concerned with survival:** William T. Bowers et al., *Black Soldier, White Army: The 24th Infantry Regiment in Korea* (Honolulu: University Press of the Pacific, 2005), 186–187. President Truman later reduced the death penalty sentence to twenty years, and the soldier served only five years before being released.

77 **When word of the:** Diary, Thurgood Marshall Papers, Library of Congress, B57914.

77 **At the club:** Marshall, who had already battled his share of racists in the United States, was unimpressed with MacArthur's explanations. The lawyer reminded the general that the Air Force and Navy were already integrated but the Army, particularly those men under his charge, was not. MacArthur claimed he couldn't find any qualified Negroes. But when he did, they would be integrated.

"Well, look, General," said Marshall. "You've got all those guards out there with all this spit and polish and there's not one Negro in the whole group."

"There's none qualified," MacArthur replied.

"Well, what's the qualification?" asked Marshall, to which MacArthur gave a discourse on battlefield accomplishments and the like.

"Well," Marshall impatiently responded, "I just talked to a Negro yesterday, a sergeant, who has killed more people with a rifle than anybody in history. And he's not qualified?"

"No."

"Well, now, General, remember yesterday you had the big band playing at the ceremony over there?"

"Yes, wasn't it wonderful?"

"Yeah. The Headquarters Band. It's beautiful," said Marshall. "Now, General, just between you and me, Goddamn it, don't you tell me that there's no Negro who can play a horn." (Stephen Smith and Kate Ellis, *Thurgood Marshall Before the Court*, American Radio Works documentary. Transcript may be viewed at http://americanradioworks.publicradio.org/features/marshall/.

77 *Meanwhile, hearing about:* ELPOH, 33.

78 *Getting home was:* ChDe, 4/28/1951, 1.

79 *In enormous disrepair:* Peter Irons, *Jim Crow's Children: The Broken Promise of the* Brown *Decision* (New York: Penguin Books, 2004), 80–95.

85 *In early April 1951:* The religious analogy was inspired by similar veneration from others in the black press, such as "destined to be known as 'the Negro bible.'" (*Ebony,* October 1970, 62); Timuel Black quoted in Alan Ehrenhalt, *The Lost City: The Forgotten Virtues of Community in America* (New York: Basic Books, 1995), 148.

85 *In stark contrast:* ChDe, 4/28/1951, 2 and 4/28/1951, 14; Vernon Jarrett (The HistoryMakers A2000.028), interview by Julieanna Richardson, 06/27/2000, The HistoryMakers Digital Archive. Session 1, tape 4, story 7. Jarrett hosted the first daily black radio newscast.

86 *Although it covered:* Ehrenhalt, *The Lost City,* 150.

86 *As she faced:* Most women on newspaper staffs wrote for the women's page or handled society and church news. When asked if she ever considered doing society news, Payne said, "No way! No, I had no taste for society news, none whatsoever." ELPOH, 35.

87 *A natty dresser:* ELPOH, 34.

88 *An elaborate system:* Douglas S. Massey and Nancy A. Denton,

American Apartheid: Segregation and the Making of the Underclass (Cambridge, MA: Harvard University Press, 1993), 47; Lorraine Hansberry, *A Raisin in the Sun: Thirtieth Anniversary Edition* (New York: Samuel French, Inc., 1958), 137.

88 **Health care, even:** Richard Wright, *Black Boy* (New York: Harper Perennial, 1993), 356.

89 **In no time:** ChDe, 5/5/1951, 14; ChDe, 6/16/1951, 14.

89 **As she became:** Ehrenhalt, *The Lost City*, 160.

90 **The articles were:** ChDe, 6/30/1951, 13. At one plant, a manager provided a summation of the pattern of race relations. "If two white people have a quarrel, it's just another quarrel. If two Negroes quarrel, it's a disturbance; but if a white person and a Negro quarrel, it becomes an 'incident.'" (*ChDe*, 7/28/1951, 13.)

90 **On the other hand:** ChDe, 7/14/1951, 13.

90 **Her output was:** ELPOH, 30.

91 **On a sunny:** ChDe, 1/19/1952, 1.

91 **Twenty-six years after:** ChDe, 1/26/1952, 15.

92 **When they reached:** ChDe, 2/2/1952, 15.

92 **In fact, the:** Guild Reporter, 2/22/1952, 3.

93 **Within a few:** ChDe, 4/21/1951, 3.

93 **Payne had not:** Victor Groza, Karen F. Rosenberg, *Clinical and Practice Issues in Adoption: Bridging the Gap Between Adoptees Placed as Infants and as Older Children* (New York: Praeger, 1998), 110; Donna L. Franklin, *Ensuring Inequality: The Structural Transformation of the African-American Family* (New York: Oxford University Press, 1997), 138.

93 **As a result:** Ellen Herman, *Kinship by Design: A History of Adoption in Modern America* (Chicago: University of Chicago Press, 2008), 129.

94 **In the spring:** ChDe, 4/12/1952, 1.

95 **For four weeks:** ChDe, 5/3/1951, 1.

95 **The series was:** ChDe, 6/28/1952, 4; ELPOH, 36.

95 **The editors assigned:** ChDe, 6/07/1952, 1.

96 **In subsequent installments:** ChDe, 6/14/1952, 1.

96　*There was little:* ChDe, 6/28/1952, 2.

97　*The series resonated:* ChDe, 10/18/1952, 3.

98　*This was a direct:* ChDe, 7/26/1952, 1.

99　*Instead of seeking:* Crisis, August-September 1952, 413.

99　*Slender in build:* Keith M. Finley, *Southern Opposition to Civil Rights in the United States Senate: A Tactical and Ideological Analysis, 1938–1965* (PhD dissertation, Louisiana State University, 2003.)

102　*Reaching Washington on:* ChDe, 1/31/1953, 13; details about the inauguration may be found at http://www.eisenhower.archives.gov/all_about_ike/presidential/1953_inauguration.html.

103　*A more demure:* See the oral history interview with Philleo Nash, who served variously as a high-ranking special assistant in the Roosevelt and Truman administrations. HSTPL.

103　*"As the last":* ChDe, 1/31/1953, 1.

103　*But her stories:* ELPOH, 37.

104　*On the other hand:* ChDe, 6/6/1953, 4; 6/14/1953, 14; 3/21/1953, 15.

104　*Quite to her:* ChDe, 6/13/1953, 3; 11/7/1953, 15.

104　*While in Tulsa:* ELPMSRC, B1657.

106　*She drafted a request:* ELP to LM, ELPMSRC, correspondence, B1657.

107　*Five days earlier:* Herald Tribune, 2/11/1954; NYT, 2/11/1954; WaPo, 2/11/1954, 8; ChDe, 2/13/1954, 1.

108　*The exclusion of:* Paul William Schmidt, *The History of the Ludwig Drum Company* (Fullerton, CA: Centerstream Publications, 1991), 64; ELP telegram to Sherman Adams, 2/6/1954, Correspondence, ELPMSRS Box 1657; Cross Reference Sheet, Payne, Miss Ethel L., 2/6/1954, Papers of Dwight D. Eisenhower as President, 1953–61, DDEPL; ChDe, 2/13/1954, 1.

108　*A few months:* ELPOH, 37.

109　*Since the end:* ChDe, 2/7/1953, 3.

109　*With the fanfare:* ChDe, 11/28/1953, 1.

109　*E. Frederic Morrow:* David Halberstam, *The Fifties* (New York: Villard Books, 1993), 425–426; *Milwaukee Wisconsin Sentinel*

Journal, 1/16/2009; Simeon Booker, the only black reporter on the staff of the *Washington Post,* said he couldn't even eat lunch in the cafeteria of the Interstate Commerce Commission, where he went to cover stories on segregation. (Simeon Booker with Carole McCabe Booker, *Shocking the Conscience: A Reporter's Account of the Civil Rights Movement* (Jackson: University of Mississippi Press, 2013), 43–44).

110 **In late November:** Waters to ELP, 11/30/1953, Correspondence Folder, ELPMSRC B1657; Autobiographical Notes, ELPMSRC B1672.

110 **A few weeks:** ELP to EPW, 12/5/1953, Correspondence Folder, ELPMSCR, Box 1657; *AfAm,* 11/3/1979, 7.

110 **That night Maxwell:** Louis Martin, Memoirs Draft 1, LMLOC Box 8.

111 **Rabb and other:** Washington to Wilton B. Persons (assistant chief of staff in the White House), 6/3/1953, Negro Newspapers and Clippings Folder, Maxwell Rabb Box 53, DDEPL.

111 **In his talk:** Morrow quoted in Ivan A. Zasimczuk, *Maxwell M. Rabb: A Hidden Hand of the Eisenhower Administration in Civil Rights and Race Relations* (master's thesis, University of California Davis, 1997), 36; ELP to EPW, 12/5/1953, Correspondence Folder, ELPMSRC B1657.

111 **In the corridor:** *ChDe,* 8/13/1955, 18B; Donald A. Ritchie, *Reporting from Washington: The History of the Washington Press Corps* (New York: Oxford University Press, 2005), 28.

112 **In 1948, for:** Ritchie, *Reporting from Washington,* 37; Rodger Streitmatter, *Raising Her Voice: African-American Women Journalists Who Changed History* (Lexington: University Press of Kentucky, 1994), 112.

112 **Female reporters had:** Streitmatter, *Raising Her Voice,* 112; Franklin D. Mitchell, *Harry S. Truman and the News Media: Contentious Relations, Belated Respect* (Columbia: University of Missouri Press, 1998), 130 and 141.

113 **But before he:** Ruth Edmonds Hills, ed., *The Black Women Oral*

History Project, Vol. 3 (Westport, CT: Meckler, 1991), 100. The reporter, Lacey Reynolds, was also known to have a keen sense of humor. When Interior Secretary Harold Ickes complimented Reynolds on a story, he said. "Your words of praise almost rendered me speechless."

"I guess," replied Reynolds, "I am about the only one in Washington who ever accomplished that result, Mr. Secretary." (Drew Pearson, Merry-Go-Round column, *Palm Beach Post*, 7/8/1942, 4.)

113 **A couple of:** Streitmatter, *Raising Her Voice*, 113.

113 **At first, neither:** ELPOH, 48; Ted (last name not indicated) on *New York Post* stationery to MMR, 3/37/1953, Negro Newspapers and Clippings Folder, Maxwell Rabb Box 53, DDEPL; Ritchie, *Reporting from Washington*, 42.

114 **Despite her fury:** Melvin Cray taped interview with Ethel Payne 1984 for the Dollie Robinson documentary, Media Genesis Productions, LLC; Sherrod, *Ethel L. Payne*, 32.

115 **"Mr. President," she:** Presidential Press Conference Transcript, 2/10/1953, APP.

115 **When the press:** Autobiographical notes, ELPMSRC, Box 1672.

116 **Payne's question to:** *New York Herald Tribune*, 2/11/1954; *LaTi*, 2/11/1954, 7; *WaPo*, 2/11/1954, 8. "Because Miss Payne raised the question at the president's press conference," the *Defender* proudly noted in an editorial a week later, "daily papers throughout the nation, which had ignored the incident, filled their readers in on the background to report the president's apology." (*ChDe*, 2/20/1954, 11.)

116 **Payne was no:** ELPOH, 53.

116 **"From then on":** ELPOH, 45.

116 **Two days after:** *ChDe*, 2/27/1954, 5.

117 **Dressed in a:** ELP to JHS, 1/28/1954, Correspondence folder, ELPMSCR B1657; *ChDe*, 4/9/1955, 12.

117 **In both meetings:** *ChDe*, 2/27/1954, 5; Correspondence in Rabb folders, DDEPL.

117 **Rabb was not:** *ChDe*, 3/20/1954, 14.

119 ***Ethel Payne was:*** ELP to JHS 2/22/1954, ELPMSRC B1657.

119 ***She was concerned:*** ChDe, 1/1/1955, 12.

119 ***Payne submitted twelve:*** Correspondence and memorandums can be found in RMNPL, Box 144 of Vice-President General Correspondence, *Chicago Defender.*

120 ***In the end:*** ELP to JHS 2/22/1954, ELPMSRC B1657.

120 ***To some, Payne's:*** Essence, 3/1974, 94, 96.

121 ***Communists had never:*** ELPOH, 39, 41.

121 ***She believed McCarthy:*** ELPOH, 39. For an account of Payne's involvement with the McCarthy hearings, see Jon Marshall, "The First Lady of the Black Press vs. Joseph McCarthy: Ethel Payne's Coverage of the Annie Lee Moss Hearings," presented at the American Journalism Historians Conference, Kansas City, MO, October 2011.

122 ***Payne made sure:*** ChDe, 3/6/1954, 1.

123 ***To Payne, the:*** ELPHO, 39.

123 ***With the television:*** Edward R. Murrow and Fred W. Friendly, *See It Now* (New York: Simon & Schuster, 1955), 55–67.

123 ***McCarthy resumed the:*** ChDe, 3/30/1954, 1.

125 ***Payne went back:*** The day was actually not Wednesday, as Payne wrote, but Thursday.

125 ***By April 1954:*** ChDe, 4/24/1954, 7.

126 ***The first was:*** ChDe, 4/3/1954, 3.

126 ***Payne's second, even:*** ELP to EPW, 3/16/1954, Correspondence Folder, ELPMBRC B1657.

126 ***Waters followed Payne's:*** ChDe, 4/3/1954, 12.

127 ***Payne's flattering assessment:*** NYT, 4/4/1954, WaPo, 4/4/1954, ChDe 6/5/1954, 2.

127 ***At the White:*** MMR to ELP, 4/1/1954; EFM to ELP, 4/2/1953, Correspondence, ELPMSRC, B1657; ELPMSRC, B1665.

127 ***Two weeks later:*** ChDe, 4/17/1954, 14.

129 ***As she had:*** ChDe, 12/19/1953, 1, 4.

130 ***The Mondays of:*** Juan Williams, *Thurgood Marshall: American Revolutionary* (New York: Times Books, 1998), 225; Lerone Ben-

nett Jr., "D-Day at the Supreme Court," *Ebony*, May 2004.

130 **But as the:** Richard Kluger, *Simple Justice: The History of Brown v. Board of Education and Black America's Struggle for Equality* (New York: Knopf, 1976), 705.

131 **At 12:52 PM:** LAT, 5/18/1954, 1; ChDe, 5/29/1954, 2.

131 **At last Warren:** Jim Newton, *Justice for All: Earl Warren and the Nation He Made* (New York: Riverhead, 2006), 325.

132 **For Payne it:** ChDe, 5/29/1954, 4. *Ebony*, May 1979, 174; NYT, 5/18/1954, 1.

132 **When the decision:** Helen Reed interview with author.

133 **Even though its:** Eisenhower Press Conference, 5/19/1954, APP.

135 **Prior to May:** ELPOH, 44; Eisenhower Press Conference, 4/7/1954, APP.

136 **A few weeks:** Eisenhower Press Conference, 5/5/1954, APP.

136 **Payne's two attempts:** "Old Hands in Washington: Portrait of Black Journalists," *Horizons*, National Public Radio, aired January 1, 1984, copy on file at the Library of Congress.

137 **Payne could not:** ChDe, 8/13/1950, 18b.

137 **Payne made it:** ChDe, 6/19/1954, 4.

138 **"You know," she:** ELPOH, 45; Ritchie, *Reporting from Washington*, 41.

138 **Payne appreciated the:** Henry G. LaBrie, *Perspectives of the Black Press* (Kennebunkport, ME: Mercer House Press, 1974), 158; ELPOH 38, 41.

139 **Louis Lautier didn't:** ELP Autobiographical Notes, ELPMSRC, B1672.

139 **Mitchell publicly rebutted:** AfAm, 5/25/1954, 3.

139 **The president resumed:** Hagerty diary 6/16/1954 Box 1, DDEPL.

139 **Two days later:** Eisenhower News Conference, 6/16/1954, APP.

141 **For forty-four years:** Jet, 7/29/1954, 6–7.

141 **If for no:** ChDe, 4/24/1954, 2.

142 **Payne complained to:** ELP to Waters and Martin, 6/24/1954, correspondence, ELPHMSCR, B1657.

144 **The president drew:** The audio recording of the president's

response makes his anger clear, unlike the printed transcripts. ELPOH, 46.

145 *Payne was gratified:* Washington Star, 7/7/1954, 1; NYT, 7/7/1954, 14; *Panama Tribune* clipping, ELPMSRC, Box 1657.

145 *Payne's own paper:* ChDe, 7/17/1954, 1.

145 *Dunnigan rallied to:* ChDe, 7/24/1954, 1.

146 *But Lautier didn't:* Alice Allison Dunnigan, A *Black Woman's Experience: From Schoolhouse to White House* (Philadelphia: Dorrance & Company, 1974), 96–97; Hagerty to McCaffree, 2/9/1955, Central files DDEPL.

146 *When Payne entered:* Autobiographical Notes, ELPMSRC B1672; WaPo, 4/27/1959, 59.

147 *The rules of:* Both the Senate and House rules have carried this phrase since the inception of press regulations. For more on this see, Stephen Hess, ed., *Live from Capitol Hill: Essays on Congress and the Media* (Washington, DC: Brookings Institution Press, 1991), 30.

148 *The White House remained:* ChDe, 8/7/1954, 12; 8/7/1954, 1.

149 *After clawing her:* ELPOH, 48.

149 *Her reporting grew:* ELPOH, 50.

149 *In the time:* Women in the Federal Service: 1954 Women's Bureau Pamphlet, U.S. Department of Labor, Washington, DC, 1954; ELP to LEM, 11/22/1954, correspondence folder, ELPMSRC Box 1657.

150 *For a newspaper:* ChDe, 1/7/1955, 1; *Milwaukee Sentinel*, 1/3/1955, 7.

151 *Payne's phone rang:* ELPOH, 63.

152 *In Paris, writer:* Richard Wright, *The Color Curtain: A Report on the Bandung Conference* (New York: World Publishing Co, 1956), 14.

152 *On the floor:* Adam C. Powell, *Adam by Adam* (New York: Kensington Books, 2002), 103.

153 *It was the:* Quoted in Cary Fraser, "An American Dilemma: Race and Realpolitik in the American Response to the Bandung Conference, 1955," *Window on Freedom* (Chapel Hill: University of North Carolina Press, 2003), 120.

153 *The administration told:* Powell, *Adam by Adam*, 103.

153 **The black press:** If Lautier worked for an impoverished news agency, he gave no hint of it. "I went home and nonchalantly announced that I was going to fly around the world," Lautier said. "My wife became interested and decided she wanted to accompany me." (*AfAm*, 4/5/1955, 3)

153 **The flurry of:** Shaw Livermore to Nelson A. Rockefeller, 6/6/1955, Record Group 4, Special Assistant to the President, Afro-Asia: Colonialism, Neutralism—Bandung Conference. NARA.

153 **On the suggestion:** F. A. Jamieson to Nelson A. Rockefeller, 3/9/1955, Record Group 4, Special Assistant to the President, Afro-Asia: Colonialism, Neutralism—Bandung Conference. NARA.

154 **Meanwhile, unaware that:** The best book on the CIA's involvement with the media, keeping track of the various players, is Hugh Wilford, *The Mighty Wurlitzer: How the CIA Played America* (Cambridge, MA: Harvard University Press, 2008). See also Carl Bernstein, "The CIA and the Media," *Rolling Stone*, 10/20/1977.

154 **"One of Life's:** C. D. Jackson to Nelson A. Rockefeller, 3/28/1955, Record Group 4, Special Assistant to the President, Afro-Asia: Colonialism, Neutralism—Bandung Conference. NARA.

155 **If not money:** *Guild Reporter*, 2/22/1952, 3.

155 **He had just:** Carl Rowan, *Breaking Barriers: A Memoir* (New York: Harper Perennial, 1992), 128.

155 **Even Richard Wright's:** Michael Faber, *The Unfinished Quest of Richard Wright* (Urbana: University of Illinois Press, 1993), 416–417. For more on Wright and the Congress for Cultural Freedom, see Wilford, *The Mighty Wurlitzer*, 201–202.

156 **Cartwright, the Hunter:** AmNe, 4/9/1955, 1.

156 **But if it:** AtWo, 4/30/1955, 1; ELP to LEM, 3/22/1955, and ELP to LEM, 3/28/1955, Correspondence File, ELPMSRC B1657. Until the end of her life, Payne credited the *Defender* with paying for the trip. "I was a little astonished that my publisher would open up his purse to send me," she said in the 1980s. (Terry, *Missing Pages*, 2.) It was uncharacteristic of her not to have been a bit suspi-

cious, especially when she knew that the government was funding Lautier's trip.

157 *On April 13:* ChDe, 4/16/1955.

157 *As the plane:* ELP, "Reflections from a Mountain Top," undated typescript, 1, ELPLOC B41F2.

157 *Attending the Bandung:* ELP "Reflections," 1.

157 *Including a refueling:* ELPOH, 64.

158 *In the short:* ChDe, 4/30/1955, 12.

158 *At the airport:* ELPOH, 64.

159 *Reaching the tarmac:* Powell, *Adam by Adam*, 106.

159 *Nor were the:* Payne, "Reflections," 2; Wright, *The Color Curtain*, 177; ELPHO, 65.

160 *The city of:* Christopher Rand, "Four Hours by Rail from Jakarta," *New Yorker*, 6/11/1955, 39; Rowley, *Richard Wright*, 465.

160 *The city's fourteen:* AtWo, 4/21/1955, 2; Hartford Courant, 3/25/1955, 34A; ELP, "Reflections," 3; ChDe 8/6/1955, 4.

161 *The work got:* ELPOH, 66.

161 *Without question the:* ChDe, 3/4/1972, 26; Rand, "Four Hours by Rail from Jakarta," 62.

162 *Payne's enthusiasm turned:* ChDe, 5/7/1955, 12.

162 *For Payne, the:* ChDe, 3/30/1955, 12.

163 *On the fourth:* Payne, "Reflection," 4.

163 *Payne spent most:* ELPOH, 72.

164 *After each long:* ELPOH 71; Rowan, *Breaking Barriers*, 129.

164 *"Years later," Payne:* Payne, "Reflections," 4–5.

165 *For the trip:* ELPOH, 69–70; Terry, *Missing Pages*, 31.

165 *"The Sterno is:* ELP cites the loss of the Sterno in a letter to TG 4/28/1955, ELPLOC B4F1.

166 *Not a single:* Payne, "Reflections," 6; ELPOH, 67–68.

168 *The conference achieved:* Saturday Review, 5/21/1955, 8.

168 *Delegates and others:* Chapter title in Carl Rowan, *The Pitiful and the Proud* (New York: Random House, 1956); Powell, *Adam on Adam*, 118.

168	*Likewise, Payne was:* ELPOH, 74; *ChDe,* 4/16/1955, 1.

168	*"This is the hottest":* ChDe, 5/21/1955, 1; *ChDe* 5/14/1955, 1.

169	*Only in Germany:* ChDe, 7/23/1955, 12.

170	*Her reporting also:* ChDe, 7/16/1955, 12.

171	*The soiree underlined:* ChDe, 3/26/1955, 1.

172	*But in his column:* NYT, 4/28/1955, 14; *WaPo,* 4/28/1955, 62; *LaTi,* 4/28/1955, 12; *ChDe,* 5/7/1955, 1.

172	*The Hagerty matter:* Untitled Manuscript, 6–7, ELPLOC B40F3.

172	*The optimism Payne:* ChDe, 8/20/1955, 4.

173	*Even the Supreme:* ChDe, 6/11/1955, 1.

174	*The Defender opened:* ChDe, 9/10/1955, 1; Davis W. Houck and Matthew A. Grindy, *Emmett Till and the Mississippi Press* (Jackson: University Press of Mississippi, 2008), 31.

174	*The two white:* Autobiographical notes, ELPMSRC, B1672.

175	*In Washington, Payne:* ChDe, 9/17/1955, 1.

175	*It had been believed:* WaPo, 10/15/1955, 26; Houck and Grindy, *Emmett Till and the Mississippi Press,* 135.

175	*Mamie Bradley had:* ChDe, 5/12/1956, 18; *ChDe,* 10/22/1955, 1; *AfAm,* 11/5/1955, 18; Mamie Till-Mobley, *Death of Innocence: The Story of the Hate Crime That Changed America* (New York: One World/Ballantine; reprint edition, 2004), 203.

176	*Payne immediately sought:* ChDe 10/21/1955, 1; *ChDe,* 10/29/1955, 1; *WaPo,* 10/15/1955, 26.

177	*The arrest of:* Life, 2/20/1956, 28.

177	*Payne was convinced:* Autobiographical Notes, ELPMSRC B1672.

177	*On Tuesday, February 7:* ChDe, 2/8/1956, 3, 5, 10.

178	*Publicly the students:* E. Culpepper Clark, *The Schoolhouse Door: Segregation's Last Stand at the University of Alabama* (New York: Oxford University Press, 1993), 67.

178	*"You are in":* ChDe 2/9/1956, 3; *ChDe,* 2/18/1956, 2.

179	*Before escaping from:* Clark, *The Schoolhouse Door,* 63.

179	*"It is for":* ChDe, 2/18/1956, 2.

179	*Hicks and Payne:* DaDe, 2/14/1956, 18.

179	*As her first:* Garrow, *Bearing the Cross,* 7–23.

180 *Only a few:* Nomination form, ELPLOC, B18F9, and correspondence with Sig Gissler, administrator of the Pulitzer Prizes.

180 *Beyond attracting Rowan:* Gene Roberts and Hank Klibanoff, *The Race Beat: The Press, the Civil Rights Struggle, and the Awakening of a Nation* (New York, Knopf, 2006), 128.

181 *For Ethel Payne:* ChDe, 2/18/1956, 1.

182 *"A new type":* ChDe, 2/15/1956, 8.

183 *In Chicago the editors:* ChDe, 2/15/56, 11. Louis Martin also devoted a column to Payne's reporting on this issue (see 3/17/1956, 9).

183 *Payne followed up:* ChDe, 2/27/1956, 8.

184 *Her articles and:* ChDe, 2/15/1956, 3.

184 *The unity was:* ChDe, 3/7/1956, 4.

184 *From Montgomery, Payne:* ChDe, 3/1/1956, 1.

185 *In the Masonic:* NYT, 3/4/1956, E2; NyAm, 3/10/1956, 1.

186 *Lucy and her:* ChDe, 3/17/1956, 2.

186 *In the company:* ChDe, 3/17/1956, 8.

187 *Payne and Lucy:* DaDe, 3/8/1956, 12; WaPo, 3/5/1956, 2.

187 *Butler was already:* DaDe, 2/4/1956, 1; 2/6/1956, 2.

188 *The three-day:* ChDe, 12/8/1956, 1.

188 *Again Payne made:* DaDe, 3/19/1956, 4.

189 *As she had:* Roberts and Klibanoff, *The Race Beat,* 139.

189 *Dean Drug Store, a:* ELPOH, 79.

189 *King, who was:* DaDe, 3/20/1956, 4.

190 *At the end:* Payne even managed to sell some coverage of the trial to the London *Daily Herald,* whose New York editor said he might want more. "There is terrific interest in England in the segregation crisis," he wrote to her. (John Sampson to ELP, 3/28/1956, ELPLOC B4F1.)

190 *The trial lasted:* St. Petersburg Times, 3/23/1956, 2.

190 *A few hours:* DaDe, 3/26/1956, 4.

191 *Montgomery had been:* ELPOH, 80.

191 *Upon her return:* DaDe, 3/28/1956, 2.

191 *In Chicago, Payne:* DaDe, 4/26/1957, 8.

192 *Scribbling in her:* ChDe, 4/21/1956, 1.

193 **In the four years:** *DaDe*, 8/20/1956, 3.

193 **With the summer:** *DaDe*, 8/20/1956, 8.

193 **Republican operatives discerned:** Val Washington to Maxwell Rabb, 7/17/1956, Fisher Howe to Maxwell Rabb, 8/2/1956, Maxwell Rabb to Val Washington, 8/7/1956, Central Files, DDEPL. The delegation of Americans who did attend the Paris conference "all had the hallmarks of a CIA front operation," according to Hugh Wilford, *The Mighty Wurlitzer*, 201.

194 **The supposition that:** Taylor Branch, *Parting the Waters: America in the King Years, 1954–63* (New York: Simon & Schuster, 1988), 220; *DaDe*, 11/8/1956, 1.

194 **In a front-page:** *DaDe*, 11/8/1956, 1.

195 **But as frustrated:** *ChDe*, 12/8/1956, 1.

195 **Despite Ethel Payne's:** Wright, *The Color Curtain*, 182–189.

196 **Readers would certainly:** "He made that tall tale up himself out of whole cloth," according to writer Margaret Walker, who interviewed Payne in 1981. See Walker, *Richard Wright: Daemonic Genius* (New York: Harper Paperback, 2000), 266–267; various interviews with friends of Payne.

196 **In January 1957:** Dwight Eisenhower to Richard Nixon, 1/29/1957, African Trip, 1957, Series 351, Box 1, Folder African Trip—1957—administration, RMNPL.

197 **In addition to:** *ChDe*, 2/16/1957, 3. Kwame Nkrumah to JHS, 1/22/1957, A-SFP.

197 **Ghanaians promised to:** *WaSt*, 4/4/1957.

197 **While the potential:** *ChDe*, 2/23/1957, 4.

197 **An estimated 10,000:** *DaDe*, 3/4/1957, 3. The incident was alluded to in *Ebony*, June 1957, which has a photo of Nixon with the armband. Argus, "Nairobi Roundabout," *Sunday Post*, 3/24/1957. Africa Trip, 1957, Press Clippings Africa to Kenya, Series 349, Box 1, RMNPL.

198 **Later that night:** *DaDe*, 3/5/1957, 1; *AmNe*, 3/16/1957, 1.

198 **As the hour:** *DaDe*, 3/6/1957, 3. UPI dispatch, *Bonham Daily Favorite*, Bonham, TX, 3/5/1957, 1.

198 **"Mr. Vice-President":** *PiCo*, 3/9/1957, 2.

199   *American domestic politics: PiCo,* 5/13/1974, 25.

199   *In the days:* Itinerary and Press List, African Trip, 1957, Series 351, Box 1, folder Africa Trip—1957—administration, RMNPL.

199   *The stops in: ChDe,* 4/6/1957, 4; *ChDe,* 3/30/1957, 12. Not all Payne observed was as weighty. At one stop, she telegraphed her Chicago editors with sartorial news about Pat Nixon. She had confided in Payne that she managed to keep a fresh look in the absence of a maid by packing lightweight nonwrinkle suits rolled in tissue paper. But in an emergency, she also swapped clothes with Rose Mary Woods, her husband's secretary, "such as at Khartoum when Pat stepped off plane in dark silk faille suit and black hat loaned to her by Rose." Woods remained Nixon's personal secretary his entire career and became famous for claiming that she inadvertently erased a critical part of a White House tape relating to the Watergate scandal by stretching to press two different controls several feet apart. Silk faille is a slightly glossy silk. (Undated telegram to *Chicago Defender* from Tripoli, "Writings by, Dispatches from Africa" folder, ELPSMRC, B1657.)

200   *After visits to: ChDe,* 3/23/1957, 2.

200   *Back home Payne: DaDe,* 4/8/1957, 2.

201   *As the date:* Payne also reported that leaders of the rally said they were aware that Communists were attempting to infiltrate the march but that there was no chance of their "capturing" the meeting. Although Payne added that "fellow travelers" Paul Robeson and his wife, Eslanda, would be joining the pilgrimage; *DaDe,* 5/15/1957, 9; *DaDe,* 5/20/1957, 2.

202   *The Sunday after: DaDe,* 5/22/1957, 1.

202   *Payne continued to:* Payne's boss, Louis Martin, was also at times favorably impressed with Nixon, although he remained suspicious. (See Memoirs, Draft I, 140, LBMLOC, B8.) Booker, *Shocking the Conscience,* 165.

203   *Two days after:* Branch, *Parting the Waters,* 219; *DaDe,* 6/18/1957, 6.

204   *Ethel Payne was optimistic: ChDe,* 6/8/1957, 3.

205   *From the press: DaDe,* 7/9/1957, 1.

205 *Payne sought to:* ChDe, 7/20/1957, 12.

206 *By the end:* DaDe, 7/31/1957, 7.

206 *In early August:* ChDe, 8/10/1957, 3.

207 *To Payne the treachery:* ChDe, 5/31/1958, 11.

207 *Thurmond's speechifying resistance:* Branch, *Parting the Waters,* 221.

208 *Payne and civil:* Garrow, *Bearing the Cross,* 98; ChDe, 9/7/1957, 1.

208 *In the Defender:* DaDe, 8/5/1957, 5.

209 *The nine children:* Rowan, *Breaking Barriers,* 155.

209 *After landing at:* DaDe, 9/11/1957, 1.

210 *After a night's:* DaDe, 5/1/1956, 8. The first part of the two articles appeared on 4/30/1956.

211 *Payne was particularly:* ChDe, 9/21/1957, 1.

212 *Payne spent her:* ChDe, 9/21/1957, 3.

212 *Payne caught up:* DaDe, 9/16/1957, 4; NYT, 9/14/1957.

213 *At his press:* DaDe, 9/16/1957, 5.

214 *"Grimly," said Payne:* DaDe, 9/17/1957, 19.

214 *The next morning:* DaDe, 9/16/1957, 1.

215 *What with the traveling:* PiCo, 4/6/1974, 6.

215 *In Washington, a:* DaDe, 10/3/1957, 1

215 *As the Little Rock:* DaDe, 10/21/1957, 14.

215 *White House press:* DaDe, 10/21/1957, 24.

217 *If white America:* DaDe, 10/28/1957, 1.

218 *The next morning:* DaDe, 10/28/1957, 6.

218 *In Payne's eyes:* ChDe, 1/11/1958, 12.

218 *On her Defender:* Remarks by Alice Samples, 6/12/1982, ELP-LOC B7F5; Expense Account, ELPMSRC B1657.

219 *In September, she:* ELP to JHS, 9/27/1957, Correspondence, ELPMSRC B1657.

219 *Payne opened 1958:* ChDe, 1/4/1958, 11.

220 *Shortly after the:* ELP to JRH, 1/3/1958, Payne, E. folder, DDEPL. Hagerty was then in the sixth year of the eight years he would serve as press secretary, the longest anyone ever held that position.

220 *The truth of:* Booker, *Shocking the Conscience,* 137; ChDe, 4/5/1958, 3.

221 *In February, Ethel:* ELPOH, 123–125.

221 *So the gang:* ELP to RMN, 2/13/1958, Correspondence, ELPM-SRC, Box 1657.

222 *On the night:* Joseph B. Samples to RMN, 3/17/1958, Box 582 of Vice-President General Correspondence, Payne, Ethel L. (Miss), RMNPL; Booker, *Shocking the Conscience*, 167.

222 *Several days later:* DaDe, 3/4/1958, A3; RMN to ELP, 3/7/1958, Box 582 of Vice-President General Correspondence, Payne, Ethel L. (Miss), RMNPL; Pat Nixon to ELP, Correspondence, ELPMRS, B1657.

223 *A few weeks:* Expense Accounts and ELP to LEM, 4/24/1958, Correspondence, ELMPSRS, B1657.

224 *The conflict was:* DaDe, 3/19/1956, 4; ChDe, 9/21/1957, 5.

224 *John Sengstacke was:* ChDe, 5/10/58, 11.

225 *The answer to:* Daniel T. Sullivan to ELP, 6/28/1958, Correspondence, ELPMSRC, B1657.

225 *In August, Sengstacke:* JHS to ELP, 8/7/1958, Expense Account, ELPMSRC B1657.

226 *If the Chicago:* Documents in PMWP and Personal Bio Folder, ELPMSCR B1667 date ELP work for the AFL-CIO.

226 *In June 1958:* Personal Bio Folder, ELPMSRC, B1667; *Jet*, 7/31/1958, 29.

226 *Payne put her:* COPE records, RG22–001, Committee on Political Education, Research Division Files, 1944–1979, GMMA. Personal Bio Folder, ELPMSCR B1667.

227 *But the union:* Jet, 9/3/1959, 11; ELP Memo to James L. McDevitt, 4/24/1959, Payne, Ethel, 1959, 61, B5, PMWP.

227 *With the hike:* Roy Wilkins to ELP, 12/19/1958, ELPMSRC, correspondence, B1657; *The Crisis*, April 1959, 236; Mildred Bond to ELP, 2/5/1959, NAACP III, BA214, NAACP.

227 *Working for a:* ELP to Clare B. Williams, 5/20/1959, 109-A–1 1959–1960, DDEPL.

228 *Payne also found:* In 1958, Payne told a relative she was working on landing Johnson a page position. (ELP to Philip A. Johnson, 6/5/1958, JAJP); James A. Johnson, interview with author, 5/22/2012.

228 ***In the summer:*** *AfAm,* 1/31/1959, 2. In 2013, House historians uncovered records that revealed the House had an African American page in 1871, and other records indicate the Senate employed a black "riding page" who delivered messages between the Senate and executive offices at some point in the nineteenth century. The Supreme Court, following Earl Warren's appointment as chief justice, had employed three black pages prior to Johnson's attempt to become a House page. In fact, Payne had written a front-page story about the appointment of the first one five years earlier. (See *ChDe,* 7/31/1954, 1.)

228 ***In a chamber:*** *ChTr,* 1/28/1959, 1.

229 ***Thinking everything was:*** An inkling that something might go wrong surfaced when O'Hara called Payne to let her know there might be a slight delay because two pages had not yet vacated their posts. Nonetheless, Johnson left Chicago for Washington. But Payne ignored the warning signs.

229 ***Only when the two:*** *ChDe,* 2/14/1959, 10.

229 ***Meanwhile the press:*** *ChTri,* 1/28/1959, 1; *ChTr,* 1/29/1958, 1.

229 ***With the Page:*** *ChTr,* 2/17/1959, A2; James A. Johnson interview with author, 5/22/2012.

230 ***With a partial:*** Johnson's family was Lutheran, while Payne remained nominally an AME Baptist but rarely if ever attended services. Her older sister Avis, Jimmy's mother, had retained their mother's religiosity but switched to the Salem Evangelical Lutheran Church when they moved to the Park Manor neighborhood of Chicago. Herman Davis interview with author, 2/20/2013.

230 ***Johnson did well:*** *Ebony,* May 1960.

231 ***Representative William H.:*** William H. Ayres to Clarence Mitchell, 1/25/1960, Jimmy Johnson Folder, ELPMSCR B1664.

231 ***Mitchell was beside:*** Clarence Mitchell, 1/28/1960, Jimmy Johnson Folder, ELPMSCR B1664.

232 ***More odious to:*** Andrew Edmund Kersten, A. *Philip Randolph: A Life in the Vanguard* (Lanham, MD: Rowan & Littlefield, 2007), 152.

232 *"Now the letters"*: ELP to BP, 2/18/1960, JAJP.

233 *Payne was elected*: ELP Memo to You, undated by early spring 1961, Correspondence, ELPMSCR.

233 *The Metropolitan Women's*: ELPOH, 86.

233 *Payne was soon*: DaDe, 4/14/1973, 8.

234 *In the fall*: ELP to family, 11/15/1960, ELPLOC.

235 *The year 1961*: Walter Mosley, *Black Betty* (New York: Washington Square Books, 1994), 45.

235 *For Payne the*: ELP to family (undated), Spring 1961, JAJP.

235 *After the new*: Jet, 2/16/1961, 9; ELP Memo, undated but early spring 1961, Correspondence, ELPMSCR Box 1657.

235 *On Monday, June*: Remarks by Vice-President Lyndon B. Johnson, 6/12/1961, Statements of Lyndon B. Johnson, Box 55, LBJPL.

236 *"Although his family"*: ELP to family, (undated) Spring 1961, JAJP.

236 *A year into*: Jet, 2/8/1962, 51; PiCo, 2/10/1962.

236 *At first it*: Jet, 4/19/62, 3.

237 *In September, the*: Reading Eagle, 9/7/1962, 10; Jet, 9/20/1962, 13.

238 *One night she*: "Civil Rights and Journalism: Then and Now," 1989 video, Department of Special Collections and Archives, Queens College Libraries, CUNY, Queens, NY.

239 *The scope and*: ChDe, 8/24/1963, 6.

240 *The changing political*: AtWo, 1/9/1963, 2.

241 *But at age*: ELP to Family (undated) 1963.

241 *A. Philip Randolph*: NYT, 8/29/1963, 21.

241 *As King began*: "And all of a sudden this thing came to me that . . . I'd used many times before . . . 'I have a dream.' And I just felt that I wanted to use it here . . . I used it, and at that point I just turned aside from the manuscript altogether. I didn't come back to it" (King, November 29, 1963).

242 *The reporters sitting*: Sherrod, *Ethel Payne*, 71; Robert Camfiord, who directed the television pool coverage for the networks, recalled that in a television news career spanning six decades, the March on Washington stands out clearly in his memory. "The raw emotions of Dr. King's speech and its effect on all who were there

to witness it will always remain with me. I am indeed grateful. (Robert Camfiord, USA [2003] http://news.bbc.co.uk/onthisday/hi/witness/august/28/newsid_3171000/3171155.stm.)

242 *A few days:* ELP to APR, 9/3/1963, ELPLOC B4F1.

242 *Payne sought to:* Jet, 10/31/1963, 13; Jet, 8/15/1963, 12, Jet, 3/26/1964, 13; *Denver Post*, 4/8/1964, 23.

243 *It was so:* Carl B. Stokes to ELP, 2/26/1963, ELPLOC B4F1.

243 *Like most everything:* ELPOH, 87.

243 *Now Texan Lyndon:* NYT, 11/28/1963, 1.

244 *On July 2, 1964:* Lawrence F. O'Brien to President, 7/2/1964, courtesy of Allen Fisher, LBJPL.

246 *Payne could not:* ELP to President Lyndon Baines Johnson, 3/17/1965, W.H. Central File, Subject File, LBJPL.

246 *Taking her pledge:* ELPOH, 82.

247 *Another life was:* Charles E. Fager, *Selma: 1965* (New York: Charles Scribner's Sons, 1974), 150–153; ELPOH, 82.

247 *A Johnson aide:* Streitmatter, *Raising Her Voice*, 125.

247 *The DNC Christmas:* ChDe, 12/25/1965, 2.

248 *Payne deftly skirted:* Meriden Journal, 1/22/1966, 4; Press Release, ELPMSRS B1657.

248 *Payne could see:* Katie E. Whickam to Margaret Price, 3/11/1965, MBPP.

249 *The election in:* Cal Jillson, *Texas Politics: Governing the Lone Star Sate* (New York: Routledge, 2011), 80.

249 *Now, five years:* Sean P. Cunningham, *Cowboy Conservatism: Texas and the Rise of the Modern Right* (Lexington: University of Kentucky Press, 2010), 76–77.

249 *On August 28:* By any measure, Payne was neither comfortable nor facile as a public speaker. At first she stuck to her prepared remarks. But Payne's anger toward Republican opposition to the Great Society stirred her. "When I think about all the lies those ornery critters of the opposition are telling," she said, "well, I just get turned on and come out fighting." Her developing stump

speech opened with a recounting of the Selma marches, President Johnson's "We Shall Overcome" address to Congress, and the eventual passage of the Voting Rights Act, triggering amens from her audiences. More talk of expanding the rolls of voters with Negroes and closing with an evangelical call to support the president and Negro soldiers in Vietnam would bring a roar of amens, Payne said. "And you just hope you've succeed in translating apathy into action." ELP letter, 11/9/1966, Correspondence Folder, ELPMSRC B1657.

250 *Moreover, her candidate:* Cunningham, *Cowboy Conservatism,* 106; Van Pell Evans, "Texas Politics," *The Informer and Texas Freeman,* 11/5/1966, 4.

250 *On Election Day:* ELP letter, 11/9/1966, Correspondence Folder, ELPMSRC B1657.

251 *But the end:* ELPOH, 92.

255 *After an absence:* The *New York Times* assigned Tom Johnson, an African Amercian, in December of 1967. Wallace Terry, whom Payne met at the Gov. Faubus press conference, went to the war for *Time* magazine that year as well. A few months after Payne departed from Vietnam, the concert pianist Philippa Schuyler was killed when the helicopter she was in crashed. She had written some freelance articles but on this instance was volunteering to help evacuate orphans from danger. Payne missed meeting Schuyler by a few days when in Vietnam (*DaDe,* 5/18/1967, 3). Frances FitzGerald and Martha Gellhorn were both in Vietnam at the time. The two white women were well-known writers, particularly Gellhorn, a famous war correspondent who had once been married to Ernest Hemingway. (Joyce Hoffman, *On Their Own: Women Journalists and the American Experience in Vietnam* [New York: Da Capo, 2008], 149–151)

255 *Even before agreeing:* ELP to JHS, 11/29/1966, *Defender* Correspondence File, ELPMSRC B1667.

256 *Ahead of the:* Nikolas Kozloff, "Vietnam, the African American

Community, and the *Pittsburgh New Courier*," *The Historian*, Vol. 63, No. 2, 2001, 523.

256 ***But with each**: Ebony*, August 1968, 60–61; Herman Graham III, *The Brothers' Vietnam War: Black Power, Manhood, and the Military Experience* (Gainesville: University Press of Florida, 2003), 17–24; *DaDe*, 4/11/1967, 1.

257 ***The White House**: SB to LEM, 8/13/1965, Correspondence, ELPMSRC, Box 1657.

257 ***Martin forwarded a**: Memorandum by LEM to Bill Moyers, Lee White, Marvin Watson, and Cliff Carter, 8/16/1965, Correspondence, ELPMSRC, Box 1657. By 1966, 35 percent of African Americans opposed the war (Kozloff, "Vietnam," *The Historian*, Vol. 63, No. 2, 2001, 526).

258 ***After twenty hours**: DaDe*, 1/3/1967, 4.

259 ***A representative from**: Thomas E. Barden, ed. *Steinbeck in Vietnam: Dispatches from the War* (Charlottesville: University of Virginia Press, 2012), 105.

259 ***Print and broadcast**: ELP to TG, 12/25/1966, JAJP.

259 ***Early the following**: ELPOH, 94; *News & Courier*, Charleston, SC, 1/15/1967, 3.

260 ***A Christmastime truce**: ChDe*, 12/27/1975. A mistake in the printed version is corrected by an earlier unpublished version found in ELPLOC, B4F1.

261 ***By the time**: ELPOH, 94.

261 ***Recalling her impressions**: DaDe*, 1/3/1967, 4.

261 ***The military public**: Richard West, a British freelance journalist, quoted in Phillip Knightley, *The First Casualty: From the Crimea to Vietnam; The War Correspondent as Hero, Propagandist, and Myth Maker* (New York: Harcourt Brace Jovanovich, 1976), 382; ELPOH, 95.

261 ***Among her first**: ELP to TG, 1/5/1967, JAJP. Outfitted in a life jacket, Payne wondered why the plane's seats were placed backward and straps held her in place vise-like. "I soon found out," she said. "When

the plane hits the deck, the impact is so great that unless you're strapped in properly, your neck might snap like that of a chicken."

262 *As was true:* ELPOH, 96.

262 *Payne also used:* DaDe, 1/16/1967, 5.

262 *Back on dry:* DaDe, 1/25/1967, 8.

263 *Saigon hardly offered:* DaDe, 2/7/1967, 1.

263 *Every reporter who:* ELP to TG, 1/5/1967, JAJP.

264 *For Payne's tour:* DaDe, 1/23/1967, 1. The source for what Payne was thinking is her own account of her thoughts.

265 *Forest and the:* DaDe, 1/24/67, 9.

266 *"It is the battle":* DaDe, 1/26/1967, 1.

266 *As the days:* DaDe, 3/14/1967, 1.

268 *Ethel Payne had:* DaDe, 4/11/1967, 1.

268 *This was not:* DaDe, 3/20/1976, 1.

270 *"In general," Payne:* ELP to BP , 2/23/1967, JAJP.

270 *Leaving Vietnam, Payne:* ELP to BP, 2/23/1967, JAJP.

271 *"I didn't really":* ELPOH, 96.

271 *She paused in South:* DaDe, 3/16/1967, 1.

272 *Making one last:* DaDe, 3/28/1967, 4.

273 *As a member:* DaDe, 3/9/1968, 14.

273 *Her new apartment:* ELP to TG, 9/8/1967, JAJP; Biographical Notes, Personal Bios, EP, ELPMSRC B1667.

274 *"During the day":* Robert H. Fleming to Howard B. Woods, 6/13/1967, White House Central File Subject File PR, LBJPL.

274 *In early June:* DaDe, 6/14/1967, 2.

274 *The club had:* NYT, 4/7/1967, 36; WaPo, 4/6/1967, A10.

275 *Even the Defender:* DaDe, 4/11/67, 1; ChDe, 4/22/1967, 10.

275 *"He knew he":* DaDe, 6/14/1967, 2.

276 *Less impressed with:* Garrow, *Bearing the Cross*, 576–577.

276 *It was indeed:* DaDe, 1/20/1968, 1.

276 *Lady Bird Johnson:* DaDe, 1/22/1968, 7.

277 *Payne pursued the:* DaDe, 6/24/1967, 1.

277 *In August 1967:* ChDe, 8/19/1967, 1.

278 *Three years after:* Garrow, *Bearing the Cross,* 497; DaDe, 7/18/1967, 4.

278 *It was a somber:* DaDe, 7/26/1967, 2.

279 *"The use of":* DaDe, 7/17/1967, 2.

279 *The disunity did:* DaDe, 8/21/1967, 12.

279 *Over the fall:* Garrow, *Bearing the Cross,* 583.

279 *Senator John McClellan:* DaDe, 12/7/1967, 7.

280 *King's planned protest:* DaDe, 1/15/1968, 8.

280 *A few weeks:* DaDe, 1/30/1968, 4.

280 *She followed the:* DaDe, 2/8/1968, 2.

281 *Carmichael lived up:* DaDe, 2/17/1968, 2.

281 *By mid-March:* DaDe, 3/14/1968, 1.

282 *Ethel Payne watched:* Quoted in Mark Engler, "Dr. Martin Luther King's Economics: Through Jobs, Freedom; How would Dr. King have responded to the current crises of recession, unemployment, and foreclosure?" *The Nation,* 1/1/2010.

283 *There remained only:* DaDe, 4/4/1968, 10; ELP letter to friends and family, 4/12/1968, ELPLOC, B4F1.

284 *The anger in:* James Brown flew into Washington in his private jet at the invitation of the mayor, who hoped the singer might help restore calm there after having walked the streets in Boston and Harlem with a message of "Cool it." Payne met up with him at a command post set up by law enforcement in a municipal building. Before going on television to appeal for calm, Brown described to her his experience in Boston. "The people were mad, you know," he said, "but I just walked along the streets talking to them. We dig each other, you know. I'm one of them, yeah. I'm a millionaire, but I got a poor heart, you understand?" *PiCo,* 4/13/1968, 2.

284 *Despite her allusion:* Florence Ridlon, *A Black Physician's Struggle for Civil Rights: Edward C. Mazique, MD* (Albuquerque: University of New Mexico Press, 2005), 251.

285 *Ralph Abernathy, whom:* DaDe, 5/2/1968, 12.

286 *At first, Payne:* DaDe, 5/14/1968, 7.

286 *Caravans of buses:* DaDe, 5/20/1968, 5.

286 *Payne was skeptical:* DaDe, 5/21/1968, 2.

287 *Andrew Young, who:* DaDe, 6/1/1968, 16.

287 *Sympathetic to the:* DaDe, 5/21/1968, 2.

288 *Payne's doctor, Edward:* Ridlon, *A Black Physician's Struggle*, 268, 272.

288 *One day Payne:* DaDe, 6/22/1968, 24.

288 *John Conyers Jr.:* DaDe, 5/28/1968, 8.

289 *Conditions were indeed:* DaDe, 6/4/1968, 19.

289 *Compounding the troubles:* DaDe, 6/3/1968, 7.

289 *As organizers struggled:* DaDe 6/1/1968, 2.

290 *But within days:* DaDe, 6/5/1968, 7; DaDe, 6/11/1968, 5.

290 *In the midst:* DaDe, 6/10/1968, 4.

291 *The encampment's population:* DaDe, 6/22/1968, 1.

291 *Talking to sources:* DaDe, 6/29/1968, 13.

292 *Three days later:* DaDe, 6/19/1968, 13.

292 *Payne came across:* DeDe, 7/1/1968, 4.

294 *"If nothing else":* DaDe, 8/7/1968, 1.

295 *From Miami it:* That is not to say the Republican gathering in Miami was entirely quiet. The city experienced a race riot in Liberty City during the convention. DaDe, 8/24/1968, 11.

295 *In assessing the:* DaDe, 7/13/1968, 31 and 8/31/1968, 1.

296 *But the convention:* DaDe, 9/4/1968, 4.

296 *In the fall:* DaDe, 10/28/1968, 2.

296 *In December the:* DaDe, 12/14/1968, 8.

297 *At first President:* Lawrence Allen Eldridge, *Chronicles of a Two-Front War: Civil Rights and Vietnam in the African American Press* (Columbia: University of Missouri Press, 2012), 160–162.

298 *The appointment didn't:* DaDe, 1/9/1969, 1; 4/10/1969, 2; 5/15/1969, 4.

298 *On the other:* DaDe, 5/1/1969, 5, 8; 5/10/1969, 9.

299 *Weeks later, from:* DaDe, 6/26/1969, 12.

299 *The Richard Nixon:* DaDe, 7/7/1969, 8.

299 *In April, one:* DaDe, 4/23/1969, 3; DaDe, 4/14/1973, 8.

300 *Payne and her:* ELP to Family, 8/22/1969, unlabeled folder, ELPMSRC B1667; WaPo, 12/9/2011.

300 *Meanwhile* **Defender** *publisher:* ELP to JHS and LPM, 6/23/1969, Defender Correspondence, ELPMSRC B1667.

300 *Payne told Sengstacke:* ELP to JHS, 12/30/1969, Defender Correspondence, ELPMSRC B1667.

301 *Payne's frustration with:* ChTr, 3/7/1972, 9; DaDe, 3/11/1972, 5.

301 *The* **Defender** *gave:* DaDe, 3/13/1972, 1.

302 *"We reject the":* DaDe, 3/13/1972, 4.

302 *The 1972 political:* DaDe, 7/11/1972, 9.

302 *As she had:* DaDe, 7/15/1972, 36; 7/29/1972, 8; 8/26/1972, 5.

303 *That autumn Nixon:* DaDe, 11/9/1972, 8.

303 *Still, the tone:* DaDe, 12/13/1972, 1; 12/23/1972, 6.

305 *An immensely frustrated:* Circumstantial evidence indicates that the Nigerians paid for all, or at least most, of the costs associated with the journey. Neither of their newspapers had a budget for such a trip.

305 *In late January:* ELP to ARJ, 1/27/1969, JJP.

305 *Unlike life in:* Elsie Olusola Interview with Miss Ethel Payne, Voice of America, 2/4/1969, National Archives Record Group 306: Records of the U.S. Information Agency, 1900–2003; DaDe, 2/19/1969, 2 and 2/4/1969, 7.

305 *But as far:* "Part II of My African Adventure," ELPLOC B39F8.

306 *"Adekunle's particular reason":* ELPOH, 99.

306 *The following morning:* DaDe, 2/12/1969, 8.

307 *After two days:* "Part II of My African Adventure," ELPLOC B39F8.

308 *Payne raised the:* The National Negro Publishers Association had changed its name to the National Newspaper Publishers Association.

308 *The group traveled:* DaDe, 2/24/1970, 6; DaDe, 2/21/1970, 2; DaDe, 2/23/1970, 6; DaDe, 3/4/1970, 8; DaDe, 3/5/1970, 6; DaDe, 3/28/1970, 26; DaDe, 4/7/1970, 6.

309 *Unbeknownst to her:* Quoted in Seymour Hersh, *The Price of Power: Kissinger in the Nixon White House* (New York: Summit Books, 1983), 111. The comment caught by Nixon's tape record-

ing system in the White House was not to be revealed until years
later.

309 **When Congo president:** *DaDe*, 2/24/1970, 6; *DaDe*, 2/21/1970, 2;
DaDe, 2/23/1970, 6; *DaDe*, 3/4/1970, 8; *DaDe*, 3/5/1970, 6. During the question-and-answer period at the National Press Club,
Mobutu was asked to comment on the new Afro hairdos popular
in the United States. The translator was stymied by the question.
"Then," said Payne, "Marion Barry, director of Pride, Inc., stood
up with his modified bush and dashiki." In the confusion, the
president believed he was to make a comment on Barry's shirt, but
an aide whispered to him about the hairstyle query. "Voilà," said
Mobutu, waving his hand over his head. "We are already doing
that in the Congo." (*DaDe*, 8/5/1970, 2; 8/15/1970, 14); ELP to TG,
8/9/1970, JAJP.

309 **Payne soon torpedoed:** *WaPo*, 10/21/1970; *Newark Evening News*,
10/21/1970.

310 **The film showed:** *DaDe*, 10/17/1970, 14; *Jet*, 11/5/1970, 4.

311 **To bring Young's:** Booker, *Shocking the Conscience*, 290.

311 **Landing in Lagos:** *DaDe*, 3/16/71, 2; 3/15/1971, 1.

311 **When it was:** *Ebony*, May 1971, 42; *DaDe*, 3/27/1971, 8.

312 **At the grave site:** *Ebony*, May 1971, 31–39.

312 **No more than:** *DaDe*, 8/7/1971, 8.

313 **Ethel Payne was:** ELPOH, 103.

313 **Robinson liked the:** ELPSCRBC, B7.

313 **Upon her return:** ELPOH, 105.

314 **Robinson was pleased:** Maurice Robinson to ELP, 6/12/1972.
Scripts may be found in ELPSCRBC Box 7.

314 **In 1972, with:** Interview with author, 12/13/2011.

315 **Payne was completely:** *DaDe*, 7/10/1972, 8.

315 **If nothing else:** *AfAm*, 8/22/1972, 11.

317 **The dust had:** *AfAm*, 5/19/1984, 3; ELP "Notes on China" 11/10/1975,
ELPLOC B39F9.

317 **However, because Manton's:** "Notes on China" 11/10/1975, ELP-
LOC B39F9.

318 *After landing in:* NYT, 1/16/1973, 16; AfAm 5/19/1983, 3.

318 *Now inside China:* ChDe, 2/17/1973, 4; small Chinese notebook, SSP, B127F2.

319 *Almost every day:* Description drawn from small Chinese note-book, SSP, B127F2.

319 *During a visit:* ChDe, 3/10/1973, 6.

320 *Payne was dazzled:* ELP to TG, 1/26/1973, JAJP.

320 *In Shanghai, Payne's:* Tri-State Defender, 3/10/1973, 6.

320 *Reg Murphy, an:* Atlanta Constitution, 11/18/1974.

321 *In addition to:* AfAm 5/19/1983, 3.

322 *For their work:* Fox Butterfield, China: *Alive in the Bitter Sea* (New York: Times Books, 1982), 29.

322 *On April 11:* FBI File in possession of author.

322 *Payne, of course:* George Derek Musgrove, *Rumor, Repression, and Racial Politics: How the Harassment of Black Elected Officials Shaped Post–Civil Rights America* (Athens: University of Georgia Press, 2012), 56.

323 *In June, the:* FBI File in possession of author.

324 *As the summer:* ELP to TG 6/18/1973, JAJP; ELP to Friends, 12/25/1973, ELPMSRC B1657.

324 *Payne put the:* ChDe, 7/7/1973, 8.

324 *By early August:* ELPOH, 108.

325 *One day on:* Letter from Shirley Small-Rougeau to the author, 5/10/2013.

326 *Payne felt the:* ELPLOC B2F5.

326 *After an absence:* ELPSCRBC Box 9.

326 *Statistically speaking, Payne:* ChTr, 7/8/2012.

327 *"Super Fly and":* DaDe, 1/21/1974, 1.

327 *Payne was entering:* Faustin C. Jones, "On Respect for the Law: 'Law and Order,'" *The Crisis,* April–May 1971, 91; Cynthia Flem-ing, *Yes We Did?: From King's Dream to Obama's Promise* (Lexing-ton: University Press of Kentucky, 2009), 73.

328 *On Sunday evening:* ChDe, 2/25/1974, 1 and 2/28/1974, 2.

328 *"This could not"*: *Atlanta Constitution*, 11/18/1974.

328 *Despite her crime-fighting"*: Coretta Scott King to ELP, 2/9/1975, Lee Lorch to ELP, 12/11/1974, Daniel James to ELP, 1/8/1974 ELP-SCEBC B36; Lady Bird to ELP from LBJ Ranch ELPMSRC 1664; Hubert Humphrey to ELP, 2/4/1975, ELPCHM.

328 *Given the chance*: ELP to ARJ, 1975 postcard, JAJP.

329 *In the spring*: ELP to ARJ, 2/4/1987, ELPLOC B5.

329 *To pay for*: Carlton Goodlett to NNPA members, ELPLOC B15.

329 *The strategy worked*: Department of State, Tanzania Dar es Salaam, US Delegation Secretary to Department of State, Secretary of State, 4/25/1976.

330 *The problem resolved*: ELP to ARJ, 2/4/1987, ELPLOC B5; See Kissinger to ELP, 6/28/1976, ELPSCRBC B15.

330 *At its various stops*: Richard Valeriani, *Travels with Henry* (Boston: Houghton Mifflin, 1979) 361–362.

331 *At one point*: Valeriani, *Travels with Henry*, 84–85; ELP to ARJ, 2/4/1987, ELPLOC B5.

331 *Payne questioned Kissinger's*: *AfAm*, 6/29/1976, 2; Typescript, LOC B39F9.

331 *The same issue*: National Security Advisor's Memoranda of Conversation, 6/2/1976 and 8/3/1976, GRFPL.

332 *Kissinger nonetheless went*: *PiCo*, 8/21/1976, 6; AP report, *The Bulletin* 8/3/1976, 10; *ChTr*, 8/6/1976, A4.

332 *It was a heady*: ELP to TG, 8/13/1996, JAJP.

332 *Payne began by*: *Atlanta Constitution*, 10/19/1976; ELP to Jody Power, 7/16/1976, LOC 41, 4; PiCo 10/9/1976, 6.

333 *In the midst*: ELP to Rev. Addie Wyatt, ACWP B33F42; ELP to Richard Ferris, 10/29/1976; ELPSRBC B28.

333 *Next it was*: I-Chen Loh to ELP, 8/15/1977, JAJP; *ChDe*, 9/3/1977, 12.

333 *After the journey*: OMB forms, ELPSRBC B37; ELPOH, 109.

334 *"Ethel, we have"*: JHS to ELP, 10/11/1977, ELPSCRBC B36.

334 *Unapologetic, Payne challenged*: ELP to JHS, 1/17/1978, ELP-SCRBC B36.

336 *As had happened:* ELPOH, 142.

336 *The foundation liked:* ELP, *Black Colleges: Roots, Reward, Renewal* (Delta Sigma Theta, 1979), 47–50.

337 *Delta Sigma Theta:* Sidney Hook letter in letter to Samuel Halperin, the former deputy assistant secretary of health, education and welfare for legislation. ELPSCRBC B36.

337 *The report done:* Eddie Williams to ELP, 6/12/1978, ELPSCBC B36.

337 *It was dispiriting:* ELPOH, 132.

338 *Three allies in:* John Raye letter to author; Census folder, ELPSCRBC B4.

338 *In her new:* Various interviews. The use of eggshells was described by Rita Bibbs-Booth, who learned about them when she house-sat for Payne. Payne later donated her collection of dolls, as well as dolls once owned by her sister Thelma, to the Charles Sumner School Museum and Archives in Washington, DC.

339 *She chose her:* By the end of 1980, she was an officer of the Capital Press Club. *Washington Informer*, 10/23/1980, 19. Gil to ELP, Dated October 8 no year, ELPSCEBC B5.

339 *At 2:05 in:* Scott M. Bushnell, *Hard News, Heartfelt Opinions: A History of the Fort Wayne Journal Gazette* (Bloomington: Indiana University Press, 2007), 170–171.

340 *Payne had known:* Vernon Jordan to ELP, 8/2/1973, ELPSCRBC B36

340 *Now Payne was:* ChTr, 6/15/1980, B14. (The article was written by Payne's friend Barbara Reynolds.)

340 *"There's one thing":* ELPOH, 151.

340 *This was not:* ChTr, 7/31/1988, section 6, page 3.

341 *"The truth is":* WaPo, 6/14/1982, c6; ChDe, 2/4/1978, 6; ELPOH, 150.

341 *From his hospital:* Vernon E. Jordan Jr., *Vernon Can Read!: A Memoir* (New York: Public Affairs, 2008), 294.

341 *When he was:* Looking back on the contretemps many years later, Jordan called it "a little incident in an otherwise outstanding career as an important journalist." Author interview 11/21/2012.

341 ***When they first:*** Barbara Reynolds, *No, I Won't Shut Up* (Temple Hills, MD: JFJ Publishing, 1998), 285.

342 ***Payne predicted in:*** "Carter's High Risk Re-Election Gamble," *Dollars & Cents*, Fall, 1980.

342 ***Payne's optimism, however:*** *Sepia*, Fort Worth, TX, 1/1/1981, 14.

342 ***In August, Payne:*** An essay and a radio commentary for WBBM, ELPLOC, Box 39, 9 and Box 40, 3.

343 ***Like the president:*** Originally the chair was to be named after Payne; then as the project got under way it was named after journalist Ida B. Wells. Confusion over the name persisted, and when Payne was on campus in 1982–1983 it was again referred to as the Payne Chair.

343 ***Leonard and Reynolds:*** AfAm, 6/22/1982, 3.

343 ***"They came from":*** WaPo, 6/14/1982, C6.

344 ***As she was:*** Interview with author 11/22/2011.

344 ***"Come fall, when":*** AfAm, 6/22/1982, 3.

345 ***She had been:*** Scandinavian study quoted in Aderanti Adepoju, "The Dimension of the Refugee Problem in Africa," *African Affairs*, Vol. 81, No. 322 (January 1982), 21.

345 ***In March, Payne:*** Interview with author, 6/17/2013.

346 ***Payne told Lucas:*** ChDe, 10/26/1973, 6. See, for example, *ChDe*, 5/24/1975, 10; ELP to C. Payne Lucas, 3/12/1982, ELPSCBC Box 5.

346 ***Lucas bought into:*** ELP, *Focus on Africa: A Report on Refugee Camps and Settlements in Somalia, Sudan, Zambia, Zimbabwe* (Africare, 1982), i; *Black Enterprise*, February 1986, 142.

346 ***Payne, the veteran:*** ELP to Patricia Scales, 6/25/1982, ELPSCFBC B5.

346 ***An overnight flight:*** ELP, *Focus on Africa*, 1, 3 Somalia.

347 ***The Somali government:*** ELP, *Focus on Africa*, 12–13 Somalia.

348 ***For five days:*** UNDP, *Human Development Report, 2001—Somalia* (New York: 2001), 42; ELP, *Focus on Africa*, 14 Somalia.

348 ***They landed at:*** ELP, *Focus on Africa*, 1–2 Sudan.

348 ***Sudan consisted of:*** At the Lusaka International Airport, she reflexively answered "journalist" when immigration officials asked

her profession rather than explaining she was a board member of Africare visiting the organization's projects. Journalists could enter Zambia only with prior approval from the Ministry of Information. Kevin Lowther, the Africare representative in Zambia, tried to come to her aid. The officials, however, were unwilling to take his word. So Lowther drove back the twenty miles into Lusaka in hopes of finding the commissioner of refugees in his office. Good fortune was with Lowther. He obtained a typed letter on stationery, signed and officially stamped. (In African nations, noted Lowther, "a letter that hasn't been stamped isn't a letter.") Suitably armed, he returned to the airport to further plead with the officials. However, the two agents in charge continued to debate whether to admit Payne. The delays did not sit well with Payne. "She was accustomed to being known and respected," said Lowther. "To be confronted far from home by officious immigration officers was not the welcome she had expected." The agents, who were not seeking bribes but were more concerned with the safety of their jobs if they erred, finally relented, and Payne headed to the hotel in Lowther's company.

349 *The camp now:* ELP to family, 7/31/1982, JJP.

349 *At the end:* ELP, *Focus on Africa*, 5 Zambia.

350 *Upon her return:* AfAm, 9/14/82, 5.

350 *In January 1981:* ELP to family, 1/15/1981.

350 *Payne was assigned:* Interview with author, 5/27/2013.

351 *In class, Haynes:* ChMe, 5/30/1981, 10.

351 *Haynes was not:* Interview with author.

352 *Haynes and Bibbs:* Interview with author.

352 *A year and:* Convocation Speech, ELPLOC, B28F6.

353 *Speech concluded, journalist:* She lived at 1809 Morena St. 37208; "The students just loved it," recalled President Leonard. (Author interview.)

353 *The seminar series:* "The Great Issues of Today Seminar," ELPLOC B28F4.

354 *Payne's post at:* Omaha World-Herald, 2/25/1983, 33.

354 *Normally winning a:* ELP to Hal Chase, 5/3/1983, ELPLOC, B5F1.

355 *Her column was:* Bruce Tucker to ELP, 4/29/1983, ELPLOC B5F1.

355 *A week later:* ELP to Bruce Tucker, 5/6/1983, ELPLOC B5F1.

356 *As the spring:* "The Great Issues of Today Seminar," ELPLOC B28F4.

357 *To Ethel Payne's:* Laura Ross Brown to ELP, 4/4/1984, ELPLOC B5F2.

359 *For Payne, Coleman:* ELPOH, 127.

359 *Three years before:* Brown returned the salvo with one of his own. "Ethel Payne," he wrote, "should have said that she was not in San Francisco and given the reasons why it was necessary to brand 150 black people who are looking for ways and means to stop the tide of the white liberal black professional leader 'march to the rear' in the so-called civil rights fight as 'hasty switcher' opportunities." (*Columbus Times,* Columbus, GA, 2/4/1981, 5.)

360 *Payne's fight with:* Milton Coleman interview with author 5/7/2013.

360 *Her anger also:* Edwin Emery and Michael Emery, *The Press and America: An Interpretive History of the Mass Media* (Englewood, NJ: Prentice-Hall, 1984), 580–581.

360 *"Ethel and the":* Ernest Green interview with author, 1/4/2013. Looking back on the time, Green said, we didn't know what a rich and important period it was. "The Ethel Paynes and Bayard Rustins of the world ran their business on three-by-five cards and changed the world."

361 *The civil rights:* WaIn, 3/26/1986, 18.

361 *A black journalist:* Audrey Edwards to ELP, 3/22/1984, ELPLOC B40F1.

361 *Even work from:* ELP to Max Green, 2/7/1984, ELPSCBC B36.

363 *In the cold:* Payne's companion that day was Sylvia Hill, a criminal justice professor at the University of the District of Columbia. When contacted, Hill said she didn't recall getting inside the embassy, but the press accounts consistently report that the two women did enter the building.

363 *For Payne, ending:* ANC Donation form, ELPSCRBC Box 5; ChDe, 1/22/1955, 1.

364 *During her years:* ChDe, 6/5/1976, 6; ChDe, 12/21/1974, 8.

364 *South Africa, however:* ELPSRBC B28; AfAm, ELP to Kinfolks and Friends, 8/22/1985, ELPLOC, B5F4.

364 *The embassy called:* WaPo, 1/5/1985, B1; AfAm, 1/12/1985, 1; ELP to Kinfolks and Friends, 8/22/1985, ELPLOC B5F4; Catherine Brown interview with author, 6/5/2013.

365 *February brought back:* MiTi, 2/28/1985.

365 *But Payne hardly:* ELP to Kinfolks and Friends, 8/22/1985, ELPLOC B5F4; ELP Memo, ELPSRBC B22; Miami Folder, ELPSRBC B5; ELP to Family, 5/15/1985, ELPLOC B5F3.

365 *In the fall:* WaPo, 11/23/1985, G3; ELP Speech, ELPLOC B2F4; Africare Board Minutes, 6/24/1988, ELPLOC B14F8.

367 *Several months later:* Minutes of 9/12/1986 Africare Executive Committee Meeting, ELPSBRC B22; Kevin Lowther interview and letters with author.

367 *Outside of her:* ELP to Hortense Canady, 1/10/1987, Howard University.

368 *Payne recommended to:* AfAm, 5/5/1987, 48; Jet, 4/27/1987, 7.

369 *Payne rushed to:* MiTi, 5/28/1987, 5.

369 *Nothing would weaken:* ELP to Winnie Mandela, 7/1/1988, ELPLOC B5F8.

369 *In her defense:* USA Today, 2/25/1987, 4A.

369 *"I hate to":* ELPOH, 143–144.

370 *The Miller Brewing:* Chicago Sun-Times, 4/11/1987, 10.

371 *It was an easier:* ELPOH, 133–134.

371 *But Payne's generosity:* ELP to T and Ruth, 12/17/1985, ELPSCRBC B5.

372 *What Payne lacked:* Letter, Shirley Small-Rougeau to author, 4/26/2013.

372 *"We, our little":* Letter, Shirley Small-Rougeau to author, 5/29/2013.

372 *When Payne turned:* Jet, 9/22/1986, 30; ELP to friends January 1987, ELPSCBC B5.

374 *After waiting for:* AfAm, 10/3/1987, 12; WaPo, 10/3/1987.

375 *Payne told caucus:* ELP to Mervyn Dymally, 9/30/1987, ELPJJP.

375 ***Dymally was quick:*** Mervyn Dymally to ELP, 9/29/1987, ELPJJP.

375 ***The 1988 presidential:*** *The City Sun*, Brooklyn, NY, 6/8–14/1988, 19.

376 ***Attending the convention:*** "New Recognition for the Black Press," 7/19/1988, ELPLOC B36F3.

376 ***Payne was keenly:*** ELP to Ruth and David, 2/4/1987, ELPLOC; ELP to David Payne Johnson, 1/23/1989, ELPLOC B6F1.

377 ***Barry replied that:*** Associated Press report in *Observer-Reporter*, Washington, PA, 4/3/1989, 13.

377 ***In the fall:*** ELP to Maureen Bunyan, 10/11/1989, ELPLOC B6F2.

377 ***In the end:*** "Coming to Terms with Reality," ELPLOC B40F3.

378 ***She remained for:*** ELP to Mitsuko Shigomura, 11/30/1989, ELP-LOC B6F2; ELP to Frances Draper, 11/11/1989, ELPLOC B6F2.

379 ***The trip was:*** Letter from Joseph Dumas to author.

379 ***In the living:*** C. Payne Lucas interview with author.

380 ***A month later:*** *Philadelphia Inquirer*, 7/1/1990.

380 ***At the end:*** *WaTi*, 2/28/1991; *WaPo*, 2/21/1991, DC2; ELPOH, 116–117.

381 ***In April, Payne:*** ELP to Ruth and David, 2/4/1987, ELPLOC; ELP to David Payne Johnson, 1/23/1989, ELPLOC B6F1; *Washington Times*, 2/28/1991; copy of eulogy in author's possession.

381 ***On May 23:*** Dean Mills to ELP, 5/23/1991, JAJP.

382 ***Upon reflection, Payne:*** Interview with author.

384 ***As a reporter:*** *ChDe*, 3/26/1977; Layfield, "Chasing the Dream," 132–133.

385 ***On Capitol Hill:*** *Congressional Record*, E2072.

386 ***Then, from the:*** James M. Christian interview with author, 6/25/2013.

387 ***Indeed, two years:*** Interview with author, 6/14/2013.

387 ***The first two:*** Tracey Scruggs-Yearwood interview with author; Fred Harvey interview with author.

388 ***Civil rights activist:*** NYT, 9/28/2011, 13.

389 ***A decade before:*** *Tennessean*, Nashville, TN, 2/28/1981, 2.

INDEX

Garvey, Marcus, 197
Gates, Mahlon Eugene, 269
Gellhorn, Martha, 270
George Washington University, 336
Germany, 56, 169–70
Ghana, 196–99, 202, 304, 378
Goldwater, Barry, 248, 249
Goodlett, Carlton, 329
Goodwin, Edward L., Sr., 104–5,
    223
Granger, Lester, 141–43, 155, 198
Grass, Martha, 291
Gray, Fred, 182, 184
Gray, Louis Patrick, III, 322
Gray, Thelma Elizabeth (sister), 11,
    12–13, 26, 27–29, 69, 102, 163,
    309, 320, 324, 371–73
Gray, William, III, 386
Great Books, 69
Green, Dwight, 50, 51
Green, Ernest, 361
Green, Victor H., 105
Gregory, Dick, 343–44
Grooms, Harlan Hobart, 184

Hagerty, James, 114–16, 135, 139,
    146–47, 171–72, 215, 220
Haiti, 156, 157
Halberstam, David, 323
Haley, Alex, 349, 370
Haley, George, 370
Hall, Robert, 123, 124
Hamer, Fannie Lou, 325
Hansberry, Carl A., 88
Hansberry, Lorraine, 88
Harriday, Mamie, 300
Harriman, Averell, 193
Harris, Louis, 249
Hart, John, 313
Harvard University, 382
Harvey, Fred, 388

Hatcher, Andrew, 237
Hatcher, Richard, 302
Hayes, Ira, 306
Haynes, Gillie, 351
Hays, Brooks, 212, 213
Hayward, J. C., 372
Hearst, William Randolph, 21
Height, Dorothy, 291
Hemingway, Ernest, 24–26
Hicks, James L., 71–74, 178–80, 185,
    209
Higgins, Marguerite, 388
Hill, J. Lister, 101
Hill, Oliver, 81
Himes, Chester, 36
Hooks, Benjamin, 337, 340
Hoover, J. Edgar, 299
Hope, Bob, 259, 260, 262
housing, 135–36, 139, 142, 149; in
    Chicago, 42, 88
Howard University, 102, 201, 279,
    325; choir of, 107–8, 114–16, 119,
    386
Huff, William Henry, 176
Hughes, Langston, 125
Humphrey, Hubert, 5, 99, 188,
    295–96, 302, 314, 328
Huntley, Chet, 163, 164
Hurley, Ruby, 175, 185

If He Hollers Let Him Go (Himes),
    36
Indonesia, 150–51, 152–59, 160–68,
    172, 180, 195, 200, 304
Inland Steel, 90
Interracial Commission, 51, 52–55,
    57
Iyalla, Joe, 304, 305

Jack, Homer A., 163
Jackson, C. D., 154

ABOUT THE AUTHOR

JAMES MCGRATH MORRIS is an author, columnist, and radio show host. His books include *Pulitzer: A Life in Politics, Print, and Power*—which the *Wall Street Journal* deemed was one of the five best books on American moguls and *Booklist* placed on its 2010 list of the ten best biographies—and *The Rose Man of Sing Sing: A True Tale of Life, Murder, and Redemption in the Age of Yellow Journalism*, a *Washington Post* Best Book of the Year. He is one of the founders and past presidents of Biographers International Organization (BIO) and makes his home in Santa Fe, New Mexico.